Strategies for Protein Purification and Characterization

Strategies for Protein Purification and Characterization

A LABORATORY COURSE MANUAL

Daniel R. Marshak Cold Spring Harbor Laboratory

James T. Kadonaga University of California, San Diego

Richard R. Burgess University of Wisconsin, Madison
& Mark W. Knuth Promega Corporation, Madison, Wisconsin

William A. Brennan, Jr. Pennsylvania State University
& Sue-Hwa Lin University of Texas M.D. Anderson Cancer Center

COLD SPRING HARBOR LABORATORY PRESS 1996

Strategies for
Protein Purification
and Characterization
A LABORATORY COURSE MANUAL

ISBN 0-87969-449-1 (cloth bound)
ISBN 0-87969-385-1 (comb bound)
LC 95-69760

Design by Emily Harste

Cover: Schematic representation of the preparation of the components of a protein mixture by chromatography.

All Cold Spring Harbor Laboratory Press publications may be ordered directly from Cold Spring Harbor Laboratory Press, 10 Skyline Drive, Plainview, New York 11803-2500. Phone: 1-800-843-4388 in Continental U.S. and Canada. All other locations: (516) 349-1930. FAX: (516) 349-1946.

To Professor John T. Edsall

who has inspired us to think about proteins as entities
with unique and wonderful properties

Contents

UNIT II • PURIFICATION OF TRANSCRIPTION FACTOR AP-1 FROM
        HeLa CELLS
        James T. Kadonaga

UNIT IV • SOLUBILIZATION AND PURIFICATION OF THE RAT LIVER INSULIN RECEPTOR

William A. Brennan, Jr. and Sue-Hwa Lin

Preface

This manual has evolved from the curriculum of the Protein Purification and Characterization Course taught at Cold Spring Harbor Laboratory each April since 1989. The course is designed to introduce biologists to techniques of protein purification and to provide selected examples of protein characterization. The intent is to permit the student to discover some of the fundamental procedures commonly used in protein biochemistry so that such methods can be brought to a pressing problem in biology. The students of this course usually range from advanced graduate students to senior faculty, the majority being in the latter category.

The course was conceived to fill a void created by the trend from the mid-1970s to the 1990s toward increased training in cloning of nucleic acids and away from classical education in protein chemistry and biochemistry. One of the best applications received was from a faculty member in a microbiology department at a major university. This individual had identified a new genetic regulatory element and demonstrated that there was a proteinaceous activity that bound to this DNA sequence. After submitting an application for a grant on this topic, the referees indicated that it was essential to purify and characterize the protein factor. In applying to the Protein Purification and Characterization Course, the professor wrote, "It is clear from my study section that I must purify the protein. However, I have never run a column in my life and I don't know where to start. (I once ran an oligo-dT column to purify poly-A$^+$ RNA, but that doesn't really count!)." The professor became a student in the course, became more familiar with and no longer afraid of proteins, and eventually received his grant funding. Although this example is somewhat extreme, it does point out that much of the inertia to learning protein methodologies is fear of the complexity.

None of us learned to purify and characterize proteins by reading books. Everyone who practices these procedures successfully learned inductively, by doing one purification after another. It is impossible to predict perfectly the behavior of every protein using theoretical purification methods. Therefore, the course and this manual were constructed to introduce scientists to protein purification by taking them step by step through four representative sets of experiments comprising non-redundant methodologies for proteins from four different starting materials. After completing the program, it is unlikely you will know exactly how to purify a particular protein of interest, but you should be capable of attacking the problem in a logical fashion, given the resources available.

Most of all, we would like to thank the students who have participated in the course, and who have contributed enormously to the refining of the material in this manual. The efforts of the former course instructors were invaluable, and we gratefully acknowledge John A. Smith and Bruce W. Erickson. We are particularly thankful to Guido Guidotti who introduced membrane protein purification to the course and inspired us in our teaching. Several of the guest lecturers in the course contributed to the success of the program and to the concepts behind this manual, including George Rose, C. Nick Pace, James Garrels, Yvonne Paterson, James Rothman, Ruedi Aebersold, and Arthur Kornberg. We thank the administration and scientists at Cold Spring Harbor who have helped and encouraged us in this endeavor, particularly Jim Watson, Terri Grodzicker, John Inglis, and Bruce Stillman. We gratefully recognize the contributions of Carl Anderson and Ryuji Kobayashi to this volume, and Tom Lucas for reagents. Several assistants in the course contributed to the development of some of the protocols, including Leslie Kerrigan, Thomas Burke, Karen Earley, Nicholas Carpino, Catherine George, and Anthony Grabski. Finally, many thanks are due Catriona Simpson, Maryliz Dickerson, and Nancy Ford for editing, typesetting, and production of the book.

December 1995

D.R.M.
J.T.K.
R.R.B.
M.W.K.
W.A.B.
S.-H.L.

Foreword

The central goal of modern biological and biomedical research is to understand the phenomena associated with organisms in terms of molecular mechanisms. Attaining this goal requires attention to both "molecular" and "mechanisms" and essentially proceeds in two stages with regard to every new process whose dissection is undertaken. First, the pertinent molecules must somehow be identified from among the tens of thousands present in most organisms. Second, the mechanisms by which these molecules interact to give rise to the phenomenon in question can then be determined from studies of sequential, pairwise, and combinatorial interactions of the molecules themselves, and/or the products they generate, and from analysis of their structures in relation to these tests.

As the molecular machinery is almost always protein, it is easy to see why protein purification and characterization, the subject of this book, has always been and will continue to be center stage in biological discovery.

The traditional approach to identifying molecular machinery is to purify the pertinent components according to a functional assay in which the biological process in question is reproduced in its essential aspects in a cell-free system. This is still the core approach and is much emphasized in this course, as is appropriate since there is every reason to expect the continued importance of "classical biochemistry" for modern biology. After all, this approach has an enviable record of success, beginning before the turn of this century, in which processes of increasing complexity have been understood in chemical terms, ranging from glycolysis to oxidative phosphorylation to the discovery of protein kinases and mechanisms of signal transduction, to the synthesis of macromolecules (including DNA, RNA, and protein), and more recently the translocation and transport of proteins and neurotransmission at synapses.

With the rise of modern molecular genetics and the accompanying confluence among the previously distinct intellectual disciplines of anatomy (and its more modern lineal descendants, cell and structural biology), biochemistry, and genetics, there are now several important new ways to discover protein machinery that are uniquely applicable to complex phenomena that have so far resisted cell-free reconstitution. For example, mutants can be obtained that affect multicellular processes such as patterning in embryos, and the affected gene can be efficiently cloned. Genes specifying proteins used in simpler fashion, such as cell surface receptors, can be cloned according to function after expression in a recipient cell.

Discovering proteins by these and other means following essentially genetic schemes can provide powerful shortcuts while at the same time allowing some level of insight into function (as defined by the phenotype of the mutation), but such approaches can never, as a matter of first principles, reveal a molecular mechanism. This is because genetics, by its very nature, describes biological systems in the language of information flow. When we demand a molecular mechanism, however, we expect an answer in the language of chemistry, an answer that can only be obtained through studies that employ that language—experiments employing the protein molecules themselves in a chemically tractable system. So, even when proteins are first discovered through genetic means (the "molecular" of "molecular mechanism"), it is still necessary to express and purify them and then to study these proteins in cell-free systems.

Many proteins are now being discovered without any prior knowledge of their function, as would naturally follow from isolation according to a functional cell-free assay or according to a well-defined phenotype. This is due to the ease of cloning and sequencing DNA as well as profound simplifications and improvements in methodology for analyzing proteins. It is probably the case that most new proteins are now described according to structural criteria alone, sometimes accompanied by a correlation in space or time (guilt by association) with a biological process of interest. A few years ago it would have seemed hopeless to then go on to discover the molecular mechanism by which such a protein acts, with no assay and no chemical insight, but with the now impressive database of proteins and modular domains of known function an approach is possible, and although this is still hit-or-miss, it works often enough to be respectable. For this we can thank both the generations of biochemists who discovered a large number of proteins according to their function to construct the database of functional units and the law of evolution that assures that new proteins are assembled by variation and linear recombination of old proteins and domains. But an homology with a functional unit in the database can be no more than suggestive, and so even the structure/correlation-based discovery scheme requires expression, purification, and assay of the protein in question to confirm the ascribed function and move to molecular mechanism.

In light of the above analysis of the history and trends in discovery of molecular mechanisms in biology, it should be clear that the purification and characterization of proteins has and will always play an essential role. It must be admitted that protein purification is more of an art than the cloning and manipulation of DNA, for although DNA has a standard physical chemistry despite extraordinary diversity of sequence (hence its unique suitability as genetic material), each protein has its own physical chemistry as dictated by its sequence (hence the use of protein to carry out most biological functions). Although it is these differences in physical properties among proteins that allow their purification, it also means that a new methodology needs to be developed for each protein to be purified.

Fortunately, despite this inherent difficulty, many methods are now available, and strategy is indeed possible in protein purification. As this manual emphasizes, the key first step in any protein purification is establishing the assay to be used throughout. This is strategically the most important decision to be made because the assay is always honest: You will purify whatever *can* give a signal in the assay. That is, you will not necessarily purify what you intend to purify unless your assay is as clear-cut as your concept is (hopefully) pure. The next most important aspect of strategy is to take advantage of what you already known about the protein in designing the purification, avoiding redundancy among purification steps. Here what is needed is a little clever common sense, and this manual provides many nice illustrations of how to think about the various distinct "handles" each protein provides in its unique set of physical properties (size, charge, hydrophobicity, ligand affinity, etc.). Finally, a key element is to maintain the mentality of an accountant. A quantitative approach in which every unit of activity is accounted for will be richly rewarded in the purest protein in the highest yield, for in the end protein purification is a numbers game, seeking to maximize both specific activity and yield.

This book succeeds admirably and perhaps uniquely as a manual to teach the strategy and execution of protein purification by actually doing it, as it is best learned. Thus, various chromatographic and other fractionation methods are taught in the context of specific examples, with enough general comments to allow application to other problems, which no doubt will be most users' goals. The book is extensively cross-indexed so that readers can find their way to specific methods quickly.

It is entirely fitting that this manual should be dedicated to Professor John T. Edsall, a great biochemist who has singularly influenced the course of protein work, and I join with the authors in saluting him. In addition, it should be said that the biomedical community owes a great debt to the authors for making available this excellent manual that no doubt will have a major impact in making protein purification and characterization more accessible to many researchers, and in so doing extend the traditions that Professor Edsall has been so pivotal in developing.

James E. Rothman
Vice Chairman, Sloan-Kettering Institute, and
Chairman, Cellular Biochemistry and Biophysics Program
Memorial Sloan-Kettering Cancer Center

Strategies for Protein Purification and Characterization

Introduction

The magnitude of the challenge of protein purification becomes more clear when one considers the mixture of macromolecules present in a cell extract. In addition to the protein of interest, several thousand other proteins with different properties are present in the extract, along with nucleic acids (DNA and RNA), polysaccharides, lipids, and small molecules. The proteins present in the bacterium *Escherichia coli* may be dramatically visualized after resolution by two-dimensional gel electrophoresis as shown in Figure 1. A given protein may be present at more than 10% or at less than 0.001% of the total protein in the cell. The challenge, therefore, is to separate the protein of interest from all of the other components in the cell, especially the unwanted contaminating proteins, with reasonable efficiency, speed, yield, and purity, while retaining the biological activity and chemical integrity of the polypeptide.

PROTEIN PROPERTIES THAT CAN BE USED AS HANDLES FOR PURIFICATION

The reason one is able to purify one protein from a mixture of thousands of proteins is that proteins vary tremendously in a number of their physical and chemical properties (Burgess 1987). These properties are the result of proteins having different numbers and sequences of amino acids. The amino acid residues attached to the polypeptide backbone may be positively or negatively charged, neutral and polar, or neutral and hydrophobic. In addition, the polypeptide is folded in a very definite secondary structure (α helices, β sheets, and various turns) and tertiary structure to create a unique size, shape, and distribution of residues on the surface of the protein.

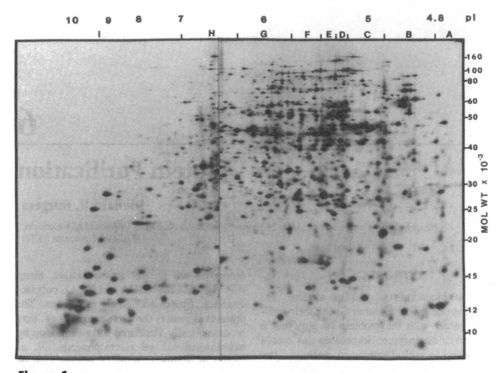

Figure 1
E. coli proteins resolved on a two-dimensional gel. The approximate isoelectric point and molecular weight scales are indicated. *E. coli* K12 strain
W3110 was labeled with $^{35}SO_4$ during growth in glucose minimal medium at
37°C. A composite autoradiogram was made from nonequilibrium (*left side*)
and pH 5–7 (*right side*) isoelectric focusing gels. (Adapted, with permission,
from Neidhardt and Phillips 1985.)

By exploiting the differences in properties between the protein of interest and other proteins in the mixture, one can design a rational
series of fractionation steps. These properties include:

Size.   Proteins may vary in size from peptides of a few amino acids
(with molecular weights of a few hundred) to very large proteins containing over 10,000 amino acids (with molecular weights of over
1,000,000). Most proteins have molecular weights in the range
10,000–150,000 (see Fig. 1). Proteins that are part of multisubunit
complexes may reach much larger sizes.

Shape.   Protein shapes range from approximately spherical (globular)
to quite asymmetric. The movement of a protein through a solution
during centrifugation or through small pores in membranes, beads
during gel filtration, or gels during electrophoresis is influenced by its
shape. For example, consider two monomeric proteins of the same

mass where one is spherical and the other cigar-shaped. During centrifugation through a glycerol gradient, the spherical protein will have a smaller effective radius (Stokes' radius) and thus will encounter less friction as it sediments through the solution. It will sediment faster and thus appear to be larger than the cigar-shaped protein. On the other hand, during size exclusion chromatography, the same spherical protein with its smaller Stokes' radius will more readily diffuse into the pores of a gel filtration bead and will elute later, thus appearing smaller than the cigar-shaped protein.

Charge. The net charge of a protein is determined by the sum of the positively and negatively charged amino acid residues. If a protein has a preponderance of aspartic and glutamic acid residues, it has a net negative charge at pH 7.0 and is termed an acidic protein. If it has a preponderance of lysine and arginine residues, it is considered to be a basic protein. The equilibrium between charged and uncharged groups and hence the charge of a protein is determined by the pH of the solution. The charge of the ionizable groups found on unmodified proteins as a function of pH is shown below in Table 1.

Isoelectric point. The isoelectric point (pI) is the pH at which the charge on a protein is zero and is determined by the number and titration curves of the positively and negatively charged amino acid residues on the protein. Protein pI values generally range from 4.0 to 10.0 (Fig. 1). An example of a theoretical titration curve and pI determination of *E. coli* RNA polymerase transcription factor, sigma-32 (σ^{32}) (see Unit III), is shown in Figure 2.

Charge distribution. The charged amino acid residues may be distributed uniformly on the surface of the protein or they may be clustered

Table 1 Charge of the Ionizable Groups Found on Unmodified Proteins as a Function of pH

Ionizable Group	pKa	pH2 <-------- pH7 --------> pH12
C-terminal (COOH)	4.0	0 0 0 0 0 − − − − − − − − − − − − − − − − − − −
Aspartate (COOH)	4.5	0 0 0 0 0 0 − − − − − − − − − − − − − − − − − −
Glutamate (COOH)	4.6	0 0 0 0 0 0 − − − − − − − − − − − − − − − − − −
Histidine (imidazole)	6.2	+ + + + + + + + + 0 0 0 0 0 0 0 0 0 0 0 0
N-terminal (amino)	7.3	+ + + + + + + + + + + 0 0 0 0 0 0 0 0 0 0
Cysteine (SH)	9.3	0 0 0 0 0 0 0 0 0 0 0 0 0 0 0 0 − − − − − − −
Tyrosine (phenol)	10.1	0 0 0 0 0 0 0 0 0 0 0 0 0 0 0 0 0 0 − − − − −
Lysine (amino)	10.4	+ + + + + + + + + + + + + + + + + + 0 0 0 0
Arginine (guanido)	12.0	+ 0

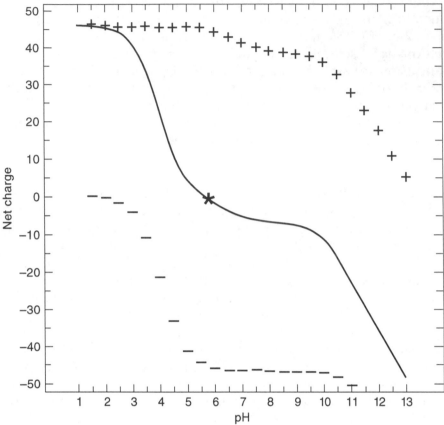

Figure 2
Titration curve and isoelectric point (pI) of *E. coli* σ^{32}. This graph shows theoretical plots of the number of positively charged and negatively charged groups and the net charge as a function of pH for the *E. coli* RNA polymerase transcription factor σ^{32}, based on its amino acid sequence. The pI is indicated by the asterisk and is 5.78. The charged groups are Arg (23), Lys (16), His (6), Tyr (7), Glu (22), and Asp (23). This plot was generated using the Genetics Computer Group Sequence Analysis Software package.

such that one region is highly positive while another region is highly negative. Such nonrandom charge distribution can be used to discriminate between proteins. An example is the *E. coli* σ^{32} protein, whose purification is described in Unit III of this manual. At pH 7.9, σ^{32} has a negative charge of −46 and a positive charge of +40, giving a net charge of −6. It is able to bind reasonably tightly to both anion- and cation-exchange columns, apparently because its charged residues are not evenly distributed on the surface. This property can be used to purify this protein because most proteins will not bind to both types of ion-exchange columns under a single solvent condition.

In contrast, calmodulin (see Unit I) is highly acidic and will only bind to cation-exchange resins under very extreme conditions of pH (e.g., pH 2).

Hydrophobicity. Most hydrophobic amino acid residues are buried on the inside of a protein, but some are found on the surface. The number and spatial distribution of hydrophobic amino acid residues present on the surface of the protein determine the ability of the protein to bind to hydrophobic column materials and therefore can be exploited in fractionation.

Solubility. Proteins vary dramatically in their solubility in different solvents, all the way from being essentially insoluble (<10 µg/ml) to being very soluble (>300 mg/ml). Key variables that affect the solubility of a protein include pH, ionic strength, nature of the ions, temperature, and the polarity of the solvent. Proteins are generally less soluble at their isoelectric point (see Unit I).

Density. The density of most proteins is between 1.3 and 1.4 g/cm^3 and this is not generally a useful property for fractionating proteins. However, proteins containing large amounts of phosphate (e.g., phosvitin, density = 1.8) or lipid moieties (e.g., β-lipoprotein, density = 1.03) are substantially different in density compared with the average protein and may be separated from the bulk of proteins using density gradient methods.

Ligand binding. Many enzymes bind substrates, effector molecules, cofactors, or DNA templates quite tightly. This binding affinity can be used to bind an enzyme to a column to which the appropriate ligand or template has been immobilized. For example, in Unit II the transcription factor AP-1 is purified by binding to a specific DNA affinity column.

Metal binding. Many enzymes bind certain metal ions (e.g., Cu^{++}, Zn^{++}, Ca^{++}, Co^{++}, and Ni^{++}) quite tightly, usually through interactions with cysteine or histidine residues. This binding can be used to bind an enzyme to a column to which the appropriate chelated metal ion has been immobilized (Porath 1992).

Reversible association. Under certain solution conditions, some enzymes aggregate to form dimers, tetramers, etc. For example, the ability of *E. coli* RNA polymerase to be a dimer under one condition (0.05 M NaCl) and a monomer under another condition (0.3 M NaCl) can be used if two fractionations based on size are carried out sequentially under those two different conditions (Burgess 1969).

Posttranslational modifications. After protein synthesis, many proteins are modified by the addition of carbohydrates, acyl groups, phosphate groups, or a variety of other moieties. In many cases, these modifications provide handles that can be used in fractionation. For example, proteins containing carbohydrates on their surface can often be bound to columns containing lectins, which are molecules capable of binding tightly to certain carbohydrate moieties (see Unit IV). Phosphoproteins will in some cases bind to a chelated Fe^{++} column (Porath 1992).

Specific sequence or structure. The precise geometric presentation of amino acid residues on the surface of a protein can be used as the basis of a separation procedure. For example, an antibody that recognizes only a particular site (epitope) on a protein can usually be obtained. An immunoaffinity column can be prepared by attaching a monospecific antibody (which binds only to the protein of interest) to a resin. Immunoaffinity chromatography can result in highly selective separation and provides a very effective purification step (see Unit III).

Unusual properties. In addition to the types of properties mentioned above, certain proteins have unusual properties that can be exploited during their purification. An example is unusual thermostability. Most proteins unfold and coagulate or precipitate when heated to 95ºC. A protein that remains soluble and active after such heat treatment can be separated easily from the bulk of the other cellular proteins. Another such property is unusual resistance to proteases. These two properties often go hand in hand. An interesting example of a purification involving these properties is that of *E. coli* alkaline phosphatase. The cellular extract is heated and the insoluble coagulated proteins are removed by centrifugation. The supernatant that contains the phosphatase is then treated with a protease, which digests the remaining contaminating proteins, leaving an essentially pure preparation of alkaline phosphatase.

Genetically engineered purification handles. With the advent of genetic engineering, it has become relatively easy to clone the cDNA encoding a given protein. It is then possible to construct an overproducing strain of *E. coli* that can be induced to produce large amounts of a desired gene product (see Unit III). Recently, it has become common to alter the cDNA in such a way as to add an extra few amino acids on the amino terminus or the carboxyl terminus of the protein being expressed. This added "tag" can be used as an effective purification handle (Ford 1991). One of the most popular tags is to add 6–10 histidines onto the amino terminus of a protein. One then purifies the protein by its ability to bind tightly to a column containing chelated Ni^{++} where it can be washed and then eluted with free imidazole or by lowering the pH to 5.9 where histidine becomes fully protonated and no longer binds to Ni^{++}.

TYPES OF MOLECULAR INTERACTIONS AND VARIABLES THAT AFFECT THEM

In thinking about protein structure and stability and the interaction between an individual protein and other proteins, DNA, or materials used in protein purification, one must understand the molecular forces involved and how the strength of these forces varies as one varies conditions such as temperature, pH, and ionic strength of a solution. The atomic interactions that seem to be the most important with regard to protein interactions are hydrogen bonds, hydrophobic interactions, and ionic interactions. These are described briefly below. For a more detailed discussion, see Creighton (1993).

Hydrogen bonds. Hydrogen bonds (Fig. 3) occur when a proton is shared between a proton donor (–NH and –OH) and a proton acceptor (O = C– and :N–). Optimal hydrogen bonds have a linear geometry and a distance between the donor and acceptor atoms of between 2.6 and 3.1 Å. Hydrogen bonds are stronger at low temperature and are weakened as the temperature is raised.

Hydrophobic interactions. Nonpolar residues (isoleucine, leucine, valine, phenylalanine, and tryptophan) cannot make favorable hydrogen bonds with water. In order to avoid water, they tend to come together in a so-called hydrophobic interaction (see Fig. 4) usually resulting in their being buried in the interior of a protein. Hydrophobic interactions are strengthened at high salt and high temperature.

Ionic interactions. Ionic interactions (see Fig. 5) occur between charged molecules, with like charges repelling and opposite charges attracting. The force of the electrostatic interaction is given by an approximation

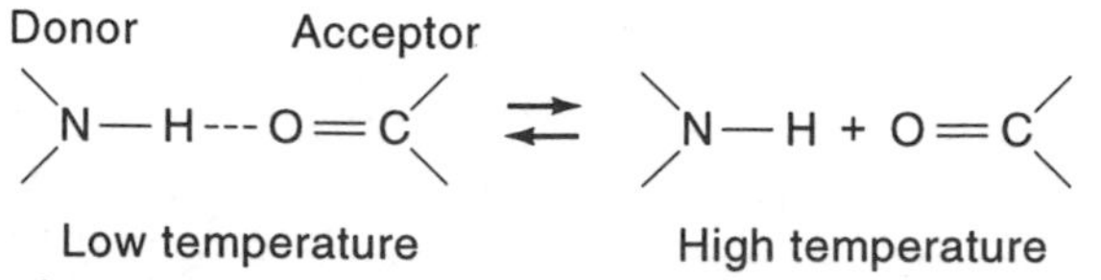

Donor   Acceptor

Low temperature   High temperature

Figure 3
Hydrogen bonds.

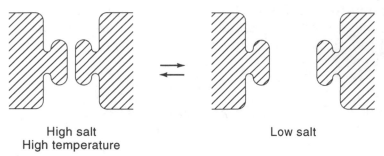

High salt
High temperature   Low salt

Figure 4
Hydrophobic interactions.

of Coulomb's law $E = Z_A Z_B e^2 / D r_{AB}$, where r_{AB} is the distance between two charges, A and B, Z_A and Z_B are their respective number of unit charges, e is one unit of electronic charge, and D is the dielectric constant of the solvent. The strength of ionic interactions is therefore inversely proportional to the distance between the charges and the dielectric constant of the solvent, which varies from 2 in nonpolar solvents to 80 in highly polar solvents such as water. Ionic interactions are weakened as the ionic strength of the solvent increases and the charge is shielded by counterions. Ionic interactions are affected by the pH of the solution, since pH determines the number of charged residues.

TYPES OF SEPARATION METHODS

There are a large number of separation processes that can be utilized to fractionate proteins based on the properties listed above. These are summarized in Table 2. The sequential use of several of these separation processes will allow the progressive purification of almost any

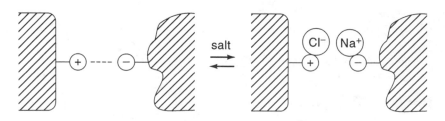

Low ionic strength   High ionic strength

Figure 5
Ionic interactions.

Table 2 Separation Processes That Can Be Utilized to Fractionate Proteins

Separation Process	Basis of Separation
Precipitation	
ammonium sulfate	solubility
acetone	solubility
polyethyleneimine	charge, size
isoelectric	solubility, pI
Phase partitioning (e.g., with polyethylene glycol)	solubility
Chromatography	
ion-exchange	charge, charge distribution
hydrophobic interaction	hydrophobicity
reverse-phase HPLC	hydrophobicity, size
affinity	ligand-binding site
DNA affinity	DNA-binding site
lectin affinity	carbohydrate content and type
immobilized metal affinity	metal binding
immunoaffinity	specific antigenic site
chromatofocusing	pI
gel filtration	size, shape
Electrophoresis	
gel electrophoresis	charge, size, shape
isoelectric focusing	pI
Centrifugation	size, shape, density
Ultrafiltration	size, shape

protein. If the processes are chosen carefully and if proper attention is paid to separation conditions and to maintaining the stability of the protein, the purification will result in reasonable efficiency, speed, yield, and purity while retaining the biological activity and chemical integrity of the polypeptide.

Many of the above separation processes are described in detail in the Units of this manual. The explanations, notes, and comments accompanying each unit are intended to help the reader learn how to use these separation processes judiciously and effectively. Good luck and happy purification!

REFERENCES

Note: For additional literature on protein purification, see Appendix 9.

Burgess, R.R. 1969. A new method for the large scale purification of *E. coli* DNA-dependent RNA polymerase. *J. Biol. Chem.* **244:** 6160–6167.

————. 1987. Protein purification. In *Protein engineering* (ed. D. Oxender and C.F. Fox), pp. 71–82. A.R. Liss, New York.

Creighton, T.E. 1993. *Proteins: Structures and molecular properties*, 2nd edition. W.H. Freeman, San Francisco.

Ford, C.F., I. Suominen, and C.E. Glatz. 1991. Fusion tails for the recovery and purification of recombinant proteins. *Protein Expr. Purif.* **2:** 95–107.

Neidhardt, F.C. and T.A. Phillips. 1985. The protein catalog of *E. coli*. In *Two-dimensional gel electrophoresis of proteins* (ed. J.E. Celis and R. Bravo), pp. 417–444. Academic Press, New York.

Porath, J. 1992. Immobilized metal ion affinity chromatography. *Protein Expr. Purif.* **3:** 206–281.

How to Use This Manual

Proteins are complex macromolecules. Because they are made up of 20 different encoded amino acids, plus the modified amino acids, proteins are chemically much more diverse than nucleic acids. This fact makes every new protein a challenge to scientists employing purification and characterization methods. It would take hundreds of volumes to document all known procedures for protein analysis, and to a large extent, such a series already exists in *Methods in Enzymology*. In addition, there are a number of books already published that attempt to document fundamental procedures of protein purification in general terms. Our approach is to teach protein purification and characterization in the way that most of us who are practitioners learned our trade. We learned by purifying proteins in the laboratory, and after multiple attempts at a wide variety of proteins, some guiding principles were extracted.

This manual can be used in at least three ways. First, it can be used as a programmed study guide to protein purification methods. The four examples shown in the manual have been carefully selected so that together they cover most of the major sources of protein and types of bulk fractionation methods, chromatography procedures, and other techniques. The proteins purified are: a soluble protein from an animal tissue, a recombinant protein overproduced in bacteria, a protein from cultured human cells, and a plasma membrane-bound receptor molecule. There is a minimum of overlap in the bulk fractionation methods employed and the columns used for separations. By systematically performing most or all of the experiments in each unit, you should obtain a useful survey of the major techniques in the field. No one should expect to learn exactly how to purify the protein in which he or she is interested. However, after performing the experiments in all four units, most students have reported that they are no longer afraid to attack a protein purification problem. It is for just this reason that we have tried to emphasize the strategies of purification, since none of the protocols in this manual will isolate anything except the particular protein indicated in the example.

Second, the manual can be used as a reference for the techniques employed in each unit. For example, if you want to learn how to perform ion-exchange chromatography, but do not want to go through the entire calmodulin preparation, you can go directly to that technique using either the Table of Contents or the Techniques or Subject Index. If you use the manual as a reference, it is recommended that you take a few minutes to read some of the accompanying information in the unit. Sometimes the context in which a column method is utilized is as important as the method itself. There are also very useful general procedures in the Appendices. These are methods used in all of the units, such as how to measure pH and conductivity or how to perform polyacrylamide gel electrophoresis.

Third, each unit is self-contained, so an entire set of protocols can be studied without performing the experiments in all four units. This strategy might be very helpful if your specific problem involves a particular class of protein. For example, if you are trying to isolate a new membrane-bound receptor molecule, you might choose to study only the unit on the insulin receptor. Likewise, if you are attempting the purification of a new transcription factor, the section on AP-1 is most appropriate. However, there are lots of useful tips in each of the units, so any one unit alone is not sufficient to cover all of the methods that might be useful.

We hope the protein purification schemes, specific techniques, and practical tips discussed here will serve to guide you toward successful protein purification.

UNIT I

Purification of Calmodulin

The goal of this unit is to introduce you to the purification and characterization of milligram amounts of a protein from an animal tissue. You will purify and characterize calmodulin, a small calcium-binding protein that is ubiquitous among eukaryotic organisms (Klee et al. 1980; Means et al. 1982; Forsén et al. 1986; Means 1988). This is interesting and instructive in itself because calmodulin plays a central role in cellular calcium metabolism, which interacts with other signal transduction mechanisms. However, the intended objective is to show an example of a protein that is soluble in dilute aqueous media and is relatively easy to purify in large amounts.

You will learn basic purification techniques, which one might refer to as classical methods because they have been in use for several decades. The purification procedure employs two classes of methods for protein isolation, bulk fractionation and low-pressure chromatography. The bulk fractionation section consists of ammonium sulfate and isoelectric point precipitation methods, and the chromatography section consists of ion-exchange and hydrophobic interaction procedures. These procedures are, in general, some of the most useful bulk precipitation and column chromatography methods available, without resorting to affinity-based techniques. A flowchart that illustrates the purification strategies employed in this unit is shown in Figure 1.

Following the purification of calmodulin, you will be introduced to techniques for the basic characterization of proteins that are available in at least microgram quantities. During the characterization, you will analyze the structure and function of the protein using a variety of quantitative and qualitative methods. Function will be examined using enzyme assays and calcium ion binding as examples of biological activity. At the end, you will assemble a purification table

13

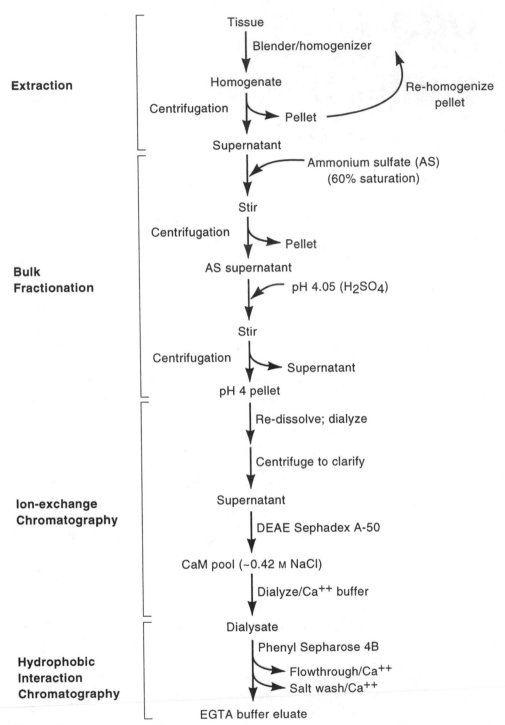

Figure 1
Flowchart for the purification of calmodulin.

that shows the quantitative recovery of the protein from the tissue, including the fold purification and specific activity. The structure of the purified calmodulin will be addressed by electrophoretic methods as well as by proteolytic digestion and analysis of the peptide products. Physical and chemical analysis of the fragments of calmodulin can be evaluated by mass spectrometry and protein sequencing when facilities are available for these procedures. This will allow you to verify that the protein isolated is the 148-residue polypeptide (Watterson et al. 1980) called calmodulin. There are a few surprising post-translational modifications and unusual occurrences that are interesting problems in structural analysis, as well as several extra experiments that will fascinate you.

Overall, you should come away understanding the principles of purification using nonaffinity chromatography methods and the principles of characterization for relatively abundant proteins. This unit is therefore a good place to start if you have had little or no exposure to the methods of protein purification and characterization.

OVERVIEW OF CALMODULIN

Calmodulin is a small protein consisting of 148 amino acids in a single polypeptide chain (Watterson et al. 1976, 1980). The protein has a highly acidic isoelectric point (pI = 4.05) and contains no tryptophan or cysteine residues. Calmodulin has been found in all eukaryotic cells examined (Van Eldik et al. 1982) and it has a very highly conserved primary structure. For example, the amino acid sequence of the spinach leaf and human brain calmodulin are identical in all but 13 amino acids. This degree of conservation of structure has led to the conclusion among evolutionary biologists that most of the structural motifs in calmodulin became fixed very early in the emergence of eukaryotes, and selective pressures have maintained the amino acid sequence intact for millions of years (Kretsinger 1980; Van Eldik et al. 1982). Calmodulin is a member of the family of calcium-modulated proteins that bind calcium ions reversibly under physiological conditions of ionic strength and pH. The protein was identified as a calcium-dependent activator of cyclic nucleotide phosphodiesterase (Kakiuchi and Yamazaki 1970; Cheung 1971), and later of several protein kinases, phosphatases, and ATPases. It was purified and characterized as a troponin-C-like protein from nonmuscle tissue (Watterson et al. 1976). Overall, calmodulin is a calcium-dependent regulator of a variety of enzymes and transduces the signals that produce transient fluxes in intracellular calcium ion concentrations. Calmodulin is central to cell physiology and to the action of hormones, neurotransmitters, and growth factors.

History of Calmodulin

The history of the discovery and characterization of calmodulin is an interesting lesson in the convergence of ideas in the history of biology. Several excellent reviews of calmodulin have been published (Klee et al. 1980; Means et al. 1982; Means 1988), so in this section the history of calmodulin will be summarized only as an anecdotal account. Three lines of research in biochemical physiology all approached the concept of calmodulin over a period of about 15 years, from 1962 to 1977. During the early 1960s, the idea of a calcium-dependent regulator of muscle contraction was established, particularly from the work of Ebashi and coworkers (Ebashi et al. 1969), who characterized the troponin complex of striated muscle. Troponin (Tn) consists of three subunits, Tn-T, Tn-I, and Tn-C, of which Tn-C is the calcium-binding component. Troponin is not an enzyme by itself, but it confers calcium ion dependence on the actomyosin ATPase of skeletal and cardiac muscle, so that muscle contraction is coupled to calcium ion release from the sarcoplasmic reticulum upon stimulation of the neuromuscular junction (Collins et al. 1977). This was championed as a clear system that employed calcium ions as a second messenger. In this way, Tn-C represented a model of stimulus-response coupling in muscle tissue, a concept later extended to other, non-muscle tissues (Tan et al. 1992). Among the other models of such coupling was stimulus-secretion coupling in neuronal, neuroendocrine, and endocrine tissues.

During the late 1960s and early 1970s, the coupling of hormonal signals to metabolic pathways had attracted the attention of researchers interested in calcium ions. Glycogen metabolism had been studied for many years by the Cori's in St. Louis, and various of their scientific progeny (for a review, see Flockhart and Corbin 1982). It was clear that adrenergic hormone coupling to glycogenolysis was mediated by cyclic adenosine 3'-5' monophosphate (cAMP) via stimulation of a cascade of activating protein kinases. The study of insulin action was clouded, however, by various research suggesting the action of cyclic nucleotides or calcium ions as mediators of responses involving multiple phosphorylation events. Thus, in those days, before signal transduction was acknowledged as a general biochemical principle, debates ensued about the roles of cAMP and calcium ions and which was the second messenger of greatest import in hormonal stimulation of tissues. This field was further complicated by two research groups, those of Cheung (1971) and Kakiuchi (Kakiuchi and Yamazaki 1970), who were studying the cyclic nucleotide phosphodiesterase family of enzymes, which catalyze the hydrolysis of cAMP. One of the relatively minor isoforms of phosphodiesterase found in mammalian brain tissue showed a calcium ion dependence to its activity, and a heat-stable, low-molecular-weight, proteinaceous material was described as the element that conferred the calcium ion dependence to this enzyme. This was virtual heresy in the field of hormone research, because it suggested that calcium ion and cyclic nucleotide pathways were intertwined. Most investigators in the field dismissed the results as relatively insignificant compared to the central second messenger pathways, involving either calcium ions (as in muscle contraction) or cAMP (as in glycogen metabolism).

During this period of polarization in the second messenger field, studies of the protein biochemistry of muscle continued in earnest. Muscle tissue was found to be the source of another calcium-binding protein, parvalbumin, first isolated from carp muscle. R.H. Kretsinger crystallized parvalbumin and solved the three-dimensional structure of the protein by X-ray diffraction (for a review, see Kretsinger 1980). In addition, he identified the calcium-binding moieties of the protein as consisting of a helix-loop-helix motif, in which the helices were amphipathic in nature, harboring one surface of hydrophobic amino acids and one of hydrophilic residues. The calcium-binding ligands arose from the loop region, and the ligand field consisted of oxygen-containing moieties arranged in an octahedral fashion. Using one of these units as a model, Kretsinger described the "E-F hand" structure based on the E and F helices of the third calcium-binding domain of carp parvalbumin (Kretsinger 1980). As the structures of other calcium-binding proteins emerged, it became clear that E-F hands were the structures of choice for intracellular proteins that bound calcium ions reversibly under physiological conditions. This also prompted investigators to search for analogs of muscle proteins in nonmuscle tissues. The quest for such muscle proteins ultimately led to the crucial description of the major elements of the cytoskeleton, including the microfilaments containing actin fibers. It was logical, at least in hindsight, that other muscle proteins might have homologs in nonmuscle tissues, such as brain.

Into this morass of knowledge wandered the members of a protein biochemistry laboratory at Duke University, headed by T.C. Vanaman. Together with postdoctoral fellow D.M. Watterson and others, Vanaman made a significant leap forward in the understanding of signal-response coupling by calcium ions in tissues other than striated muscle. As part of the laboratory of R.L. Hill, Vanaman had previously characterized the acyl carrier protein from *E. coli* (Vanaman et al. 1968a,b). That small, acidic protein was one of the first examples of a protein that was neither an enzyme nor a structural element, but served an essential regulatory component of the fatty acid biosynthetic apparatus. Vanaman set out to characterize other small acidic proteins that might act as regulators also. He was attracted by the S100 protein fraction that had been described by

B.W. Moore in St. Louis as an apparently brain-specific, acidic protein fraction (Moore 1965). By employing the then novel technique of polyacrylamide gel electrophoresis in sodium dodecyl sulfate (Laemmli 1970), Vanaman identified a component of the S100 protein fraction that migrated more slowly than the rest and was found in other tissues besides brain. In fact, Watterson and Vanaman recognized that this "post-S100" protein was similar in size and amino acid composition to Tn-C. Therefore, they purified and characterized this Tn-C-like protein from bovine brain, with the notion that it was a calcium-binding protein and possibly an enzyme regulator.

Upon searching the literature, the similarity of the Tn-C-like protein from brain to the partially purified protein of Kakiuchi and Cheung was recognized. The results of testing this hypothesis became the basis of the landmark paper in 1976, which linked the Tn-C-like protein from nonmuscle tissue to the calcium-dependent activators of cyclic nucleotide phosphodiesterase (Watterson et al. 1976). This concept brought together the idea that calcium and cyclic nucleotides might work in concert to transmit cellular signals and the idea that a Tn-C-like protein in nonmuscle tissue might mediate stimulus-response coupling. This union was reinforced by Vanaman's later observation, while visiting the laboratory of P. Cohen in Scotland, that this same Tn-C-like, calcium-binding protein served as the integral δ subunit of phosphorylase b kinase, the hallmark enzyme of cyclic nucleotide-regulated glycogen metabolism (Cohen et al. 1978). Thus it was that the calcium and cyclic nucleotide factions in hormone regulation were united, shortly to be inundated with other signal transduction pathways, involving phospholipases, protein kinase C, inositol phosphates, tyrosine phosphorylation, and guanyl nucleotides.

Structure and Function

In 1979, Cheung proposed that the name of the Tn-C-like protein that acted as a calcium-dependent activator of cyclic nucleotide phosphodiesterase be changed to calmodulin, to emphasize the activity of the protein as a calcium-dependent modulator (for a review, see Klee et al. 1980). The primary structure of calmodulin was determined by Watterson, Vanaman, and their colleagues (Watterson et al. 1980). The modifications and amidation states of the protein were subjects of discussion between 1980 and 1985 (Sasagawa et al. 1982). The protein has four E-F hand units, arranged in two pairs, and a bridging sequence central to the molecule. The three-dimensional structure, first determined in 1988 (Babu et al. 1988), revealed that the two pairs of E-F hands were connected by a central α-helix. The protein therefore appeared to adopt a shape similar to a dumbbell, with two domains at either end of the helix (Strynadka and James 1989). Upon calcium binding, the molecule undergoes dramatic changes in conformation, which presumably lead to the allosteric effect on target enzymes. The exact nature of the conformational change is still debated. It may reflect a single bend in the central helix, arising from the alteration of the phi-psi angles of one peptide bond, or it may result from a more complex flexibility arising from an accordion-like expansion and flexing of the helix. The dynamic nature of the conformational change continues to be a subject of research.

Regardless of the exact geometry of the conformational change, calcium binding does result in the activation of a variety of target enzymes by calmodulin. In some cases, particularly for the calcium/calmodulin kinase II, it appears that calcium ions and calmodulin form a complex first, followed by the association of the complex with the target enzyme (Kennedy and Greengard 1981). This appears to be most prominent in the postsynaptic density of neuronal junctions. In many other cases, however, calmodulin is already bound to the target enzyme as an integral subunit (Van Eldik et al. 1982; Shoemaker et al. 1990). Calcium ions bind to calmodulin and induce an activation without an intermediate calmodulin-binding step. Such responses can be very rapid, as they do not require the diffusion of macromolecules, but only of ions. In the following purification and characterization experiments, we will use the calcium-dependent activation of an enzyme as an assay for calmodulin, as well as calcium-dependent changes in electrophoretic mobility (Burgess et al. 1980). Calmodulin also has the property of binding to various heterocyclic and aromatic compounds in the presence of calcium ions (Levin and Weiss 1979; Marshak et al. 1981). Some of these compounds, such as the phenothiazines and naphthalene sulfonamides, can be used as inhibitors of calmodulin-dependent activities. We will also utilize the calcium-dependence of this interaction with aromatic compounds to assist in the purification.

Purification Strategy

In this unit and throughout the manual, we will emphasize that an efficient purification of a protein should take advantage of the physical/chemical characteristics of the protein that distinguish it from others in the source material. In the case of calmodulin, the purification utilizes classical methods because the protein is freely soluble in neutral, dilute aqueous solutions. Besides its high solubility, calmodulin also has distinctive properties of small size, net negative charge, and calcium-dependent hydrophobic behavior. The strategy of purification takes advantage of each of these properties in three very efficient steps. The strategy for the purification of calmodulin that is given in this unit is the product of many years of refinement. For example, it was typical practice to take advantage of calmodulin's size by using gel filtration for separating the many larger, contaminating proteins. This required a day or two of work with a large (typically 10 x 200 cm) Sephadex column at low flow rates for high resolution. However, the development of hydrophobic interaction chromatography for calmodulin obviated the need for that step. In the beginning, the purification of a hitherto unknown protein is always less than ideal. No protocol can be developed without systematic refinement of each step. In fact, it is not always necessary to optimize a purification, particularly if the protein is not to be used as a reagent. However, if one aspires to characterize the structure and function of the protein, developing a rapid and simple purification strategy is essential.

INTRODUCTION TO ANALYTICAL METHODS

During the course of this unit, you will find several sets of experiments that concern the characterization of calmodulin. Some of these should be performed in conjunction with the purification protocol, particularly the enzyme activator assays and polyacrylamide gel electrophoresis procedures. Other characterization methods may be performed at any time on previously purified calmodulin. The primary structural analysis of the protein is addressed by the long-standing, traditional methods of proteolytic or chemical cleavage, followed by separation of the fragments by reverse-phase, high-performance liquid chromatography (HPLC). The peptide fragments are analyzed by methods that are dependent upon the availability of automated instruments, including a protein sequencer, amino acid analyzer, and mass spectrometer. This portion of the unit provides information only on the basic principles and interpretation of the methods, and does not cover operation of instruments, as these vary considerably and change continuously. Most instrument manufacturers offer training courses on the operation of their machines. Many other kinds of analyses of calmodulin are possible, including spectroscopy of many sorts. These are not covered in any detail, but ultraviolet absorption spectroscopy is discussed because it is usually available in laboratories and, in the case of calmodulin, is quite revealing.

Activity Assays

The most important part of the protein purification is the assay. The assay is the measurement that defines the entity that you will purify.

If there are two proteins with the same activity, you may find two different proteins in the product. Your assay must be rapid and simple. If the assay is, for instance, to inject a sample into an animal and wait six months to see if the animal develops a disease, it is unlikely that you will find it easy to isolate the protein with that activity. In general, an assay should take a few minutes to a few hours. Since proteins are subject to unwanted modifications, such as proteolysis, oxidation, dehydration, alkylation, and denaturation, the faster the procedure, the less likely are irreversible, artifactual modifications. The assay should be rather simple, so that artifactual results do not cloud the analysis. For example, if the assay requires modifications to the protein, such as chemical derivatization, adsorption to a surface, heat treatment, or an unusual pH, then there could be effects on protein structure that account for an anomalous activity. The assay should be specific. If there are many different ways to obtain a positive result, the significance of the purification is in question. Finally, the assay must be quantitative. It is essential to establish beyond any doubt that the protein purified accounts quantitatively for the activity. This is essentially the fundamental and age-old problem of biochemistry: How does one establish that a particular molecule is the active species? The answer to that question is the ultimate justification for purification of a protein to homogeneity. Incidentally, genetics and molecular biology are also important to the proof of activity.

One of the difficulties with the purification of calmodulin compared to the isolation of an enzyme concerns the assay. The assay for calmodulin is the calcium-dependent activation of an enzymatic activity, rather than an intrinsic activity. Thus, one can be misled by false positive results if fractions are contaminated with compounds that change the free calcium ion concentration in the sample. False positives can also be observed if fractions contain endogenous enzymatic activity that mimics the enzyme of interest. One could imagine that calcium ion-binding could be used as an assay, but there are now many known calcium-binding proteins, so that would not be a particularly specific assay. These considerations are becoming even more important in modern biology, since many proteins have binding activities and activation or inhibition functions for target enzymes or other proteins.

Electrophoresis

Three sorts of electrophoresis are discussed in this unit for the analysis of calmodulin. First is the common method of electrophoresis in polyacrylamide gels containing sodium dodecyl sulfate (SDS-PAGE), using the discontinuous Tris-glycine buffer system of Laemmli (1970).

Because this procedure is used in all the units of the course, details on its use have been relegated to Appendix 5. An interesting twist on the SDS-PAGE method for calmodulin is the fact that the mobility of the protein is different depending upon the presence or absence of calcium ions in the buffers. Thus, you can identify a calcium ion binding activity of calmodulin qualitatively as an altered electrophoretic mobility. Second, nondenaturing or "native" gels are useful for calmodulin because of its small size and large net negative charge (Watterson et al. 1976). A procedure for such native gels is given in this unit. Third, calmodulin's domain structure can be probed by the use of urea gradient gels, as described by Goldenberg and Creighton (1984). Calmodulin is a particularly interesting example of the application of this technique due to its stepwise denaturation and altered electrophoretic mobility.

Protein Cleavage and Peptide Separation

The first goal of this section is to demonstrate the use of endoproteinases and chemical reagents in the cleavage of calmodulin into component peptides. It is instructive to compare and contrast these methods by the size and yield of fragments generated. This is not an exhaustive survey of proteolytic methods, but rather a useful guide to the general principles. As an added attraction, calmodulin has various anomalous cleavage sites, and discovering some of these exceptions to the rules is designed to teach you how the chemistry of real proteins, isolated as natural products, is different from theoretical analysis of the translation product of a cDNA sequence by a computer program.

The second goal is to introduce the use of HPLC as a tool in protein chemistry. In this case, the experiment is limited to the separation of peptide fragments of calmodulin by reverse-phase HPLC using quite common protocols. There are a wide range of uses for HPLC in the purification and characterization of proteins, as well as other molecules, and entire volumes and series are devoted to this topic (Hancock 1984). The methods employed here require only the most basic instrumentation, and so should be accessible to many scientists and students.

Protein Sequencing, Amino Acid Analysis, and Mass Spectrometry

As noted above, protein sequencing, amino acid analysis, and mass spectrometry are commonly performed with automated instruments, which are often available in core protein chemistry facilities. The intent here is to introduce how these procedures can be used by biologists, not to explain how to run the instruments. Of particular importance are general do's and don'ts of how to prepare the sample for analysis. Many analyses fail as a result of improper sample preparation and not because of the limitations of the instruments or their operators. The major problems that arise in interpretation of protein sequence, compositional, and mass spectrometry data are summarized for the specific case of calmodulin. These problems are typical of those one might encounter with other proteins, but the scope of the unit is not exhaustive, and undoubtedly there are new anomalies of protein chemistry as yet undiscovered. Foremost among problems of structural analysis are posttranslational modifications. The examples of modifications from calmodulin are helpful in learning to recognize that proteins are more than just the amino acid sequence translated from a cDNA and that chemistry is of tremendous value in understanding the nature of protein structure.

BON VOYAGE NOTE

Before you enter the world of protein purification and characterization, you may ask a few questions arising from the occasional bewilderment that accompanies your first steps with proteins. What is the point of all this demanding and often excruciating purification and characterization work? Why have we selected a protein with annoyances like posttranslational modifications, anomalous gel electrophoretic mobility, and divalent cation binding sites? These challenges are designed to convince you that proteins are complicated beasts, chemically and biologically. They deserve considerable respect because they are more than the gene products, they are the molecular phenotype of the cell. There is no substitute for careful, *quantitative* analysis of proteins. All the DNA sequence and predictive computer programs are insufficient to prove the chemical structure and function of a protein. Even genetic analysis by mutagenesis cannot prove mechanistic properties of protein function. The structural and functional analysis of proteins is and will remain an essential part of biology. It is also a fascinating discipline that deserves your attention, as much today as more than half a century ago when the foundations of the field were established (see Cohn and Edsall 1943).

• Experiment 1
Activity Assays: Assay of Calmodulin Fractions

INTRODUCTION

Starting a Protein Purification

Many scientists spend very little time in careful consideration of the initial steps in a protein purification and subsequently find themselves exhausting every form of chromatography available to separate the desired protein from contaminants. Upon starting a protein purification, you must first establish a few parameters regarding the protein of interest.

Although it is often assumed that a biological activity is the consequence of a protein, there are a plethora of small molecules, as well as macromolecules, that are active in many circumstances. The best criteria for the involvement of a protein are: (i) sensitivity to endoproteinases; (ii) retention in dialysis; (iii) inactivation by denaturants; and (iv) inactivation by chemical modification reagents. All of these criteria are subject to exceptions. Although most proteins are sensitive to proteases such as trypsin, some proteins retain a protease-resistant core that may continue to be active or even become more active than the intact protein. Unlike small molecules, proteins should be retained upon dialysis, but of course this depends on the nominal molecular weight cutoff rating of the dialysis membrane. Membranes with nominal cutoff values of from 1000 to 30,000 are available, but a protein close to the cutoff value may not be retained due to its shape. Also, some biological activities may reside in peptides with molecular weights of less than 1000, so technically, these are proteinaceous materials that would be dialyzable. Common denaturants are heat or chaotropic agents such as urea or guanidinium ions. Many proteins are sensitive to irreversible inactivation upon heating, but there are significant exceptions, such as calmodulin, which are heat-stable. Also, denaturation by chaotropic agents is, in many cases, reversible. This is also true of certain chemical modifications, particularly reduction of disulfides. Reduction of disulfides, followed by alkylation, is often used as a means to demonstrate protein involvement in a biological activity. However, not all proteins contain disulfide bonds (e.g., calmodulin) or have activities dependent upon a sulfhydryl group. The best course of action is to use several criteria to establish that the biological activity in question is due to protein *before* starting the purification.

Establishment of an Assay

It is worth repeating that the most important part of the purification is the assay. You must have a relatively rapid, simple, and quantitative assay to enjoy any hope of isolating a particular protein. The specificity of the assay is important, but often impossible to know a priori. Often after a single activity is purified, antisera for proteins and molecular tools for DNA manipulation, such as molecular cloning and polymerase chain reaction (PCR), permit the identification of molecules that are structurally related. However, such analysis does not guarantee functional identification of related molecules. There could be proteins with similar functions that are structurally unrelated to the original protein. Alternatively, structurally related molecules might have different functions, and therefore show no activity in the assay used. Overall, it is the assay that defines the entity that will be purified.

Measurements can be of direct enzymatic activity, modulation of enzymatic activity, binding to a ligand, binding to a macromolecule (such as another protein, a carbohydrate, or a nucleic acid), or a biological activity of a cell, tissue, or organism. The farther removed the measurement is from molecular assays, the less likely it is that the measurements can be done quickly, inexpensively, and quantitatively. Immunological assays are very useful, as the specificity of antibody molecules can be very high. However, some antibodies react with epitopes that are common to several different molecules. It must be kept in mind when using immunological assays that the criteria are structural (i.e., immunoreactivity) and not functional. In some cases, however, antibodies are defined by inhibition of a biological activity. In such cases, isolating the immunoreactive protein ought to yield a functional molecule. When utilizing ligand or macromolecule binding assays, it is important to remember that these measure the interaction of two (or more) molecules, and not a specific enzymatic activity. This is true for transcription factors, for example, which can be isolated and assayed by DNA binding but are not clearly transcriptional activators until proven so in vitro and in vivo (see Unit II).

ASSAY OF SAMPLES FOR CALMODULIN

Calmodulin will activate a wide variety of enzymes in a calcium-dependent manner, including cyclic nucleotide phosphodiesterase

(PDE), several protein kinases, protein phosphatases, Ca^{++}/Mg^{++} ATP-ases, and NAD kinase. How do we choose the assay that will be most useful for monitoring purification? Although calmodulin was first identified as an activator of PDE (Kakiuchi and Yamazaki 1970; Cheung 1971), there is at present no compelling reason to use that enzyme in the assay. A partially purified preparation of PDE can be made from bovine brain, but there are also several PDE activities that are not calmodulin-dependent, and these may raise the background levels of the assay. Also, assays with PDE, like those with ATPases and NAD kinase, require a step to separate the substrate nucleotides from the products. Many methods are available for such separations, using thin-layer, ion-exchange, or other chromatography, and these are readily adaptable to your laboratory. We have chosen to assay a protein kinase because the assays are amenable to rapid, large-scale results using adsorption of the products to phosphocellulose papers. The kinase substrates are synthetic peptides, which are available commercially or can be synthesized in the laboratory or core facility. The specificity of the assay lies in utilizing purified enzyme, added exogenously, as well as the specific peptide substrate. Two of the most popular protein kinases for assay of calmodulin are Ca^{++}/calmodulin kinase II and myosin light chain kinase (MLCK) (Gorecka et al. 1976; Kennedy and Greengard 1981). These kinases have the advantage that they can be purified and separated from endogenous calmodulin under mild conditions, and therefore fractions to be assayed can be added back to assay for Ca^{++}-dependent activation (Lukas et al. 1986; Haiech et al. 1991). Other protein kinases, such as phosphorylase b kinase, are inconvenient because the endogenous calmodulin is tightly bound. In addition, the activation kinetics of phosphorylase b kinase is complicated by the additional requirement for phosphorylation of the regulatory subunits.

In this unit, calmodulin is measured as the Ca^{++}-dependent activator of MLCK, isolated from smooth muscle tissue. Unlike striated muscle, smooth muscle does not utilize troponin-C for Ca^{++}-dependent activation of actomyosin ATPase and the subsequent cycle of contraction. In smooth muscle, the actomyosin ATPase is controlled by phosphorylation of the regulatory light chain, a small protein that binds to the myosin head (Tan et al. 1992). This phosphorylation is catalyzed by MLCK, a Ca^{++}-dependent enzyme that is activated by calmodulin. The substrate for the enzyme used in the assay in vitro is a synthetic peptide based on the light chain sequence at the phosphorylation site. Phosphate is transferred from the γ-position of ATP to a hydroxyl moiety on the peptide. By using [γ-^{32}P]ATP, radioactivity appears in the peptide as a function of time, temperature, Ca^{++} ion concentration, enzyme concentration, ATP and peptide concentrations, and calmodulin concentration. By keeping all other variable components of the reaction constant, and ATP and peptide levels well above the K_m, calmodulin levels in unknown samples can be measured. Separating the phosphopeptide product from the ATP substrate is the critical step. The peptide contains several basic residues, so that it is easily bound to phosphocellulose paper under acidic conditions. By repeated washing in aqueous phosphoric acid, the ATP is removed, and the peptide remains on the paper.

MATERIALS AND EQUIPMENT

Polypropylene microcentrifuge tubes (1.5-ml)
Peptide substrate for MLCK (10 mM concentrated stock solution; for the assay, dilute 1:20 in H_2O to give a 0.5 mM solution)
ATP (2 mM stock solution containing 5 μCi of $[\gamma\text{-}^{32}P]ATP/5$ μl)
Calmodulin stock solutions (0.1 μg/ml or 1 μg/ml)
MLCK enzyme (Keep the concentrated stock solution at –70ºC; for the assay, dilute 1:200 in 1 mg/ml bovine serum albumin)
Water bath
Whatman® P81 phosphocellulose paper (cut into strips)
Phosphoric acid (75 mM) (3 x 4 liters)
Glass beakers (3–4-liter capacity)
Pipettes (3–10-ml)
Scintillation vials
Scintillation counter
Acetone (optional)
Blow dryer (optional)

SAFETY NOTE

• Wear gloves when handling radioactive substances. Consult the institutional environmental health and safety office for further guidance in the appropriate use of radioactive materials.

REAGENT

MLCK assay buffer (10x)
(For recipe, see Preparation of Reagents, pp. 120–122)

PROCEDURE

1. For each assay, combine the following in a 1.5-ml polypropylene microcentrifuge tube:

MLCK assay buffer (10x)	5 µl
Peptide substrate for MLCK (0.5 mM)	5 µl
[γ-^{32}P]ATP (2 mM; 5 µCi/5 µl)	5 µl
Calmodulin (0.1 µg/ml or 1 µg/ml) or unknown fraction from purification procedure	0–20 µl
Milli-Q H$_2$O	10–30 µl
MLCK enzyme (1:200 dilution of stock solution)	5 µl
Total volume:	50 µl

Note: Each fraction from the purification procedure, if it contains EDTA or EGTA, should be made 1 mM excess in CaCl$_2$.

Assay several dilutions of each fraction, such as 1:10, 1:100, and 1:1000. Under these conditions, 4 ng of calmodulin is approximately half maximal. For a standard curve of calmodulin (0.2–20 ng/assay) in the MLCK assay, see Figure 2.

2. Initiate the assays by adding the MLCK enzyme. Incubate for 20 minutes at 25°C.

3. Place the assay tubes on ice. Remove a 10-µl aliquot from each assay and apply it to a small area of P81 paper. You can use a strip of P81 paper on which you have marked with a pencil sequential numbers (corresponding to the assay tubes) approximately 2–3 cm apart.

4. Wash the paper strips three times in 75 mM phosphoric acid, stirring manually with a pipette. Perform each wash in a glass beaker, and transfer the strips of paper with a pipette. Place the first wash in the radioactive waste. After washing, air dry the paper, cut the strips into pieces, and place them in scintillation vials for counting. Alternatively, the papers can be washed in acetone and dried more quickly with a hand-held blow dryer (Marshak and Carroll 1991).

TROUBLESHOOTING THE ASSAY

The calmodulin assay has several potential pitfalls that are generally instructive as examples of problems that might arise in an assay used in any protein purification.

• Samples may have endogenous MLCK activity, and therefore would show higher phosphotransferase activity without actually measur-

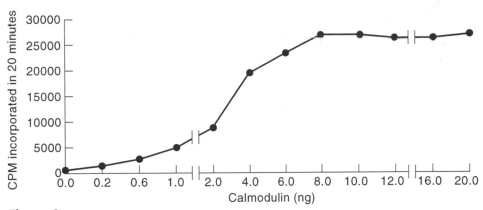

Figure 2
Standard curve for calmodulin in the MLCK assay.

ing activation of the exogenous MLCK enzyme. To avoid this, samples can be heat-treated, which will destroy kinase activity but preserve calmodulin. The easiest procedure is to treat the samples for 10 minutes at 80°C, followed by centrifugation to remove precipitated protein. Remember that the protein concentration of the sample should be measured before boiling so that you can normalize the activator activity to the total protein in the sample. Instead of heat treating, this problem can be avoided by performing experiments to measure the kinetics of activation, to demonstrate that there is more enzyme present, rather than more calmodulin. However, these experiments are relatively tedious, and inactivation of the endogenous MLCK is simple. In cases where the activity of interest is not heat-stable, dilution of samples or altering the time course should be used to analyze endogenous activities.

- Small-molecular-weight compounds in the samples to be tested can interfere with the assay. Samples may contain a calcium chelator, and, as noted in the protocol, excess calcium ions should be added to saturate any effects of the chelator. Otherwise, activator activity will be masked. Similarly, high salt or extremes of pH can affect the assay. Therefore, it is often useful to use high dilutions of the samples or to exchange the buffer by dialysis. If dialysis is used, remember that the volume of the sample can change, particularly when the ionic strength is lowered substantially. Therefore, volumes should be measured before and after dialysis to correct for this in the final determination of specific activity.

• Experiment 2
Preparation of a Tissue Extract

INTRODUCTION

Starting Material

Before commencing the purification from an arbitrary source, there is much to be profited from investigating alternate sources of the activity. Of course, one does not know if similar activities found in different tissues arise from the same molecules, so one is potentially limited by the definition of the assay. However, some of the preliminary purification and characterization steps can limit the risks. For example, if extracts of different tissues have activities that are identical in solubility, sensitivity to denaturants and proteases, and approximate size, as well as in the biological or biochemical assay, then it is probably worth pursuing the tissue that is most readily available or in which the activity is most abundant.

Choice of species. One of the first decisions in extracting animal tissues is—what animal? Choosing a species is usually dependent on the abundance and nature of the activity, as well as the size, cost, and availability of the animal. First, question the phylogeny of the activity. If the assay is performed on mammalian targets, should you use an avian, insect, fish, or amphibian starting material? The activity may be highly conserved, but the protein structure may not. How will you know if you have isolated a new protein, or just the avian version of a mammalian protein that is already known? These questions should be considered before choosing the species. Second, is the animal large enough to produce a substantial amount of protein? Do not be afraid of large animals. Much of successful biochemical analysis of proteins is due to the choice of domesticated animals such as cows, sheep, pigs, and goats, since they are raised as food sources. Rodents are convenient and less expensive per animal, because of size, but often the weight of tissue is not available without sacrificing many animals. This problem is magnified in isolating insect proteins. Obviously, if there is a homologous protein in an abundant domestic animal, it is usually more convenient to purify from this source than from insects. In urban areas, local slaughterhouses often allow scientists to gather tissues at nominal cost, or without charge, if the tissues have no commercial value. Alternatively, there are companies that sell animal tissues to scientists either frozen or freshly prepared on ice. It can be advantageous to seek out colleagues who are doing projects on animals in order to share organs from the sacrifice of a single animal. Your neighbor may be discarding the organ that you desperately need for starting material.

Choice of tissue. Once the species has been chosen, you must pick a tissue. Using an isolated tissue from an organism is itself a purification step. If the desired protein is enriched in a particular tissue, the simple procedure of removing the organ containing that tissue from an animal is a purification, compared to using the entire animal. It is usually not a good idea to take an entire organism as starting material, unless dissection is impossible, as in the case of tiny insects, very early embryos, or protozoa. Screening for the activity in various tissues is a recommended first step to deciding on a starting material. For such a survey, only a small amount of tissue is needed, sufficient only to measure the specific and total activity. Even if the specific activity is high, expressed in units per weight of protein, always calculate the total activity present in units per wet weight of tissue. It does no good to have a tiny tissue with high specific activity, unless larger amounts of that tissue are available. You will often find that it is impossible to predict which tissues have an abundance of the activity; it is usually only in retrospect that one can rationalize the presence of a particular protein in a tissue.

At the outset, do not be afraid to obtain small samples of every tissue that you and your friends can identify. Some tissues may turn out to be much easier to use than the one you first imagined to be the source of the protein. Besides total activity, you might consider the potential contaminating proteins. In highly differentiated, homogeneous tissues, you may find that a large fraction of the contaminating proteins are eliminated in the early steps. Tissues with high cell heterogeneity, like whole brain, may be more difficult to use because only one or a few specific cell types contain the protein of interest. If other cell types contain structurally or functionally related proteins, these can complicate the purification. Furthermore, a protein may reside in a particular subcellular compartment, and isolation of the appropriate organelle or subcellular fraction can greatly enrich the starting material. This concept will be discussed in more detail in Units II and IV in connection with nuclear and plasma membrane proteins, respectively.

Finally, when choosing a tissue as starting material, do not forget the major focus of your project. For example, if you are searching for a protein involved in cell division, use tissue containing proliferating cells in the first approximation. Similarly, if you are isolating a protein involved in a metabolic pathway, such as glycogen metabolism, you should probably first look at tissues abundant in glycogen. Although seemingly trivial, these principles are often ignored because investigators, or more frequently their students, feel bound by previous work in the field to utilize a particular tissue. Sometimes tissue sources are established in a field just because the first person to examine the activity chose to look at a particular tissue that was convenient. Always look systematically at the tissue distribution of the activity and use existing knowledge of physiology and pathology. The beginning of a purification provides a good opportunity for basic scientists in the fields of molecular biology and biochemistry to consult with organismal biologists and clinical scientists.

Tissue Extraction

Successful extraction of the protein from a tissue can be assessed in terms of the yield of the activity studied and the physical nature of the collected material. The yield is determined by the quantitative assay of a small aliquot of the extract. It is important to record the total volume of the extract to determine the total activity obtained. Extraction conditions, unfortunately, must be optimized empirically, although sometimes information about the protein or the activity can be helpful in guessing. If it is known that the protein is an integral membrane protein, for instance, then it is likely that detergents will be required for solubilization. Membrane proteins and detergent extraction are discussed in Unit IV in connection with the isolation of the insulin receptor. The physical characteristics of the extract are also at issue because of logistical concerns. For example, if the optimal condition for extraction is one liter per gram of tissue when performed on a small scale, then a kilogram of tissue will produce a thousand liters of material, which may be impossible to manipulate without large, pilot plant facilities. Thus, you may have to sacrifice some overall yield to obtain a usable extract. In the following discussion, each parameter of the extraction for aqueous media is considered separately. It is also possible and sometimes profitable to utilize organic solvents in extractions of proteins. This has been notably successful in the isolation of bioactive peptides, but is not typical for larger proteins.

Buffers. The pH of the extraction buffer is a critical parameter, and the optimal pH should be determined initially. An acidic protein, like calmodulin, is most soluble at a pH higher than neutrality. Basic proteins are more soluble at acidic pH. Proteins with neutral isoelectric points (pIs) are often most soluble at a pH either above or below the pI. However, this also depends to some extent on ionic strength. In general, one should use a pH for extraction that is far from the pI of the protein, without endangering the chemical nature of the protein. There are exceptions to this rule. If a protein is being copurified with another protein because they are bound tightly together, optimal extraction will be at a pH different from the net pI of the complex. Depending on later steps in the purification, it may be advantageous or disadvantageous to maintain the protein complex intact. Thus, a highly acidic protein bound to a larger neutral or basic protein might be best solubilized as a complex under acidic conditions. There are also cases (e.g., fibroblast growth factor [Burgess and Maciag 1989]) in which choosing an acidic or basic extraction buffer leads to the isolation of different proteins with similar activities.

It is a good idea to avoid extremes of pH, as chemical changes in the protein structure can occur (Whitaker 1980). Above pH 9.0, deamidation of glutamine and asparagine side chains can occur, resulting in protein containing abnormal numbers of glutamic and aspartic acid residues, thus changing the pI. Alkaline conditions also promote β-elimination of serine and threonine residues, particularly if they are esterified to a leaving group, such as phosphate. Partial hydrolysis of the peptide bonds can occur at high pH, and certain modifications, particularly carbohydrate, can also degrade. Proteins are chemically quite stable under mildly acidic conditions (pH 4.0–6.0). However, very low pH can lead to denaturation and precipitation of some proteins, resulting in loss of biological activity. Precipitation does not always destroy activity, as will be discussed during the bulk fractionation section of this unit. Acidic conditions can also result in partial hydrolysis of peptide bonds, as well as in acid-catalyzed β-elimination. Certain modifications, such as phosphohistidine, are destroyed at low pH.

Careful consideration should be given to the type of buffer used. A paramount consideration in choosing a buffer is that the effective buffering range overlaps the desired pH. A common mistake, for example, is to use Tris as a buffer at pH 7.0, which is just on the edge of the range. Additions to the buffer, such as the proteins and other ionic molecules extracted from the tissue, can alter the pH of such a solution tremendously. Therefore, always use a buffer in the middle of its effective buffering range. Some buffers, notably Tris, have pKs that vary greatly with temperature. Preparing such a buffer at room temperature and using it at 4ºC can result in large errors in pH. Buffering *capacity* is an issue when extracting tissues, and it is closely linked to the volume of solution used. If small extraction volumes are used, the concentration of protein and other molecules from the tissue will be high, demanding a higher molarity of buffer. In many instances, larger volumes can be used conveniently, allowing dilute buffers to be adequate. It is usually insufficient to use buffers below 10–20 mM when extracting a tissue with volumes that produce protein concentrations above 2 mg/ml. Typically, buffer concentrations of 20–50 mM are utilized. Finally, chemical compatibility is a consideration in the choice of buffer. Buffers containing primary amines are not suitable if the amino groups will interfere with a subsequent step, such as cation-exchange chromatography. Similarly, phosphate buffers might interfere with subsequent anion-exchange procedures. Very useful buffers are those developed by Good et al. (1966), which consist of substituted piperazine sulfonates (see Appendix 2). These are available in different forms (e.g., HEPES, PIPES) with discrete buffering ranges, and the family of buffers covers the entire useful pH range.

Ionic strength. The solubility of proteins depends on ionic strength, and the optimal ionic strength varies greatly among proteins. High ionic strength can lead to aggregation and precipitation of many proteins, so it is common practice to use hypotonic conditions. However, some enzymatic activities are sensitive to low ionic strength, resulting in loss of activity. In those cases, isotonic solutions are recommended. Remember that the buffer contributes to the overall ionic strength, as well as added salt. Some proteins are more soluble under hypertonic conditions. Notably, peripheral membrane proteins can be isolated without detergent by extraction of membranes with hypertonic buffers. In such cases, it may be useful to perform a hypotonic extraction first, followed by a hypertonic extraction, resulting in a partial purification simply by changing salt concentration. The choice of salts used to alter the ionic strength of an extraction buffer is another significant issue. Some proteins are more active in sodium or potassium ions, so these options should be studied. Chloride is very common as the accompanying anion, but some solutions demand sulfate or other counteranion. Although it is possible to change ionic strength and type of salt in the solution by dialysis later in the preparation, it is best to find the optimal conditions initially, to avoid time-consuming subsequent steps.

Metal ion chelators. Tissues contain various metal ions, particularly divalent cations such as Mg^{++}, Ca^{++}, and Mn^{++}. Vascularized tissues, muscle, and blood have large amounts of iron cations as well. There are also varying amounts of other heavy metal ions, including Zn^{++}, Hg^{++}, and Pb^{++}, among others. Chelators, such as EDTA and EGTA, are often used to remove these metal cations from interactions with proteins and other compounds in the extract. Without chelators, tissue extracts are often very sticky, resulting in incomplete solubilization of proteins. Some of this is due to mixing of Ca^{++} from extracellular fluids with the intracellular phosphates, leading to insoluble or partially soluble precipitates. The heavy metal ion salts, particularly chloride salts, are frequently poorly soluble, and the absence of exogenous chelating agents can result in some inorganic salt precipitation. The chelator EGTA has a greater specificity for Ca^{++} than for Mg^{++}, but EDTA has a higher overall affinity for the divalent metal cations (Kretsinger and Nelson 1977). Unless there is a compelling reason to chelate Ca^{++} without affecting Mg^{++}, it is usually best and less expensive to use EDTA. Note that the free acid form of these chelators is not soluble in water in the absence of buffers above pH 7.0. Add the chelator to the buffer solution before adjusting the pH. It is also possible to use the disodium or dipotassium salts of the chelators, but these add sodium ions to the solution. The concentration of chelator required in the extraction buffer varies with the tissue used, but generally 2–10 mM is adequate.

Reducing agents. Oxidation can occur at several sites on proteins, and it is usually advantageous to include reducing agents in the extraction buffer. Strong reducing agents, such as borohydrides, should not be used, as they will produce chemical modifications of proteins. Most often used are sulfhydryl reducing agents, including 2-mercaptoethanol and dithiothreitol. Proteins contain sulfhydryl groups that can assume a variety of oxidation states, and sufficient reducing agent concentration should maintain the proteins in their fully reduced state. Some disulfide bonds are resistant to reduction without denaturants, so it is not useful to destroy biological activity just to reduce the disulfides. Oxidation of methionine and tryptophan residues by oxidizing species in the extract is also suppressed by using sulfhydryl reducing agents. Dithiothreitol is a more efficient reducing agent than 2-mercaptoethanol because the former operates through an intramolecular reaction, whereas the latter requires a bimolecular reaction (Cleland 1964). In both cases, a mixed disulfide is formed, followed by reaction of a second sulfhydryl group to produce a reduced cysteine and a disulfide form of the reducing agent. Typical concentrations of reducing agent are 1–10 mM. When large volumes of buffers are used, it is less expensive to use 2-mercaptoethanol, despite its strength. Always add fresh reducing agent to the buffer, as the mercaptans are volatile and susceptible to air oxidation.

Protease inhibitors. Animal tissues contain a wide variety of proteases that can lead to degradation of the desired protein and, in some cases, alterations in activity. It is common to use small-molecular-weight compounds, including peptides, as inhibitors of the proteases. Since some of these inhibitors are expensive, it is important to think about which classes of proteases are targets for different inhibitors, to avoid redundant use of expensive inhibitors or the exclusion of inhibitors to an entire class of proteases. Some proteases will be inhibited already by other components of the buffer. Metalloproteases, for example, are usually blocked by EDTA, which chelates the required divalent metal cation. Sulfhydryl proteases are blocked by sufficient concentrations of reducing agents, which prevent the successful attack of the peptide bond during the hydrolysis reaction. Calcium-ion-dependent proteases are also blocked by chelators. The common serine proteases can be blocked by inhibitors such as phenylmethyl-sulfonyl fluoride (PMSF), which covalently inactivates the enzyme. Although PMSF must be added as a solution in ethanol or other miscible organic solvent, there are now alternative inhibitors that are freely soluble in water. Other useful compounds include benzamidine and the family of chloromethyl ketones, such as TPCK and TLCK, which are specific to chymotryptic- and tryptic-like activities. Remember that compounds that covalently react with proteases require a few minutes to inactivate the enzymes completely. Several peptide and protein inhibitors of proteases, such as leupeptin and soybean trypsin inhibitor, act by binding so tightly to the protease active site as to be essentially irreversible. Generally, it is most important to utilize protease inhibitors at early steps in the purification, such as the extraction step. Later on, most of the contaminating proteases have been removed or inhibited, so it is not necessary to add protease inhibitors to a nearly purified protein. In fact, if chemical analysis of the protein is to be performed, it is ridiculous to add large concentrations of proteinaceous inhibitors, such as soybean trypsin inhibitor, since this only serves to contaminate the preparation with an exogenous protein.

Temperature. Efficient extraction of protein can be temperature dependent. In general, proteins are more soluble at 20–40°C than at low temperatures, but this varies widely among proteins. The optimal thermodynamic stability of a protein can be at even more diverse temperatures (Whitaker 1980; Pace et al. 1989). Low temperature suppresses proteolysis, so it is customary to work at 4°C. However, for proteins that are relatively stable and in the absence of wholesale proteolytic degradation, it is often possible to purify proteins at room temperature. Elevated temperature can lead to denaturation and precipitation of protein. In addition, undesired chemical modifications, such as deamidation, hydrolysis, and oxidation, are accelerated at high temperature. Therefore, heat treatment is not recommended for purification of proteins. Some protocols utilize heat treatment to precipitate other proteins while a heat-stable activity remains soluble, but such procedures should be used with caution if chemical characterization of the product is to be accurate.

Tissue disruption. There are many methods for tissue disruption, and one should be chosen that produces high yields of the desired protein without significant denaturation. Preparation of the tissue is helpful, including the removal of any unwanted connective tissues that are difficult to disperse. Often mincing a tissue with a knife or scalpel leads to a more efficient extraction of protein. Commercial mechanical tissue homogenizers or blendors are very good at disrupting and homogenizing tissues. The major drawback of these machines is the possibility of foaming. Bubbles and foaming arise when proteins in aqueous solution form films at an air-water interface. Protein can denature at the surfaces formed by these interfaces, so that foaming is to be avoided to obtain active protein. Most homogenizers are equipped with a rheostat mechanism to control the speed and limit foaming. Gentle disruption of tissue can be done with manual homogenizers, such as glass or Teflon Dounce units. The extent of disruption will depend on how tight the pestle fits with the body of the unit, so always check this before manual operation. Another approach is to lyse the cells of the tissue with hypotonic shock, such as with distilled water. This can be effective, in some instances, but the solubility of the protein remains a key consideration.

An often ignored area is the type of material used in the vessel for extraction and homogenization. Glass may contain heavy metals chelated to the silica, and the silica surface might bind the desired protein nonspecifically. Also, heavy metals can deplete the solution of chelator. Different glasses, for example, borosilicate and soda-lime glass, can have different properties, so they should be tested for use in any protein purification. Glass can be treated with silanes, such as dichlorodimethylsilane, a procedure popular in nucleic acid biochemistry. Unlike nucleic acids, which are large anionic polymers, some proteins may actually stick more tightly to a silane-treated surface, which is more neutral and slightly hydrophobic compared to the glass surface. When using glass, it is also essential that all cleaning solutions, including acids, alkali, and detergents, are completely removed.

For many proteins, including calcium-binding proteins, the use of plastics is recommended. There are many different sorts of plastics, and you should consult the manufacturer for chemical compatibility. Polycarbonate materials are stiffer than polyethylenes, and they are useful as the material for bottles that will not deform upon centrifugation. Polycarbonate is brittle, however, and degrades with high salt, such as ammonium sulfate, and certain organics, notably acetone (see Table 1). Metallic (e.g., stainless steel) vessels are very strong, but nonspecific binding and metal contamination can be problematic. Remember that stainless steel is made in a variety of grades, of which the lower quality ones can deposit iron

Table 1 Resistance of Some Plastics to Chemicals and Sterilization

Chemicals	Conventional polyethylene	Linear polyethylene	Polyallomer	Polypropylene	Polymethyl-pentene	Polytetra-fluoroethylene	Fluoroethylene-propylene	Chlorotri-fluoroethylene	Polycarbonate	Phenylene-oxide resin	General purpose polystyrene	Styrene-acrylonitrile	Acrylics	Polyvinyl chloride	Acetal resins
Acids, inorganic	E	E	E	E	E	E	E	E	E	E	E	E	E	N	
Acids, organic	E	E	E	E	E	E	E	E	E	N	E	G	G	G	
Alcohols	E	E	E	E	E	E	E	E	E	G	G	E	E	G	
Aldehydes	G	G	G	E	E	E	E	G	E	G	F	F	F	G	
Amines	G	G	G	E	E	E	E	N	N	N	G	G	N	G	
Bases, inorganic	E	E	E	E	E	E	E	E	E	G	E	N	E	E	
Dimethyl sulfoxide	E	E	E	E	E	E	E	E		N	N	N	N		
Esters	E	E	E	G–N	N	E	E	F		N	N	N	N	E	
Ethers	G	G	G	N	E	E	E	G		F	G	E	F	E	
Glycols	E	E	E	E	E	E	E	E	E	G	E	E	F	E	
Hydrocarbons, aliphatic	G	G	G	N	E	E	E	F	F	N	F	E	F	G	

Hydrocarbons, aromatic	G	G	G	N	E	E	N	N	N	N	N	G
Hydrocarbons, halogenated	G	G	G	N	E	F	N	N	N	N	N	G
Ketones	G	G	G	F	E	E	N	N	N	N	N	G
Mineral oil	E	E	E	E	E	E	E	E	G	G	G	E
Oils, essential	G	G	G	G	E	E	G	G	N	F	N	E
Oils, lubricating	E	E	E	E	E	E	G	E	G	G	G	E
Oils, vegetable	E	E	E	E	E	E	E	G	G	E	G	E
Proteins, unhydrolyzed	E	E	E	E	E	E	E	E	G	E	G	E
Salts	E	E	E	E	E	E	E	E	E	E	E	E
Silicones	G	G	G	G	E	E	G	G	G	G	G	E
Water	E	E	E	E	E	E	E	E	E	E	E	E
Sterilization												
Autoclaving	no	yes[a]	yes	yes	yes	yes	yes[b]	no	no	no		
Gas (ethylene oxide)	yes	yes	yes	yes	yes	yes	yes	yes	yes	yes		
Dry heat (160°C)	no	no	no	no	no	no	no	no	no	no		
Chemical (e.g., ethanol)	yes	yes	yes	yes	yes	yes	yes	yes	yes	yes		

Adapted, with permission, from ISCO (1982).

E = excellent; long exposures (up to one year) at room temperature cause no damage. G = good; short exposures (<24 hours) at room temperature have no effect. F = fair; short exposures at room temperature cause little or no damage under unstressed conditions. N = not recommended; short exposures may cause permanent damage.

[a]Can be autoclaved at 121°C for 20 minutes.

[b]Autoclaving reduces mechanical strength.

and zinc into the solution. In general, brief use of stainless steel instruments and polypropylene vessels is often satisfactory in homogenization.

EXTRACTION OF CALMODULIN FROM CHICKEN GIZZARDS

Calmodulin is found in all mammalian tissues, as well as in other eukaryotic organisms. It is one of the most ubiquitous and highly conserved proteins known. Why use chicken gizzards for the purification of calmodulin? Gizzards are an abundant and cheap source of smooth muscle without too much vascularization, fat, or connective tissue. Smooth muscle is an outstanding source of calmodulin because the tissue does not contain the structurally related protein, troponin-C, which is found in striated muscle. Uterus is another useful source of smooth muscle, but it is more highly vascularized and usually more expensive and less readily available than gizzards. Since mammalian and avian calmodulins are identical, there is no compromise to specificity using chickens. Thus, chicken gizzards have an abundance of calmodulin and very few other related proteins that would make the preparation more difficult.

It is essential to remove the connective tissue from the gizzards before homogenization because it can foul the homogenizer quite easily. Mincing the smooth muscle tissue before homogenization also aids extraction. The volume of the extract is relatively small, and the extract is therefore quite dense and viscous due to high protein concentration. To obtain a high yield of calmodulin while maintaining a high protein concentration, it is crucial to re-extract the pellets from the first centrifugation step. This high concentration of total protein is helpful in the subsequent bulk precipitation steps. Much of the insoluble material in the extract is myosin fibrils from the muscle. By using very low ionic strength, high pH, and calcium chelators, the calmodulin is easily solubilized, but the myosin remains insoluble. Myosin solubilization requires very high ionic strength, typically 4 M KCl. The protocol is strategically designed to solubilize the protein of interest, calmodulin, while leaving the most abundant contaminating protein, myosin, insoluble. Choice of tissue and extraction procedures has been optimized to produce high yields of calmodulin. Protease inhibitors are not used because there are few contaminating proteases in this tissue extract, compared to brain, pancreas, or liver, and because calmodulin is relatively resistant to proteolysis. Chelators and reducing agents are employed, partly to inhibit proteases but mainly to help release calmodulin from bound sites in the tissue, principally MLCK.

MATERIALS AND EQUIPMENT

Chicken gizzards (25; stored at –20°C) (e.g., Pel-Freez, Inc.)
2-Mercaptoethanol (2-ME; M.W. 78.13; density 1.114)
Polypropylene beaker (4-liter)
Homogenizer (e.g., Brinkmann Polytron)
Polycarbonate centrifuge bottles (6 x 500-ml)
Superspeed centrifuge with rotor to hold up to 3-liter volume
Polypropylene graduated cylinder (4-liter)
Cheesecloth
Polypropylene funnel (large, wide-mouth)

SAFETY NOTE

- 2-Mercaptoethanol may be fatal if swallowed and is harmful if inhaled or absorbed through the skin. High concentrations are extremely destructive to the mucous membranes, upper respiratory tract, skin, and eyes. Use only in a chemical fume hood. Gloves and safety glasses should be worn.

REAGENT

Buffer H (10x)
(For recipe, see Preparation of Reagents, pp. 120–122.)

PROCEDURE

1. Thaw the gizzards for 2 hours at room temperature and then overnight at 4°C.

2. Using a scalpel, remove the white connective tissue between the two lobes of each gizzard, but do not worry about the small amount surrounding the main lobes. Discard the connective tissue, and cut the gizzards into pieces approximately 1 cm^3.

3. Weigh the trimmed gizzard tissue and record the weight.

4. Make up 2 liters of 1x buffer H by diluting the 10x stock with distilled H$_2$O and adding 70.1 µl of 2-ME/liter to give a final concentration of 1 mM 2-ME.

5. Add the gizzard tissue to two volumes (i.e., 2 ml/g) of 1x buffer H in a 4-liter polypropylene beaker. For example, if you have 400 g

of tissue, add 800 ml of buffer. In the cold room, transfer the tissue in the buffer to a homogenizer and homogenize at nearly top speed for three bursts of 30 seconds.

6. Pour the homogenate into 500-ml polycarbonate centrifuge bottles and balance using a pasteur pipette broken off at the end to give a larger opening (the homogenate is quite viscous). Spin in a superspeed centrifuge at 8000 rpm for 30 minutes at 4°C.

7. Remove the supernatant by pouring it into a polypropylene gradu- ated cylinder through two layers of cheesecloth placed in a polypropylene funnel. Pour the supernatant down the side of the cylinder so that the extract does not foam a lot (as you would pour a beer with no head). Remove the pellets with a spatula and pool them back in the polypropylene beaker. Add one volume of 1x buffer H (based on the *original* wet weight of starting material [see step 3 above]). Repeat the homogenization and the centrifugation.

8. Pool the second supernatants with the first supernatants and record the total volume. Retain 0.1% (~1 ml) of the volume for as- say later. You will need to know these two volumes to do calcula- tions.

• Experiment 3
Bulk Fractionation

INTRODUCTION

The tissue extract is a complex mixture of proteins and other compounds that were soluble in the extraction buffer. Usually, this extract contains a high total protein concentration, in excess of 2 mg/ml. Under these conditions, it is possible to alter the composition of the buffer to force the precipitation of a portion of the proteins. This procedure takes advantage of the differential solubility of proteins under varying conditions as well as the high protein concentration of the solution which allows aggregates of protein to form over a short period of time (minutes to hours). Precipitation of one group of proteins permits their separation from other proteins that remain in solution by low-speed centrifugation. If the activity of interest quantitatively follows either group of proteins, then the specific activity should increase. It is common to use high salt concentrations to promote precipitations. Ammonium sulfate is used widely as the salt of choice because it has been found to preserve protein activity and precipitation of protein is promoted at lower concentrations of ammonium sulfate than those of sodium or potassium chloride.

Theory of Precipitation

Precipitation arises when individual monomers or small complexes of soluble proteins interact to form large aggregates that can be recovered by centrifugation. Conceptually, you might think of the precipitation process as the proteins interacting with each other rather than with the solvent, in this case, water. To accomplish this, the conditions of the solution are altered to thermodynamically favor the binding of hydrophobic surfaces on the proteins and to negate charge interactions. By increasing the concentration of salt in the solution, charged and polar groups on the protein surfaces are paired with the ions in the solution, disrupting protein-protein interactions on the basis of charge. Moreover, high salt promotes the interaction of surface hydrophobic regions on proteins, and aggregates of protein form and separate from the water. The best explanation of this phenomenon arises from the consideration of the structure of water around the surface hydrophobic patches. These water molecules are highly ordered to maximize hydrogen bonding with each other rather than with the hydrophobic surface. Such cages of water surrounding the protein generate a relatively low entropy system. At higher salt, it is thermodynamically beneficial for the water to interact with the ions, as the free exchange of water with the bulk solution rather than the protein surface is a higher entropy, more disordered state. Because the protein surface hydrophobic regions are less likely to be protected by an ordered water structure, the most energetically favorable state is when those surfaces bind to each other and form van der Waals interactions with each other. Therefore, as more protein molecules bind to each other, the aggregate is excluded from the aqueous environment. In this way, the system is thermodynamically driven by the hydrophobic effect to precipitate (Tanford 1973; Timasheff and Arakawa 1989).

A successful precipitation for protein purification depends upon several factors. First, the total protein concentration must be high enough to rapidly produce aggregates and the resulting precipitate. At very low protein concentrations, the formation of aggregates may be kinetically unfavorable, either requiring an unacceptable period of time (weeks to months) or reaching an equilibrium state in which the aggregate size is too small to be collected by centrifugation. Second, the activity of the protein of interest must be preserved during the precipitation process, so that active proteins are obtained and recovery can be monitored. Similar precipitation effects can occur if the protein becomes denatured. Under those conditions, hydrophobic portions of the protein core, rather than the surface, are exposed during unfolding, and similar thermodynamic forces promote aggregation. Very high concentrations of certain "chaotropic" salts can cause this denaturation, so every activity must be tested empirically to avoid unacceptable loss (Pace et al. 1989). Sometimes, useful fractionation can be accomplished by the addition of organic solvents to the extract, rather than salt, resulting in the reduction of the fraction of water in the solvent and the partial denaturation of the proteins. Organic solvents that are miscible with water in all proportions, such as ethanol and acetonitrile, are sometimes used to fractionate an extract if the activity of interest can tolerate the treatment. Ethanol precipitates are very convenient as they are free of high salt concentrations, but they are sometimes difficult to redissolve in aqueous buffer. Third, the pH can affect the precipitation, as well as the activity, because the surface charge will be altered as a function of pH. Measuring the solubility of the desired activity at various pH levels is a useful, preliminary experiment that can be done with a small portion of the extract. Finally, temperature can also affect precipitation, but the temperature is usually that point where the protein remains active and proteolysis is minimal, often 4°C.

Ammonium Sulfate Precipitation

Ammonium sulfate is a very useful salt for the differential precipitation of proteins. For a diagrammatic representation of the theory of ammonium sulfate precipitation, see Figure 3. The most productive protocol is to add increasing proportions of ammonium sulfate to the extract, with intermittent centrifugation steps. These stepwise precipitations are often referred to as ammonium sulfate "cuts." Typically, a pilot experiment is performed first to identify the precipitation range of the desired activity using broad cuts. It is convenient in the first attempt to use intervals of 20% saturation. A chart, shown in Appendix 4, gives the amount of solid ammonium sulfate to be added to a known volume in order to obtain the desired percentage saturation.

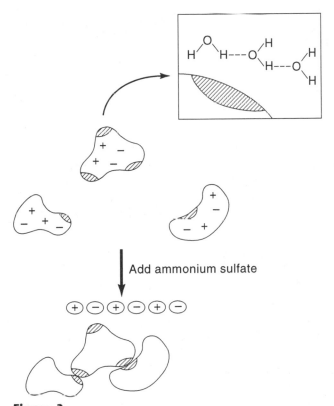

Figure 3
Schematic illustration of the theory of ammonium sulfate precipitation. Hatched areas represent hydrophobic patches on the surface of the protein.

Solid ammonium sulfate should be added slowly while the solution is stirring to allow a uniform increase in the concentration. It is helpful to grind the ammonium sulfate crystals in a mortar and pestle to produce a fine powder. Lumps or large crystals will not dissolve immediately, so the solution near the surface of the lump will have a much higher concentration of ammonium sulfate than does the bulk solution. This can lead to the uneven and unreproducible precipitation of protein.

In the suggested preliminary experiment, the initial extract is brought to 20% saturation in ammonium sulfate, stirred for a short time (e.g., 60 minutes), and the resulting precipitate collected by centrifugation. The supernatant, which is still 20% saturated in ammonium sulfate, is transferred to another vessel and additional ammonium sulfate is added to obtain 40% saturation. This solution is allowed to precipitate with stirring, and the 20–40% precipitate is collected by centrifugation. Continuing in this way, one obtains pellets that contain the protein precipitated by ammonium sulfate cuts at 20% saturation steps. Upon assay, the precipitation range of the protein is roughly determined by which pellet contains activity. If one finds activity spread over the entire range of ammonium sulfate, without a discrete precipitation point, then there are three options: (i) abandon ammonium sulfate fractionation as a useful purification step; (ii) repeat the experiment in case uneven precipitation occurred; or (iii) conclude that multiple forms of the activity exist, and focus on one of them for purification. Following the preliminary fractionation, it is helpful to go back to the original extract, and do narrower intervals of ammonium sulfate cuts to obtain better fractionation. For example, if the activity precipitates between 20% and 40% saturated ammonium sulfate, bring the initial extract to 20% saturation, and then do cuts of 5% intervals to 40%, and test the precipitates for activity. This procedure can be extrapolated to very narrow cuts of 1% saturation ammonium sulfate, but it is rare that a protein will precipitate at such a discrete concentration.

There are generally three strategies that one can pursue in using ammonium sulfate fractionation. First, the desired protein might precipitate at a discrete concentration of ammonium sulfate, permitting a huge increase in the specific activity and an excellent purification step. Second, one can precipitate the protein of interest in a broad cut, producing an acceptable increase in specific activity and the removal of many contaminating proteins. Third, if the desired protein is highly soluble under a particular set of conditions, one can precipitate a large proportion of the protein contaminants and retain the desired protein in the supernatant. Ammonium sulfate fractionation is best used at the beginning stages of a purification protocol, due to the dependence on total protein concentration. It is usually not a good idea to do an ammonium sulfate precipitation at the end of the purification when one has a nearly purified protein, often at concentrations of much less than 1 mg/ml total protein. Overall, use ammonium sulfate fractionation at an early step in the purification, such as on the initial tissue extract, and do pilot experiments on small aliquots of the extract to determine the best strategy of fractionation.

Isoelectric Point Precipitation

The isoelectric point (pI) of a protein is defined as the pH at which the net charge on the protein is zero. At that point, proteins generally have their lowest solubility in aqueous solutions, and it is possible to take advantage of that property to enrich a preparation for a fraction of proteins with a particular pI. One way to think about pI precipitation is shown in Figure 4. With an overall net charge of zero, the solvent water component of the system excludes the protein from the bulk solvent as described above. Similarly, the protein molecules in-

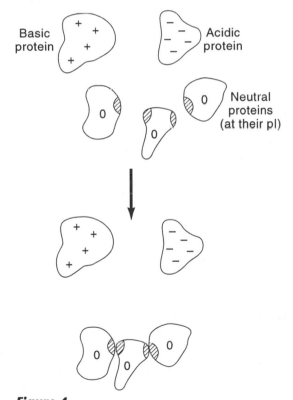

Figure 4
Schematic illustration of the theory of isoelectric point (pI) precipitation. Hatched areas represent hydrophobic patches on the surface of the protein.

teract to form aggregates as in the ammonium sulfate procedure. However, in this case, molecules of similar pI are favored to interact, including identical molecules of protein. In addition, the interactions may be not only through hydrophobic surfaces, but also by dipole or ionic interactions, limited only by the fact that the net charge on the aggregate will be zero. Thus, ion pairs and dipole pairs may also contribute to aggregate formation near the protein pI.

In practice, pI precipitation is most successful when the required pH is very different from the pH of the extraction buffer. For example, a basic protein might be solubilized under acidic conditions and precipitated at high pH, whereas an acidic protein might be solubilized under alkaline conditions and precipitated at low pH. Proteins with neutral pIs are often solubilized at near neutral pH using isotonic or slightly hypertonic buffers. It may be possible to precipitate the protein merely by diluting the buffer to a lower ionic strength. In some cases, it may be difficult or impossible to precipitate a protein with a neutral pI because it contains domains of widely different net charges, although the overall charge at the pI is zero. These domains maintain the protein's solubility in solutions with buffers and salts as counterions, but it is sometimes possible to precipitate such a protein by dialysis against distilled water.

BULK FRACTIONATION OF CALMODULIN

The bulk fractionation of smooth muscle tissue extract utilizes two different steps for the purification of calmodulin:ammonium sulfate and pI precipitations. These procedures take advantage of two different properties of calmodulin, its high solubility at pH above neutrality and its acidic pI. First, ammonium sulfate precipitation at pH 8.0 is used to precipitate the majority of the protein, while leaving calmodulin in the supernatant. At neutral or slightly basic pH and in the absence of calcium ions, calmodulin is highly soluble. Even at high salt concentrations (60% saturation with ammonium sulfate), the protein stays in solution at pH 8.0. Therefore, one can precipitate a large fraction of the other proteins and leave the calmodulin in the supernatant. If this procedure was attempted in the presence of calcium, calmodulin would bind to other proteins and would be much more prone to bind nonspecifically to hydrophobic moieties. You will take advantage of this latter property during the hydrophobic interaction chromatography later in the purification (see Experiment 5).

The second step employs pI precipitation to concentrate and precipitate calmodulin at pH 4.0. The pH of the solution is adjusted to between pH 4.0 and 4.1 using 50% (v/v) sulfuric acid. This permits lowering the pH without changing the major anionic species in the solution, the sulfate ion. The volume of acid required is small, so that the pH can be lowered quickly, avoiding precipitation of other proteins at intermediate pH. Following centrifugation, the pH 4.0 pellet is dark brown, due mainly to the myoglobin, and it is quite sticky and hard. To obtain a high yield of calmodulin, it is critical to resuspend this pellet thoroughly. The pellet contains not only protein, but also ammonium sulfate at pH 4.0. To resuspend such a pellet, add a small volume of distilled, deionized water and gently break up the lumps of protein pellet using a flexible spatula or rubber policeman. The volume of this suspension is considerably smaller than that of the original extract, several milliliters as compared to liters. To dissolve the protein, it is necessary to raise the pH to approximately 7.5–8.0 by the addition of a few drops of a 1 M solution of Tris base. This is the free base of Tris, which is approximately pH 11.0 and has not been adjusted by the addition of acid. The large quantity of sulfate in the resuspended pellet acts as the counterion, and the addition of Tris results in a Tris-sulfate mixture. It is essential to take the time to dissolve the pellet carefully, without vigorous agitation, because any protein not dissolved will be lost to the subsequent ion-exchange step. Rapid dialysis of the redissolved sample will bring the sample to the required pH and ionic strength.

MATERIALS AND EQUIPMENT

Supernatant from Experiment 2 (~700–1000 ml)
Solid ammonium sulfate
Polypropylene beakers (2 x 4-liter)
Stir plate and magnetic stir bars
Polycarbonate centrifuge bottles (6 x 500-ml)
Superspeed centrifuge with rotor to hold up to 3-liter volume
Polypropylene graduated cylinders (2 x 4-liter)
Cheesecloth
Polypropylene funnel (large, wide-mouth)
Concentrated sulfuric acid (diluted to 50% v/v in H_2O)
Rubber policemen/spatulas
Tris base (1 M; ~10 ml)
Small polypropylene funnel with a long stem
Dialysis tubings (6000–8000 nominal M.W. cutoff; washed)

SAFETY NOTE

- Concentrated acids should be handled with great care; gloves and a face protector should be worn. Add acid to H_2O and keep it cool because dilution of sulfuric acid in H_2O is exothermic.

REAGENT

Buffer B (10x) (Immediately before use, prepare 4 liters of 1x buffer B
and add 2-mercaptoethanol to 1 mM)
(For recipe, see Preparation of Reagents, pp. 120–122.)

SAFETY NOTE

- 2-Mercaptoethanol may be fatal if swallowed and is harmful if inhaled or absorbed through the skin. High concentrations are extremely destructive to the mucous membranes, upper respiratory
tract, skin, and eyes. Use only in a chemical fume hood. Gloves and
safety glasses should be worn.

PROCEDURE

1. On the basis of the volume of the supernatant from Experiment 2
   (subtract the aliquot removed for assay), look up in the ammonium sulfate table (see Appendix 4) the amount of solid ammonium sulfate required to give 0–60% saturation. This should
   be 361 g/liter. Weigh out the appropriate amount of ammonium
   sulfate and crush any lumps to a smooth powder.

2. Place the supernatant in a 4-liter polypropylene beaker containing a large magnetic stir bar. Stir slowly on a large stir plate in the
   cold room. Add the ammonium sulfate slowly by shaking it in
   over a period of 20 minutes. If solid ammonium sulfate appears
   at the bottom of the beaker, stop for a few minutes to allow it to
   dissolve. Let the mixture stir for an additional 40 minutes (i.e., 1
   hour total).

3. Transfer the mixture to 500-ml polycarbonate centrifuge bottles
   and balance them. Spin in a superspeed centrifuge at 8000 rpm
   for 60 minutes at 4°C.

4. Remove the supernatant by pouring it into a polypropylene graduated cylinder through two layers of cheesecloth placed in a
   polypropylene funnel. Discard the pellet. Record the volume of
   the supernatant. Retain 1% of the volume for assay later. You will
   need to know these two volumes to do calculations.

5. Transfer the supernatant to a 4-liter polypropylene beaker. At the
   pH meter, add with moderate stirring 50% (v/v in H_2O) sulfuric
   acid until the pH reaches approximately 4.05. Try to attain a pH
   of below 4.1 and above 4.0.

6. Put the beaker in the cold room and stir for 1 hour.

7. Transfer the suspension to 500-ml polycarbonate centrifuge bottles. Spin in a superspeed centrifuge at 8000 rpm for 60 minutes at 4°C.

8. Remove the supernatant and discard. Using a rubber policeman, resuspend the pellets in a few milliliters of distilled H_2O containing a few drops of 1 M Tris base. Use a minimum volume to resuspend the pellets.

9. Wearing gloves, transfer the suspension to dialysis tubing. Fill the tubing using a small polypropylene funnel with a long stem. Remove excess air and leave 50% of the tubing empty (collapsed, no air). Tie off both ends with at least double knots or clips.

10. Dialyze for 4 hours against two changes of distilled H_2O at 4°C. Then transfer into 4 liters of 1x buffer B. Continue to dialyze overnight at 4°C. In all cases of dialysis, have a small stir bar in the beaker stirring slowly to mix the dialysate. Do not let the stir bar hit the dialysis tubing or it may rupture.

NOTES ON DIALYSIS

Dialysis in cellulose bags is a very useful way to change the buffer composition of a solution of proteins. Cellulose dialysis tubings are available in a variety of sizes. The two critical dimensions are the diameter of the tubing and the nominal pore size of the holes in the membrane. In principle, the cellulose membrane comprising the tubing has uniform pores that allow passage of low-molecular-weight materials, such as buffers, salts, and small organic compounds. The solvent, water, passes freely through these pores as well. Proteins and other molecules with molecular weights above the cutoff are retained by the membrane. The cutoff is a nominal measure, because it is based on the assumption of the size of an average globular protein. If the protein of interest has an extended shape, it may not be retained by the membrane even if it is above the cutoff limit. Therefore, it is good practice to use a nominal molecular weight cutoff significantly below the molecular weight of the protein of interest to avoid loss. In cases where the molecular weight is not known, it may be necessary to determine suitable membranes by empirical trials.

The rate of dialysis depends on several factors, all of which relate to the diffusion of the components in the sample. The rate of diffusion is related to the molecular weight of the species, so smaller molecules, such as salts, will dialyze faster than molecules of higher mass. A large gradient of concentration of solute between the sample in the dialysis bag and the solvent will permit depletion of salts in the sample in a relatively short time. The relative volumes also play a role. If you dialyze against a volume similar to that of the sample, the theoretical limit of the dialysis is only one half the concentration of solute ions, at equilibrium against pure water. However, by using a very large volume for dialysis compared to the sample, a larger dilution can be obtained. However, reaching equilibrium in a large volume may take a long time. It is therefore useful to use stirring to mix the dialysis solution, although care must be taken to avoid damaging the cellulose membrane by the stirring action. Another useful procedure is to use a large, but not vast, volume of dialysis buffer. Since the approach to equilibrium is exponential with respect to time, most of the dilution occurs in the first few hours. By changing the dialysis solution with fresh buffer, it is possible to force the approach to equilibrium.

During the first dialysis of the redissolved pH 4.0 pellet in the calmodulin purification, a very high concentration of Tris sulfate, along with some chelator and chloride ions, is dialyzed against pure water. By using a very high differential of ionic strength, there is a large dilution of salts in the sample. Changing this once or twice in the first few hours of dialysis leads to a very fast dilution of the Tris sulfate. However, care should be taken to avoid extended dialysis against pure water, as eventually all the buffers and salts in the sample will be lost, leading to the possibility of protein insolubility. The extended dialysis of the sample occurs against the buffer for the following step, the anion-exchange column buffer B. This contains Tris-HCl buffer at pH 8.0 as well as 0.2 M NaCl. The presence of sodium chloride also helps remove the remnants of the sulfate, as the exchange of anions proceeds faster than the simple dilution of one solvent ion. In theory, it would be best to carry out the entire dialysis procedure against buffer B, but this would take many changes of buffer that would be expensive and time consuming. By utilizing a limited initial dialysis against water, most of the sulfate is lost rapidly, and the buffer is subsequently equilibrated with buffer B for the next step. Temperature can also affect dialysis, as higher temperature increases the rate of diffusion. However, 4°C is usually maintained to avoid proteolysis. In addition, the sample is certainly not sterile, so cold temperature and chelator help to suppress bacterial growth.

Remember that the sample will increase in volume due to the osmotic pressure. The sample should fill only half the dialysis bag at the outset, with the remainder being empty and collapsed, not filled with air. If the sample volume expands against the air in the bag, the air will not escape, and the pressure in the bag will increase. This can lead to rupture of the membrane or deformation of the pores. In either case, the protein will be lost in the dialysis medium.

In practice, if the purification is started in the morning, the pH 4.0 pellet can be redissolved and in dialysis within about eight hours after the initial extraction. During the Cold Spring Harbor course, the students usually started cutting up the gizzard tissue around 8:30 a.m., had lunch during the ammonium sulfate precipitation, and collected the pH 4.0 pellet by about 4 p.m. The dialysis against water proceeded during dinner, with changes during the evening. The last one to bed, usually between 10 p.m. and midnight, put the sample into dialysis against buffer B overnight.

• Experiment 4
Ion-exchange Chromatography

INTRODUCTION

The purpose of ion-exchange chromatography lies in using the charged groups on the surface of a protein to bind to an insoluble matrix with opposite charge. More precisely, the protein dipolar ion displaces the counterions (e.g., chloride or sodium) of the matrix functional group and will itself be displaced with an increasing proportion of a counterion. This is usually done by increasing the concentration of ions in the elution buffer; for example, elution with an ascending gradient of salt concentration. Alternatively, a pH gradient may be employed so that the net charge on the adsorbed protein decreases. Under specific starting conditions of buffer, pH, and ionic strength, the net charge on the protein of interest can be manipulated to interact with the matrix. Thus, the most important parameters to consider in an ion-exchange separation are the choice of ion-exchange matrix and the initial conditions.

The Ion-exchange Matrix

There are two broad classes of ion exchangers, cation and anion exchangers. Cation exchangers consist of an insoluble support bonded with functional groups that are negatively charged at neutral pH, such as carboxymethyl or sulfopropyl moieties. These resins are useful for separating proteins with pIs above neutrality. To adsorb the protein to a cation-exchange matrix, one should be at a pH below the pI of the protein and above the pK of the functional groups on the resin. For example, at pH 6.0, a sulfated resin will be negatively charged and a basic protein will have a net positive charge, resulting in adsorption of the protein to the matrix at low ionic strength and constant pH. Likewise, anion exchangers, such as diethyl aminoethyl (DEAE)-derivatized or quaternary ammonium ethyl (QAE)-derivatized matrices, will be positively charged at neutral pH, and they will be able to interact with acidic proteins at neutral pH.

Remember, anion exchangers are themselves basic groups that are positively charged below their pKs and cation exchangers are acidic groups that are negatively charged above their pKs. One should select a weak or strong ion exchanger based on the properties of the protein to be adsorbed. For example, carboxymethyl is a weakly acidic cationic exchanger, whereas sulfopropyl is a strong cation exchanger, since the pK for the acidic proton is lower for sulfate than for acetate. A cationic protein will bind to both types of cation exchangers, but a higher concentration of counterions will usually be required to desorb the protein from the "stronger" ion exchanger, sulfopropyl. Similarly, DEAE is a weakly basic anion exchanger, whereas the quaternary ammonium ions are strong anion exchangers.

If your protein requires very high salt concentrations to elute it from an ion-exchange resin, you can switch to a weaker ion exchanger. If it still requires high salt to elute, altering the pH of the experiment can be helpful. Remember that raising the pH of a cation-exchange experiment will decrease the salt concentration required to elute the protein, whereas lowering the pH of an anion-exchange experiment will have a similar effect. Conversely, if your protein is not being retained by the ion exchanger even at low ionic strength, you can use a stronger ion-exchange resin and/or manipulate the pH. Raising the pH of an anion-exchange experiment will increase the salt concentration needed to elute the protein, and lowering the pH will have the same effect on a cation-exchange experiment.

The Starting Conditions

Buffer. The first parameter to consider when using an ion exchanger is the choice of buffer. In general, one should choose a buffer that does not interact with the matrix. For example, use Tris buffers with anion exchangers and phosphate buffers with cation exchangers. If you use a buffer whose buffering ion is positively charged (e.g., Tris), it will bind to a cation exchanger, setting up a complex equilibrium among the ion exchanger, the buffer, and the proteins. The ion exchanger will lower the buffering capacity, and the buffer will lower the capacity of the matrix. Similarly, it is not advisable to use phosphate buffers with anion exchangers. Although frequently found in the scientific literature, phosphate buffers will interact with DEAE and cause problems in anion exchange. When used, the concentration of phosphate is usually very low, such as 5–10 mM. At such low buffering levels, the protein load and the source of water can severely affect the success and reproducibility of the separation. Overall, excellent choices for ion exchange are the Good's buffers, which have buffering capacity over a wide pH range (Good et al. 1966) (see Appendix 2). This is due to the zwitterionic character of the functional group, the piperazine sulfonic acid moiety. HEPES buffer, for example, can be used for both anion- or cation-exchange chromatography at pH 7.4.

pH. The initial pH of the experiment must be determined empirically, unless the activity being purified cannot withstand changes in pH. For example, if an enzyme or other activity is only stable at pH 7.4, then there is no point determining the optimal pH for separation. In those cases, it may be advantageous to explore the possibility of renaturing the activity following denaturation (see Unit III). In most cases, however, it is best to determine the optimal initial pH by a simple test-tube experiment. Equilibrate the ion-exchange resin at various pHs, ranging from 5.0 to 9.0 in units of 0.5. It will require different buffers to accomplish this. For consistency, the Good's buffers are useful, as described above. Add a small aliquot of the sample to each of the resin samples, and incubate each tube for 30–60 minutes at the temperature that is intended for the experiment, usually 4°C. Mix the tubes gently every 5 minutes or use a rotating platform for continual mixing. At the end of the incubation, spin the tubes briefly in a table-top, low-speed centrifuge to pellet the resin, remove the supernatant, and measure the activity in an aliquot of each supernatant. For anion exchange, the activity should be present in the supernatants at low pH, and it will begin to disappear once the pH is high enough to allow protein-matrix binding. Above that pH, all the activity will disappear, as it will be bound to the resin. Choose an initial pH for the experiment about 0.5 of a pH unit higher than the point at which the activity begins to be bound by the ion exchanger. The pH must be high enough for all the active material to bind, but not so high as to require very high salt to elute (see comments on ionic strength below). For cation-exchange chromatography, the results will be inverse; the activity should be bound at low pH and be present in the supernatant at higher pH. It is not necessary to use an entire preparation for this experiment. One can use just enough activity in each tube to detect in a few assays. Successful ion-exchange test-tube experiments can be done using less than 1 ml of resin in 1.5-ml plastic centrifuge tubes. This experiment can be performed in a short time, usually 2 hours, and it is extremely useful for optimal ion-exchange separations. Unfortunately, many scientists choose to neglect this step and stubbornly use only pH 7.4 or a pH chosen arbitrarily by themselves, a colleague, or a competitor. Do this test-tube experiment first; it is well worth the hours required, and it may save weeks of further preparation in the future.

Ionic strength. The starting ionic strength of the ion-exchange experiment should be determined empirically in a test-tube experiment similar to that described above for pH. This time, fix the buffer and pH at the predetermined conditions, and set up several tubes with increasing salt concentrations, usually ranging from 0 to 1 M salt in units of 0.1 or 0.05. Add an aliquot of the protein sample and incubate with agitation for 30–60 minutes at 4°C. Upon centrifugation, the activity remaining in the supernatants should be measured. In this case, activity will be absent at low ionic strength because the protein in question binds to the resin. At higher salt concentrations, the activity should begin to appear in the supernatants. As your initial conditions, choose an ionic strength *just below* that required to elute the protein. In fact, it is often desirable to be at least 0.1 M salt below the point of elution. It is not necessary to load at zero salt because there can be enormous purification potential gained by allowing contaminating proteins to "flow through" or not be adsorbed to the resin.

Capacity. Most ion exchangers have a fairly high capacity for protein, and this parameter is critical for an efficient separation. If you exceed the capacity of the resin, then valuable activity will be lost in the nonadsorbed material. If you use an enormous excess of resin, then the recovery of activity will be severely decreased. Do not put microgram quantities of protein on hundreds of milliliters of an ion-exchange resin because it is unnecessary and you are unlikely to find the activity again. Determine the capacity of the resin for your particular activity and protein mixture empirically by a third test-tube experiment. Under the predetermined buffer, pH, and ionic strength conditions, add increasing amounts of the sample and incubate with agitation for 30–60 minutes at 4°C. After centrifugation, little or no activity should be observed in the supernatants at low sample loading, but at a certain sample protein to resin bed volume ratio, some of the activity will begin to appear in the supernatants. Choose an amount of resin below that point. Remember to scale up in a linear fashion—keep the total sample protein to resin bed volume ratio constant. You should have some excess capacity for protein binding, but keep it to a minimum. Remember that the capacity involves the total protein applied, not just the activity in question. Do not rely on capacities determined for other proteins, such as albumins or γ-globulins. These are accurate numbers, but are not always useful for proteins of very different compositions.

Strategic Use of Ion-exchange Chromatography

Ion-exchange chromatography is an example of adsorption-desorption type chromatography. In such methods, the proteins of interest are *adsorbed* to the surface of the resin matrix, and nonadsorbed proteins flow through the column in the void or excluded volume. This process is in contrast to gel filtration chromatography in which, ideally, protein components are differentially separated according to their average inclusion in the matrix pores (see Unit II). Adsorption-desorption methods include various forms of affinity and hydrophobic interaction chromatography, as well as ion exchange. One of the great advantages of adsorptive methods is the ability to use high volumes of sample, avoiding concentration steps. This saves an enormous amount of time and generally leads to higher overall yields in protein preparations. For example, one can load ion-exchange resins in batch mode by stirring the sample (which could be in volumes of liters) with the resin. Subsequently, the resin can be poured into a column for gradient elution, or batch eluted on a sintered glass funnel. Thus, one can move rapidly through large volume steps at the early stages of the preparation.

Another useful strategy is to find conditions under which the protein of interest does *not* interact with the ion-exchange matrix while a majority of the contaminating proteins are adsorbed. It is thus possible to filter the sample through the ion exchangers and retain the nonadsorbed material, discarding the adsorbed protein. The nonadsorbed protein mixture, containing the desired protein, can be then directly applied to another column. The purification of the mitotic form of the cdc2 protein kinase (Marshak et al. 1991) took advantage of just such a strategy. The enzyme is not retained by DEAE-cellulose at neutral pH and 80 mM salt, whereas many of the known protein kinases are adsorbed under these conditions. Application of the diluted ammonium sulfate fraction directly to DEAE-cellulose resulted in flowthrough of the desired kinase. This could be applied to a cation exchanger, sulfopropyl Sepharose, for further purification. It is thus possible to go through at least four steps of purification on the first day of the preparation.

In general, it should not be necessary to use the same type of ion exchanger more than once during a protein purification. It is not uncommon to see a published protocol that calls for two or three successive DEAE-cellulose columns. If well-designed, one column should be sufficient. Often multiple column steps arise because the purification has been done only once or twice. Many investigators do not want to spend the time to optimize a step, citing the adage, "If it works, don't fix it." If a DEAE column has to be run twice, the size or the gradient was probably too small or the starting conditions were not properly assigned. It is not bad to use two anion- or cation-exchange steps at very different pH or with very different resins. For example, a batch adsorption/desorption of protein on to DEAE-cellulose at pH 8.0 at an early stage in the preparation might serve to eliminate a large fraction of proteins with very different pIs than the protein of interest. Subsequently, at a later step in the procedure, one might turn to a high-resolution QAE column at pH 7.5 to effect complete separation of proteins with characteristics very similar to those of the protein of interest.

Notes on Instrumentation

Ion-exchange chromatography will require the use of some basic types of instrumentation. Column chromatography will require the use of, minimally, a column, solvent reservoir/gradient apparatus, and a fraction collector. Such equipment is available from a variety of manufacturers, and selection depends on cost, availability, features, service, and laboratory restrictions (e.g., space, personnel, and administrative policies). Preparation of buffers requires the use of an analytical balance and optional items, such as magnetic stirrers. Because ion-exchange chromatography is so highly dependent upon pH, it is essential to know how to use a pH meter. A brief explanation of the theory and practice of pH measurement is presented in Appendix 1. Ion-exchange chromatography is also highly dependent upon ionic strength measurements, and a convenient means to accomplish this is the use of a conductivity meter. The theory and practice of conductivity measurements are described in Appendix 3.

ANION-EXCHANGE CHROMATOGRAPHY OF CALMODULIN ON DEAE SEPHADEX A-50

The next step in the purification of calmodulin is anion-exchange chromatography on DEAE resin. This procedure takes advantage of the fact that calmodulin is a highly acidic protein, and therefore carries a high net negative charge at neutral or slightly alkaline pH. Under conditions of low ionic strength, calmodulin will bind to a positively charged matrix, whereas many proteins of higher pI (i.e., less acidic) will not bind. Bound proteins can then be differentially desorbed from the matrix by altering the conditions. In this case, the pH is set at 8.0, which is nearly four pH units higher than the pI of calmodulin. Under these conditions, calmodulin binds very well to the anion exchanger. It is not necessary to use a strongly basic ion exchanger, such as a quaternary amine; DEAE will suffice, since calmodulin at pH 8.0 is such a strong anion. Indeed, using a QAE resin might lead to binding of contaminating weakly anionic proteins other than calmodulin, so a weakly basic ion exchanger has been selected. The ionic strength of the starting buffer is relatively high (0.2 M NaCl). This is also designed to avoid binding of the more weakly anionic proteins. The vast majority of the purification of calmodulin on this column arises from the adsorption of the strongly anionic (acidic) proteins to the DEAE resin and flowthrough of the bulk of the proteins, which are weakly acidic, neutral, or basic. For example, all of the dark brown color in the sample will flow through the DEAE column. This color is mainly due to the porphyrin moiety in the muscle myoglobin.

Note that it would have been possible to load at a lower pH, but the ionic strength would have to be lower. Such conditions would enable fractionation of contaminating proteins, and calmodulin would be left at the high end of the salt gradient for elution. This would be of interest only if other proteins were being purified from the same extract. Note also that one could use a quaternary ammonium anion exchanger, but calmodulin would elute at a higher salt concentration. Thus, the resin and the starting conditions have been optimized on the basis of many years experience and many attempts at purification of calmodulin. Remember that a protein purification will not be optimal the first time that it is attempted. It is very useful to observe where the other protein contaminants appear in the chromatography, and to determine analytically the best ways to remove these contaminants. It is a good idea to know your "enemies" (undesired contaminants) as well as your "objective" in the battle for protein purification!

A slightly more sophisticated application of the anion-exchange column is also in use here. As noted above, the bulk of the purification is simply done by the adsorption and desorption of calmodulin to the column. Why then is it necessary to perform chromatography at all? Why not use batch adsorption/desorption of the protein without setting up a column? The answer is that it *is* possible to use batch mode for this step, but there is an added dimension provided by the chromatography. As with many types of chromatography, the anion-exchange resin used here provides a "mixed-mode" type of chromatography that is not pure ion exchange but a mixture of ion exchange and gel filtration. The resin chosen, DEAE Sephadex A-50, employs a matrix that is comparable to Sephadex G-50 in gel filtration characteristics, but one that is derivatized with DEAE functional groups. Therefore, if one uses a modest excess of resin, such that the bulk of the protein sample is adsorbed to the top 10% of the column bed, then when the calmodulin is eluted by the appropriate salt concentration (~0.42 M NaCl), it will experience some of the gel filtration characteristics of the column. This is important because several of the major contaminants to the calmodulin at this step are of high molecular weight (>70 kD), whereas calmodulin is relatively small (~17 kD). Therefore, as the calmodulin and these contaminating proteins are eluted from the DEAE, the higher-molecular-weight materials are excluded from the matrix pores, and calmodulin is somewhat retarded by partial inclusion in the matrix, resulting in added separation. The calmodulin elutes in fractions later than many of the higher-molecular-weight contaminants that normally would elute along with calmodulin according to salt concentration. Typically, this sort of mixed-mode usage is either discovered empirically (i.e., fortuitously) or after very careful analysis of the column fractions. One should generally not consider this until the basic preparative steps have been well-defined.

MATERIALS AND EQUIPMENT

DEAE Sephadex® A-50 (dry powder) (Pharmacia Biotech, Inc.)
Concentrated NaOH (10 N)
Retentate from dialysis in Experiment 3
Superspeed centrifuge
Glass column (5 cm in diameter)
Chromatography equipment: peristaltic pump, ultraviolet (UV) monitor, fraction collector, and borosilicate glass tubes (16 x 150 mm)

SAFETY NOTE

- Concentrated bases should be handled with great care; gloves and a face protector should be worn.

REAGENT

Buffer B (10x) (Immediately before use, prepare 4 liters of 1x buffer B and add 2-mercaptoethanol to 1 mM)
(For recipe, see Preparation of Reagents, pp. 120–122.)

SAFETY NOTE

- 2-Mercaptoethanol may be fatal if swallowed and is harmful if inhaled or absorbed through the skin. High concentrations are extremely destructive to the mucous membranes, upper respiratory tract, skin, and eyes. Use only in a chemical fume hood. Gloves and safety glasses should be worn.

PROCEDURE

1. Swell the DEAE resin in 1x buffer B overnight at 4°C or for 1 hour in a boiling water bath. Since the resin swells to approximately 30 ml/g at pH 8.0 (see reference *Ion Exchange Chromatography*), you will need approximately 15 g of dry resin for a 400-ml column.

2. Adjust the pH of the slurry to 8.0 with concentrated NaOH. The resin is supplied as the acid form, so this will require a few mil-

liliters. Do not stir with a stir bar or you may break the beads. Use a pipette or glass rod to stir manually. After adjusting the pH, let the resin settle, and decant the supernatant. Wash in this way three times with 1x buffer B, rechecking the pH after each wash until it is pH 8.0 and not changing.

Note: DEAE-cellulose is provided as the free base, so the pH of this resin must be adjusted with concentrated acid (e.g., 12 N HCl).

3. Carefully transfer the retentate from the dialysis bag into a beaker. Transfer into 30-ml plastic centrifuge tubes. Spin in a superspeed centrifuge at 20,000 rpm for 1 hour at 4°C.

4. Decant the supernatants into a beaker. Measure the conductivity of the sample at 4°C compared to that of 1x buffer B at 4°C. The sample must be at or below the conductivity of the buffer. If it is too high, add distilled H_2O until it is the same as buffer B. Keep the volume as low as possible (that is why you dialyzed instead of just diluting). Record the volume. Retain 1% for assay and record that volume.

5. Pour the column and assemble the apparatus for the chromatography as illustrated in Figure 5. Replace the lower nylon screen, if necessary. Leave approximately 2 cm of buffer above the bed of the column to allow gradient mixing. Make sure the baseline has been established on the recorder by allowing the effluent to flow through the UV monitor. Adjust the fraction collector to collect approximately 10–12-ml fractions.

6. Apply the sample by placing the inlet to the peristaltic pump into the sample beaker. Keep an eye on it so it does not pull air. Wash the column with 1x buffer B until the recorder UV signal approaches the original baseline. Collect the effluent in a beaker. There is no need to collect fractions until the gradient begins.

7. The gradient will be a total of 1000 ml: 500 ml of 1x buffer B to 500 ml of 1x buffer B containing 0.7 M NaCl. Note that 1x buffer B starts at 0.2 M salt, so to make 0.7 M NaCl, add 14.62 g of NaCl to 500 ml of 1x buffer B. Use a concentric plastic gradient maker: high salt on the outside, low salt on the inside. The stir bar goes in the inside chamber stirring moderately.

8. Collect the entire gradient in 10–12-ml fractions in borosilicate glass tubes. For typical results from the DEAE anion-exchange chromatography step in the purification of calmodulin, see Figure 6.

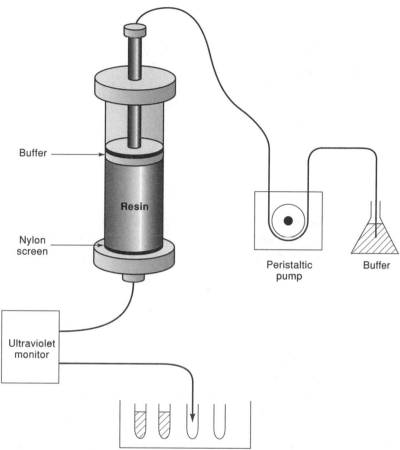

Figure 5
Diagrammatic representation of the apparatus required for low-pressure ion-exchange chromatography.

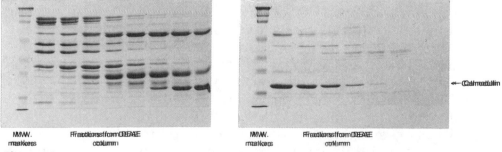

Figure 6
Polyacrylamide gel electrophoresis of fractions eluted from DEAE-Sephadex A50. Protein eluting at increasing salt concentrations from left to right. Two gels are shown following staining with Coomassie Brilliant Blue, and molecular weight markers are shown in the leftmost lane of each gel. Calmodulin migrates just above the lysozyme marker (14.4 kD).

Experiment 5
Hydrophobic Interaction Chromatography

INTRODUCTION

The purpose of hydrophobic interaction chromatography (HIC) is to take advantage of the surfaces of the protein that are prone to interact with nonpolar materials under nondenaturing conditions. Globular proteins usually have hydrophobic residues buried in the interior, and these regions are only accessible to bulk solvent if the protein is at least partially denatured. There are also hydrophobic patches on the surface of proteins that will interact with nonpolar moieties without denaturation. These surface hydrophobic interactions are promoted by increasing salt concentrations. At high salt concentrations, typically 1 M ammonium sulfate or 2 M sodium chloride, even very soluble, hydrophilic proteins can be forced to bind to hydrophobic materials.

The theory of HIC is shown schematically in Figure 7. As with bulk fractionation by ammonium sulfate precipitation, a high salt concentration promotes interactions between surface hydrophobic patches on the protein molecules. However, by raising the ionic strength to just below the point of precipitation, using a more dilute protein concentration, and suspending the solution of protein in the presence of an immobilized hydrophobic matrix, proteins bind to the column matrix rather than tending to precipitate. One takes advantage of this property by adsorbing proteins to immobilized nonpolar moieties under high salt conditions and desorbing the proteins selectively with decreasing salt concentrations. As the concentration of salt decreases, desorption of proteins will occur in the order of binding to the hydrophobic matrix by surface interactions. At very low ionic strength, there may still be proteins retained by the column, and these must be removed by the addition of nonpolar or chaotropic components to the matrix. Unfortunately, these solvent modifiers can lead to denaturation of proteins, as well as desorption from the matrix. Under these conditions, HIC becomes similar to reverse-phase systems using organic solvents. The most useful portion of HIC is the separation during the decreasing ionic strength gradient, rather than when resorting to desorbant materials to remove tightly bound proteins. The prime advantage of HIC is the ability to use the

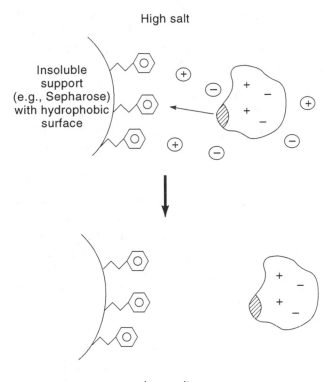

High salt

Insoluble
support
(e.g., Sepharose)
with hydrophobic
surface

Low salt

Figure 7
Schematic illustration of the theory of hydrophobic interaction chromatography. Hatched areas represent hydrophobic patches on the surface of the protein.

relative hydrophobic properties of the surface of the protein in a salt-dependent manner without denaturation in organic solvents.

The Hydrophobic Interaction Chromatography Experiment

Matrix. The two classes of materials used for hydrophobic interaction chromatography are immobilized aromatic compounds, such as phenyl agarose, and immobilized alkyl moieties, such as octyl agarose. Although both have hydrophobic properties, individual proteins may behave differently on these resins. Specific interactions with aromatic species rather than alkyl ones may be due to a slight affinity-based interaction. For example, calmodulin interacts with a variety of phenothiazine and benzodiazapine derivatives, substituted naphthalenes, and other heterocyclic and polycyclic compounds in a calcium-dependent manner. The binding to phenyl Sepharose may reflect this preference for aromatic compounds, but it falls short of true affinity chromatography and is simply a version of HIC. When purifying unknown proteins, it is prudent to test both octyl and phenyl matrices to see which gives more efficient separation. A wider variety of HIC matrices are becoming available commercially.

Loading conditions. In general, protein solutions should be supplemented with a salt to promote HIC. One of the dangers is that high salt can also result in protein-protein interactions through surface hydrophobic domains, as we saw in bulk precipitation using ammonium sulfate. Generally, the concentrations of salt used for loading an HIC column are below those that cause precipitation. This must be determined empirically, and may already be known from preliminary studies on ammonium sulfate precipitation. Ammonium sulfate is a popular salt for HIC, since concentrations of 1 M are usually sufficient for initial conditions. Sodium or potassium chloride can be used, but often concentrations of 2 M or higher are needed to force interactions with the HIC column. The dynamic range of separation ends up with very high concentrations of these chloride salts and may produce precipitation.

CHROMATOGRAPHY OF CALMODULIN ON PHENYL SEPHAROSE

As described above, the usual use of HIC for the calmodulin purification would be to apply the sample after DEAE chromatography in a buffer containing high salt, and to elute proteins with a descending gradient of salt concentration. Since you already know that calmodulin is highly soluble in 60% saturated ammonium sulfate at pH 8.0 in the absence of Ca^{++}, it would not be unreasonable to collect the fractions from the DEAE experiment that contain calmodulin (identified on the basis of electrophoresis and activity assay), to add ammonium sulfate to the pooled fractions, and to apply them to an HIC column. This is a strategy that is commonly exploited in protein purification. Because ion-exchange columns often leave sample pools in buffers containing salt, it is convenient to avoid dialysis, gel filtration, or other methods of removing salt, and to simply progress directly to HIC following ion exchange. This strategy has a good conceptual basis because the two separation techniques take advantage of very different properties of the proteins, namely, charge and hydrophobic characteristics. Alternatively, one could use the pH 4.0 ammonium sulfate precipitate or the 60% ammonium sulfate supernatant prior to precipitation as the starting material for HIC. This avoids dialysis or dilution of the sample to change salt concentration.

Chromatography of calmodulin on phenyl Sepharose, however, is a nontraditional application of HIC. This is possible because the surface hydrophobic nature of calmodulin is strongly increased when the protein binds Ca++. The pool of DEAE fractions containing cal-modulin has very low free Ca++ due to the chelators added to the buffer. The chelators were necessary to obtain good separation of cal-modulin from the ion-exchange column, as the elution position varies with the addition of Ca++ (Burgess et al. 1980). It is therefore important to exchange the buffer for one containing Ca++. In this ex-ample, we use dialysis to avoid more complicated procedures such as gel filtration and because there is a natural break after the DEAE step when you can dialyze overnight. This also serves to lower the salt concentration to the starting conditions prescribed. It is also possible simply to add excess Ca++ and Mg++ to the pooled fractions and ad-sorb the proteins to the phenyl Sepharose column.

The rationale for the chromatography is as follows. If you used HIC on partially purified fractions containing calmodulin without Ca++, calmodulin would be separated from other proteins during the descending salt gradient elution, but analysis of all the fractions would be required and there might be marginal separation from some proteins, demanding that you take losses in yield to obtain purified calmodulin. If, however, HIC is done on the pooled fractions in the presence of Ca++, then calmodulin is retained by the matrix and is not eluted, even at very low ionic strength (no added salt). It is therefore unnecessary to do the entire elution as a complicated gradient, but rather easier to adsorb the sample to the matrix as a batch and then wash extensively to remove contaminating proteins. However, since the high salt steps have been eliminated, it is possible that some proteins might bind to calmodulin, rather than to the matrix per se. The wash with Ca++-containing buffer supplemented with 200 mM NaCl is intended to remove these piggybacked proteins, and is not part of the HIC nature of the experiment directly. Buffers containing chelators are then used to elute calmodulin, which is obtained in es-sentially pure form from this procedure. Note that the buffers contain excess Mg++ and EGTA, which has a higher affinity for Ca++. Under these conditions, there is not wholesale depletion of all divalent cat-ions in the buffer, but selective depletion of Ca++ in the presence of Mg++. This is a precautionary step to avoid copurification of con-taminating proteins that might show divalent cation interactions with the HIC matrix. Certain proteins, such as kinases, contain nucle-otide-binding sites that permit interaction with various hydrophobic dyes particularly in the presence of divalent cations such as Mg++ or Mn++. Although this dye-ligand chromatography can be exploited for the purification of nucleotide-binding proteins, it is specifically avoided in the purification of calmodulin by using conditions of altering Ca++ in the presence of Mg++.

This protocol has evolved over many years, and it is not typical of a first attempt at protein purification by HIC. In fact, this procedure is not pure HIC chromatography, since part of the interaction of calmodulin with phenyl Sepharose arises from the protein's affinity for aromatic compounds in a Ca^{++}-dependent manner. The phenyl Sepharose procedure arose after the discovery that calmodulin specifically interacts with phenothiazine and naphthalene sulfonamide drugs (Hidaka et al. 1979; Levin and Weiss 1979). Affinity-based adsorption chromatography similar to the HIC procedure can be performed using immobilized drugs, although this procedure requires the preparation of the matrix, and is therefore more tedious. Thus, for calmodulin, phenyl Sepharose is the preferred HIC matrix.

MATERIALS AND EQUIPMENT

Pooled calmodulin-containing fractions from the DEAE column
    (see Experiment 4)
Dialysis tubings (6000–8000 nominal M.W. cutoff; washed)
Phenyl Sepharose® 4B resin (preswollen) (Pharmacia Biotech, Inc.)
Glass column (2.5 cm diameter x 10 cm)
$CaCl_2$ (solid)
Chromatography equipment: peristaltic pump, ultraviolet (UV)
    monitor, fraction collector, and borosilicate glass test tubes
    (13 x 100 mm)
Ammonium bicarbonate (10 mM; pH 8.0) (8 liters)
Lyophilizer/freeze dryer

REAGENTS

Buffer E (500 ml)
Buffer E containing 0.2 M NaCl (200 ml)
Buffer E containing 8 M urea (100 ml)
Buffer F (500 ml)
Buffer F containing 0.2 M NaCl (200 ml)
(For recipes, see Preparation of Reagents, pp. 120–122.)

PROCEDURE

Dialysis

1. Wearing gloves, transfer the pooled calmodulin-containing fractions from the DEAE column to dialysis tubing. Tie off both ends of the tubing with at least double knots or clips.

2. Dialyze against buffer F overnight.

Hydrophobic Interaction Chromatography

1. Wash the phenyl Sepharose resin in buffer E (without NaCl) to remove the ethanol in which the resin is stored. Leave as a 50% slurry in buffer E for storage.

2. Pack approximately 40 ml of the phenyl Sepharose resin into a 2.5 x 10-cm glass column. Equilibrate with buffer F (without NaCl) for several column volumes at a flow rate of approximately 2 ml/minute.

3. Carefully transfer the retentate from the dialysis bag into a beaker. Record the volume. Retain approximately 1% for assay and record that volume. Add solid $CaCl_2$ to a final concentration of 1 mM above whatever is in the sample from dialysis to ensure it is saturated for calcium ions.

4. Apply the sample to the phenyl Sepharose column, allowing 30–60 minutes for the sample to bind during application.

5. Wash the column with approximately 2–4 volumes (60–120 ml) of buffer F containing 0.2 M NaCl. Collect the wash in a beaker or flask.

6. Remove all the buffer on the top of the column. Step elute the column with buffer E containing 0.2 M NaCl, collecting 2–4-ml fractions. Monitor the UV absorbance and stop after the peak returns to baseline.

7. Strip the column with buffer E containing 8 M urea. Regenerate and store the column with buffer E.

8. Perform SDS-polyacrylamide gel electrophoresis on the fractions to monitor the elution of calmodulin from the column. For typical results from the HIC experiment, see Figure 8.

9. Pool the fractions that contain calmodulin, dialyze against 10 mM ammonium bicarbonate (pH 8.0), and lyophilize. Weigh the final dry sample of calmodulin. Typical yields are 25–40 mg of pure calmodulin per kilogram wet weight of gizzard tissue. Although ammonium bicarbonate is volatile, there may be some dry weight that is not protein. The sample can be dissolved in water and relyophilized. Alternatively, exhaustive dialysis against pure water is possible, but precipitation under these conditions can occur, leading to mechanical losses in recovery.

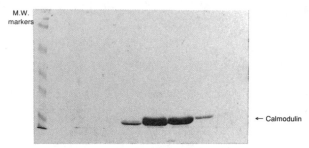

Fractions from phenyl Sepharose column

Figure 8
Polyacrylamide gel (12%; w/v) electrophoresis of aliquots (10 μl) of fractions eluted from phenyl Sepharose. Sequential fractions (from left to right) eluted in 3–5 ml each in buffer E (with NaCl).

• Experiment 6
Characterization of Calmodulin: Calculation of Recovery

PURIFICATION TABLE

Quantitative Recovery of Calmodulin

During each step of the calmodulin purification, you saved an aliquot of the preparation. By quantitating the calmodulin activity in each aliquot and knowing the total volume of the preparation at each step, you can calculate the total recovery of calmodulin at each step. By measuring the total amount of protein at each step, the calmodulin activity can be normalized to determine the specific activity, that is, the activity per unit total protein. As the purification proceeds, the total activity recovered will decrease, in general, since no step gives perfect recovery of activity. However, the specific activity should increase significantly at each step, as contaminating proteins are removed and the calmodulin is recovered as a larger fraction of the total protein. The relative increase in specific activity is often termed the fold purification. The various parameters of yield can be displayed in a table, such as the one shown below. This format allows the rapid and clear evaluation of each step in the purification.

Procedure	Total protein (mg)	Total activity (units)	Recovery (%)	Specific activity (units/mg)	Purification (fold)
Homogenate supernatant					
$(NH_4)_2SO_4$ precipitation					
pH 4.0 precipitation					
DEAE Sephadex®					
Phenyl Sepharose®					
Pure calmodulin					

For calmodulin, units are defined as the amount of sample required for 50% activation of MLCK. In general, units can be defined in any consistent way. However, the activity measured must show linear dependence on the sample in order to be accurate. It is often most convenient to use half-maximal activation, because this point is the most linear and sensitive portion of a sigmoidal activation curve. For enzyme activities measured directly, a linear portion of the velocity curve is necessary. Often an arbitrary aliquot of a crude sample may not fall on the linear portion of the activity curve. Therefore, it is usually necessary to use several dilutions of the sample to achieve an accurate determination of the specific activity. Do not forget to account for the removal of the aliquot in calculating the total activity at each step. For example, if 1% of the sample was removed at a step, the following step should be normalized to represent 99% of the starting material. Thus, you can estimate the total activity recoverable from the original tissue.

Sometimes, particularly in the early steps of the purification, the total activity might show an increase. This is usually indicative of the removal of an inhibitor present in the initial extract. It is also possible that the activity does not show linear dependence on the amount of crude extract due to the very large variety of material in the sample. In these cases, very high dilutions of the extract can often solve the problem, by diluting the interfering contaminants while preserving the activity. Alternatively, as with calmodulin, it is sometimes possible to treat the extract in some way, such as heating, to remove interfering components. However, the total protein measurements must refer back to the original, untreated samples.

STRATEGY

Interpreting the Purification Table

Several general concepts can be learned from a careful accounting of the activity in a purification. As a general rule, a step that results in an increase of specific activity of less than twofold is probably not very worthwhile. At very early steps, low-fold purification can be acceptable for the removal of a large fraction of the protein or to reduce the volume of the sample, if there is high overall yield (>95%) of the desired activity. You should not do the same step twice, under exactly the same conditions. You may see purification protocols that call for two ion-exchange steps of the same type (e.g., DEAE) at exactly the same pH and other conditions. This is usually a sign of a poorly designed preparation. If the step is optimized correctly, a subsequent step of exactly the same type should not be helpful. It is permissible, however, to perform two different ion-exchange steps (anion and cation) or to use the same technique with a different matrix or at a different pH. You should try at each step to exploit one property of the protein, such as charge, size, hydrophobicity, or affinity. At every step, you will have to sacrifice yield for purity. For example, as you evaluate fractions from the DEAE column, there will be those fractions that clearly contain a large amount of calmodulin, and those on the sides that contain some calmodulin, but lots of contaminating proteins. It is your decision whether to include some of these fractions. Given a very specific next step, such as the phenyl Sepharose column, in the case of calmodulin, it is useful to include most of the side fractions, as the contaminating proteins will be eliminated in the following step. This is true of the highly specific affinity chromatography steps as well. However, if you had used brain, for example, rather than gizzards, there would be other proteins that bind to phenyl Sepharose with the same Ca^{++} dependence as calmodulin. In that case, judicious sacrifice on the DEAE column fractions is helpful in obtaining highly purified calmodulin.

•Experiment 7
Characterization of Calmodulin: Electrophoresis

INTRODUCTION

In this section, we discuss three types of electrophoresis on polyacrylamide gels as they apply to calmodulin: (i) polyacrylamide gel electrophoresis (PAGE) in sodium dodecyl sulfate (SDS) in the presence and absence of Ca^{++}; (ii) native PAGE without detergents; and (iii) urea gradient PAGE to analyze folding states. The theory of electrophoresis is not reviewed in detail here, but we examine the applications of a few useful methods of PAGE to calmodulin.

Polyacrylamide Gel Electrophoresis in Sodium Dodecyl Sulfate

The most important point to remember about SDS-PAGE is that the technique allows you to measure the relative mobility of a detergent-protein aggregate in an electric field within a matrix that mechanically restricts movement of macromolecules. The technique of SDS-PAGE does not measure molecular weight directly; it is an interpretation of the relative mobility compared with that of other detergent-protein complexes. Anomalous mobilities on SDS-PAGE are more common than usually acknowledged. Highly charged proteins, either acidic or basic, can deviate from the norm because their intrinsic charge alters the charge-to-mass ratio of the SDS-protein complex. Thus, a highly acidic protein, like calmodulin, may have abnormally high mobility, whereas a highly basic protein, such as a histone, may have abnormally retarded mobility. Modifications may also change the mobility. It is common to find that phosphorylation of a protein results in a slower migrating species. Although the phosphate adds negative charge to the protein, it probably also lowers the total amount of SDS bound to the protein, due to either conformational changes or charge exclusion. Finally, protein ligands can alter the conformation of proteins and thereby change the binding of SDS and the relative mobility on SDS-PAGE. In ideal theory, proteins bound to SDS are unfolded into rod-like structures decorated with detergent molecules yielding constant charge-to-mass ratios of the complexes. In reality, some proteins retain structure, even in SDS, and ligand-binding functions can be retained as well.

Calmodulin retains the ability to bind Ca^{++} even in the presence of SDS (Burgess et al. 1980). As you saw in the purification, calmodulin has dramatically different hydrophobic properties in the presence and absence of Ca^{++}. Therefore, during SDS-PAGE in the presence of Ca^{++}, calmodulin binds more SDS and has a faster mobility than it does in the absence of Ca^{++} (with chelators present). In either case, the calculated molecular weight of calmodulin, measured by relative mobility in SDS-PAGE, is incorrect. In the presence of Ca^{++}, the apparent molecular weight is 12,000–14,000; in the absence of Ca^{++}, the apparent molecular weight is 19,000–20,000; and the true molecular weight is 16,700 (Watterson et al. 1980). Calmodulin maximally binds four moles of Ca^{++} per mole of protein. At subsaturating levels of Ca^{++}, calmodulin displays several bands on SDS-PAGE between relative mobilities of 12 kD and 19 kD. These probably correspond to intermediate states in which less than four moles of Ca^{++} are bound per mole of protein and a parallel, intermediate amount of SDS is also bound, leading to differential mobility. This interesting phenomenon points out the importance of remembering that SDS-PAGE is only a relative measure of electrophoretic mobility and not an absolute measure of molecular mass.

To demonstrate this Ca^{++}-dependent mobility shift of calmodulin on SDS-PAGE, the gels (12.5% or 15% acrylamide) should be cast in buffer containing either 1 mM EGTA or 0.1 mM $CaCl_2$. Note that you should not use 1 mM $CaCl_2$ because SDS will precipitate at higher levels of Ca^{++}. Anyway, 0.1 mM Ca^{++} is sufficient to greatly exceed the association constants for Ca^{++} calmodulin binding. Also, add $CaCl_2$ or EGTA to the samples and to the running buffers for SDS-PAGE. Aside from these modifications, electrophoresis can be performed normally. Remember to run several lanes of low-molecular-weight marker proteins so that accurate R_fs can be measured. An interesting and informative application of this technique is to run aliquots of the samples eluted from the DEAE column in two sets of gels, one with added $CaCl_2$ and one with EGTA. Although various proteins will be visible on the gels upon staining with Coomassie Brilliant Blue, there will be a noticeable shift in mobility of the band corresponding to calmodulin. This method can be used to screen column fractions for the presence of calmodulin without resorting to enzyme activator assays. However, it should be noted that this electrophoresis assay is a qualitative measure of gel mobility shift, and not a true quantitative assay of calmodulin function.

A general protocol for SDS-PAGE using the Laemmli buffer system is given in Appendix 5.

● ───

Native Polyacrylamide Gel Electrophoresis without Detergent

Electrophoresis without detergent is a useful qualitative method for analysis as well as a technique for separation and purification. Large-scale native gels can be used for the purification of active proteins under conditions that do not denature the protein. It is most convenient to perform native PAGE on proteins that have a strong net charge at neutral pH. Otherwise, very high or low pH might be required to obtain a net charge large enough to produce significant migration in polyacrylamide gels. Depending upon the pH of the buffer and the pI of the protein of interest, the direction of electrophoresis (toward the anode or cathode) should be selected appropriately. Calmodulin is highly acidic and therefore carries a strong net negative charge, particularly at pH 8–9. Under these conditions, calmodulin, as an anion (negatively charged), migrates toward the anode (positively charged). Also, because calmodulin is relatively small, compared to many of the contaminating proteins found in smooth muscle tissue, it migrates quickly even through relatively high percentage polyacrylamide gels.

One useful method for native PAGE is to cast gels according to the normal Laemmli buffer system (see Appendix 5), but without SDS. By running the gels under normal conditions, but without SDS, calmodulin and other acidic proteins enter the gel and migrate toward the anode. An alternative is the native PAGE method of Watterson et al. (1976) which utilizes a highly discontinuous Tris-glycine buffer at high pH without a stacking gel. This method is quite useful for very rapid analysis of fractions containing calmodulin in relatively crude extracts or fractions from the DEAE chromatography step. The procedure described below is adapted from Watterson et al. (1976).

MATERIALS AND EQUIPMENT

Acrylamide
Bisacrylamide
Tris base
Sucrose
HCl (1 M)
Ammonium persulfate (0.3 g/ml)
N,N,N',N'-Tetramethylethylenediamine (TEMED)
Slab gel electrophoresis apparatus

Power supply (250 V)
Coomassie® Brilliant Blue dye

SAFETY NOTES

- Acrylamide and bisacrylamide are potent neurotoxins and are absorbed through the skin. Their effects are cumulative. Wear gloves and a mask when weighing acrylamide and bisacrylamide. Wear gloves when handling solutions containing these chemicals. Although polyacrylamide is considered to be nontoxic, it should be handled with care because of the possibility that it might contain small quantities of unpolymerized acrylamide.
- Ammonium persulfate is extremely destructive to tissue of the mucous membranes and upper respiratory tract, eyes, and skin. Inhalation may be fatal. Exposure can cause gastrointestinal disturbances and dermatitis. Wear gloves, safety glasses, respirator, and other protective clothing and work in a chemical fume hood. Wash thoroughly after handling.
- TEMED is extremely destructive to tissue of the mucous membranes and upper respiratory tract, eyes, and skin. Inhalation may be fatal. Prolonged contact can cause severe irritation or burns. Wear gloves, safety glasses, respirator, and other protective clothing and work in a chemical fume hood. Wash thoroughly after handling. Flammable: Vapor may travel a considerable distance to source of ignition and flash back.

REAGENTS

Upper reservoir buffer
Lower reservoir buffer
Sample buffer (5x)
(For recipes, see Preparation of Reagents, pp. 120–122.)

PROCEDURE

1. Dissolve the following components in H_2O and adjust the final volume to 47.9 ml:

Acrylamide	6.0 g
Bisacrylamide	0.144 g
Tris base	2.18 g
Sucrose	4.80 g
HCl (1 M)	2.88 ml

2. De-gas the solution in a sidearm flask under vacuum.

3. Add 100 μl of 0.3 g/ml ammonium persulfate and gently swirl it into the solution.

4. Add 5 μl of TEMED, quickly mix, and pour the gel solution into the plates.

5. Tap the glass to release any air bubbles, insert the comb, and overlay the gel with H_2O until set.

6. Attach the gel to the electrophoresis apparatus. Pour the upper reservoir buffer and lower reservoir buffer into the appropriate tanks.

7. Mix the samples 4:1 with 5x sample buffer (e.g., 80 μl of sample + 20 μl of 5x sample buffer).

8. Load the samples onto the gel and subject to electrophoresis at 200 V constant voltage.

9. Stain the gels with Coomassie Brilliant Blue as you would for Laemmli gels (see Appendix 5).

● ──

Urea Gradient Polyacrylamide Gel Electrophoresis and the Analysis of Folding

Goldenberg and Creighton (1984) introduced the use of polyacryl-amide gels containing a gradient of urea concentrations to analyze the folding states of a protein. In this method, the gel is cast vertically with a 0–8 M gradient of urea. After solidifying, the gel is turned sideways one-quarter turn (90º), so that the gradient extends across the gel. A sample of the protein is loaded across the new top edge of the gel, so that the electrophoresis proceeds down, perpendicular to the urea gradient. As the protein migrates toward the anode, it en-counters different concentrations of urea across the gel. Acting as a chaotropic agent, the urea causes denaturation of the protein to vari-ous extents, depending upon the urea concentration. As denaturation occurs and the protein unfolds, its mobility in the polyacrylamide un-der the influence of the electric field is altered. Generally, the un-folded protein is somewhat retarded in mobility compared to the folded, globular protein. After staining, the protein band extends across the gel, bending upwards at transitions in folding states. For calmodulin, this is particularly instructive, as at least two transitions can be detected. An extensive description of this procedure together with technical considerations and theoretical interpretations are found in Goldenberg (1989). The procedure below is adapted from Goldenberg and Creighton (1984) and Goldenberg (1989).

MATERIALS AND EQUIPMENT

Acrylamide
Bisacrylamide
Tris-acetate buffer (0.5 M; pH 8.0)
Riboflavin (0.04 mg/ml in H_2O)
Urea (crystalline; commercial ultrapure grade or deionized to remove cyanates)
Linear gradient-forming chamber with stir platform
N,N,N',N'-Tetramethylethylenediamine (TEMED)
Peristaltic pump with silicone rubber tubing
Slab gel casting stand
Glass plates for casting gels (use square plates only, not those notched for multiwell combs)
Spacers (two side spacers and two bottom spacers for standard gels)

H_2O-saturated butanol
Fluorescent light
Glycerol
Bromophenol blue (0.1 mg/ml)
Slab gel electrophoresis apparatus
Power supply (250 V)
Coomassie® Brilliant Blue dye

SAFETY NOTES

- Acrylamide and bisacrylamide are potent neurotoxins and are absorbed through the skin. Their effects are cumulative. Wear gloves and a mask when weighing acrylamide and bisacrylamide. Wear gloves when handling solutions containing these chemicals. Although polyacrylamide is considered to be nontoxic, it should be handled with care because of the possibility that it might contain small quantities of unpolymerized acrylamide.
- TEMED is extremely destructive to tissue of the mucous membranes and upper respiratory tract, eyes, and skin. Inhalation may be fatal. Prolonged contact can cause severe irritation or burns. Wear gloves, safety glasses, respirator, and other protective clothing and work in a chemical fume hood. Wash thoroughly after handling. Flammable: Vapor may travel a considerable distance to source of ignition and flash back.

PROCEDURE

1. Prepare the following gel solutions:

   N Solution (15% acrylamide; no urea)

Acrylamide (30%; w/v)/bisacrylamide (0.8%; w/v)	50 ml
Tris-acetate buffer (0.5 M; pH 8.0)	10 ml
Riboflavin (0.04 mg/ml)	12.5 ml
H_2O	27.5 ml
Total volume:	100 ml

   D Solution (11% acrylamide; 8 M urea)

Acrylamide (30%; w/v)/bisacrylamide (0.8%; w/v)	36.7 ml
Tris-acetate buffer (0.5 M; pH 8.0)	10 ml
Riboflavin (0.04 mg/ml)	12.5 ml
Urea	48.1 g
H_2O	4 ml
Total volume:	100 ml

2. De-gas the solutions in sidearm flasks under vacuum.

3. Set up the gradient maker with solutions N and D in the appropriate places, depending on the orientation of gel loading. If you are loading the gel from the top, place the D solution in the forward chamber and the N solution becomes the limiting solution of the apparatus. If you are loading the gel from the bottom, place the N solution in the forward chamber and the D solution is limiting.

   Note: You can use gradient makers with either concentric or adjacent chambers, but be careful which solution is in the forward chamber.

4. Set up the gel plates using the bottom spacers for standard gels as the side spacers. These usually require trimming so that they do not extend past the edge of the glass plates when the cast gels are turned sideways. Use a standard side spacer on the bottom.

5. Begin stirring the solutions in the gradient maker. Add 100 μl of TEMED to each solution. Open the valve and start the peristaltic pump flowing at approximately 1 ml/minute. It is best to set up this apparatus in a dark room so that fluorescent light does not initiate polymerization.

   Note: Volumes can be scaled up or down to accommodate the total volume of the gel casting apparatus.

6. Overlay the gel with H_2O-saturated butanol and expose to direct fluorescent light for 1 hour or until the gel is set.

7. Remove the H_2O-saturated butanol and wash the surface of the gel with H_2O. Insert a standard side spacer at the top of the gel. Rotate the gel 90°. Remove the standard bottom spacers from the new top and bottom of the gel. The urea gradient should now run side to side across the gel.

8. Mix the sample (at least 1 mg/ml) 10:1 with glycerol and 0.1 mg/ml bromophenol blue.

9. Assemble the gel in the electrophoresis apparatus. For running buffer, use a 1 in 10 dilution of 0.5 M Tris-acetate buffer (pH 8.0) (final concentration 50 mM).

10. Layer the sample (50–100 μl) evenly over the top of the gel. Subject the sample to electrophoresis at 10 mA toward the anode. Calmodulin is an anion and it will move toward the anode at pH 8.0.

11. Remove the gel and stain it with Coomassie Brilliant Blue, as described for standard Laemmli gels in Appendix 5.

MODIFICATIONS TO THIS TECHNIQUE

The calmodulin sample can be run with or without Ca^{++} ions (i.e., you can add 0.1 mM $CaCl_2$ or 1 mM EGTA to the sample and to the gel solutions). In a separate experiment, you can dissolve the calmodulin sample in 50 mM Tris-acetate buffer containing 8 M urea to observe where the fully unfolded protein migrates.

SILVER STAINING OF CALMODULIN

Coomassie Brilliant Blue is a standard and useful stain for proteins, including calmodulin. However, silver staining of calmodulin and other divalent-cation- and metal-binding proteins can produce unusual results. Unless the gels are fixed first, using glutaraldehyde or an equivalent cross-linker, calmodulin displays a negative staining pattern with silver. Unfixed calmodulin excludes the deposition of silver from the area of the gel in which the protein resides, and this is visible as a clear area surrounded by low background staining. Many of the other proteins show a black or dark brown color over a lighter background. After silver staining, it is therefore common to identify fractions of protein as being without calmodulin, when in reality there are large amounts of the protein. This emphasizes the fact that silver staining is not quantitative for all proteins, and the silver staining characteristics of the protein of interest should be understood before attempting to evaluate gels in this way. Several silver staining protocols for calmodulin have been compared (Schleicher and Watterson 1983).

• Experiment 8
Proteolytic Digestion

INTRODUCTION

The purpose of proteolytic digestion of a protein is the division of the protein into smaller polypeptides that are more amenable to physical and chemical characterization. Proteolytic digestion refers to the hydrolysis of a number of specific peptide bonds in the target protein molecule. Ideally, a specific proteolysis method would quantitatively cleave a limited number of peptide bonds reliably, producing peptides that could be recovered in very high yields. Unfortunately, all methods give some heterogeneity in specificity of peptide bond cleavage and no procedure consistently gives 100% yield. In this respect, any proteolysis procedure should be considered experimental and the products should be characterized in detail. It is possible to predict some of the fragments of a protein that will be generated upon proteolysis with a particular reagent on the basis of a known protein or translated cDNA sequence. However, such predictions are consistently an incomplete picture of the actual products as they cannot reliably foretell modifications, incomplete digestion products, and side reactions. As you will see from this experiment, unexpected, interesting, and functionally important results may arise from the careful analysis of proteolysis products. There are two general classes of reagents for proteolysis: (i) chemical compounds that react covalently with particular amino acid side chains and their adjacent peptide bonds, promoting peptide bond hydrolysis, and (ii) enzymes, known collectively as endoproteinases, that catalyze the hydrolysis of peptide bonds adjacent to specific amino acid residues. Here we present two separate protocols for the fragmentation of calmodulin, one utilizing the chemical reagent cyanogen bromide (CNBr) and the other using the endoproteinase trypsin. In recent years, a new class of molecules has emerged, known as catalytic antibodies, which in the future might be the most useful reagents for specific proteolytic cleavage.

Chemical Cleavage

Several sorts of chemical reagents are useful in specific cleavage of proteins. The most important elements for such reagents to be useful are specificity and uniformity. It is, of course, an absolute requirement that the covalent reaction that is necessary to produce the fragments does not result in products that are resistant to further chemical procedures. The most popular and useful reagent is CNBr (Gross and Witkop 1962), which results in cleavage of the peptide bonds between the carboxyl moiety of a methionyl residue and the amino moiety of another amino acid, except threonine. Other useful reagents include acid, which cleaves at aspartyl-proline peptide bonds (Allen 1989), and hydroxylamine, which cleaves at asparaginyl-glycine bonds (Bornstein 1970). Several reagents are available that specifically cleave proteins at tryptophan residues. The cysteine cleavage reagent NTCB is not widely used because the peptide liberated as the carboxy-terminal fragment is modified and refractory to Edman degradation (Allen 1989). Overall, CNBr is used most often, unless the protein is found to be devoid of methionyl residues or the methionyl side chain sulfurs have been oxidized.

The mechanism of CNBr action is outlined in Figure 9. Briefly, CNBr reacts with the sulfur of the methionyl thioether bond, resulting in a methylthiocyanate derivative of the amino acid. The sulfur retains a positive charge as a sulfonium ion. The point is to make the γ-carbon of the side chain an attractive site for intramolecular, nucleophilic attack by the oxygen of the carbonyl involved in the adjacent peptide bond. In an unmodified methionine side chain, a methanethiol unit in the thioether linkage is quite stable and completely unattractive to attack by the carbonyl oxygen. However, as the sulfonium ion resulting from the cyanylation, the methyl thiocyanate becomes an excellent leaving group. The carbonyl moiety is not isolated, of course; it is part of the conjugated double bond system of the peptide amide linkage. You can imagine this as having a partial double bond character, or as an equilibrium between keto- and enol-tautomers. Under acidic conditions, that equilibrium is shifted toward the enol form. The presence of the wonderful leaving group on the γ-carbon of the derivatized methionine favors formation of a five-membered ring and the loss of the methyl thiocyanate. The resulting structure is no longer a peptide bond, but a Schiff base that is rapidly hydrolyzed by water. This liberates a free amino group of the carboxy-terminal peptide product and the homoserine lactone of the amino-terminal peptide product. The lactone form can open via another molecule of water to the free acid form of homoserine, depending upon the pH. In anhydrous acid, the homoserine is forced to the lactone, whereas under basic, aqueous conditions, the open form is preferred. Typically, in dilute aqueous acid (pH 2–4), there is an equilibrium between the lactone and open forms, resulting in a mixture of products. This is a significant consideration during HPLC separation of peptide fragments. Such analysis is performed in dilute aqueous

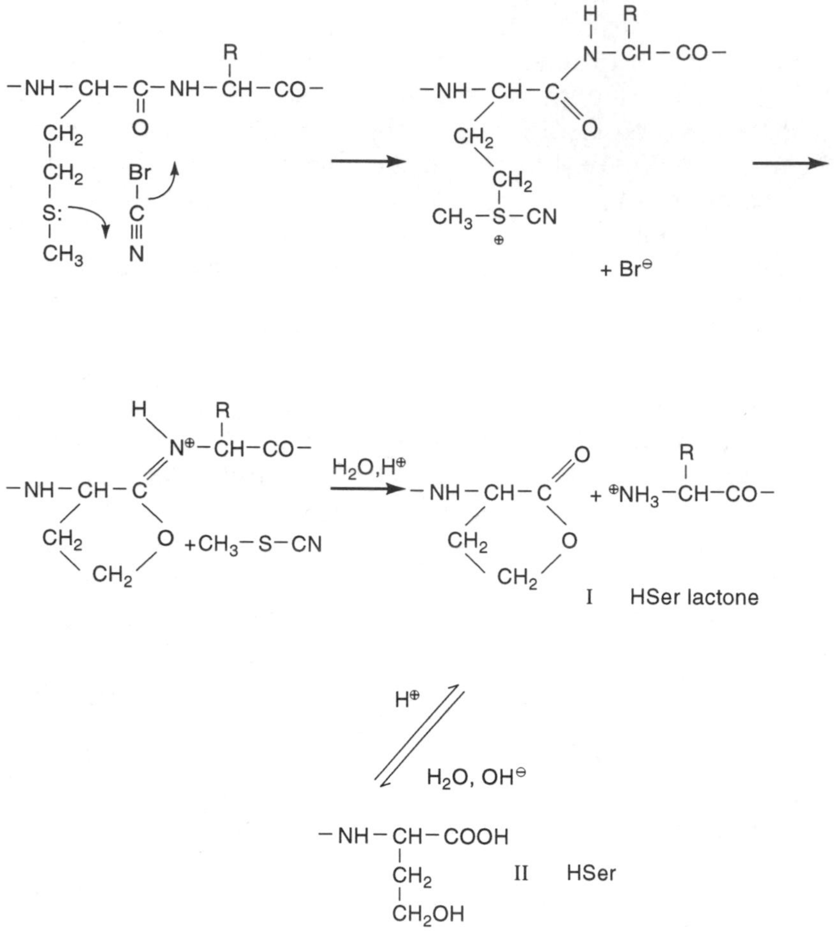

Figure 9
Chemistry of cyanogen bromide cleavage. (Adapted, with permission, from Gross and Witkop 1962.)

acid at pH 2–4, and peptides resulting from CNBr cleavage often yield twin peaks on the chromatogram. This can be avoided by treating the lactone form with methylamine to form an α-carboxyamide.

Endoproteinase Digestion

Enzymes for the proteolytic digestion of proteins are commercially available with a variety of different specificities. In most of these enzymes, the specification site constitutes one or two amino acids, although there are now several commercial enzymes in which the specification site constitutes a larger segment. Table 2 lists some of the most popular enzymes. Trypsin is widely used because it was one of

Table 2 Proteolytic Enzymes Commonly Used in Protein Digestion

Enzyme	Specificity	Comments
Trypsin	K-X or R-X;	aminoethylated C-X is a good substrate
	X not P	K-D and K-E are poor substrates
Lys-C	K-X; X not P	active in 0.1% SDS
Arg-C	R-X; X not P	R-E is a poor substrate
S. aureus V8	D-X or E-X	buffer pH changes specificity
Asp-N	X-D	cysteic acid is also a substrate
Chymotrypsin	F-X, F=F,Y,W	best for aromatics
	L-X, L=L,I,V	weaker for aliphatics
Thermolysin	X-F,L and other nonpolar residues	requires zinc ions

Amino acids are represented by one-letter symbols: C, cysteine; D, aspartic acid; E, glutamic acid; F, phenylalanine; I, isoleucine; K, lysine; L, leucine; P, proline; R, arginine; V, valine; W, tryptophan; Y, tyrosine.

the first proteinases available commercially in high purity. An enormous number of structural and enzyme mechanistic studies have been performed on pancreatic trypsin, and it is one of the prime examples of a serine protease. The specificity of trypsin is the hydrolysis of peptide bonds following a lysyl or arginyl residue. The basic side chain is required for binding to the catalytic site. However, when followed or surrounded by acidic residues, the lysyl peptide bond often becomes refractory to hydrolysis by trypsin. Also, a peptide bond from a basic residue to a proline is not suitable for tryptic hydrolysis. It is possible to create a site for trypsin digestion by aminoethylation of cysteine (Allen 1989). In recent years, enzymes with recognition sites similar to those of trypsin but with greater specificity have become more popular, particularly endoproteinases Lys-C and Arg-C (Marshak et al. 1984). These enzymes catalyze the hydrolysis of peptide bonds specifically on the carboxy-terminal side of lysyl or arginyl residues, respectively. Lys-C is quite useful in the digestion of proteins exposed to polyacrylamide gel electrophoresis because the enzyme is stable in low concentrations of SDS (see Appendix 8).

The trypsin protocol presented here calls for digestion in the presence of 1 mM EGTA as chelator. This is important because the conformation of calmodulin changes significantly in the presence of Ca^{++} and only limited digestion by trypsin occurs. It is a useful exercise to do parallel digests with 1 mM chelator or 1 mM $CaCl_2$ and to compare the pattern of fragments obtained. In the older literature on trypsin, there are protocols that demand 1 mM $CaCl_2$ as a requirement for the activity of trypsin. However, if you use highly purified trypsin, this is not necessary as the Ca^{++} is only required for the conversion of the zymogen, trypsinogen, to the active trypsin. Purified trypsin is quite active in the presence of chelator. Trypsin activity is optimal at approximately pH 8.0 and the enzyme is not active in dilute acid. The trypsin is dissolved in 1 mM HCl and kept on ice to preserve its activity, but the final reaction conditions (pH 8.0 at 37°C) are more like the intestinal environment where trypsin functions in vivo.

A list of expected fragments from a trypsin digest of calmodulin is shown in Table 3. The prediction is based on quantitative hydrolysis of all Lys-X and Arg-X peptide bonds. As discussed above, there are occasions when these bonds do not hydrolyze or do so in low yield. Therefore, you should examine the sequence of calmodulin (see Fig. 10) yourself to predict which bonds may or may not be susceptible to trypsin.

Other enzymes that are useful for digestion include those with specificities for peptide bonds adjacent to acidic or neutral residues. The *Staphylococcus aureus* strain V8 produces a protease that cleaves sites on the carboxy-terminal side of glutamyl or aspartyl bonds, and this specificity is altered depending upon the type of buffer employed (Allen 1989). The Asp-N protease cleaves sites that are amino-terminal

Table 3 Predicted Fragments from a Trypsin Digest of Calmodulin

Fragment	Protease	Site	Length	Site	Protease	M.W.
F1	trypsin	(38)	37	(74)	trypsin	4071.7
F2	trypsin	(127)	22	(148)	–	2490.8
F3	–	(1)	13	(13)	trypsin	1521.7
F4	trypsin	(95)	12	(106)	trypsin	1265.4
F5	trypsin	(116)	11	(126)	trypsin	1349.6
F6	trypsin	(22)	9	(30)	trypsin	907.0
F7	trypsin	(78)	9	(86)	trypsin	1093.1
F8	trypsin	(107)	9	(115)	trypsin	1028.3
F9	trypsin	(14)	8	(21)	trypsin	956.1
F10	trypsin	(31)	7	(37)	trypsin	805.0
F11	trypsin	(87)	4	(90)	trypsin	521.6
F12	trypsin	(91)	4	(94)	trypsin	507.6
F13	trypsin	(76)	2	(77)	trypsin	277.4
F14	trypsin	(75)	1	(75)	trypsin	146.2

This prediction is based on a computer analysis of the sequence of calmodulin using the IntelliGenetics PEP program, DIG routine.

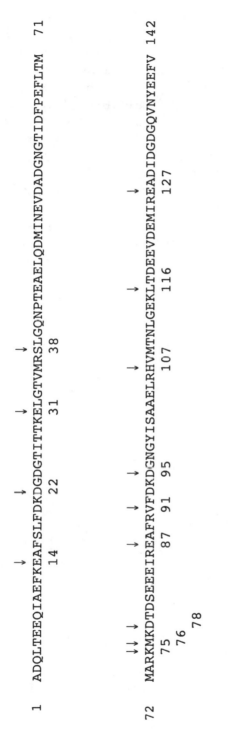

Figure 10

Amino acid sequence of vertebrate calmodulin. The vertical arrows indicate the amino acid residues that follow the cleaved peptide bond and that become the amino terminal residue of the new predicted peptides. The primary structure of calmodulin was determined by Watterson et al. (1980) and Sasagawa et al. (1982).

to aspartyl residues. If you digest an acidic protein, such as cal-modulin, with the V8 protease, for example, you may obtain tiny peptides, consisting of 2–5 amino acids, which are not helpful in structural analysis. Similarly, a basic protein, such as a histone, digested with trypsin may yield many different small peptide products. In general, you should use a protease that will cleave the protein of interest infrequently to obtain moderate to large fragments. Therefore, might use trypsin or Lys-C to digest an acidic protein, such as calmodulin, and use V8 or Asp-N protease to digest basic proteins, such as histones. Neutral proteases, such as thermolysin, are often too promiscuous to obtain useful fragments of an intact protein. In general, it is best to use enzymes such as thermolysin and chymotrypsin for the digestion of fragments already purified from a protein. These sub-digestions can be helpful in identifying the exact sites of modifications.

Digestion of Calmodulin with Cyanogen Bromide

MATERIALS

Formic acid (highest grade available) (e.g., Aldrich Chemical Co., Inc.)
Purified calmodulin (dry powder; salt-free) (0.1–1 mg)
Cyanogen bromide (CNBr) (crystalline) (e.g., Aldrich Chemical Co., Inc.)
Acetonitrile (e.g., Burdick & Jackson or J.T. Baker)

SAFETY NOTES

- Cyanogen bromide is highly toxic and volatile. Wear gloves and always handle this compound in a fume hood.
- Acetonitrile is very volatile and extremely flammable. It is an irritant and a chemical asphyxiant that can exert its effects by inhalation, ingestion, or absorption through the skin. Cases of severe exposure are treated as cyanide poisoning. Handle acetonitrile in a chemical fume hood. Wear gloves and safety glasses.

PROCEDURE

This procedure is adapted from Gross and Witkop (1962).

1. Dilute formic acid in H_2O to give a final concentration of 70% (w/v). For formic acid that is >99%, use 2.1 ml of formic acid and 0.9 ml of H_2O. For formic acid that is 88%, use 2.1 ml of formic acid and 0.54 ml of H_2O.

2. Dissolve calmodulin in the 70% formic acid to give a final concentration of 1 mg/ml. Place on ice.

3. Weigh a 1.5-ml capped polypropylene centrifuge tube. Wearing gloves, open the CNBr jar in a fume hood and transfer a small crystal to the preweighed tube. Close the tube and the jar of CNBr in the fume hood. Weigh the closed tube containing the CNBr crystal and subtract the weight of the tube to calculate the weight of CNBr.

4. Dissolve the CNBr in acetonitrile to give a final concentration of 6 M (0.64 g/ml). Remember to wear gloves and to open the tube only in the fume hood.

5. Add an aliquot of the CNBr solution to the calmodulin. The aliquot should contain a 400-fold molar excess of CNBr over the total amount of methionine residues expected in the protein.

6. Cap the tube tightly and mix thoroughly. Cover the tube with foil to exclude light. Incubate the reaction mixture in the fume hood for 22 hours at room temperature.

7. Add an equal volume of pure H_2O to the reaction mixture and subject the sample to vacuum centrifugation until it is dry. Redissolve the sample in 0.1% (w/v) trifluoroacetic acid for analysis by HPLC or mass spectrometry.

● ───────────────────────────────────────

Digestion of Calmodulin with Trypsin

MATERIALS

TPCK-treated trypsin (available as a dry powder from Worthington
    Biochemical Corp.)
HCl (1 mM)
Purified calmodulin (dry powder; salt-free) (0.1–1 mg)

REAGENTS

Digestion buffer
(For recipe, see Preparation of Reagents, pp. 120–122.)

PROCEDURE

1. Weigh 0.1–1 mg of trypsin in a 1.5-ml polypropylene centrifuge
   tube and dissolve in 1 mM HCl to give a final concentration of 1
   mg/ml. Place on ice.

2. Dissolve the calmodulin in digestion buffer to give a final concentration of 1 mg/ml. Place on ice.

3. Add an aliquot of trypsin to the calmodulin. The aliquot should
   contain 1/100 of the amount of calmodulin by weight. For example, add 5 μg of trypsin (5 μl of the 1 mg/ml trypsin stock solution)
   to 0.5 mg of calmodulin.

4. Cap the tube tightly and incubate the reaction mixture for 2 hours
   at 37°C.

5. While the digestion reaction is incubating, keep the remainder of
   the trypsin stock solution on ice. After 2 hours, add a further aliquot of trypsin (again 1/100 of the amount of calmodulin by
   weight) to the digestion mixture. Cap the tube tightly and continue the incubation for another 4–8 hours (or overnight if possible) at 37°C.

6. At the end of the reaction, you can freeze the sample until it is required, subject it to vacuum centrifugation to reduce the volume, or inject it directly onto the HPLC for separation. The sample can be acidified with HCl or trifluoroacetic acid to pH 2–3 to stop the reaction. However, with this procedure you risk precipitating some of the peptides with low pIs.

• Experiment 9
Reverse-phase HPLC

INTRODUCTION

The technique of high-performance liquid chromatography (HPLC) has grown and changed over the last few decades to encompass a variety of high-resolution separation methods. In general, HPLC refers to chromatographic separation methods performed with matrices that are: (i) stable under high pressures and (ii) comprise small particles, giving a large effective surface area. These matrix characteristics, combined with relatively high flow rates, result in separations that are rapid (occurring in minutes) and of very high resolution. One of the most common matrices for HPLC is silica. Underivatized silica particles were originally used to separate lipid molecules with different hydrophilic characteristics. Thus, in normal- or straight-phase HPLC on silica, lipid mixtures in an organic solvent are applied to the column, and molecules with increasing hydrophilicity are eluted by increasing the proportion of aqueous or other polar solvent. Separations by normal-phase HPLC on silica take advantage of the marginal polar quality of hydrophobic molecules, such as lipids. Proteins, however, are dipolar ions with marginal hydrophobic qualities. Therefore, HPLC of proteins utilizes silica derivatized with aliphatic or aromatic moieties, and mixtures of proteins are adsorbed in aqueous solutions. Increasingly hydrophobic proteins are eluted with an ascending gradient of organic solvents. This separation of proteins is referred to as reverse-phase HPLC (RP-HPLC) to indicate that the basis of the separation is opposite to that used for lipids in normal-phase HPLC. This nomenclature is purely historical.

It should be noted that HPLC does not automatically refer to reverse-phase separation of proteins. Ion exchange, gel filtration, and affinity chromatography can be performed quite well using HPLC instrumentation and media. In this section, RP-HPLC on silica-based columns is discussed because it is one of the most powerful and widely used techniques of HPLC and because you will use RP-HPLC to separate the fragments of calmodulin. Remember that RP-HPLC utilizes organic solvents, such as acetonitrile, to separate molecules, and such solvents may denature the three-dimensional structure of a protein. When preparing proteins or fragments of proteins for chemical analysis, the three-dimensional structure is not an issue. However,

RP-HPLC is often avoided when preparing proteins for crystallography or NMR analysis because of the denaturation question. As you have seen in the purification of calmodulin, it is possible to use HIC under nondenaturing conditions to separate proteins on the basis of hydrophobicity. Nevertheless, RP-HPLC does produce very high resolution separations, and if it is feasible to use it in an application, then it has the advantages of speed and performance over HIC on soft gels. One of the most frustrating parts of RP-HPLC can be trying to choose a column. There are now many different varieties and manufacturers of silica-based HPLC columns, and distinguishing between these options is often daunting to a scientist new to the field. There are several basic parameters of silica-based, reverse-phase HPLC columns that are important to consider. These include the characteristics of the silica matrix, the nature of the derivatizing side chain, and the physical dimensions of the column.

Silica. Silica is a crystalline array of silicon and oxygen atoms in which each silicon atom has single bonds to four oxygens and each oxygen atom has single bonds to two silicons, as shown in Figure 11. Raw silica is mined on a very large scale and is used in the manufacture of many products, including abrasives, desiccants, and toothpaste. Silica particles are sized by sieving procedures, and different size particles are processed for use in HPLC matrices. The size of the particles refers to the average diameter of the particles. The smaller the particle size, the higher the back pressure on the column, which will limit the flow rate. For many applications, particles of 5 or 10 μm are acceptable,

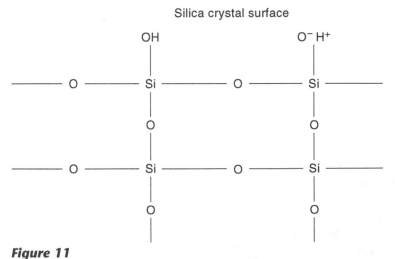

Figure 11
Schematic representation of the crystalline structure of silica. Note the silanol groups at the crystal surface.

giving very high resolution and a reasonable flow rate for columns 1–10 mm in diameter. In cases where larger diameter columns are used, 15-μm particles may be necessary to preserve the flow rate, and 25–40-μm particles are necessary for larger scale projects, for example, with a 50-mm diameter column and a flow rate of 75 ml/minute. The silica particles can be irregularly shaped or, by processing, can assume a spheroidal shape. Irregular particles have a greater surface area overall and pack more densely. Spheroidal particles pack more regularly and give good, reproducible results, although columns have a lower capacity. For proteins and peptides, it is often wise to choose spheroidal silica particles that are 10 μm in diameter.

The silica particles have holes, called pores, that permit molecules of solute and solvent to penetrate. If the pores are too small, then larger macromolecules will be excluded from the pores. In RP-HPLC, it is advantageous to have the proteins or peptides to be separated exposed to the largest surface area possible. Manufacturers use alkali, heat, and pressure to treat silica, generating average pore sizes that vary from 75 Å to 1000 Å. Columns with 75–125-Å pores are used for small molecules, including very small peptides, consisting of two to a few amino acids. For larger peptides and small proteins, it is often wise to use 300-Å pore size silica. This size is readily available from various manufacturers.

Derivatives. To accomplish reverse-phase separations, silica is derivatized with silanes so that one or more substituents of the silica is an aliphatic or aromatic moiety. The reactive groups on the silicon atom of the silane consist of halogens, usually chlorine, or oxy derivatives, such as methoxy or ethoxy. The silanes are reacted with the silica in refluxing toluene under strictly anhydrous conditions. The aliphatic or aromatic functionality thus becomes incorporated onto the silica crystal surface by reaction with the surface silanol groups. The type of derivatization affects the separation. Generally, the longer the aliphatic chain, progressing from C2 to C18, the more effective the binding of solute peptides and proteins. However, larger proteins and hydrophobic peptides may bind too tightly to long aliphatics, such as C18, and even very high proportions of organic solvent may not elute the desired molecules. Small peptides, however, will be separated better on C18. A good compromise for a mixture of long and short peptides is C8.

The extent of derivatization is often referred to as the carbon loading. HPLC column manufacturers generally give this parameter a qualitative, rather than a quantitative, value. High carbon loading may be good for separating small organic compounds, but it is not desirable for peptides and proteins. Moderate to low carbon loadings are usually adequate to separate peptides. A carbon loading that is too high can result in very low yields. The silanol groups on the silica surface that are not derivatized are acidic, donating protons to the solvent. The anionic form, carrying a negative charge, can set up cation-exchange properties on the matrix that are not desired in the reverse-phase separation. Therefore, the matrix should be fully end-capped. This means that the unsubstituted silanol groups should be derivatized with a neutral silane that blocks the ion-exchange effect, but does not contribute much to the overall reverse-phase separation. Often, dichlorodimethylsilane is used, resulting in one carbon capping of the silanols. Note that this is the same compound widely used for "silanizing" glass surfaces.

Column size. The diameter and length of the HPLC column will affect the separation. Analytical and micropreparative work is currently done on columns 2 mm in diameter, and there is increasing use of microbore columns ≤1 mm in diameter, as well as microcapillary HPLC using fused silica columns. Typical columns at larger scales are 4–5 mm, 8–10 mm, and 20 mm in diameter. Large systems are available with columns ≥50 mm for gram-scale preparative work. A rough rule of thumb for peptides is micrograms on 1–2-mm columns, milligrams on 5-mm columns, 10–20 mg on 10-mm columns, 100 mg on 20-mm columns, and 0.5–1 g on 50-mm columns. Column length has a significant effect on separation, but this is dependent upon the diameter and the load. For very small loads, the sample generally undergoes most of the adsorption and desorption in the first few centimeters of the column length. Often, increasing column length for tiny samples adds no more practical separation, so short columns of a few centimeters are adequate. For larger samples on narrow-bore (2-mm diameter) columns, added length can improve resolution significantly. Typical columns are 15–30 cm in length.

Mobile phase. As described above, the sample is applied in an aqueous solvent, and the adsorbed peptides are eluted with increasing proportions of miscible organic solvent. A popular system is 0.1% (w/v) trifluoroacetic acid (TFA) as the aqueous component and acetonitrile (methyl cyanide) as the organic component. Alcohols can be used up to isopropanol, the largest organic alcohol that is miscible with water in all proportions. However, mixing alcohols, particularly methanol, with the aqueous solvent leads to heating and can cause bubbles of dissolved gas to form in the flow. TFA is the smallest of the perfluoroalkanoic acids (see Hancock 1984). It serves to acidify the solution to pH 2.1, so the carboxylates are all protonated and neutral. The trifluoroacetate anion also serves to ion pair with the charged amino, imidazole, and guanidinium moieties on the proteins, helping to mask their charge. Thus, all the substituents of the protein side chains are neutralized, aiding the adsorption to the hydrophobic surface. Highly basic peptides and proteins will elute abnormally early in this system, so stronger ion-pairing reagents, altered pH, or different columns are more useful for those basic molecules. Silica columns are not stable above pH 7.0, so acidic pH is necessary. A useful technique is to employ ammonium acetate or other volatile buffers for aqueous systems at higher pH. The use of volatile solvents, such as dilute organic acids and acetonitrile, is very helpful after the separation, so that concentration of the solute can be achieved without transfer.

REVERSE-PHASE SEPARATION OF CALMODULIN FRAGMENTS BY HPLC

There is no set protocol for this procedure as it is highly dependent upon the type and extent of HPLC equipment. A simple linear gradient of acetonitrile from 5% to 70% (by volume) is adequate to separate most of the fragments of calmodulin. The sample can be injected directly after the digestion and vacuum centrifugation step. If necessary, all dilutions of the sample should be in the 0.1% TFA solvent. Most HPLC systems are equipped with a detector that measures ultraviolet light absorbance at a wavelength of 200–300 nm. Remember to monitor at low wavelength (e.g., 210 nm) where the peptide bonds and all conjugated double bond systems absorb. If you monitor at 280 nm, tryptophan- and tyrosine-containing peptides will be visible, but none of the others. Of course, calmodulin has no tryptophan. Collect the fractions corresponding to the absorbance peaks that appear on the monitor. Remember to calculate or measure the delay time between the flow cell and the outlet, so you do not miss the peak-containing peptide. Fraction collectors can be used, but manual collection is still the most useful and reliable method for a small number of fractions. For a typical profile of a trypsin digest of calmodulin on RP-HPLC, see Figure 12.

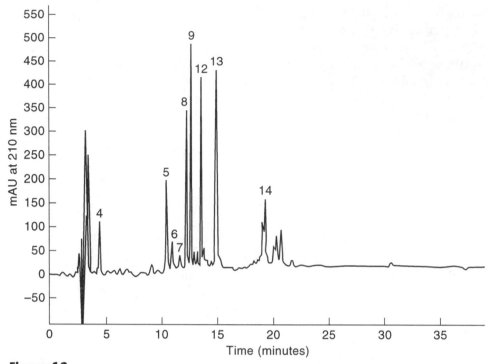

Figure 12
Profile of a trypsin digest of calmodulin separated on RP-HPLC. The numbers indicate the positions of the 14 individual fragments generated by the digestion. Individual peaks can be collected for further characterization by mass spectrometry (see Experiment 10). This profile was generated during the 1993 Cold Spring Harbor Protein Purification and Characterization Course.

• Experiment 10
Physical Analysis of Calmodulin

INTRODUCTION

The goal of this section is to introduce you to two useful methods of physical analysis of proteins, ultraviolet (UV) absorption spectroscopy and mass spectrometry. These methods can be applied to intact proteins, such as the purified calmodulin prepared in this unit, or to peptide fragments of proteins obtained from HPLC separations of proteolytic digestions. Physical methods take advantage of some intrinsic property of the protein or peptide being analyzed. UV absorption spectroscopy measures the light absorbed (or transmitted) by a protein solution across the useful portion of the UV spectrum. Mass spectrometry measures the mass-to-charge ratio of an ionized form of the protein or peptide. Both techniques give clues about the polypeptide structure, without the addition of exogenous chemical for prior reaction. Physical analysis alone, however, is usually insufficient to prove the nature of a protein structure. The strongest evidence for structural characterization of a polypeptide is a combination of physical and chemical procedures. By adding these analyses to biological assay of the intact protein, you will produce the strongest case for the identity of the structure with a particular biochemical function.

Ultraviolet Absorption Spectrometry

The conjugated double bond systems found in polypeptides absorb UV light in the range of 200–300 nm wavelength. Various functional groups have different absorption maxima, so examination of the overall absorption spectrum of a protein or peptide reveals significant information about the amino acid composition and amount of the protein. If the amino acid composition of the protein is known, it may be possible to estimate purity by examining the spectrum. For example, if a protein is known to contain no tryptophan, any evidence of the characteristic absorbance of the indole ring is likely due to contamination. The technique is rapid, and a UV-visible spectrophotometer is standard equipment in most biochemistry laboratories. Spectrophotometry is a nondestructive method, so the entire sample is recovered. Overall, UV absorption spectroscopy is an easy way to obtain information on your protein, and it is astounding how often this simple method is overlooked.

Characteristic absorbance peaks due to protein constituents are found in the range 190–220 and 250–285 nm wavelength. At low wavelength, conjugated double bonds, such as that found in the peptide bond itself, show strong absorbance. Therefore, proteins display an intense absorbance peak in this range, but it is not diagnostic, since many other organic compounds have similar absorbance bands. Notable among these are the organic acids, such as formic, acetic, and trifluoroacetic acid, that are often used to dissolve proteins. The absorbance of the peptide bonds is most useful when monitoring the effluent from the HPLC separation of peptides. By following the absorbance at 210 nm, for example, it is possible to detect very small amounts (<1 pmol) of a short peptide containing no other UV-absorbing moieties. Even greater sensitivity can be achieved by using 10 mM HCl rather than 0.1% trifluoroacetic acid in the mobile phase, as the background absorbance of high purity HCl in pure water is very low.

The diagnostic portion of the spectrum for proteins is 250–285 nm. The aromatic side chains of amino acids absorb in that range. It is a common misconception that an absorbance peak at 280 nm is the only characteristic absorbance peak. The indole ring of tryptophan has an absorption maximum at 274.8 nm and the phenolic group of tyrosine maximally absorbs at approximately 280.4 nm. The relative extinction coefficients are about fourfold higher for tryptophan than for tyrosine, so the spectrum of protein or peptides containing tryptophan is dominated by this peak. Phenylalanine gives a very interesting fine spectrum, producing a series of four relative maxima at

247, 252, 258, and 264. The phenylalanine fine spectrum is often overshadowed by the tryptophan peak at 280, but it can easily be seen in proteins such as calmodulin, which has no tryptophan and a high phenylalanine-to-tyrosine ratio. Cystine also contributes to absorbance at 280 nm, so peptides without aromatics and containing cystine can be identified spectrophotometrically. Finally, the imidazole ring of histidine has a modest absorbance maximum between 250 and 260 nm. Two important notes of practical use in the molecular biology and biochemistry of proteins and nucleic acids are: (i) the absorbance of an average protein at 260 nm is not zero, and (ii) certain proteins have relatively low absorbance at 280 nm. Ignoring these concepts and assuming that all proteins must show absorbance at 280 nm and that absorbance at 260 nm is solely due to nucleic acid and not protein can lead to incorrect assumptions about the abundance of specific proteins during purification protocols.

ULTRAVIOLET ABSORPTION SPECTRUM OF CALMODULIN

To determine the UV spectrum of calmodulin, dissolve a dry, lyophilized, salt-free sample of the protein in 10 mM ammonium bicarbonate (pH 8.0) at a concentration of 1 mg/ml. Measure and record the absorption spectrum between 200 and 300 nm using the 10 mM ammonium bicarbonate (pH 8.0) solution as the blank. No tryptophan peak should be seen, and the phenylalanine fine spectrum should be very clear. The tyrosine peak should be significant but it should not obscure the phenylalanine (see Fig. 13).

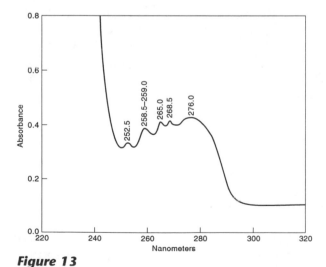

Figure 13
UV absorption spectrum of calmodulin. The phenylalanine fine spectrum has four peaks at 252.5, 258.5–259.0, 265.0, and 268.5 nm. The tyrosine peak is at 276.0 nm.

● ——

Mass Spectrometry of Proteins and Peptides

There are now a wide variety of instruments available commercially to assist in the measurement of the mass of a protein or peptide. These instruments consist of a mechanism to ionize the molecule of interest and an analyzer to measure the mass-to-charge ratio (m/z) of the ions produced, relative to known standards. Although several types of ionization methods and analyzer units are appropriate for proteins and peptides, the most affordable and most easily operated instruments are presently time-of-flight spectrometers. Following ionization, the ion of interest is desorbed from a solid phase surface into a high vacuum phase by a large electric potential, typically 15–30 kV. This acceleration occurs in a short region (a few millimeters), followed by a field-free region of known length, typically 0.1–1 meter. At a constant accelerating potential, measuring the amount of time required for the ion to travel through the field-free region and hit a detector is related to the m/z of the ion. It is easy for a microprocessor to record the time the ion hits the detector; what is difficult to measure is the time it leaves the surface. This can be approximated by using an ionization source that is, itself, intrinsically timed. Two types of sources are generally in use—lasers producing pulses of light absorbed by the matrix surrounding the protein and massive fission fragments of the transuranium isotope, californium-252. These sources generally produce ions with a small number of charges, usually $z = 1$, 2, or 3, resulting from the transfer of 1–3 H^+ from the matrix to the intact protein or peptide. The ions produced in this way are referred to as molecular ions, and denoted as $[M+H]^+$, $[M+2H]^{2+}$, $[M+3H]^{3+}$, and so on. The pattern of singly and multiply charged molecular ions detected can be interpreted to arise from a molecular species, and the molecular mass can be calculated from the inferred number of charges. However, concluding a mass value for a peptide or protein from such a spectrum is only an interpretation, since the quantities measured are actually m/z.

MASS SPECTROMETRIC ANALYSIS OF CALMODULIN

Several sorts of mass spectrometry experiments are helpful in the analysis of calmodulin. First, obtaining molecular ion information on the intact, purified protein leads to some surprising results. The predicted molecular weight of calmodulin is 16,732, based on the amino acid composition or the amino acid sequence translated from the cDNA. However, the measured mass is nearer 16,816, a difference of 84 mass units. This suggests that there are modifications on calmodulin that account for the additional mass. Second, following trypsin digestion or other fragmentation procedure, a sample of the whole, unfractionated digest product can be analyzed by mass spectrometry. This mixture generates a collection of peaks, corresponding to the molecular ions of each of the peptide products. This can be very informative in deciding if the digestion has reached completion and if there are anomalous cleavages. Third, once peptides have been purified by HPLC, their mass analysis can help in deducing their structures. Mass spectrometry alone is usually not sufficient to prove the structure of a peptide or protein. The strongest evidence comes from a combination of mass spectrometric and chemical analyses.

Figure 10 (p. 89) shows the sequence of calmodulin and Table 3 (p. 88) shows a list of the predicted peptide fragments of calmodulin following trypsin digestion. The intensity of the molecular ion peak, under positive ionization, will be greater for peptides that are more easily able to carry a positive charge. Therefore, peptides with higher pI are likely to be represented with more intense ion peaks. The peak size is not linearly related to the amount of each peptide, since the pI and ionization potentials are different. A typical spectrum of the trypsin digest of calmodulin is shown in Figure 14. By comparing the recorded spectrum to the predicted peptide masses, several conclusions can be made. It is apparent that there are a number of molecular ions that do not match the list, and quite a few smaller peptide masses do not appear on the spectrum. This might arise if certain peptide bonds have not been cleaved. Based on the previous discussion of proteolysis, the most likely trypsin-resistant bonds might be those with lysyl residues in Asp-Lys-Asp sequences, which appear twice in calmodulin. Try to match the molecular ions with those predicted if these bonds do not hydrolyze. Remember that you are inferring that a peptide bond exists between the carboxy-terminal and the amino-terminal residues of two peptides; adding together two peptide masses, you must subtract 18 mass units to account for the water molecule that is eliminated when the peptide bond if formed. Also remember that an [M+H]+ value is 1 mass unit higher than the molecular weight of the peptide, due to the additional proton.

Modifications to calmodulin can be identified on peptides analyzed by mass spectrometry. This is most clearly done on the HPLC-purified peptides. Two peptides are found to have an additional mass of 42 mass units. This value is consistent with several potential modifications, so it is impossible to conclude the nature of the modification without additional data. Fragmentation of the peptide under mass spectrometry is a useful way to demonstrate peptide structure, as

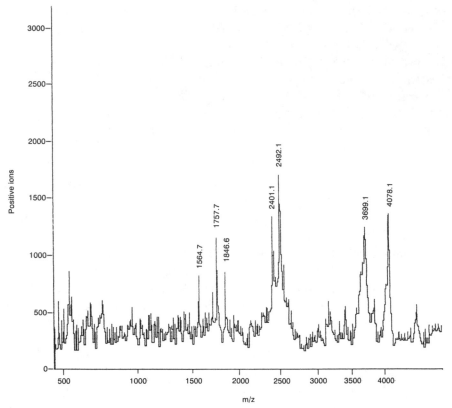

Figure 14
Profile of an entire trypsin digest of calmodulin on mass spectrometry. This profile was generated during the 1994 Cold Spring Harbor Protein Purification and Characterization Course.

the peptide tends to be most easily fragmented by ionizing radiation at peptide bonds. Extensive discussions of peptide fragmentation in mass spectrometry are available elsewhere.

In this analysis, it is convenient to combine data from chemical characterization with the mass spectrometric data. One peptide with an additional 42 mass units is also refractory to Edman degradation, suggesting that the amino-terminal residue of the peptide is blocked. You can conclude that this is the amino-terminal peptide of the entire calmodulin molecule, since it too is refractory to Edman degradation and all other peptide fragments are susceptible to sequencing. A common blocking group found biologically is the acetyl moiety in amide linkage to the amino-terminal nitrogen. Thus, the data are consistent with the interpretation that there is an amino-terminal acetylation of calmodulin. Another peptide also carries an additional mass of 42 mass units. Sequence analysis indicates that this corresponds to residues 107–126, including lysine residue 115 which did not cleave with trypsin. However, this lysine is adjacent to a leucine residue, which should not compromise its ability to be a substrate. Therefore, you must infer an explanation that is consistent with a modification that: (i) will not permit the lysine to act as a trypsin substrate and (ii) accounts for the 42 mass units. Among known modifications to lysine, these are consistent with N-ε-trimethyllysine (Watterson et al. 1980; Marshak et al. 1984). Conformation of this modification can be made by fragmentation analysis by mass spectrometry and from direct amino acid analysis.

• Experiment 11
Chemical Analysis of Calmodulin

INTRODUCTION

The goal of this section is to introduce you to two important methods of chemical analysis of proteins—amino acid analysis following acid hydrolysis and sequence analysis by repetitive Edman degradation. These two techniques are by far the most widely used chemical methods for protein characterization. They are complementary methods that give different sorts of information. Amino acid analysis is performed on protein samples after hydrolysis of all the peptide bonds and gives the total amount of each amino acid in the mixture. The relative abundance of each amino acid can be calculated from this information. If the molecular weight of the protein is known, then the approximate number of each amino acid residue per molecule of protein can be calculated. Remember that amino acid analysis does not and cannot give sequence information. The use of repetitive Edman degradation gives amino acid sequence information, but it does not tell you the overall fraction of each amino acid in the protein. There are many other chemical modification methods that are useful in protein analysis. Most of these involve the reactive groups of a protein, mainly amino, sulfhydryl, hydroxyl, and carboxylate functionalities, as well as the indole, imidazole, and phenolic moieties. These are reviewed in other volumes (e.g., Allen 1989) and will not be discussed extensively here.

•

Amino Acid Analysis

The amino acid composition of a protein can be measured by a two-step procedure that involves: (i) hydrolysis of the peptide bonds to obtain a mixture of free amino acids and (ii) chromatographic separation and detection of the amino acids. In this section, hydrolysis and analysis are discussed separately.

Hydrolysis. Protein hydrolysis is most frequently performed by dissolving the protein in 6 N HCl and incubating in vacuo for 24 hours at 105°C (Moore and Stein 1963). Lower background can be achieved by vapor phase hydrolysis, in which the protein is dried inside a hydrolysis tube and the tube is placed inside a vessel containing 6 N HCl. By evacuating and heating the entire vessel, the HCl vapor is sufficient to hydrolyze the protein without the physical transfer of liquid to the hydrolysis tube. This avoids a potential source of contamination. Very high purity HCl is required for these procedures (e.g., from J.T. Baker or Pierce Chemical Co.). In addition, the glassware used for hydrolysis should be cleaned by baking in an annealing oven at 500°C, only ~100°C below the melting point of borosilicate glass. Following hydrolysis, the samples are dried by vacuum centrifugation and prepared for analysis.

Not all amino acids are stable to acid hydrolysis in HCl. Tryptophan is lost in this procedure, and other acids (such as mercaptoethane sulfonic acids) can be used to preserve tryptophan. Alternatively, tryptophan content can be estimated by spectrophotometry. Tyrosine can produce several side reactions in HCl at high temperature, so a small crystal of phenol is often included in the hydrolysis reaction to act as a scavenger for the phenolic ring in tyrosine. Cysteine is prone to oxidation and β-elimination, so it is not recovered quantitatively in acid hydrolysis. Chemical modification of cysteine and cystine by reduction and alkylation prior to hydrolysis is a standard method for quantitating cysteine in amino acid analysis. Amidated amino acids (i.e., glutamine and asparagine) are hydrolyzed to the free acids in HCl, so that glutamic acid and aspartic acid values in a composition reflect the sum of the amides and the free acids in the intact protein. Finally, serine and threonine are subject to β-elimination, which results in lower yields (as a function of time in hydrolysis) for those amino acids. The amounts of serine and threonine can be accurately estimated by extrapolating from values obtained after various times of hydrolysis, typically 18–72 hours.

Analysis. There are two sorts of analysis systems, utilizing precolumn or postcolumn derivatization. In precolumn derivatization, the free amino acids in the hydrolysate are allowed to react with a reagent that will covalently link a chromophore to each amino acid. Typically, reagents that modify amino groups are used, such as phenylisothiocyanate (PITC). This reagent produces phenylthiocarbamyl (PTC) amino acid derivatives, which have a strong absorbance maximum at 265 nm. Fluorescence reagents, such as dansyl chloride, can be used to create fluorescent amino acid derivatives for very high sensitivity. Both forms of amino acid derivatives are separated by RP-HPLC on very high resolution columns of C18 silica using a mobile phase consisting of aqueous sodium acetate buffer and increasing proportions of acetonitrile. Each amino acid has a unique time of elution from the column, and peaks corresponding to the amino acid derivatives are recorded by monitoring the UV absorbance or fluorescence at the appropriate wavelength. The values represented by these peaks are calculated by comparing the peak areas and retention times to those of known amino acid standards.

Postcolumn derivatization utilizes ion-exchange columns to separate the free amino acids in the hydrolysate. Various improvements to the method originally described by Moore and Stein 1963 have not changed the basic concept—free amino acids are separated on sulfonated polystyrene resin using citrate buffers of increasing pH. As the amino acids emerge from the column at unique elution times, the effluent is channeled into a reaction loop. There the amino acids react with reagents that give either a colorimetric or fluorescent product. Classically, the reagent ninhydrin is used, which reacts with amino groups to yield a product with absorbance in the visible range. *Ortho*-phthalaldehyde is the most widely used fluorescence reagent. Overall, amino acid analysis by postcolumn derivatization is slower than that by precolumn derivatization and requires longer chromatography times. Also, ninhydrin-based detection has limited sensitivity. Precolumn derivatization with PITC and RP-HPLC separation is fast, inexpensive, and sensitive to picomole levels of sample. However, precolumn derivatization systems require very careful attention to obtain good, reproducible results. In general, amino acid analyses are accurate to approximately 10%, although this can be reduced to about 5% in laboratories with a very reproducible and clean technique.

AMINO ACID COMPOSITION OF CALMODULIN

The composition of calmodulin is dominated by acidic residues (glutamic and aspartic acids). There is no cysteine in vertebrate calmodulin, although some plant species have one residue of cysteine.

With regard to aromatic residues, calmodulin contains no tryptophan and has a high phenylalanine-to-tyrosine ratio (8:2). Much of this information can be deduced from the UV absorption spectrum. Recovery of hydrophobic, aliphatic residues can be problematic, since dipeptides of the branched aliphatic residues (e.g., Val-Val, Ile-Ile, and Leu-Leu) require longer times for quantitative hydrolysis. Therefore, a time course of hydrolysis is recommended, as this will give useful values for leucine, valine, and isoleucine when extrapolated to very long times. It also serves to give good estimates of serine and threonine when those values are extrapolated to zero time. After accounting for all the amino acids, one peak will remain on the amino acid chromatogram, that corresponding to N-ε-trimethyllysine. The identity of this residue can be demonstrated by comigration of pure standards of the methylated lysine derivatives.

Sequence Analysis

Above all, proteins are linear polymers of amino acids. The information contained in a protein resides primarily in the linear arrangement of the amino acids. The work of Anfinsen, Stein, and Moore established the principle that all the information required for a protein to fold into an active species is contained in the amino acid sequence. However, recent advances in the field suggest that there are situations in which correct protein folding requires other proteins or small molecule ligands. In any case, the amino acid sequence of a protein not only is key to its function, but also allows the investigator access to the nucleic acid structures that encode the protein. Elucidating the complete amino acid sequence of a protein is a difficult task to accomplish by chemical analysis alone. It requires that several sets of overlapping peptide fragments be obtained from the protein of interest, along with proper, quantitative recovery data to ensure that no fragments have been lost. The sequence of each peptide is established by repetitive Edman degradation, and the order of peptides is deduced from the overlapping fragments of different digests. The advent of molecular cloning methods, DNA sequencing, and knowledge of the genetic code has permitted us to infer amino acid sequences from translation of cDNAs. However, protein sequencing is still required to evaluate protein fragments to identify the piece of DNA that corresponds to the coding sequence for the protein. Thus, it has become commonplace to perform partial sequence analysis of proteins by repetitive Edman degradation, and to complete the sequence by inference from the cDNA. It is useful to remember that amino acid modifications will be detected by chemical and physical analysis, but not necessarily by inspection of the cDNA. Therefore, stringent chemical analysis of proteins is still a discipline that is critical to understanding structure and function.

SEQUENCING CHEMISTRY

The heart of protein sequencing by chemical means remains the Edman degradation reaction. The basic chemistry of the Edman degradation is the same as when it was first introduced, although the instrumentation available for automation has improved considerably. The Edman chemistry and the subsequent identification of the amino acid derivatives is now automated to a large degree, although manual methods can be used quite successfully for laboratories with limited budgets or without access to a central core instrumentation facility. The procedure consists of four segments, often described as the four Cs—coupling, cleavage, conversion, and chromatography. It is instructive to examine each of these procedures and to understand the pitfalls of each, so that sequencing data can be interpreted correctly (see Fig. 15).

Coupling. The coupling reaction occurs between the Edman reagent (phenylisothiocyanate [PITC]) and the α-amino group of the peptide or protein. There are two simple requirements for this to be successful. First, the amino group must not be blocked. The most common blocking groups are: (i) acyl moieties (e.g., acetyl, myristoyl, or palmitoyl groups) in amide linkage and (ii) pyroglutamic acid formed by cyclization of glutamine. Second, the pH of the reaction must be elevated above the pK of the amino terminus, so that its lone pair of electrons is not protonated and can attack the carbon of the PITC. The base used to raise the pH must not be a primary or secondary amine, since these would react with the Edman reagent. Typically, trimethylamine or triethylamine are used, since they are relatively volatile and easily removed from the sample. Coupling results in formation of the phenylthiocarbamyl (PTC) derivative of the protein This structure is really a substituted thiourea, in which one substituent is the phenyl group of the Edman reagent and the other is the peptide chain from the Cx of the first amino acid. This thiourea derivative becomes reactive when the pH is reduced in the subsequent steps.

Cleavage. This reaction is performed in anhydrous organic acid (such as trifluoroacetic [TFA] or heptafluorobutyric acid) at elevated temperature (45–55°C). The Edman reagent is ingenious because it enables the sulfur atom of the PTC derivative to be positioned so that nucleophilic attack of the carbon of the peptide bond is favored. The resulting five-membered ring is produced in high yield following protonation of the peptide nitrogen and cleavage of the peptide bond. The amino acid derivative is known as the anilinothiazolinone (ATZ). The central problem of the sequence analysis is not in the cleavage reaction, but in the separation of the amino acid derivative from the rest of the protein. "Solid-phase" sequencing utilizes covalent attachment of the protein to a support membrane or resin, so that severe solvents (such as liquid TFA) can be used to extract the ATZ-amino acid. Without covalent attachment, differential solubility of the ATZ-amino acid must be used. The ATZ-amino acid is much more soluble in organic solvent (such as butyl chloride or ethyl acetate) than is the protein, so organic extraction is often used. Many procedures utilize a carrier for

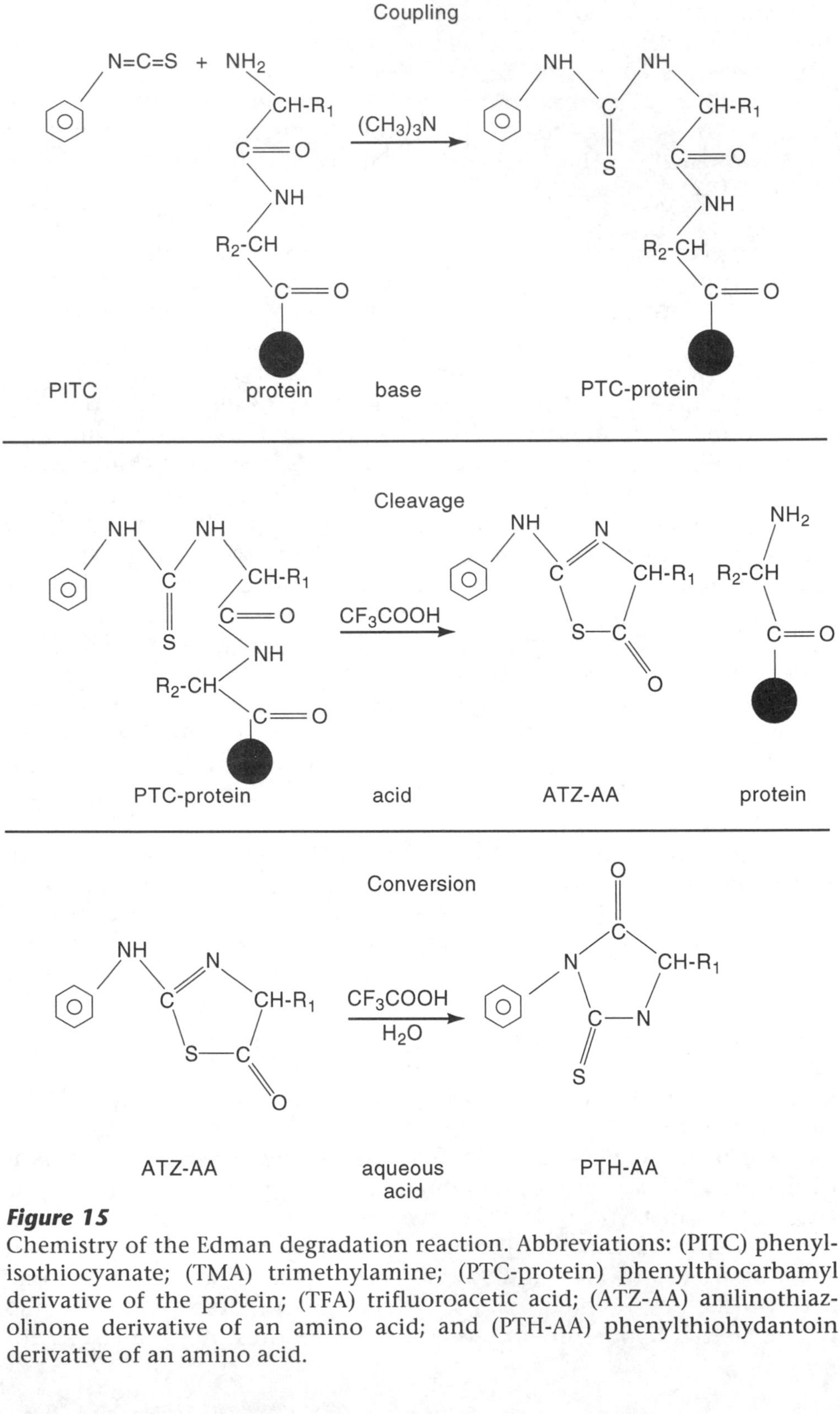

Figure 15
Chemistry of the Edman degradation reaction. Abbreviations: (PITC) phenyl-isothiocyanate; (TMA) trimethylamine; (PTC-protein) phenylthiocarbamyl derivative of the protein; (TFA) trifluoroacetic acid; (ATZ-AA) anilinothiaz-olinone derivative of an amino acid; and (PTH-AA) phenylthiohydantoin derivative of an amino acid.

the protein, such as the basic polymer (Polybrene) that helps retain the protein during solvent extraction. Because of the prior acidic conditions, all the amino acid side chains are protonated, so all but the basic residues are uncharged and highly soluble in the solvent. Lysine acts as a hydrophobe, since the ε-amino group exists as the PTC derivative from the original coupling reaction. Arginine and histidine yields are often low because the investigator fails to extract the charged amino acid derivatives in the organic solvent. This can be avoided by not removing all of the acid from the cleavage step before solvent extraction. The ion pair of arginyl and histidinyl derivatives with, for example, trifluoroacetate, is quite soluble in organic solvent.

Conversion. This is the third step of sequencing chemistry, following separation of the ATZ-amino acid from the remaining protein. The ATZ derivative is susceptible to several reactions, including oxidation and reversion to the PTC form. It is therefore necessary to convert the ATZ derivative to a more stable form. In aqueous acid at 60°C, the ATZ ring spontaneously rearranges to form a thiohydantoin, in this case, the phenylthiohydantoin (PTH) derivative. Several problems can occur during conversion. If the organic extraction solvent is not removed completely, then the introduction of aqueous acid results in an unmixed, two-phase system in which the ATZ derivatives of the hydrophobic amino acids, particularly the aliphatics such as leucine, can partition into the organic phase. A large fraction of the ATZ-amino acid is not converted, and analysis of the PTH derivative at that cycle is abnormally low. On the other hand, if the organics are removed completely, but the dried derivative is not redissolved quickly in aqueous acid, then serine and threonine derivatives can be severely dehydrated. Some dehydration occurs anyway, but heating under dry conditions leads to very poor yields of serine and threonine.

Chromatography. The final analysis of the PTH-amino acid derivative is performed by RP-HPLC under conditions similar to those used for amino acid analysis of the PTC-amino acid derivatives. Over many years, the chromatography systems have been optimized using high resolution columns and complicated buffer systems to separate all the common amino acid derivatives. On every sequencer run, a set of PTH-amino acid standards should be run for calibration. It is unacceptable to use a calibration that is weeks to months old, and fresh standard should be prepared routinely. Unprotected cysteine will not survive Edman chemistry, so reduction and alkylation is recommended. This is most conveniently done prior to sequencing by reaction with 4-vinylpyridine, although several other excellent reagents are also available. Arginyl and histidinyl derivatives are particularly troublesome, since their elution position on the chromatography is highly dependent upon pH and ionic strength. Be sure that a standard PTH-amino acid mixture shows good separation of PTH-arginine and PTH-histidine, and that the retention times are not constantly changing.

SEQUENCE ANALYSIS OF CALMODULIN

Repetitive cycles of sequence data are analyzed by inspecting the abundance of the amino acid derivatives in the cycle of interest (n) as well as in the previous (n–1) and following cycles (n+1). A true amino acid assignment generally displays an increase followed by a decrease. The usual pattern, therefore, of PTH-amino acid yields in the n–1, n, and n+1 cycles is low-high-low. If two of the same amino acids occur one after another, then the n+1 cycle will show a slight increase and the decrease will occur at the n+2 cycle, yielding a pattern low-high-higher-lower. There will be a general increase in background during the sequencing, usually due to partial acid hydrolysis of the protein. The first cycle of a sequence often contains some free amino acids, transferred from air or surfaces used in transfer. Usually, large amounts of glycine, serine, and glutamine in cycle 1 are due to contamination and disappear after several cycles. Deamidation of calmodulin can occur, so careful attention should be given to cycles containing amides. The presence of the corresponding free acid in a cycle containing an amidated amino acid indicates that some deamidation has occurred. For the purpose of assigning a residue, the amide should be chosen if there is a significant amount present. A free acid will not convert to an amide, so any evidence of an amide would suggest that the acid form seen resulted from deamidation of the protein.

One of the most important issues in sequence analysis is yield. There are two sorts of yield, absolute initial yield and repetitive yield. The initial yield is the amount of the PTH-amino acids recovered in the first cycle of the Edman degradation compared to the amount of protein loaded. Typical initial yields are 40–80%. If the initial yield is very low, say 5%, then it is possible that the sample being sequenced is a contaminating protein and not the one of interest. The calculation of initial yield presupposes that you know how much you are loading in the sequencing reaction. It is recommended to sacrifice 10% of the sample for amino acid analysis prior to sequencing. This is the only reliable way to measure the total amount of protein applied. Other methods can be in error by as much as two- to tenfold.

The repetitive yield refers to the loss in PTH-amino acid simply due to lack of complete reaction, extraction, conversion, or mechanical loss. Repetitive yield is calculated from the formula $[Y_B / Y_A]^{1/B\text{-}A}$, where B and A are two different cycle numbers and Y_B and Y_A are the PTH-amino acid yields during those cycles. It is most accurate for amino acids of the same type, such as a leucine at cycles 4 and 12. You will also notice that some of the amino acid derivative of a cycle, n, also occurs in cycle n+1. This value is referred to as a carryover or lag and is indicative of incomplete extraction or coupling. Some lag is unavoidable, but lag above a few percent of the main peak should be cause to investigate the efficiency of the reaction. Typical yields for commercial instruments are 92–94%, although under good optimization, instruments can run routinely at 95–96%. The difference of a few percent in repetitive yield is highly significant, since the loss of PTH derivatives with respect to the number of cycles is an exponential decay curve. In general, if the sequencer run has less than 50% initial yield and less than 92% repetitive yield, there are some major problems, and it is advisable to re-evaluate the sample, the instrument, and the operator.

A few special problems are encountered in sequencing calmodulin. Figure 16 shows nine cycles of Edman degradation performed on the peptide of calmodulin that contains trimethyllysine-115 (fragment 8 in Table 3, see p. 88). Note that cycle 9 shows an unusual peak that is broad and does not comigrate with the standard PTH-amino acids. Althought the cDNA sequence indicates a lysine at this position, the PTH-amino acid does not comigrate with PTH-lysine, but rather migrates nearer to PTH-arginine and shows the broad peak width characteristic of the basic (positively charged) amino acid residues. Cycle 9 is in fact PTH-N-ε-trimethyllysine. Always pay attention to the retention times of the PTH-amino acids in an unknown cycle. The system should be so reproducible that the retention times should match those of standards to less than 0.1 minute. If the times or peak shapes are off, it pays to consider modifications to the amino acid. An unusual peak, such as that seen for trimethyllysine, should not be ignored.

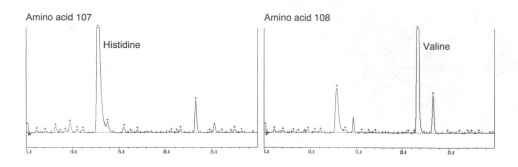

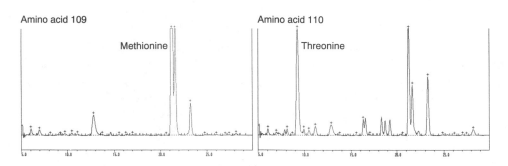

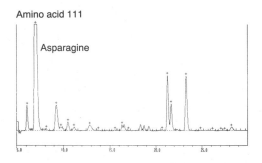

Figure 16

Nine cycles of Edman degradation performed on the peptide of calmodulin (generated by trypsin digestion) that contains trimethyllysine-115. The peptide is 20 amino acids in length from residue 107 to residue 126 (fragments F8 and F5 in Table 3, p. 88). Its sequence is His-Val-Met-Thr-Asn-Leu-Gly-Glu-trimethylLys and continues through arginine-126. The trimethyllysine does not provide a substrate for trypsin.

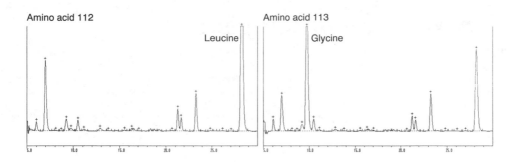

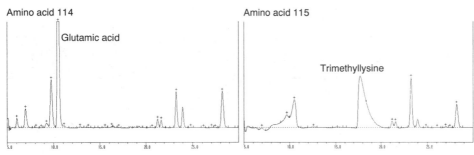

Figure 16 (*continued*)

Preparation of Reagents

Buffer B (10x)

100 mM Tris-HCl (pH 8.0)
2 M NaCl
10 mM EGTA

Store 10x buffer B at 4°C. Immediately before use, dilute the 10x stock 1 in 10 with distilled H_2O and add 70.1 µl of 2-mercaptoethanol/liter of 1x buffer B to give final concentrations of 10 mM Tris-HCl (pH 8.0), 0.2 M NaCl, 1 mM EGTA, and 1 mM 2-mercaptoethanol.

SAFETY NOTE

- 2-Mercaptoethanol may be fatal if swallowed and is harmful if inhaled or absorbed through the skin. High concentrations are extremely destructive to the mucous membranes, upper respiratory tract, skin, and eyes. Use only in a chemical fume hood. Gloves and safety glasses should be worn.

Buffer E

10 mM Tris-HCl (pH 8.0)
1 mM $MgCl_2$
2 mM EGTA
1 mM 2-Mercaptoethanol (see Safety Note above)

Buffer F

10 mM Tris-HCl (pH 8.0)
1 mM $MgCl_2$
2 mM $CaCl_2$
1 mM 2-Mercaptoethanol (see Safety Note above)

Buffer H (10x)

0.5 M Tris-HCl (pH 8.0)
20 mM EDTA

Store 10x buffer H at 4°C. Immediately before use, dilute the 10x stock 1 in 10 with distilled H_2O and add 70.1 µl of 2-mercaptoethanol/liter of 1x buffer H to give final concentrations of 50 mM Tris-HCl (pH 8.0), 2 mM EDTA, and 1 mM 2-mercaptoethanol (see Safety Note, p. 120).

Digestion buffer
(for digestion of calmodulin with trypsin)

0.1 M Ammonium bicarbonate (pH 8.0)
1 mM EGTA

Lower reservoir buffer
(for native PAGE)
(1 liter)

Tris base	12.1 g
HCl (1 M)	50 ml

Dissolve in H_2O and adjust the final volume to 1 liter.

MLCK assay buffer (10x)

50 mM HEPES (pH 7.5)
5 mM $MgCl_2$
1 mM Dithiothreitol
0.1 mM $CaCl_2$

Sample buffer (5x)
(for native PAGE)

Add glycerol to upper reservoir buffer (for native PAGE) (see below) containing 0.05 mg of bromophenol blue/ml to give a final glycerol concentration of 50% (v/v).

Upper reservoir buffer
(for native PAGE)
(1 liter)

Tris base	6.42 g
Glycine	3.98 g
2-Mercaptoethanol	0.7 ml
(see Safety Note, p. 120)	
EGTA (0.5 M; pH 8.0)	2 ml

Dissolve in H_2O and adjust the final volume to 1 liter.

References

Allen, G. 1989. Specific cleavage of the protein. In *Sequencing of proteins and peptides*, pp. 73–104. Elsevier, Amsterdam.

Babu, Y.S., C.E. Bugg, and W.J. Cook. 1988. Structure of calmodulin refined at 2.2 Å resolution. *J. Mol. Biol.* **204:** 191–204.

Bornstein, P. 1970. Structure of alpha-1-CB8, a large cyanogen bromide produced fragment from the alpha-1 chain of rat collagen. The nature of a hydroxylamine-sensitive bond and composition of tryptic peptides. *Biochemistry* **9:** 2408–2421.

Burgess, W.H. and T. Maciag. 1989. The heparin-binding (fibroblast) growth factor family of proteins. *Annu. Rev. Biochem.* **58:** 575–606.

Burgess, W.H., D.K. Jemiolo, and R.H. Kretsinger. 1980. Interaction of calcium and calmodulin in the presence of sodium dodecyl sulfate. *Biochim. Biophys. Acta* **623:** 257–270.

Cheung, W.Y. 1971. Cyclic 3',5'-nucleotide phosphodiesterase. Evidence for and properties of a protein activator. *J. Biol. Chem.* **246:** 2859–2869.

Cleland, W.W. 1964. Dithiothreitol, new protective reagent for SH groups. *Biochemistry* **3:** 480–482.

Cohen, P., A. Burchell, J.G. Foulkes, P.T.W. Cohen, T.C. Vanaman, and A.C. Nairn. 1978. Identification of the Ca^{2+}-dependent modulator protein as the fourth subunit of rabbit skeletal muscle phosphorylase kinase. *FEBS Lett.* **92:** 287–293.

Cohn, E.J. and J.T. Edsall. 1943. *Proteins, amino acids, and peptides as ions and dipolar ions.* Reinhold Publishing, New York.

Collins, J.H., M.L. Greaser, J.D. Potter, and M.J. Horn. 1977. Determination of the amino acid sequence of troponin C from rabbit skeletal muscle. *J. Biol. Chem.* **252:** 6456–6462.

Ebashi, S., M. Endo, and I. Otsuki. 1969. Control of muscle contraction. *Q. Rev. Biophys.* **2:** 351–384.

Flockhart, D.A. and J.D. Corbin. 1982. Regulatory mechanisms in the control of protein kinases. *CRC Crit. Rev. Biochem.* **12:** 133–186.

Forsén, S., H.J. Vogel, and T. Drakenberg. 1986. Biophysical studies of calmodulin. In *Calcium and cell function* (ed. W.Y. Cheung), vol. 6, pp. 113–157. Academic Press, New York.

Goldenberg, D.P. 1989. Analysis of protein conformation by gel electrophoresis. In *Protein structure: A practical approach* (ed. T.E.

Creighton), pp. 225–250. IRL Press at Oxford University Press, England.

Goldenberg, D.P. and T.E. Creighton. 1984. Gel electrophoresis in studies of protein conformation and folding. *Anal. Biochem.* **138:** 1–18.

Good, N.E., G.D. Winget, W. Winter, T.N. Connolly, S. Izawa, and R.M.M. Singh. 1966. Hydrogen ion buffers for biological research. *Biochemistry* **5:** 467–477.

Gorecka, A., M.O. Aksoy, and D.J. Hartshorne. 1976. The effect of phosphorylation of gizzard myosin on actin activation. *Biochem. Biophys. Res. Commun.* **71:** 325–331.

Gross, E. and B. Witkop. 1962. Nonenzymatic cleavage of peptide bonds: The methionine residues in bovine pancreatic ribonuclease. *J. Biol. Chem.* **237:** 1856–1860.

Haiech, J., M.C. Kilhoffer, T.J. Lukas, T.A. Craig, D.M. Roberts, and D.M. Watterson. 1991. Restoration of the calcium binding activity of mutant calmodulins toward normal by the presence of a calmodulin binding structure. *J. Biol. Chem.* **266:** 3427–3431.

Hancock, W.S. 1984. *Handbook of HPLC for the separation of amino acids, peptides, and proteins,* vols. I and II. CRC Press, Boca Raton, Florida.

Hidaka, H., T. Yamaki, T. Totsuka, and M. Asano. 1979. Selective inhibitors of Ca^{2+}-binding modulator of phosphodiesterase produce vascular relaxation and inhibit actin-myosin interaction. *Mol. Pharmacol.* **15:** 49–59.

Ion Exchange Chromatography. 1994. 2nd edition. Pharmacia Ltd., Uppsala, Sweden.

ISCOTABLES: A handbook of data for biological and physical scientists. 1982. 8th edition. ISCO, Lincoln, Nebraska.

Kakiuchi, S. and R. Yamazaki. 1970. Calcium dependent phosphodiesterase activity and its activating factor (PAF) from brain studies on cyclic 3′,5′-nucleotide phosphodiesterase. *Biochem. Biophys. Res. Commun.* **41:** 1104–1110.

Kennedy, M.B. and P. Greengard. 1981. Two calcium/calmodulin-dependent protein kinases, which are highly concentrated in brain, phosphorylate protein I at distinct sites. *Proc. Natl. Acad. Sci.* **78:** 1293–1297.

Klee, C.B., T.H. Crouch, and P.G. Richman. 1980. Calmodulin. *Annu. Rev. Biochem.* **49:** 489–515.

Kretsinger, R.H. 1980. Structure and evolution of calcium-modulated proteins. *CRC Crit. Rev. Biochem.* **8:** 119–174.

Kretsinger, R.H. and D.J. Nelson. 1976. Calcium in biological systems. *Coord. Chem. Rev.* **18:** 29–124.

Laemmli, U.K. 1970. Cleavage of structural proteins during the assembly of the head of bacteriophage T4. *Nature* **227:** 680–685.

Levin, R.M. and B. Weiss. 1979. Selective binding of antipsychotics and other psychoactive agents to the calcium-dependent activator of cyclic nucleotide phosphodiesterase. *J. Pharmacol. Exp. Ther.* **208:** 454–459.

Lukas, T.J., W.H. Burgess, F.G. Prendergast, W. Lau, and D.M. Watterson. 1986. Calmodulin binding domains: Characterization of a phosphorylation and calmodulin binding site from myosin light chain kinase. *Biochemistry* **25:** 1458–1464.

Marshak, D.R. and D. Carroll. 1991. Synthetic peptide substrates from casein kinase II. *Methods Enzymol.* **200:** 134–156.

Marshak, D.R., D.M. Watterson, and L.J. Van Eldik. 1981. Calcium-dependent interaction of S100b, troponin C, and calmodulin with an immobilized phenothiazine. *Proc. Natl. Acad. Sci.* **78:** 6793–6797.

Marshak, D.R., M. Clarke, D.M. Roberts, and D.M. Watterson. 1984. Structural and functional properties of calmodulin from the eukaryotic microorganism *Dictyostelium discoideum. Biochemistry* **23:** 2891–2899.

Marshak, D.R., M.T. Vandenberg, Y.-S. Bae, and I.J. Yu. 1991. Characterization of synthetic peptide substrates for p34cdc2 protein kinase. *J. Cell Biochem.* **45:** 391–400.

Means, A.R. 1988. Molecular mechanisms of action of calmodulin. *Recent Prog. Horm. Res.* **44:** 223–262.

Means, A.R., J.S. Tash, and J.G. Chafouleas. 1982. Physiological implications of the presence, distribution, and regulation of calmodulin in eukaryotic cells. *Physiol. Rev.* **62:** 1–39.

Moore, B.W. 1965. A soluble protein characteristic of the nervous system. *Biochim. Biophys. Res. Commun.* **19:** 739–744.

Moore, S. and W.H. Stein. 1963. Chromatographic determination of amino acids by use of automatic recording equipment. *Methods Enzymol.* **6:** 819–848.

Pace, C.N., B.A. Shirley, and J.A. Thomson. 1989. Measuring the conformational stability of a protein. In *Protein structure: A practical approach* (ed. T.E. Creighton), pp. 311–330. IRL Press at Oxford University Press, England.

Sasagawa, T., L.H. Ericsson, K.A. Walsh, W.E. Schreiber, E.H. Fischer, and K. Titani. 1982. Complete amino acid sequence of human brain calmodulin. *Biochemistry* **21:** 2565–2569.

Schleicher, M. and D.M. Watterson. 1983. Analysis of differences between Coomassie blue stain and silver stain procedures in polyacrylamide gels: Conditions for the detection of calmodulin and troponin C. *Anal. Biochem.* **131:** 312–317.

Shoemaker, M.O., W. Lau, R.L. Shattuck, A.P. Kwiatkowski, P.E. Matrisian, L. Guerra-Santos, E. Wilson, T.J. Lukas, and L.J. Van Eldik. 1990. Use of DNA sequence and mutant analyses and antisense oligodeoxynucleotides to examine the molecular basis of non-muscle myosin light chain kinase autoinhibition, calmodulin recognition, and activity. *J. Cell Biol.* **111:** 1107–1125.

Strynadka, N.C.J. and M.N.G. James. 1989. Crystal structures of the helix-loop-helix calcium-binding proteins. *Annu. Rev. Biochem.* **58:** 951–998.

Tan, J.L., S. Ravid, and J.A. Spudich. 1992. Control of nonmuscle myosins by phosphorylation. *Annu. Rev. Biochem.* **61:** 721–759.

Tanford, C. 1973. *The hydrophobic effect.* John Wiley, New York.

Timasheff, S.N. and T. Arakawa. 1989. Stabilization of protein-structure by solvents. In *Protein structure: A practical approach* (ed. T.E. Creighton), pp. 331–345. IRL Press at Oxford University Press, England.

Van Eldik, L.J., W.H. Burgess, and D.M. Watterson. 1983. *Anal. Biochem.* **??:** ??–??.

Van Eldik, L.J., J.G. Zendegui, D.R. Marshak, and D.M. Watterson. 1982. Calcium-binding proteins and the molecular basis of calcium action. *Int. Rev. Cytol.* **77:** 1–61.

Vanaman, T.C., S.J. Wakil, and R.L. Hill. 1968a. The preparation of tryptic, peptic, thermolysin, and cyanogen bromide peptides from the acyl carrier protein of *Escherichia coli. J. Biol. Chem.* **243:** 6409–6419.

———. 1968b. The complete amino acid sequence of the acyl carrier protein of *Escherichia coli. J. Biol. Chem.* **243:** 6420–6431.

Watterson, D.M., F. Sharief, and T.C. Vanaman. 1980. The complete amino acid sequence of the Ca^{2+}-dependent modulator protein (calmodulin) of bovine brain. *J. Biol. Chem.* **255:** 962–975.

Watterson, D.M., W.G. Harrelson, Jr., P.M. Keller, F. Sharief, and T.C. Vanaman. 1976. Structural similarities between the Ca^{2+}-dependent regulatory proteins of 3′:5′-cyclic nucleotide phosphodiesterase and actomyosin ATPase. *J. Biol. Chem.* **251:** 4501–4513.

Whitaker, J.R. 1980. Changes occurring in proteins in alkaline solutions. In *Chemical deterioration of proteins* (ed. J.R. Whitaker and M. Fujimaki), pp. 145–164. American Chemical Society, Washington, D.C.

UNIT II

Purification of Transcription Factor AP-1 from HeLa Cells

Many important biological processes, such as replication, transcription, and recombination, involve the action of sequence-specific DNA-binding factors. Purification is a critical, but often difficult, step in the analysis of these sequence-specific DNA-binding proteins, which typically constitute less than 0.1% of the total nuclear protein. Fortunately, there now exists a variety of related affinity chromatography procedures for the purification of sequence-specific DNA-binding proteins (for a brief review, see Kadonaga 1991). A common feature of these techniques is the use of affinity resins containing DNA with the specific recognition sites for the desired protein immobilized onto a stationary support, such as an agarose bead. The preferential binding of the desired factor to the affinity resin relative to that of other contaminating proteins typically yields substantial purification of the sequence-specific DNA-binding protein.

GENERAL STRATEGY

In this unit, we describe the purification of transcription factor AP-1 from HeLa cells as a representative sequence-specific DNA-binding protein. A flowchart that summarizes these experiments is shown in Figure 1. First, nuclei are prepared from HeLa cells, and the AP-1 is extracted from the nuclei by incubation in a buffer containing 0.42 M KCl. This mixture is subjected to centrifugation, and the AP-1 is present in the supernatant, which is a standard HeLa nuclear extract. The AP-1 is precipitated from the extract with ammonium sulfate and then partially purified by gel filtration chromatography with a

HeLa Cells

     Hypotonic swelling of cells
     Dounce homogenization
     Low-speed centrifugation

Nuclei

     0.42 M KCl Extraction
     High-speed ultracentrifugation
     Ammonium sulfate precipitation

Nuclear Extract

     S-300 Gel filtration

S-300 Peak Fractions

     Sequence-specific DNA affinity chromatography
     with AP-1 resin

Partially Purified AP-1

Figure 1

Flowchart for the partial purification of transcription factor AP-1 from HeLa cells. The sequence-specific DNA affinity resin can be prepared at the same time as the HeLa nuclear extract. The S-300 and DNA affinity fractions are assayed for AP-1 DNA-binding activity by DNase I footprinting, and the purity of the DNA affinity fractions can be determined by SDS-polyacrylamide gel electrophoresis.

Sephacryl S-300 HR column. The S-300 fractions are assayed for AP-1 DNA-binding activity by DNase I footprinting. Meanwhile, a sequence-specific DNA affinity resin is prepared, and the AP-1 is purified from the peak S-300 column fractions by chromatography with the DNA affinity resin. The purity of the AP-1 is determined by SDS-polyacrylamide gel electrophoresis, and the DNA-binding activity of the purified AP-1 is examined by DNase I footprinting.

The DNA affinity chromatography is performed by using a procedure involving covalent linkage of polymerized synthetic oligonucleotides containing the AP-1 recognition site to an agarose resin (Kadonaga and Tjian 1986; Kadonaga 1991). This specific technique has been successfully used to purify over 100 different sequence-specific DNA-binding factors from sources as diverse as bacteria, yeast, fruit flies, and mammals. It is thus possible to extend this affinity chromatography procedure to the purification of other sequence-specific DNA-binding factors. Moreover, many of the techniques described here should be generally useful for the purification of DNA-binding proteins.

TRANSCRIPTION FACTOR AP-1

AP-1 (**A**ctivator **P**rotein **1**) is a sequence-specific DNA-binding protein that regulates transcription by RNA polymerase II by interaction with promoter and enhancer regions of selected genes. It is a representative member of the class of transcription factors that display gene specificity on the basis of their ability to bind to specific recognition elements in transcriptional control regions (for reviews, see Mitchell and Tjian 1989; Johnson and McKnight 1989). AP-1 was originally discovered as a factor from HeLa cells (a human cell line) that bound to sequences resembling 5'TGAGTCA, which were present in the promoter of the human metallothionein II_A gene and in the 72-bp repeat elements of the simian virus 40 (SV40) enhancer (Lee et al. 1987). AP-1 was purified from HeLa cells by sequence-specific affinity chromatography, and it was shown that a 47-kD polypeptide in the purified AP-1 possessed DNA-binding characteristics identical to those of a preparation of affinity-purified AP-1. Further analysis revealed that AP-1 consists of a complex mixture of proteins with similar DNA-binding specificities. The predominant species in a highly purified preparation of AP-1 are Jun-Jun homodimers and Jun-Fos heterodimers, where Jun is the protein encoded by the *jun* proto-oncogene and Fos is the protein encoded by the *fos* proto-oncogene. The dimers are joined together by a coiled coil motif that is referred to as a leucine zipper (for a brief review, see Curran and Franza 1988). Thus, the study of AP-1 led to an interesting and important connection between oncogenes that encode nuclear proteins and biochemically identified transcription factors that bind to promoter and enhancer regions.

In this unit, we purify AP-1 and characterize its DNA-binding properties, as described by Lee et al. (1987). We describe the purification of AP-1 for several reasons. First, AP-1 is a well-known factor because of its central role in transcriptional regulation and its connection with oncogenes. Second, AP-1 is a somewhat stable protein, which is useful for teaching purposes. The protein can be heated to 90°C and still remain active upon cooling to room temperature. Third, the procedure for the purification of AP-1 involves the preparation of a nuclear extract from HeLa cells, which may be, in itself, useful for many investigators. Finally, the procedure for the purification of AP-1 has been performed and tested many times and is thus quite reliable.

• Experiment 1

Preparation of a Nuclear Extract from HeLa Cells

INTRODUCTION

In this experiment, we prepare a nuclear extract from HeLa cells essentially as described by Dignam et al. (1983). This basic procedure is probably the most commonly employed method for the preparation of factors for in vitro transcription and DNA-binding experiments. First, HeLa cells are incubated in a hypotonic buffer (buffer H) in which the cells become expanded due to osmotic swelling. The swollen cells are then lysed in a Dounce homogenizer, and the nuclei are collected by centrifugation. The transcription factors, including AP-1, are extracted from the nuclei by incubation of the nuclei in a buffer containing 0.42 M KCl (buffer D). The solubilized transcription factors are separated from the nuclear envelope and matrix by centrifugation at 100,000g for 1 hour. The supernatant is the crude nuclear extract. The transcription factors in the supernatant are precipitated with ammonium sulfate, suspended in chromatography buffer (TM buffer + 0.1 M KCl), and then subjected to centrifugation to remove insoluble material before being applied to the Sephacryl S-300 column.

MATERIALS

HeLa cells (See growth and storage conditions below. We have also successfully used HeLa cells grown and frozen by Cellex Biosciences, Inc.)
Glycerol
Liquid nitrogen
$MgCl_2 \cdot 6H_2O$
Ammonium sulfate

SAFETY NOTE

• The temperature of liquid nitrogen is –185°C. Handle with great care; always wear gloves and a face protector.

REAGENTS

Phosphate-buffered saline (PBS)
Buffer G
Buffer H
Buffer D
TM buffer + 0.1 M KCl
(For recipes, see Preparation of Reagents, pp. 192–200.)

PROCEDURE

Growth and Storage of HeLa Cells (12-liter scale)

1. Grow the HeLa cells exponentially to a density of 5 x 10^5 cells/ml and harvest them gently to prevent lysis.

2. Wash the cells once with PBS and pellet them again.

3. Add 2 ml of buffer G for each liter of original volume of cells (i.e., 24 ml of buffer for cells derived from 12 liters of culture). Add more glycerol until the final glycerol concentration is 20% (v/v). For example, a 12-liter culture will yield approximately 18 ml of packed cells. After adding the 24 ml of buffer G, the total volume will be 42 ml, but the glycerol concentration will only be 17.1% because of the volume of the cells. It is necessary to add a further 1.5 ml of glycerol to bring the final concentration to 20%.

4. Freeze the cells in liquid nitrogen and store them at –80°C.

Preparation of HeLa Nuclei (12-liter scale)

Maintain all solutions at 4°C and perform all procedures at 4°C, except where noted.

1. Thaw the frozen HeLa cells (prepared from 12 liters of culture at a density of approximately 5 x 10^5 cells/ml) in H_2O at room temperature. Thaw the cells as quickly as possible, but do not let the cells warm up beyond 4°C. Add PBS containing 1 g of $MgCl_2 \cdot 6H_2O$/liter to a final volume of 200 ml, and then pellet the cells in a Beckman GSA rotor at 3000 rpm for 10 minutes.

2. Wash the cells with 200 ml of 1x PBS containing 1 g of $MgCl_2 \cdot 6H_2O$/liter. Pellet the cells in a Beckman GSA rotor at 3000 rpm for 10 minutes.

3. Resuspend the cells in 60 ml of buffer H.

4. Let the cells incubate on ice for 15–30 minutes.

5. Disrupt the swollen cells with a Wheaton Dounce homogenizer (40 ml) and a B pestle. Perform 20 strokes.

   Note: It is important to work quickly after lysis of the cells to minimize loss of transcription factors by leakage out of the nuclei. In fact, high levels of nuclear factors can often be found in the cytoplasmic fraction (the supernatant of the centrifugation step in which the nuclei are pelleted). Thus, further purification of the nuclei by additional washing and centrifugation steps often results in low yields of transcription factors.

6. Pellet the nuclei in a Beckman SS-34 rotor at 3500 rpm for 10 minutes. Proceed immediately with the preparation of the nuclear extract. A typical yield is approximately 12 g of nuclei from 12 liters of HeLa cells.

Preparation of the HeLa Nuclear Extract (12-liter scale)

Maintain all solutions at 4°C and perform all procedures at 4°C, except where noted.

1. Prepare nuclei from 12 liters of HeLa cells (as described above) or thaw frozen nuclei in cold (4°C) H_2O.

2. Suspend the nuclei in 75 ml of buffer D.

   Note: The 0.42 M KCl in the extraction buffer can be substituted with 0.42 M NaCl.

3. Stir on a magnetic stirrer for 30 minutes.

4. Pellet the cell debris by spinning at 100,000g for 1 hour.

   Note: For this centrifugation step, a swinging-bucket rotor (such as a Beckman SW28) is recommended instead of a fixed-angle rotor. In a fixed-angle rotor, undesirable shearing of the nuclei can occur.

5. Measure the volume of the supernatant (usually 70–75 ml).

   Note: To prepare a standard extract for in vitro transcription experiments, the 100,000g supernatant can be dialyzed to 0.1 M KCl in TM buffer. Alternatively, the ammonium sulfate precipitate (see below) can be dialyzed against TM buffer + 0.1 M KCl. The 0.42 M KCl extract contains high levels of histone H1, which is a potent repressor of transcription (Croston et al. 1991). The ammonium sulfate precipitation removes most of the histone H1, and thus, it may be better to precipitate the 0.42 M KCl extract with ammonium sulfate before dialysis of the sample against TM buffer + 0.1 M KCl.

6. Add 0.33 g of powdered ammonium sulfate per milliliter of supernatant. Add the ammonium sulfate slowly over 5–10 minutes.

   Note: Grind the ammonium sulfate crystals about 5–10 minutes before use. The powdered ammonium sulfate is hygroscopic, and wet ammonium sulfate cannot be weighed accurately. A coffee bean grinder is a useful instrument to pulverize the ammonium sulfate—it is a lot easier to use than a mortar and pestle.

7. After all of the ammonium sulfate has dissolved, stir the mixture with a magnetic stirrer for 30 minutes.

8. Pellet the proteins by spinning in a Beckman SS-34 rotor at 15,000 rpm for 15 minutes.

9. Dissolve the pellet in approximately 3.5 ml of TM buffer + 0.1 M KCl to give a final volume of approximately 5 ml.

10. Spin the milky white mixture in a Beckman SS-34 rotor at 10,000 rpm for 10 minutes to remove insoluble material.

11. The supernatant, which is typically milky white, is now ready for gel filtration on the S-300 column. The protein concentration is usually approximately 50 mg/ml by the Bradford (Coomassie Blue) assay with bovine γ-globulin as a reference.

12. If desired, this extract can be frozen in liquid nitrogen and stored for months (and probably even years) at –80°C. It is very important to thaw the extract as quickly as possible. To do this, place the tube in H_2O at room temperature and remove any ice that may form around the tube. After thawing the extract, it is important to remove insoluble material by centrifugation in a Beckman SS-34 rotor at 10,000 rpm for 10 minutes. Alternatively, if this extract is dialyzed against TM buffer + 0.1 M KCl for several hours until the conductivity of the sample is identical to that of the buffer, the nuclear extract can be used for in vitro transcription experiments.

ALTERNATIVE PROCEDURES

One variant of the Dignam et al. (1983) procedure involves a high-ionic-strength extraction of nuclei (Soeller et al. 1988). In such preparations, however, both histone H1 and core histones (such as H2B) are extracted from the nuclei. A popular variant of the standard nuclear extract involves substitution of the Mg(II) in the extraction buffer with a spermine-spermidine mixture (Gorski et al. 1986; Shapiro et al. 1988). This method is particularly useful for the preparation of extracts from tissues, such as liver or thymus.

A very simple nuclear extract, termed the soluble nuclear fraction, can be prepared by high-speed centrifugation of nuclei at low ionic strength (Kamakaka et al. 1991; Kamakaka and Kadonaga 1994). A distinct feature of the soluble nuclear fraction is the virtual absence of histone H1 when the centrifugation is carried out in 0.1 M KCl instead of 0.4 M potassium glutamate, as originally reported (Kamakaka et al. 1991; Kamakaka and Kadonaga 1994).

Gel Filtration Chromatography with Sephacryl S-300 HR

INTRODUCTION

Gel filtration chromatography, which is also commonly referred to as size exclusion chromatography, is a method for the separation of molecules on the basis of their size and shape. In this introduction, we will briefly discuss the use of gel filtration chromatography to purify proteins. Unlike other types of chromatography, gel filtration does not, in a theoretically ideal sense, involve attractive or repulsive forces between the resin and protein. A gel filtration column consists of evenly packed porous beads, and proteins are separated on the basis of their ability to migrate through the pores, which is a function of the size and shape of the proteins. In practice, however, gel filtration resins tend to be slightly negatively charged.

If the size of a protein is very large relative to the size of the pores, it will never enter the pores and its pathway through the column will be around, rather than through, the beads. From the perspective of such a large protein, the gel filtration column consists of solid beads (or imagine small marbles), and it migrates through the column in the void space that is not occupied by the beads, which is known as the void volume, V_o. For most gel filtration resins, V_o is approximately $1/3 \cdot V_t$, where V_t is the total packed volume of the resin ($V_t = \pi r^2 l$; where r = radius of the column and l = length of the resin bed).

If a protein or a small molecule (such as a component in a buffer) is very small relative to the size of the pores in the gel filtration resin, then the small molecule will travel through the beads unimpeded—in effect, the beads will be invisible to the small molecule (imagine water passing through steel cages). Therefore, large proteins migrate more rapidly through a gel filtration resin than do small molecules.

After application of the sample to the column, a very large protein will elute in the void volume, which is approximately one third of V_t, whereas a small molecule will elute in a volume slightly less than V_t. Proteins of intermediate size will elute somewhere between V_o and V_t. Thus, according to the variable ability of proteins to migrate into the pores in a gel filtration resin, proteins can be sepa-

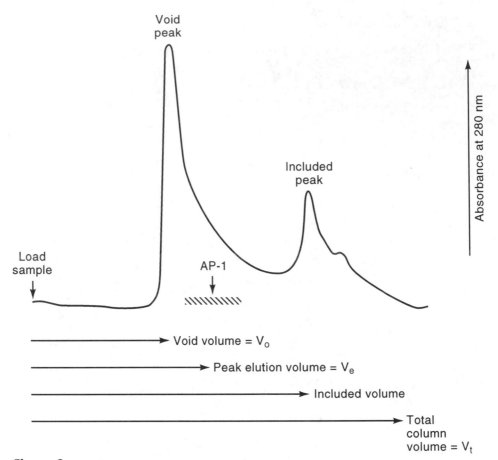

Figure 2
S-300 gel filtration chromatography of a crude HeLa nuclear extract. A nuclear extract was prepared from HeLa cells and then subjected to chromatography with an S-300 column, as described in this unit. (*Hatched area*) Location of AP-1 activity as detected by the DNase I footprinting assay. The included volume represents the volume of liquid in the column (both the liquid in the void volume as well as that within the porous gel filtration media) that is accessible to small molecules and salts. This column profile was generated during the 1995 Cold Spring Harbor Laboratory Protein Purification and Characterization Course (courtesy of R. Jiang, G. Lukacs, K. Dietmeier, and K. High).

rated by gel filtration on the basis of their size and shape. An S-300 column profile is depicted in Figure 2.

Gel Filtration Resins

Gel filtration resins are composed of a variety of materials, including dextran, agarose, and polyacrylamide. There are several considerations in the evaluation of gel filtration media. These parameters include the size range of the proteins to be fractionated, the degree of resolution, the flow rate, the cost of the resin, and the chemical composition of the medium.

Size range. Gel filtration media are available with various average pore sizes. To fractionate large proteins, it is necessary to use resins with relatively large pores. Conversely, to separate smaller proteins, it is best to use resins with smaller pore sizes. The manufacturers of gel filtration media provide information regarding the recommended resins for fractionation of proteins of specific size ranges.

Resolution. Resolution increases as the homogeneity of the size of the beads is increased and as the bead size decreases. Hence, for maximal resolution, small homogeneous beads are desired. Such beads tend, however, to be expensive and to require higher pressure for chromatography than that which may be achieved with conventional chromatography systems that are available to many investigators. In addition, it is sometimes quite informative to examine the homogeneity of bead size by microscopy.

Flow rate. Because the beads used in gel filtration are porous, they can be sensitive to moderate pressure. In a worst-case scenario (which does occur fairly often), the beads are compacted and crushed by the pressure caused by the application of the buffer or protein sample. The crushed beads then inhibit the flow of additional buffer through the column and cause further compaction and destruction of the resin and loss of the protein. It is thus desirable to use gel filtration media that can withstand high pressure. Typically, the resins with larger pore sizes (which are more fragile) should be used at lower column flow rates than the more sturdy resins with smaller pores. In addition, many resins are composed of cross-linked composite materials to increase their strength. Most manufacturers will provide information regarding recommended flow rates with each resin. The flow rates that are recommended by the manufacturers are determined for use with aqueous buffers. If there is 10% glycerol in the buffer, it is a good practice to decrease the flow rate to 50% of the recommended flow rate to compensate for the additional viscosity of the buffer. It is useful to note= that many manufacturers report the recommended flow rates in units of cm/hour. This unit of cm/hour is identical to ml/cm^2/hour, which in expanded form is **ml** (= cm^3) of buffer *per* **cm^2** cross-sectional area of the column *per* hour. Thus, if a resin has a recommended flow rate of 20 cm/hour and the column has a diameter of 1.0 cm (= cross-sectional area of 0.8 cm^2), then the flow rate should be 20 x 0.8 = 16 ml/hour (or 8 ml/hour if the buffer contains 10% glycerol).

Cost. As noted above, the better gel filtration resins tend to be more expensive. Thus, the actual resin to be used is often a compromise between performance and cost.

Chemical composition of the medium. In addition to dextran, agarose, and polyacrylamide, there are also composite copolymers that are widely used for gel filtration. The composition of the medium may also affect interactions between the resin and the sample. For example, some resins may be more charged or hydrophobic than others. If the resin is significantly charged, then it may behave as *both* an ion-exchange resin *and* a gel filtration resin. To minimize ionic interactions between the gel filtration resin and the protein sample, many investigators perform gel filtration with high ionic strength buffers containing 0.5–1.0 M NaCl.

Practical Tips for Gel Filtration

K_{av}. A protein will elute at a reproducible and characteristic position from a particular resin with a specific buffer. This property is usually reported as the K_{av}. $K_{av} = (V_e - V_o)/V_t - V_o)$ and is similar to the R_f value that is used for thin-layer chromatography. A protein that elutes in the void volume will have a $K_{av} = 0$, whereas a protein that elutes at V_t will have a $K_{av} = 1$. A gel filtration resin is most effective when the K_{av} of the protein to be purified is approximately 0.5. A related parameter is the V_e/V_o ratio. Under the conditions employed in this experiment, AP-1 will elute from the Sephacryl S-300 HR resin with a V_e/V_o of approximately 1.3–1.35.

Sample volume. Upon gel filtration, the sample will be diluted by a factor of two to three. Thus, it is necessary to have a concentrated protein sample before gel filtration. Under ideal conditions, the sample volume will be less than 2% of V_t. In practice, it is sometimes difficult to obtain such concentrated protein, and a sample volume that is up to 5% of the V_t can be used to obtain suboptimal results. The protein concentration can be as high as 50 mg/ml.

Column dimensions. For maximal resolution with gel filtration, it is better to use a long, thin column rather than a short, fat column of equivalent packed bed volumes. Successful gel filtration depends critically upon the homogeneity of the packed resin. With a short, fat column, the sample will be traveling through the column as a broad, thin disk, and any perturbation of that disk due to inhomogeneity of the resin will result in a loss of resolution. With a long, thin column, the identical sample will travel through the column as a thicker disk that is less sensitive to imperfections in the resin. The major drawback of using a long, thin column rather than a short, fat column is the lower flow rate that must be used with the thin column due to the smaller cross-sectional area.

"Fines." It is sometimes necessary to remove fine particles (including broken resin beads), "fines", from the resin. The fines will otherwise obstruct the flow of buffer through the column and contribute to the back-pressure. To remove fines, gently swirl the resin in H_2O (or chromatography buffer) in a large beaker. As soon as the beads have settled at the bottom of the vessel, pour off the supernatant, which contains the fines. Repeat this procedure several times until the fine particles are no longer visible in the supernatant. Most high-quality resins do not contain a significant amount of fine particles.

• ————————————————————————————————

How to Pour a Gel Filtration Resin

MATERIALS AND EQUIPMENT

XK 26/40 column (Pharmacia Biotech, Inc.)
Sephacryl® S-300 HR (Pharmacia Biotech, Inc.)
Blue dextran

REAGENT

TM buffer + 0.1 M KCl
(For recipe, see Preparation of Reagents, pp. 192–200.)

PROCEDURE

1. Determine the amount of resin to be used. Sephacryl S-300 HR is commercially available as a slurry at a concentration of two thirds of the packed bed volume. Thus, for a 180-ml column (diameter = 2.6 cm; length = 34 cm), remove 270 ml of S-300 slurry from the bottle.

   Note: When pouring and packing a gel filtration column, the homogeneity of the resin bed is of primary importance. Also note that a longer, thinner (diameter) column would be much more effective for high-resolution separation.

2. Wash the resin extensively with several volumes of TM buffer + 0.1 M KCl in a coarse, sintered glass funnel.

   Note: Handle the resin gently (especially when stirring) to prevent breakage of the fragile beads.

3. Suspend the resin gently in TM buffer + 0.1 M KCl to a final volume that is twice the desired packed bed volume (360 ml).

4. *(Optional, but recommended.)* De-gas the resin by subjecting the slurry to a vacuum for a few minutes. This process will remove dissolved gases in the resin and buffer.

5. Set up the column with an additional reservoir to accommodate the resin and buffer. Make sure that the column is absolutely vertical. Close the outlet at the bottom of the column.

6. Place approximately one-tenth column volume of buffer (~20 ml) into the empty column.

7. Pour the resin slurry into the column in one continuous motion.

   Note: It is important to prevent air bubbles from entering the gel filtration column. Even small air bubbles will ruin a column, which would then have to be re-poured.

8. Let the resin stand for approximately 30 minutes, and then open the outlet at the bottom of the column to allow flow of buffer through the column.

9. After the resin settles, close the outlet at the bottom of the column, remove the column reservoir, and place a column flow adapter on the top of the resin bed. *Make sure that the upper flow adapter is filled with buffer before putting it onto the column—otherwise, bubbles will be introduced into the column from the flow adapter.*

10. Attach the upper flow adapter to a pump (watch out for bubbles) and begin to pack the column with the pump. First, pack the column at the flow rate that will be used for chromatography of the sample (for the column in this experiment, 100 ml/hour). Watch the top of the resin bed as the resin is packed. As the top of the resin bed settles, lower the upper flow adapter so that it rests on the top of the resin bed. Then, after the resin has stopped settling, increase the flow rate to 150% of the chromatography flow rate (for the S-300 column, increase to 150 ml/hour). Continue to pack the column (and to adjust the upper flow adapter) until the resin does not compress any further. The column is now packed and ready to run.

    Note: The buffer does not have to contain protease inhibitors and dithiothreitol when the resin is being packed. However, before the sample is loaded to the column, it is necessary to equilibrate the column with at least one complete volume of buffer containing these reagents.

11. To test the properties of the column, it is a good practice to run a sample of 2 mg/ml blue dextran on the newly poured column. *Do not run blue dextran on a column to which protein has previously been applied.* Make a solution of 2 mg/ml blue dextran in the chromatography buffer (TM buffer + 0.1 M KCl) and filter (with a 0.22-μm filter) to remove small, undissolved particles of blue dextran. Load the blue dextran in a volume of approximately 2% of the total column volume (~4 ml, for the S-300 column). Collect 2.5-ml fractions. The chromatography with the blue dextran will provide the following information: (i) the void volume; (ii) the degree of dilution of the sample; and (iii) the overall quality of the column, as determined by visual examination of the blue dextran migrating down the column—this will reveal imperfections in the resin bed.

• _____

Sephacryl S-300 HR Chromatography of the HeLa Nuclear Extract

MATERIALS AND EQUIPMENT

HeLa nuclear extract (derived from 12 liters of cells; see pp. 130–133)
(5-ml sample)
XK 26/40 column (Pharmacia Biotech, Inc.)
Sephacryl® S-300 HR (Pharmacia Biotech, Inc.)
Liquid nitrogen

SAFETY NOTE

• The temperature of liquid nitrogen is –185°C. Handle with great care; always wear gloves and a face protector.

REAGENT

TM buffer + 0.1 M KCl
(For recipe, see Preparation of Reagents, pp. 192–200.)

PROCEDURE

Perform all procedures at 4°C.

1. Take a 5-ml sample of the HeLa nuclear extract (derived from 12 liters of cells) for the gel filtration chromatography, and set aside 50 μl of the extract for subsequent assays.

2. Use the following column parameters for the XK 26/40 column:

   Diameter = 2.6 cm
   Length = 34 cm
   Volume = 180 ml (packed bed volume)
   Flow rate = 100 ml/hour
   Buffer = TM buffer + 0.1 M KCl

3. Apply the 5-ml sample of the HeLa nuclear extract to the S-300 column. Collect 5-ml fractions.

Note: A critical step in gel filtration chromatography is the entry of the sample into the resin bed. It must go in as a thin, even disk. The resin is most evenly and tightly packed at the bottom of the column. Thus, some investigators prefer to invert the column before use and then apply the sample from the top of the column (which was previously the bottom of the column as it was being poured and packed). Alternatively, instead of inverting the column, it is also possible to apply the sample from the bottom of the column and run the sample upward. In either instance, the sample is applied to the end of the column where the resin is the most tightly and evenly packed. Also note that for high-resolution chromatography, the fraction size should be smaller—approximately one half of the volume of the applied sample.

4. Save 50-μl aliquots of each of the S-300 fractions for DNase I footprinting experiments. Transcription factor AP-1 will elute from the resin at a V_e/V_o of approximately 1.3–1.35. Many other transcription factors, such as Sp1, NF-I/ CTF, and AP-2 will elute from the S-300 column at a V_e/V_o of approximately 1.35–1.40. (See Fig. 2, p. 136, for a typical S-300 column profile.)

5. If the fractions are to be used within 24 hours, store the protein at 4°C. For long-term storage, freeze the fractions in liquid nitrogen and store at –80°C.

Note: The freezing and thawing of protein-containing solutions are critical aspects of successful protein chemistry. There are many varied opinions on this matter. It is suggested by this author that proteins should be frozen as quickly as possible by immersion in liquid nitrogen (dry ice/ethanol is adequate, whereas placement of the protein sample directly into a –80°C freezer is not recommended). In addition, it is of the utmost importance that frozen protein samples are thawed as quickly as possible. Loss of protein activity often results because thawing, as opposed to freezing, occurs too slowly. This author recommends that frozen proteins are thawed as quickly as possible by immersion in H_2O at room temperature. Moreover, to maximize the rate of thawing, it is important to remove any ice that may form around the vessel.

6. Determine the AP-1 DNA-binding activity in each of the fractions by DNase I footprinting. (See Fig. 3, p. 144, for sample results.)

7. The peak S-300 fractions containing AP-1 activity can be directly applied to the sequence-specific DNA affinity columns (see Experiment 3).

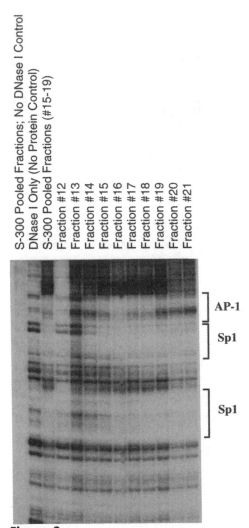

Figure 3

DNase I footprinting assay of fractions from the S-300 gel filtration column. A nuclear extract was prepared from HeLa cells and subjected to chromatography on an S-300 column as described in this unit. AP-1 (and Sp1) activity was then detected by DNase I footprinting of S-300 column fractions with the human metallothionein II$_A$ promoter. As seen in the footprint, AP-1 elutes from the S-300 column earlier than Sp1. This footprint was generated during the 1995 Cold Spring Harbor Laboratory Protein Purification and Characterization Course (courtesy of A. Strunnikov, A. Cheung, E. Miyoshi, and T. Wang).

• Experiment 3
Sequence-specific DNA Affinity Chromatography

•

INTRODUCTION

In this experiment, we describe a procedure for the purification of sequence-specific DNA-binding proteins by affinity chromatography. This technique has been demonstrated to be generally useful for the purification of over 100 different DNA-binding factors, and we use it here to purify transcription factor AP-1. The affinity resin consists of multimerized, synthetic oligonucleotides containing the AP-1 recognition sequence covalently attached to Sepharose CL-2B, an agarose-based resin.

For the preparation of the affinity resin, complementary, synthetic oligonucleotides containing an AP-1 binding site are 5'-phosphorylated with T4 polynucleotide kinase and ATP. The oligonucleotides are then polymerized with T4 DNA ligase and ATP. The multimerized DNA is separated from the residual ATP and covalently coupled to the Sepharose CL-2B by using cyanogen bromide (CNBr).

For the affinity chromatography procedure, a partially purified protein fraction (the pooled S-300 peak fractions, which contain approximately 0.1% AP-1) is combined with a nonspecific competitor DNA to which the AP-1 does not bind, and this mixture is applied to the affinity resin. The AP-1 is specifically retained on the affinity resin, whereas nonspecific DNA-binding proteins are bound to the competitor DNA and flow through the resin. The affinity resin is then washed extensively with buffer, and the AP-1 is eluted with a gradually increasing series of salt steps that is similar to a salt gradient. In this manner, AP-1 can be purified 500–1000-fold with approximately 30% overall yield in two successive affinity chromatography steps. Moreover, multiple DNA affinity resins, each with a specificity for a different DNA-binding protein, can be linked in series to purify several DNA-binding proteins simultaneously from a single protein fraction.

General Approach to the Purification of Sequence-specific DNA-binding Proteins

- Determine the sequence of the binding site of the DNA-binding protein by a technique such as DNase I footprinting (Galas and Schmitz 1978; Dynan and Tjian 1983).

- If it is possible, survey a variety of promoters and enhancers for a high-affinity binding site.

- Determine optimal conditions for binding of the factor to DNA. The effects of temperature, Mg(II) concentration, pH, and ionic strength should be examined.

- Partially purify the protein by conventional chromatography to remove nucleases and other contaminants that may adversely affect the affinity column. This is discussed later in greater detail.

- Test the effect of different competitor DNAs upon the efficiency of DNA binding by the factor by using a DNase I footprinting assay. The nonspecific competitor DNAs should include calf thymus DNA, poly(dI-dC), poly(dG-dC), and poly(dA-dT). As discussed in greater detail later, this experiment will reveal the affinity of the factor to different competitor DNAs. The competitor DNA to which the factor exhibits the lowest affinity would be the most useful as a nonspecific competitor for DNA affinity chromatography. It is very important that the competitor DNAs (including the synthetic co-polymers) are sonicated to an average length of approximately 300–500 bp. In this manner, the concentration of DNA ends (which are preferentially bound by contaminating nonspecific DNA-binding proteins, such as the Ku antigen—see later) is increased.

- Prepare two or more DNA affinity resins with naturally occurring, high-affinity binding sites. Do not attempt to guess a potential consensus sequence—the protein may not bind to it. Under ideal conditions, the DNA affinity resins would each contain the specific recognition site with different flanking DNA sequences. If a protein is purified on the basis of its specific binding to two different affinity resins that possess distinct DNA sequences except for the recognition site, then it is unlikely that the protein bound fortuitously to the flanking DNA sequences in both affinity resins.

- As a control experiment, it is also important to prepare a DNA affinity resin that does not contain the recognition sequence for the desired protein. This control resin enables the identification of proteins that bind nonspecifically to DNA-Sepharose. The DNA sequence to be used for this control resin could be any sequence that is unrelated to the binding site of the desired factor. Alternatively, a sequence that is a binding-defective, mutant form of the recognition site could be used.

• By using this approach to the purification of sequence-specific DNA-binding proteins, it is possible to identify tentatively the desired DNA-binding protein as a species that is enriched by chromatography through the specific affinity resins but is not enriched by chromatography through the control resin. Such a protein is likely to be either the desired sequence-specific DNA-binding protein or a molecule that is closely associated with the DNA-binding protein.

Inadvertent Purification of Nonspecific DNA-binding Proteins

Watch out for nonspecific DNA-binding proteins! It has been a somewhat common practice to purify nonspecific DNA-binding proteins inadvertently by DNA affinity chromatography, especially when gel mobility-shift assays (Garner and Revzin 1981; Fried and Crothers 1981) are used to monitor DNA binding. As outlined above, the use of a control DNA affinity resin that does not contain the desired factor binding sites should minimize misidentification of nonspecific DNA-binding proteins. In addition, the use of the DNase I footprinting assay rather than the gel mobility-shift assay should provide better data regarding the sequence specificity of binding by the purified protein preparations. The polypeptide(s) that binds specifically to DNA can also be identified by gel purification and renaturation of the polypeptide(s) according to the method of Hager and Burgess (1980). As an example, the gel purification and renaturation of AP-1 was performed by Lee et al. (1987) in the purification of AP-1.

In HeLa cell extracts, two proteins that are common contaminants in DNA affinity-purified protein fractions are poly(ADP-ribose) polymerase (Ueda and Hayaishi 1985; Slattery et al. 1983), which has an M_r of 116,000, and the Ku antigen, which consists of two polypeptides of M_r 70,000 and 80,000 (Mimori et al. 1986). Moreover, two nonspecific DNA-binding proteins of M_r 60,000 (also reported as 52,000 and 54,000) and 100,000 have been inadvertently purified from HeLa cells by sequence-specific DNA affinity chromatography (Zhang et al. 1993; R. Burk, pers. comm.). The 60-kD protein may have some preference for binding to octamer motifs (Yang et al. 1993), whereas both the 60- and 100-kD proteins bind to RNA and may be involved in RNA splicing (Dong et al. 1993; Patton et al. 1993; Yang et al. 1993). It is therefore important to take great care to avoid purifying nonspecific DNA-binding proteins, and adherence to the procedures and strategies described throughout this unit (particularly the use of a DNase I footprinting assay) will minimize such occurrences.

Partial Purification of DNA-binding Proteins Prior to Affinity Chromatography

Although it is usually not necessary to purify the protein extensively before DNA affinity chromatography, it is useful to separate the desired factor from nucleases and proteases that could degrade either the protein or the affinity resin. In conventional chromatography, sequence-specific and nonspecific DNA-binding proteins will often copurify. This may be due in part to their common propensity to interact with negatively charged polymers that resemble DNA. The following list of notes should be generally useful for the purification of DNA-binding proteins.

Cation-exchange chromatography. DNA-binding proteins will usually bind to cation-exchange resins in buffers containing 50–100 mM NaCl. The following conventional cation-exchange resins are known to be effective for the purification of DNA-binding proteins: SP Sepharose Fast Flow/Mono S (Pharmacia Biotech, Inc.); CM-52 (Whatman, Inc.) or CM Sepharose Fast Flow (Pharmacia Biotech, Inc.); P11 phosphocellulose (Whatman); and Bio-Rex 70 (Bio-Rad Laboratories). P11 phosphocellulose consists of phosphate groups attached to a polysaccharide (cellulose) and thus may vaguely resemble DNA. It is necessary to hydrate and "de-fine" this resin before use, as recommended by the manufacturer. It is important to note that P11 resin must be used within one week after it is hydrated because the phosphate groups hydrolyze quickly.

Heparin-agarose. Heparin-agarose is a very popular resin for the purification of DNA-binding proteins. Many, but certainly not all, DNA-binding proteins bind with high affinity to heparin-agarose resins. Heparin is a negatively charged polysaccharide and may function as an analog of DNA. A protocol for the preparation of heparin-agarose resin is given in Experiment 6 of this unit. It is important to note, however, that different preparations of heparin-agarose can possess significantly different chromatographic properties. This variation is due, in part, to distinct properties of agarose resins prepared by different manufacturers. For example, some agarose resins possess a greater ionic character than others, and in some instances, heparin-agarose chromatography might actually be a combination of *both* heparin *and* ion-exchange (from charged residues on the resin) chromatography. Unfortunately, we have also found that different preparations of heparin from different vendors exhibit vastly different properties when used for heparin-agarose chromatography. The variation in the properties of different heparin-agarose resins is also due to differences in the methods and reagents that are employed to attach the heparin to the agarose. Different methods for coupling and blocking of the agarose resin will produce different functional groups on the resin. To maximize reproducibility in heparin-agarose chromatography, it is best either to purchase heparin-agarose from a single manufacturer or to prepare heparin-agarose by using the same procedure and reagents in every batch. In practice, heparin-Sepharose CL-2B (prepared according to the procedure given in Experiment 6 of this unit) is an excellent resin for purification of DNA-binding proteins.

Nonspecific DNA-cellulose and DNA-agarose resins. Nonspecific DNA affinity resins can be useful for the purification of DNA-binding proteins. The most commonly used nonspecific DNA resins consist of either DNA adsorbed to cellulose (Alberts and Herrick 1971) or DNA covalently coupled to agarose (Arndt-Jovin et al. 1975). Calf thymus DNA and salmon sperm DNA are commonly used in the preparation of nonspecific DNA affinity resins either as double-stranded or as single-stranded DNA.

Sequence-specific DNA affinity resins that do not contain a binding site for the desired factor. In some instances, it may be useful to purify a sequence-specific DNA-binding factor by chromatography with either a sequence-specific affinity resin that *does not* contain a binding site for the factor (for an example, see Kaufman et al. 1989) or a nonspecific DNA affinity resin (for an example, see Rosenfeld and Kelly 1986). This strategy is particularly effective for the purification of sequence-specific DNA-binding proteins that possess a moderate affinity for binding to nonspecific DNA. In the purification of such factors by sequence-specific affinity chromatography, it is not possible to add nonspecific competitor DNA to the protein before affinity chromatography because the factors will bind to the nonspecific competitor. This problem may be solved as follows: The desired factor is subjected to chromatography with a nonspecific DNA affinity resin, and it is hoped that the desired factor can be eluted from the nonspecific DNA resin at a low salt concentration at which high-affinity nonspecific DNA-binding proteins remain bound to the resin. In this manner, the desired factor may be separated from the high-affinity nonspecific DNA-binding proteins (including Ku antigen and poly-[ADP-ribose] polymerase) that tend to be the major contaminants after sequence-specific DNA affinity chromatography. If such a separation of the desired protein and high-affinity nonspecific DNA-binding proteins can be achieved, then it would not be necessary to add competitor DNA during subsequent chromatography with a sequence-specific DNA affinity resin.

Wheat germ agglutinin affinity chromatography. Many sequence-specific DNA-binding transcription factors, including Sp1 and CTF/NFI, have been found to contain multiple O-linked N-acetylglucosamine monosaccharide residues (Jackson and Tjian 1988). Some of these glycosylated factors can be purified in high yield by affinity chromatography with wheat germ agglutinin-agarose (Jackson and Tjian 1989). It may thus be useful to attempt partial purification of a new factor by wheat germ agglutinin affinity chromatography.

Gel filtration chromatography. In this experiment, we employ gel filtration to purify partially the AP-1 in the HeLa nuclear extract. At first glance, gel filtration is not an obviously useful method for the purification of DNA-binding proteins, but the S-300 column does work well in practice. In the purification of sequence-specific DNA-binding proteins by DNA affinity chromatography, the major contaminants tend to be nonspecific DNA-binding proteins, such as Ku and poly(ADP-ribose) polymerase. In the course of cation exchange, nonspecific DNA affinity, or heparin-agarose chromatography, the sequence-specific factors often copurify with the nonspecific DNA-binding proteins. Thus, it is not always particularly useful to enrich a protein fraction for DNA-binding proteins prior to sequence-specific DNA affinity chromatography. Gel filtration provides a means for purification of AP-1 that does not involve its properties as a DNA-binding protein. Note, however, that gel filtration does significantly dilute the protein sample, which may not be desirable in some instances. Because the AP-1 is subsequently applied to the affinity resin, which concentrates the protein, the dilution by the S-300 column is not a problem.

Determination of the Oligonucleotide Sequence to Use for Affinity Chromatography

In the design of a DNA affinity resin, it is important to consider the following parameters.

Length of oligonucleotides. There is considerable flexibility in the length of the synthetic oligonucleotides. Oligonucleotides ranging from 14- to 51-mers have been used successfully. It may be wise to avoid using 21- and 42-mers, which contain two or four turns of the DNA helix. If the DNA is bent, then 21- and 42-mers may have a greater propensity to circularize during the ligation step, and the circular DNA would then probably couple less efficiently to the resin.

5'overhang. The oligonucleotide should be designed such that there is a single-stranded overhang. Typically, 5'GATC... works well. The DNA probably couples to the CNBr-activated agarose via primary amine groups on the single-stranded overhang that are not base-paired. It is recommended that there should be at least one A residue in the 5′ overhang.

Relation of oligonucleotide sequence to DNase I footprint. As noted previously, the DNA affinity resin should be prepared from naturally occurring, high-affinity binding sites. In the early steps in the affinity purification of a protein, it is a good practice to use a relatively long stretch of DNA that generously encompasses (several bases beyond each border) the sequence that is protected from digestion by DNase I. It is better to use a fragment that is unnecessarily too long (with which additional factors may also be copurified) than to use a short DNA fragment that does not contain a complete recognition site.

Purity of the synthetic oligonucleotides. Because the ligation step can be blocked by contaminating, incompletely synthesized oligonucleotides, it is important to use highly purified oligonucleotides. We typically purify the oligonucleotides by preparative gel electrophoresis. We have also found, however, that HPLC-purified oligonucleotides from Operon Technologies, Inc. are of sufficient purity for the preparation of DNA affinity resins.

Protein-binding capacity of the affinity resin. There is typically approximately 80–90 μg of DNA per milliliter of affinity resin. This corresponds to a maximal protein-binding capacity of 7 nmol per milliliter of resin if there is one recognition site per 20 bp.

Oligonucleotides for the purification of AP-1 and Sp1. For the purification of **AP-1**, use the following oligonucleotides:

5′GAT CGT GAC TCA GCG CG and **5′GAT CCG CGC TGA GTC AC.**

For the purification of **Sp1**, use:

5′GAT CGG GGC GGG GC and **5′GAT CGC CCC GCC CC.**

● ——

Purification of Oligonucleotides by Preparative Gel Electrophoresis

MATERIALS AND EQUIPMENT

Acrylamide

Bisacrylamide

Urea

Ammonium persulfate (10%; w/v)

N,N,N',N'-Tetramethylethylenediamine (TEMED)

Complementary synthetic oligonucleotides (containing the recognition sequence for the sequence-specific DNA-binding protein of interest)

Sec-butanol (2-butanol)

Diethyl ether

NaOAc (3 M)

$MgCl_2$ (1 M)

Ethanol (100% and 75%; v/v)

SpeedVac® rotary concentrator (Savant Instruments, Inc.)

SAFETY NOTES

- Acrylamide and bisacrylamide are potent neurotoxins and are absorbed through the skin. Their effects are cumulative. Wear gloves and a mask when weighing acrylamide and bisacrylamide. Wear gloves when handling solutions containing these chemicals. Although polyacrylamide is considered to be nontoxic, it should be handled with care because of the possibility that it might contain small quantities of unpolymerized acrylamide.
- Ammonium persulfate is extremely destructive to tissue of the mucous membranes and upper respiratory tract, eyes, and skin. Inhalation may be fatal. Exposure can cause gastrointestinal disturbances and dermatitis. Wear gloves, safety glasses, respirator, and other protective clothing and work in a chemical fume hood. Wash thoroughly after handling.
- TEMED is extremely destructive to tissue of the mucous membranes and upper respiratory tract, eyes, and skin. Inhalation may be fatal. Prolonged contact can cause severe irritation or burns. Wear gloves, safety glasses, respirator, and other protective clothing and work in a chemical fume hood. Wash thoroughly after handling. Flam-

mable: Vapor may travel a considerable distance to source of ignition and flash back.

- Diethyl ether is extremely volatile and extremely flammable. It is irritating to the eyes, mucous membranes, and skin. It is also a CNS depressant with anesthetic effects. Diethyl ether can exert its effects through inhalation, ingestion, or absorption through the skin. It should only be used in a chemical fume hood. Gloves and safety glasses should be worn. Explosive peroxides can form during storage or on exposure to air or direct sunlight.

REAGENTS

TBE (10x)
Formamide loading buffer
TE
(For recipes, see Preparation of Reagents, pp. 192–200.)

PROCEDURE

Preparation of Polyacrylamide Gel

1. Prepare a 20-cm x 40-cm x 1.5-mm gel with four wells each 3 cm in width. For oligonucleotides ranging in length from approximately 10 to 45 bases, use a 16% polyacrylamide/urea gel. For longer oligonucleotides, use either an 8% or a 6% polyacrylamide/urea gel.

2. To prepare a 16% polyacrylamide/urea gel, combine the following:

Acrylamide (38%; w/v)/bisacrylamide (2%; w/v)	50 ml
TBE (10x)	12.5 ml
Urea	62.5 g
H_2O	17 ml
Total volume:	125 ml

3. Filter, briefly de-gas, and then add 750 µl of 10% (w/v) ammonium persulfate and 50 µl of TEMED.

4. Let the gel polymerize for ≥30 minutes, and then pre-run the gel at 30 W for ≥1 hour.

   Note: Pre-running the gel helps to remove excess persulfate ions, which might degrade the DNA.

5. The amount of DNA that is prepared in a 1-μmol synthesis (~1–2 mg) can be loaded on one gel (using all four wells, with 0.25 μmol/3-cm well). This quantity of DNA is about the maximum amount that can be applied to the gel without overloading it.

   Note: The mobility of DNA in a 16% gel is as follows: Bromophenol blue co-migrates with an oligonucleotide of about 10 bases, and xylene cyanol comigrates with an oligonucleotide of about 30 bases. It is recommended that the formamide loading buffer contain only bromophenol blue if the length of the oligonucleotide is 25–35 bases.

Preparation of Sample

1. Dissolve the oligonucleotide in formamide loading buffer such that 50 μl of sample can be applied to one 3-cm well.

2. Heat the sample for 15 minutes at 65°C to remove any secondary structure in the DNA.

3. Load the sample and run the gel at 30 W. It takes approximately 4 hours for the bromophenol blue to migrate three quarters of the way down the gel, which is far enough to purify oligonucleotides of 15–30 bases.

Recovery of DNA

1. Identify the major band (which is usually the largest DNA species but is sometimes the next-to-largest oligonucleotide) by ultra-violet (UV) shadowing.

   Note: UV shadowing is performed as follows. The polyacrylamide gel is placed between two sheets of plastic wrap (such as Saran Wrap). The gel is then placed over a sheet containing a fluorescent material (such as a thin-layer chromatography plate with fluorescent backing or an autoradiography screen). By using a hand-held UV light, shine long-wavelength UV light over the gel (briefly!). Fluorescence will then be observed across the sheet of fluorescent material, *except where the bands of DNA are located* (because the DNA absorbs the UV light). In this manner, a shadow appears beneath the DNA. By using an ink pen, quickly draw an outline around the DNA bands. Then, under normal light, excise the appropriate DNA-containing segments of the gel.

2. Cut the band out carefully with a razor blade while trying to avoid shredding of the gel material. (Do not pulverize the gel slice into small pieces.)

3. Soak the gel piece in 5 ml of TE (in a 15-ml polypropylene tube) overnight at 37°C with shaking.

4. Filter the supernatant through siliconized glass wool in a pasteur pipette.

   Note: It is important to pre-rinse the glass wool plug in the pasteur pipette with approximately 5 ml of H_2O.

5. Concentrate the DNA by repeated extractions with sec-butanol.

6. Extract the DNA once with diethyl ether, and remove traces of the ether in vacuo by using a SpeedVac rotary concentrator.

7. Adjust the volume of the liquid to 180 μl with TE.

8. Add 20 μl of 3 M NaOAc and 2 μl of 1 M $MgCl_2$. Mix by vortexing.

9. Add 600 μl of 100% ethanol. Mix by inversion. Chill in dry ice/ethanol (–78°C) for 10 minutes. Let the mixture stand for 5 minutes at room temperature. Spin in a microcentrifuge for 15 minutes at room temperature to pellet the DNA.

10. Add 180 μl of TE. Dissolve the pellet by vortexing.

11. Add 20 μl of 3 M NaOAc and 2 μl of 1 M $MgCl_2$. Mix by vortexing.

12. Add 600 μl of 100% ethanol. Mix by inversion. Chill in dry ice/ethanol (–78°C) for 10 minutes. Let the mixture stand for 5 minutes at room temperature. Spin in a microcentrifuge for 15 minutes at room temperature to pellet the DNA.

13. Add 800 μl of 75% ethanol to the DNA pellet. Mix by vortexing. Spin for 5 minutes at room temperature.

14. Carefully dry the pellet in a SpeedVac rotary concentrator. (*Be careful:* Sometimes static electricity will cause the pellet to jump out of the tube.)

15. Dissolve the DNA in TE and store at –20°C.

16. Measure A_{260nm} and A_{280nm}.

    Note: For sequence-specific DNA affinity resins, assume that 1 A_{260nm} unit = 40 μg/ml DNA.

•

Preparation of the DNA Affinity Resin

MATERIALS AND EQUIPMENT

ATP (20 mM; pH 7.0)
[γ-^{32}P]ATP (5 μCi)
T4 polynucleotide kinase (10 units/μl) (Stratagene)
Ammonium acetate (10 M)
Ethanol (100% and 75%; v/v)
Phenol/chloroform (1:1; v/v)
Chloroform/isoamyl alcohol (3-methyl-1-butanol) (24:1; v/v)
NaOAc (3 M)
T4 DNA ligase (Stratagene)
Phenol (equilibrated with TE)
Isopropanol (2-propanol)
Glass-distilled H$_2$O
Sepharose® CL-2B (Pharmacia Biotech, Inc.)
Cyanogen bromide (CNBr) (Aldrich Chemical Co., Inc. C9 149-2)
N,N-dimethylformamide
NaOH (5 M)
Potassium phosphate (10 mM and 1 M; both pH 8.0)
KCl (1 M)
CNBr-activated Sepharose® 4B (Pharmacia Biotech, Inc.)
HCl (1 mM)
SpeedVac® rotary concentrator (Savant Instruments, Inc.)

SAFETY NOTES

- Wear gloves when handling radioactive substances. Consult the institutional environmental health and safety office for further guidance in the appropriate use of radioactive materials.
- Phenol is highly corrosive and can cause severe burns. Wear gloves, protective clothing, and safety glasses when handling it. All manipulations should be carried out in a chemical fume hood. Rinse skin that comes in contact with phenol with a large volume of water or PEG 400 and wash with soap and water; do not use ethanol!
- Chloroform is irritating to the skin, eyes, mucous membranes, and respiratory tract. It should only be used in a chemical fume hood. Gloves and safety glasses should also be worn. Chloroform is a carcinogen and may damage the liver and kidneys.
- Cyanogen bromide is highly toxic and volatile. Wear gloves and always handle this compound in a fume hood.

REAGENTS

T4 Polynucleotide kinase buffer (10x)
TE
Linker-kinase buffer (10x)
Ethanolamine-HCl (1 M; pH 8.0) (1 M ethanolamine [free base] adjusted to pH 8.0 with HCl)
Column storage buffer
(For recipes, see Preparation of Reagents, pp. 192–200.)

PROCEDURE

5'-Phosphorylation of the Oligonucleotides

1. Set up the following reaction mixture:

DNA (440 μg of *each* oligonucleotide in TE; i.e., 880 μg of total DNA)	65 μl
T4 polynucleotide kinase buffer (10x)	10 μl
Total volume:	75 μl

2. To denature and then to anneal the complementary DNA strands, incubate for 2 minutes at 88°C, for 10 minutes at 65°C, for 10 minutes at 37°C, and for 5 minutes at room temperature.

3. Combine the following:

DNA (from above)	75 μl
ATP (20 mM; pH 7.0; containing ~5μCi of [γ-^{32}P]ATP)	15 μl
T4 polynucleotide kinase (100 units)	10 μl
Total volume:	100 μl

4. Incubate for 2 hours at 37°C. Add 50 μl of 10 M ammonium acetate and 100 μl of H_2O to give a final volume of 250 μl.

5. Heat for 15 minutes at 65°C to inactivate the kinase.

6. Let the mixture cool to room temperature. Add 750 μl of 100% ethanol and mix by inversion. Spin in a microcentrifuge for 15 minutes at room temperature to pellet the DNA.

7. Discard the supernatant. Add 225 μl of TE and dissolve the pellet by vortexing.

8. Add 250 μl of 1:1 phenol/chloroform. Vortex for 1 minute. Spin for 5 minutes to separate the phases.

9. Transfer the upper layer to a new tube. Add 250 μl of 24:1 chloroform/isoamyl alcohol and vortex for 1 minute. Spin for 5 minutes to separate the phases.

10. Transfer the upper layer to a new tube. Add 25 μl of 3 M NaOAc and mix by vortexing.

11. Add 750 μl of 100% ethanol and mix by inversion. Spin for 15 minutes to pellet the DNA.

12. Discard the supernatant. Add 800 μl of 75% ethanol and mix by vortexing. Spin for 5 minutes.

13. Discard the supernatant, and dry the pellet in a SpeedVac rotary concentrator.

Ligation of the Oligonucleotides

1. Add 10 μl of 10x linker-kinase buffer to 65 μl of H_2O and dissolve the DNA in this solution by vortexing.

2. Add 20 μl of 20 mM ATP (pH 7.0) and 5 μl of T4 DNA ligase (30 Weiss units) to give a final reaction volume of 100 μl.

3. Incubate for ≥2 hours at room temperature. If ligation of the AP-1 oligonucleotides does not proceed, try increasing the temperature to 30°C.

    Note: Depending upon the oligonucleotides used, the optimal temperature for ligation will vary from 4°C to 30°C. Short oligonucleotides (≤ 15-mers) tend to ligate better at lower temperatures (4–15°C), whereas oligonucleotides that have a moderate degree of palindromic symmetry, which tend to self-anneal, ligate better at higher temperatures (15–30°C).

4. Monitor the progress of ligation by agarose gel electrophoresis (use 0.5 μl of ligation reaction per gel lane). The average length of the ligated oligonucleotides will typically be at least 10-mers.

    Note: (i) 5'-phosphorylated oligonucleotides often do not ligate on the first attempt. Thus, if ligation does not occur, extract the DNA once with 1:1 phenol/chloroform, once with chloroform, and ethanol precipitate (using NaOAc as the salt). Dissolve the DNA in 225 μl of TE, add 25 μl of 3 M NaOAc, and reprecipitate with 750 μl of 100% ethanol. Wash with 75% ethanol, dry in the SpeedVac, and try the ligation again. (ii) If possible, the oligonucleotides should be ligated to a length of at least 10-mers. Yet, if efficient ligation cannot be achieved, it may still be useful to make the DNA affinity resin with the poorly ligated DNA fragments, because in many instances, it has been found that effective affinity chromatography can be carried out with monomeric, complementary oligonucleotides.

Preparation of DNA for Coupling to Sepharose

Ammonium acetate-isopropanol precipitation removes residual ATP, which would otherwise interfere with the coupling of the ligated DNA to the CNBr-activated Sepharose.

1. Add 100 μl of phenol (equilibrated with TE) to each 100-μl ligation reaction. Vortex for 1 minute. Spin in a microcentrifuge for 5 minutes at room temperature. Transfer the upper layer to a new tube.

2. Add 100 μl of 24:1 chloroform/isoamyl alcohol. Vortex for 1 minute. Spin for 5 minutes at room temperature. Transfer the upper layer to a new tube.

3. Add 33 μl of 10 M ammonium acetate. Mix by vortexing.

4. Add 133 μl of isopropanol (2-propanol). Mix by inversion. Incubate for 20 minutes at –20°C. Spin for 15 minutes to pellet the DNA. Discard the supernatant.

5. Add 225 μl of TE. Vortex to dissolve the pellet. Add 25 μl of 3 M NaOAc. Mix by vortexing. Add 750 μl of 100% ethanol. Mix by inversion. Spin for 15 minutes to pellet the DNA. Discard the supernatant.

6. Wash the DNA twice with 75% ethanol. Dry the pellet in a Speed-Vac.

7. Dissolve the DNA in 50 μl of glass-distilled H_2O. Store at –20°C. *Do not dissolve the DNA in TE—the Tris buffer in the TE will interfere with the coupling reaction.*

Coupling of the DNA to Sepharose with Cyanogen Bromide

This procedure involves the activation of Sepharose CL-2B with cyanogen bromide (CNBr) and the subsequent coupling of the ligated DNA to the CNBr-activated Sepharose. Since CNBr is highly toxic, many researchers may prefer to use the alternative procedure outlined in the following section, which uses commercially available CNBr-activated Sepharose and thus does not involve direct handling of CNBr. The use of CNBr to activate the resin provides flexibility in the choice of the resin. We typically use Sepharose CL-2B, which is a sturdier, cross-linked version of Sepharose 2B. The CNBr-activated resin is available only as CNBr-activated Sepharose 4B. Another advantage of the direct use of CNBr is the lower cost of preparing the activated resin relative to purchasing the preactivated resin. Finally, the procedure outlined here has been more extensively used than that given in the following section, although it is likely that DNA affinity resins prepared by either method are equally effective in the purification of sequence-specific DNA-binding proteins.

1. Wash 10–15 ml (settled bed volume) of Sepharose CL-2B extensively with glass-distilled H_2O in a 60-ml coarse sintered glass funnel. Wash the resin with approximately 500 ml of H_2O.

2. Transfer the moist Sepharose resin to a 25-ml graduated cylinder and estimate a 10-ml volume of settled resin. Add H_2O to give a final volume of 20 ml. Transfer this slurry to a 150-ml glass beaker in a water bath (equilibrated to 15°C) over a magnetic stirrer in a fume hood.

3. In a fume hood, measure 1.1 g of CNBr into a 25-ml Erlenmeyer flask with Parafilm covering the mouth of the flask. It is better to have slightly more than 1.1 g rather than slightly less than 1.1 g. Dissolve the CNBr in 2 ml of N,N-dimethylformamide. It will dissolve instantly. Add the CNBr solution dropwise over 1 minute to the stirring slurry of Sepharose in the fume hood.

4. Immediately add NaOH as follows. Add 30 µl of 5 M NaOH every 10 seconds to the stirring mixture (at 15°C) for 10 minutes until a total volume of 1.8 ml of NaOH is added.

5. Immediately add 100 ml of ice-cold H_2O to the beaker and pour the mixture into a 60-ml coarse sintered glass funnel. AT THIS POINT, IT IS VERY IMPORTANT THAT THE RESIN IS NOT SUCTION-FILTERED INTO A DRY CAKE. If the resin is accidently dried into a cake during the filtration, do not use the dried resin. Rather, begin the procedure again from step 1.

6. Wash the resin four times with 100 ml of ice-cold H_2O (≤4°C) and twice with 100 ml of ice-cold 10 mM potassium phosphate (pH 8.0).

7. Immediately transfer one half of the resin (5 ml) to a 15-ml polypropylene screw cap tube and add approximately 2 ml of 10 mM potassium phosphate (pH 8.0) until the resin has the consistency of a thick slurry.

8. Immediately add the DNA (50 µl in H_2O; 880 µg total). Incubate on a rotating wheel overnight at room temperature.

9. Transfer the resin to a coarse 60-ml sintered glass funnel, and wash twice with 100 ml of H_2O and once with 100 ml of 1 M ethanolamine-HCl (pH 8.0).

   Note: Compare the level of radioactivity in the first few milliliters of the filtrate with the level of radioactivity in the washed resin to estimate the efficiency of incorporation of DNA to the resin. Usually, all detectable radioactivity is present only in the resin.

10. Transfer the resin to a 15-ml polypropylene screw cap tube and add 1 M ethanolamine-HCl (pH 8.0) until the mixture is a smooth slurry. Incubate the tube on a rotating wheel for 4–6 hours at room temperature. This step is to inactivate unreacted CNBr-activated Sepharose.

11. Wash the resin with the following:

10 mM potassium phosphate (pH 8.0)	100 ml
1 M potassium phosphate (pH 8.0)	100 ml
1 M KCl	100 ml
H_2O	100 ml
Column storage buffer	100 ml

12. Store the resin at 4°C (do not freeze the resin). The resin is stable for at least 1 year at 4°C.

Coupling of the DNA to Sepharose with CNBr-activated Sepharose

This procedure begins with commercially available CNBr-activated Sepharose and is safer and simpler than the method described in the previous section, which involves the preparation of CNBr-activated resin.

1. Weigh out 2 g of CNBr-activated Sepharose 4B.

   Note: 1 g of freeze-dried material gives approximately 3.5 ml of final gel volume.

2. Wash and swell the gel in 400 ml of 1 mM HCl in a sintered glass funnel for approximately 15 minutes.

3. Wash the resin with 100 ml of H_2O and then with 100 ml of 10 mM potassium phosphate (pH 8.0).

4. Immediately transfer 5 ml of the resin to a 15-ml polypropylene screw cap tube and add approximately 2 ml of 10 mM potassium phosphate (pH 8.0), until the resin has the consistency of a thick slurry.

5. Immediately add the DNA (50 μl in H_2O; 880 μg total). Incubate on a rotating wheel for 5–6 hours (or overnight, if desired) at room temperature.

6. Transfer the resin to a coarse 60-ml sintered glass funnel, and wash twice with 100 ml of H_2O and once with 100 ml of 1 M ethanol-amine-HCl (pH 8.0).

    Note: Compare the level of radioactivity in the first few milliliters of the filtrate with the level of radioactivity in the washed resin to estimate the efficiency of incorporation of DNA to the resin. Usually, all detectable radioactivity is present only in the resin.

7. Transfer the resin to a 15-ml polypropylene screw cap tube and add 1 M ethanolamine-HCl (pH 8.0) until the mixture is a smooth slurry. Incubate the tube on a rotating wheel for 4–6 hours at room temperature. This step is to inactivate unreacted CNBr-activated Sepharose.

8. Wash the resin with the following:

10 mM potassium phosphate (pH 8.0)	100 ml
1 M potassium phosphate (pH 8.0)	100 ml
1 M KCl	100 ml
H_2O	100 ml
Column storage buffer	100 ml

9. Store the resin at 4°C (do not freeze the resin). The resin is stable for at least 1 year at 4°C.

Proper Use of Nonspecific Competitor DNAs in Affinity Chromatography

In the introduction to this experiment, we discussed many of the techniques and strategies for the affinity purification of sequence-specific DNA-binding proteins, and the last remaining issue is the proper use of competitor DNAs during affinity chromatography. This parameter is an important aspect of affinity chromatography and both the type and estimated amount of DNA competitor to include are determined experimentally in DNA-binding assays that could be envisaged as scaled-down DNA affinity experiments. Commonly used competitor DNAs include calf thymus DNA, poly(dI-dC), poly(dA-dT), and poly(dG-dC). Before use in either DNase I footprinting or DNA affinity chromatography, all competitior DNAs should be sonicated to an average length of approximately 300–500 kbp. The resulting increase in the amount of DNA ends leads to much more effective binding of the competitor DNAs to nonspecific DNA-binding factors, such as Ku antigen, that exhibit high affinity for DNA ends.

Choosing a Competitor DNA and Estimating the Amount to Use

The steps involved in choosing an appropriate competitor DNA and estimating the amount to include in a DNA affinity chromatography experiment are outlined as follows: (1) DNA-binding assays (either a DNase I footprint or a gel mobility-shift experiment) are performed with a partially purified protein fraction (*the exact fraction that would be applied to the affinity resin*) in the presence of variable amounts of each of the potential competitor DNAs. The competitor DNA that inhibits DNA binding *the least* is the one to use for DNA affinity chromatography. (2) The highest amount of competitor DNA that does not diminish the binding of the sequence-specific factor under the conditions of the DNA-binding assays is determined. (3) The quantities of protein fraction and competitor DNA are scaled-up from the reaction conditions of the binding assay to those of the full-scale affinity chromatography experiment. (4) One fifth of the scaled-up amount of competitor DNA is then actually used in the affinity chromatography experiment.

The above procedure is best explained by considering the following simple hypothetical example—the purification of AP-531, the 531st AP factor:

1. A DNase I footprint assay with 10 μl of an S-300 fraction containing AP-531 revealed strong inhibition of its sequence-specific DNA binding by calf thymus DNA, poly(dG-dC), and poly(dA-dT), and weak inhibition of AP-531 binding by poly(dI-dC).

2. The results of the poly(dI-dC) competition experiments were: (i) no detectable inhibition with 1 μg or less of poly(dI-dC) in the assay; (ii) weak, but detectable, inhibition of DNA binding with 2 μg of poly(dI-dC); and (iii) strong inhibition by 4 μg or more of poly(dI-dC). With 10 μl of the S-300 fraction, the highest amount of poly(dI-dC) that does not diminish AP-531 binding is 1 μg.

3. Thus, if 10 ml (= 1000 x 10 μl) of the S-300 fraction is used for affinity chromatography, then a direct scale-up of the poly(dI-dC) competitor would be 1000 x 1 μg = 1000 μg of poly(dI-dC).

4. In the affinity chromatography experiment, however, one-fifth of the directly scaled-up amount would be used. In this instance, the appropriate amount of competitor DNA to use would be 1000 μg x 1/5 = 200 μg of poly(dI-dC).

The amount of competitor DNA is estimated as the *mass* of competitor DNA (e.g., in μg) to add per *volume* (such as ml) of protein fraction. An alternative perspective would be to consider the concentration of competitor DNA rather than the mass. In practice, the competitor DNA probably serves as a target for a pool of contaminating high-affinity DNA-binding proteins in the crude protein fraction. Thus, the mass of the competitor DNA per unit quantity of protein fraction appears to be more useful to consider than the concentration of the competitor.

The method described above for estimating the amount of competitor DNA to include in DNA affinity chromatography experiments provides only a rough guess to use as a starting point for the initial affinity chromatography experiments. To determine the optimal amount of competitor DNA to include in affinity chromatography experiments, it is then necessary to carry out parallel affinity chromatography experiments with variable concentrations of competitor DNA. In this manner, the experimental conditions that lead to the best purification of the factor (in preparative scale) can be determined.

It is essential to recognize that the optimal amount of competitor DNA will vary with the purity of the partially purified protein fraction. It appears that more competitor DNA is required when the impure protein fraction contains relatively high amounts of nonspecific DNA-binding proteins. Protein fractions that are relatively deficient in nonspecific DNA-binding proteins can be purified in the absence of competitor DNA. Thus, it is necessary to determine experimentally the optimal amount of competitor DNA to use with each protein fraction that will be subjected to affinity chromatography.

Preparation of Competitor DNAs

Poly(dI-dC), poly(dA-dT), and poly(dG-dC) are each dissolved to a final concentration of 10 A_{260nm} units in TE containing 100 mM NaCl, heated to 90°C, and slowly cooled over 30–60 minutes to room temperature before use. As mentioned above, the average length of the competitor DNA should be approximately 0.3–0.5 kbp. It is common for poly(dI-dC) to be sold in lengths greater than 9 kb. If the DNA is too long, it can be degraded by sonication. The length of the sonicated DNAs can be estimated by agarose gel electrophoresis. Note also that a mixture of different competitor DNAs can be used in a single experiment.

Procedure for Affinity Chromatography

MATERIALS AND EQUIPMENT

Econo-Column® (Bio-Rad Laboratories 731-1550)
Nonspecific competitor DNA
Liquid nitrogen

SAFETY NOTE

- The temperature of liquid nitrogen is –185ºC. Handle with great care; always wear gloves and a face protector.

REAGENTS

Buffer Z
Buffer Z^e
Column regeneration buffer
Column storage buffer
(For recipes, see Preparation of Reagents, pp. 192–200.)

PROCEDURE

The following experiment is performed with buffer Z, but good results can also be obtained with TM buffer. It is important to note that some commercially available preparations of HEPES and PIPES buffers contain contaminants that inhibit binding of proteins to DNA, and thus, in some respects, it is safer to use TM buffer. Some factors, such as Sp1, bind with higher affinity to DNA in the absence of Mg(II) than in the presence of Mg(II). Thus, it may be useful to omit Mg(II) in the chromatography buffer. As an example, buffer Z^e is identical to buffer Z, except that it does not contain $MgCl_2$. Although the procedures described here contain KCl in the chromatography buffers, the KCl could probably be substituted with NaCl. For the purification of AP-1, use either buffer Z or TM buffer.

Perform all procedures at 4ºC.

Note: DNA affinity chromatography is typically carried out at 4ºC. It has been observed, however, that some sequence-specific DNA-binding factors bind to DNA (as well as to DNA affinity resins) with higher affinity at room temperature (~22°C) than at 4°C. Therefore, for each factor, it is important to determine the optimal binding temperature.

1. Equilibrate the DNA affinity resin (1 ml settled bed volume) in a 2-ml Bio-Rad Econo-Column with 2 x 10 ml of buffer Z + 0.1 M KCl.

2. Combine the protein fraction (in TM buffer + 0.1 M KCl, buffer Z + 0.1 M KCl, or buffer Z^e + 0.1 M KCl) with nonspecific competitor DNA.

   Note: To purify AP-1, combine 0.5 ml of sonicated 10 A_{260nm} concentration poly(dI-dC) with approximately 25 ml of S-300 peak eluate (in TM buffer + 0.1 M KCl) derived from 12 liters of HeLa cells. 10 A_{260nm} concentration poly(dI-dC) ≈850 µg DNA/ml.

3. Allow the protein-DNA mixture to stand for 10 minutes.

4. Spin this mixture in an SS-34 rotor at 10,000 rpm for 10 minutes to pellet insoluble protein-DNA complexes. Transfer the supernatant to a new tube.

5. Load the column at gravity flow (15 ml/hour/column).

   Note: In the purification of AP-1 from 12 liters of cells, a single 1-ml column should be appropriate. When purifying a larger quantity of material, use multiple 1-ml columns in parallel. It is, however, a common practice to apply as much as 50 ml of protein sample onto a single 1-ml column.

6. After loading the starting material, wash the column with 4 x 2 ml of buffer Z (or Z^e) + 0.1 M KCl.

   Note: It is most important to wash the affinity column thoroughly at this step. The DNA affinity columns will often yield greater than 100-fold purification of the desired factor. When a protein is purified 100-fold, however, a 1% contamination of the starting material due to inefficient washing of the column will lead to a major contamination of the affinity-purified factor.

7. Elute the protein from the column by successive addition of 1-ml portions of buffer Z containing 0.2 M KCl, 0.3 M KCl, 0.4 M KCl, 0.5 M KCl, 0.6 M KCl, 0.7 M KCl, 0.8 M KCl, and 0.9 M KCl, and 3 x 1 ml of buffer Z containing 1 M KCl. Collect 1-ml fractions that correspond to the addition of the 1-ml portions of buffer.

   Note: When purifying a new factor, a salt elution step with 2 M NaCl should also be included, because in a few instances it has been found that sequence-specific DNA-binding proteins remain bound to the affinity resin in the presence of 1 M salt (in these cases, the factors were then eluted with 2 M salt). When carrying out salt elutions at greater than 1 M salt concentration, NaCl is preferable to KCl because of the higher solubility of NaCl relative to KCl.

8. Save two aliquots of each fraction (40 μl for the SDS gel and 25 μl for the DNase I footprint) at 4°C, and freeze the remainder of the fractions in liquid nitrogen and store them at –80°C.

9. Regenerate the affinity resin as follows. *At room temperature*, stop the flow of each column, and then add 5 ml of column regeneration buffer to each column. Stir the resin with a narrow siliconized glass rod to mix the resin with the column regeneration buffer. Let the buffer flow out of the column. Stop the flow of the column again, and repeat the addition and mixing of the column regeneration buffer with the resin. Then, equilibrate the resin with 2 x 15 ml of column storage buffer, and store the resin at 4°C.

10. Assay the protein fractions for sequence-specific DNA-binding activity. (A silver-stained 8% polyacrylamide–SDS gel of affinity-purified AP-1 is shown in Fig. 4.)

    If further purification is desired, combine the fractions that contain the activity. Then, either dilute the pooled fractions (with buffer Z without KCl) or dialyze them (against buffer Z + 0.1 M KCl) to attain a final concentration of 0.1 M KCl. Combine the protein fraction with nonspecific competitor DNA (the amount and type of which needs to be determined experimentally) and reapply to a DNA affinity resin.

TIPS FOR THE USE AND HANDLING OF AFFINITY-PURIFIED DNA-BINDING PROTEINS

- The protein concentration of affinity-purified proteins is typically 5–50 μg/ml.

- The protein should be quick-frozen in liquid nitrogen and stored at –80°C. The protein can be quickly thawed in cold (4°C) H_2O because the buffers contain 20% (v/v) glycerol. In some instances, however, it may be preferable to thaw the protein quickly in H_2O at room temperature while taking precautions to ensure that the protein sample does not warm up above 4°C. Many affinity-purified proteins retain their DNA-binding activity after several freeze-thaw cycles. It is a good idea, however, to divide protein preparations into aliquots that could be used as needed on many separate occasions.

- Minimize handling of protein—especially with regard to exposure to plastic and glass, to which the protein might be irreversibly ad-

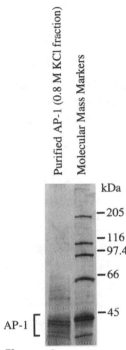

Figure 4
Purification of transcription factor AP-1 by sequence-specific DNA affinity chromatography. Transcription factor AP-1 (which is a mixture of Jun, Fos, and related species that bind to the sequence 5'TGAGTCA; see Introduction) was purified from a HeLa nuclear extract by S-300 chromatography and one cycle of sequence-specific DNA affinity chromatography, as described in this unit. The protein from the 0.8 M KCl elution step was then analyzed by 8% polyacrylamide-SDS gel electrophoresis and silver staining (ideally, a higher percentage of polyacrylamide would have been used in the gel). The mixture of polypeptides indicated by the bracket is highly purified AP-1. The purification of AP-1 from HeLa cells and SDS gel electrophoresis was carried out during the 1995 Cold Spring Harbor Laboratory Protein Purification and Characterization Course (courtesy of A. Strunnikov, A. Cheung, E. Miyoshi, and T. Wang).

sorbed. To minimize this nonspecific adsorption to plastic and glass, affinity-purified proteins should be manipulated and stored in buffers containing a detergent such as Nonidet P-40 (NP-40; a nonionic detergent) at a concentration of roughly 0.01–0.1% (v/v). The use of siliconized plastic test tubes and pipette tips will also minimize loss of protein by adsorption to plastic, but it is usually not necessary to use siliconized plasticware. Note also that the inclusion of 0.1% (v/v) NP-40 in the protein-containing buffers has not been observed (by the author) to affect protein-DNA interactions, as monitored by DNase I footprinting analysis.

- Typically, 0.2–1 µl of protein (2–10 ng) is sufficient for a "blanked-out" footprint (with ≈10 fmol of DNA probe). *Do not add competitor DNA to the footprinting reactions with purified protein—it will severely inhibit the binding of the factors.*

- After DNA affinity purification, some proteins do not exhibit DNA-binding activity in gel mobility-shift assays (this problem does not usually arise with the DNase footprinting assay). To counteract this problem, add bovine serum albumin to a final concentration of 0.1 mg/ml.

- To analyze the DNA affinity column fractions by SDS–poly-acrylamide gel electrophoresis, it is necessary to precipitate the protein with 20% (w/v) trichloroacetic acid (final concentration) and then to wash the protein pellet with acetone (to remove excess trichloroacetic acid) prior to suspending the protein in the SDS gel sample buffer. The trichloroacetic acid precipitation is performed to concentrate the dilute protein sample as well as to remove salts, such as K^+, that would form an insoluble precipitate when combined with SDS.

• Experiment 4
DNase I Footprinting

INTRODUCTION

DNase I footprinting is a useful procedure for the detection and characterization of sequence-specific binding of factors to DNA (Galas and Schmitz 1978). The technique is performed as follows. A sequence-specific DNA-binding factor is incubated with a single-end-labeled, double-stranded DNA probe to allow binding of the factor to its recognition site on the DNA fragment. Then, the factor-DNA complex is digested lightly with DNase I under conditions that give approximately one single-stranded nick per duplex DNA fragment. The region of the DNA that is bound by the factor is protected from digestion by DNase I. The resulting mixture of DNase I-digested DNA is subjected to electrophoresis using a DNA sequencing gel apparatus under denaturing conditions identical to those used for DNA sequencing. After autoradiography, the DNase I digestion ladder generated in the presence of the sequence-specific DNA-binding factor is compared with that obtained in the absence of the factor (as a reference). The region of the DNA fragment that is bound by the factor appears as a blank stretch, or "footprint," in the DNase I digestion ladder relative to the control in which the factor was omitted. A DNase I footprint of S-300 column fractions is shown in Figure 3 (p. 144), and a footprint of DNA affinity-purified AP-1 is depicted in Figure 5.

Another technique for the detection of DNA-binding factors is the gel mobility-shift assay (Garner and Revzin 1981; Fried and Crothers 1981), which is also known as the gel retardation assay or the electrophoretic mobility-shift assay (EMSA). In this procedure, the DNA-binding factor is incubated with a labeled, double-stranded probe (which is normally less than 200 bp in length), and the factor-DNA complex is then directly subjected to electrophoresis under non-denaturing conditions. Binding of the factor to the DNA is detected by the lower mobility of the factor-DNA complex relative to that of the DNA probe alone.

There are various strengths and weaknesses to the use of either DNase I footprinting or gel mobility-shift assays for the detection and characterization of sequence-specific binding of factors to DNA. The major strength of DNase I footprinting is that it directly reveals the

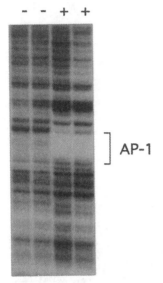

Figure 5
DNase I footprint of AP-1. Transcription factor AP-1 was partially purified from a nuclear extract of HeLa cells by S-300 gel filtration chromatography and one cycle of sequence-specific DNA affinity chromatography, and the resulting preparation was subjected to DNase I footprinting analysis with the human metallothionein II$_A$ promoter. This footprint was generated during the 1994 Cold Spring Harbor Laboratory Protein Purification and Characterization Course (courtesy of M. Grether, B.-C. Chung, T. Genetta, and D. McCarthy).

region of DNA that is bound by the factor. In contrast, the gel-shift assay indicates only that a factor (or factors) is bound to the DNA. In fact, if a gel-shift assay is performed with an impure protein fraction, it is also possible that the shifted fragment is a complex containing a nonspecific DNA-binding protein, such as the Ku antigen (Mimori et al. 1986). Thus, with the gel-shift assay, it is necessary to perform a series of control experiments to discern whether or not the DNA binding is due to a sequence-specific factor. The major drawback to DNase I footprinting is that high efficiency (>50%) binding of the factor to the DNA is required to detect a footprint. With the gel-shift assay, the shifted probe can be detected even if only a small proportion of the probe is bound by the factor. The gel-shift assay is additionally useful for the analysis of multimeric forms of bound factors as well as for DNA bending studies. For the purposes of sequence-specific DNA affinity chromatography, however, DNase I footprinting is the most useful assay because it provides direct information regarding the location of the binding site for the sequence-specific factor.

Notes on the Preparation of a DNase I Footprint Probe

- Footprint probes are single-end-labeled, double-stranded DNA fragments. The length of the probes is typically 200–800 bp.

- End-labeling of footprint probes is usually carried out either by 5′ phosphorylation with polynucleotide kinase and [γ-^{32}P]ATP or by 3′ labeling ("filling in") of a 5′ restriction fragment overhang with DNA polymerase (such as the large fragment of *E. coli* DNA polymerase I) and [α-^{32}P]deoxyribonucleoside triphosphates. If there is phosphatase activity present in a crude protein fraction, then it would be preferable to label the footprint probe with polymerase and the [α-^{32}P]nucleotides.

- If it is known, the binding site for the factor should be somewhere between 50 bp and 200 bp from the labeled end of the footprint probe. Impure protein fractions contain proteins that bind to ends of DNA fragments, and thus, if the binding site of the sequence-specific factor is near the end of the footprint probe, then its footprint may be obscured by the end-binding proteins. If, on the other hand, the sequence-specific binding site is too far from the labeled end, then it may be difficult to determine the location of the binding site due to the lower resolution of the long DNA fragments by gel electrophoresis under such conditions.

Preparation of a DNase I Footprinting Probe

MATERIALS AND EQUIPMENT

Plasmid DNA (containing the recognition site for the sequence-specific DNA-binding factor of interest)
Appropriate restriction enzymes
Phenol/chloroform (1:1; v/v)
Chloroform/isoamyl alcohol (3-methyl-1-butanol) (24:1; v/v)
Ethanol (100% and 75%; v/v)
Calf intestinal alkaline phosphatase (Boehringer Mannheim Corp. 713 023)
$[\gamma\text{-}^{32}P]ATP$ (150 µCi/µl; 7000 Ci/mmol; 21 pmol/µl)
T4 polynucleotide kinase (10 units/µl) (Stratagene)
Ammonium acetate (2.5 M)
NaOAc (3 M)
SpeedVac® rotary concentrator (Savant Instruments, Inc.)
Acrylamide
Bisacrylamide
Ammonium persulfate (10%; w/v)
TEMED (*N,N,N′,N′*-Tetramethylethylenediamine)

SAFETY NOTES

- Phenol is highly corrosive and can cause severe burns. Wear gloves, protective clothing, and safety glasses when handling it. All manipulations should be carried out in a chemical fume hood. Any areas of skin that come in contact with phenol should be rinsed with a large volume of water or PEG 400 and washed with soap and water; do not use ethanol!
- Chloroform is irritating to the skin, eyes, mucous membranes, and respiratory tract. It should only be used in a chemical fume hood. Gloves and safety glasses should also be worn. Chloroform is a carcinogen and may damage the liver and kidneys.
- Wear gloves when handling radioactive substances. Consult the institutional environmental health and safety office for further guidance in the appropriate use of radioactive materials.
- Acrylamide and bisacrylamide are potent neurotoxins and are absorbed through the skin. Their effects are cumulative. Wear gloves and a mask when weighing acrylamide and bisacrylamide. Wear

gloves when handling solutions containing these chemicals. Although polyacrylamide is considered to be nontoxic, it should be handled with care because of the possibility that it might contain small quantities of unpolymerized acrylamide.

- Ammonium persulfate is extremely destructive to tissue of the mucous membranes and upper respiratory tract, eyes, and skin. Inhalation may be fatal. Exposure can cause gastrointestinal disturbances and dermatitis. Wear gloves, safety glasses, respirator, and other protective clothing and work in a chemical fume hood. Wash thoroughly after handling.
- TEMED is extremely destructive to tissue of the mucous membranes and upper respiratory tract, eyes, and skin. Inhalation may be fatal. Prolonged contact can cause severe irritation or burns. Wear gloves, safety glasses, respirator, and other protective clothing and work in a chemical fume hood. Wash thoroughly after handling. Flammable: Vapor may travel a considerable distance to source of ignition and flash back.

REAGENTS

TE
Calf intestinal phosphatase buffer (10x)
T4 polynucleotide kinase buffer (10x)
TBE loading buffer (5x)
TBE (10x)
(For recipes, see Preparation of Reagents, pp. 192–200.)

PROCEDURE

Plasmid DNA

The plasmid DNA used for the preparation of a DNase I footprinting probe must be of high quality (CsCl purified) and must have very low levels of RNA contamination. RNA contaminants would inhibit the kinase reaction. We typically purify the DNA with two successive CsCl gradients.

First Restriction Digest

The objective of the first restriction digest is to form a 5'-overhang. The location of the restriction site should be 50–200 bp from the factor binding site.

1. Incubate the plasmid DNA (50 μg is a convenient amount) with the first restriction enzyme and monitor completion of the reaction with an agarose gel.

2. Extract the DNA once with 1:1 phenol/chloroform and once with 24:1 chloroform/isoamyl alcohol.

3. Ethanol precipitate the DNA and dissolve in TE to give a final concentration of 1 μg/μl.

Removal of the 5' Terminal Phosphate

1. Add 1 unit of calf intestinal alkaline phosphatase per microgram of DNA (e.g., to dephosphorylate 50 μg of DNA, add 50 units of phosphatase [50 units = 50 μl] in a total volume of 500 μl). Incubate for 2 hours at 37°C.

2. Extract once with phenol, once with 1:1 phenol/chloroform, and once with 24:1 chloroform/isoamyl alcohol.

3. Ethanol precipitate the DNA, and dissolve in TE to give a final concentration of 1 μg/μl.

   Note: It is convenient to digest and dephosphorylate a large quantity of the DNA (≥50 μg) as a stock and then to label smaller quantities (typically 5 μg) of the DNA when it is needed.

Labeling of the 5' End

1. Add 5 μl of digested, dephosphorylated DNA (1 μg/μl; 5 μg total; 5 pmol of 5' ends) to 2 μl of 10x T4 polynucleotide kinase buffer in 11 μl of H_2O. Mix by vortexing.

2. To this mixture, add 1 μl of [γ-^{32}P]ATP. (There should be a two- to fourfold molar excess of labeled ATP relative to 5' ends on the DNA.) Then add 1 μl of T4 polynucleotide kinase. (This is an excess of kinase.) The final reaction volume is 20 μl.

3. Incubate for 1–2 hours at 37°C.

4. Add 200 μl of 2.5 M ammonium acetate and mix by vortexing. Bring the liquid to the bottom of the tube by spinning in a microcentrifuge for 0.5 seconds.

5. Heat for 15 minutes at 70°C to inactivate the kinase. Chill on ice.

6. Add 660 µl of 100% ethanol and mix by inversion. Spin in a microcentrifuge for 15 minutes to pellet the DNA. Withdraw the supernatant with a pipette.

   Note: Be very careful not to remove the DNA pellet. Make sure that the pellet has the appropriate level of radioactivity.

7. Add 100 µl of TE and mix by vortexing to dissolve the DNA.

8. Add 100 µl of 1:1 phenol/chloroform and mix by vortexing for 1 minute. Spin for 5 minutes to separate the phases.

9. Transfer the upper layer to a new tube and add 10 µl of 3 M NaOAc. Mix by vortexing.

10. Add 300 µl of 100% ethanol and mix by inversion. Spin for 15 minutes to precipitate the DNA. Withdraw the supernatant with a pipette.

    Note: Be very careful not to remove the DNA pellet. Make sure that the pellet has the appropriate level of radioactivity.

11. Add 800 µl of 75% ethanol and mix by vortexing. Spin for 5 minutes to pellet the DNA. Withdraw the supernatant with a pipette.

    Note: Be very careful not to remove the DNA pellet. Make sure that the pellet has the appropriate level of radioactivity.

12. Dry the pellet in a SpeedVac rotary concentrator.

13. Dissolve the DNA in 10 µl of TE.

Second Restriction Digest

The objective of the second restriction digest is to generate a labeled DNA fragment of 200–800 bp.

1. Incubate the labeled DNA with the second restriction enzyme. To ensure that this reaction goes to completion, it is recommended that a large excess of enzyme is used whenever possible (e.g., 50–100 units of restriction enzyme for 5–10 µg of DNA).

   Note: Watch out for restriction enzymes with phosphatase activity. Inexpensive enzymes, such as *Eco*RI and *Hin*dIII, are usually adequate. It is convenient to perform this reaction in a volume of 80 µl. If you wish, you can monitor the progress of the reaction with an agarose gel.

2. Extract the DNA once with 1:1 phenol/chloroform. Then add 20 µl of 5x TBE loading buffer to 80 µl of DNA and load the sample directly onto a 5% polyacrylamide (nondenaturing) gel.

Polyacrylamide Gel Electrophoresis of the Labeled Restriction Fragment

1. Pour a 5% polyacrylamide gel (20 cm x 40 cm x 1.5 mm; with four 3-cm wells) by using the following recipe:

Acrylamide (30%; w/v)/bisacrylamide (0.8%; w/v)	20.3 ml
TBE (10x)	12.5 ml
H_2O	92.2 ml

   Mix, filter, and then add 750 µl of 10% (w/v) ammonium persulfate and 60 µl of TEMED.

2. Let the gel polymerize for at least 45 minutes, and pre-run the gel for at least 1 hour at 19 W ($\approx$400 V). When running, the gel should not get hot.

3. Apply the sample to the gel, and run the gel for the desired length of time. The voltage will slowly increase from 400 V to 450–500 V.

   Note: Xylene cyanol comigrates with a 300-bp restriction fragment on a 5% gel.

Elution of the DNA from the Polyacrylamide Gel

This procedure works fine for gels that are ≤8% polyacrylamide.

1. Cut out the radioactive band from the gel. Try to minimize the size of this band.

2. Poke a hole in the bottom of a 1.5-ml plastic test tube with an 18-G (pink) needle.

3. Place the bottom of the tube with a hole inside the mouth of another 1.5-ml tube (which does not have a hole).

4. Place the gel slice in the upper tube with a hole.

5. Spin both tubes together in a microcentrifuge for 15 seconds. The gel slice should be pulverized by passage through the hole into the lower tube.

6. Add 300 µl of TE. Mix by vortexing.

7. Incubate overnight at 37ºC.

8. Poke a hole in the bottom of a 1.5-ml plastic test tube with a 20-G (yellow) needle. Place approximately 200 μl (tightly packed volume) of siliconized glass wool in the bottom of the tube over the hole. *The siliconized glass wool should be tightly packed at the bottom of the tube.* Then, insert the bottom of this tube into the mouth of another 1.5-ml tube (without a hole). By using a 1000-μl (blue) pipette tip with approximately 2–3 mm of the tip cut off with a razor blade, place the TE plus pulverized gel slice mixture onto the top of the glass wool, and spin the two-tube setup briefly in a microcentrifuge for 10 seconds. The lower tube should contain the eluted DNA fragment in TE.

9. Ethanol precipitate the probe DNA, and dissolve in TE.

10. Store at –20ºC.

DNase I Footprinting

MATERIALS

^{32}P-labeled DNase I footprinting probe
Phenol/chloroform (1:1; v/v)
Ethanol (100% and 75%; v/v)

SAFETY NOTES

- Wear gloves when handling radioactive substances. Consult the institutional environmental health and safety office for further guidance in the appropriate use of radioactive materials.
- Phenol is highly corrosive and can cause severe burns. Wear gloves, protective clothing, and safety glasses when handling it. All manipulations should be carried out in a chemical fume hood. Any areas of skin that come in contact with phenol should be rinsed with a large volume of water or PEG 400 and washed with soap and water; do not use ethanol!
- Chloroform is irritating to the skin, eyes, mucous membranes, and respiratory tract. It should only be used in a chemical fume hood. Gloves and safety glasses should also be worn. Chloroform is a carcinogen and may damage the liver and kidneys.

REAGENTS

Polyvinyl alcohol (10%; w/v)
Competitor DNA
Buffer Z' (or buffer Z^e)
DNase I (2.5 mg/ml)
$MgCl_2$ (10 mM)/$CaCl_2$ (5 mM)
DNase I stop solution
Proteinase K (2.5 mg/ml)
Formamide loading buffer
(For recipes, see Preparation of Reagents, pp. 192–200.)

PROCEDURE

1. Chill 1.5-ml plastic test tubes on ice. It is not necessary to close the caps on the tubes until addition of the DNase I stop solution (see step 11, p. 182).

2. Make a combined probe DNA mix for all of the reactions according to the following recipe:

1x Probe DNA mix (for 1 reaction)

^{32}P-labeled probe DNA (10–25 fmol)	X μl
Polyvinyl alcohol (10%)	10 μl
Calf thymus DNA (1 mg/ml); poly(dI-dC), poly(dG-dC), or poly(dA-dT) (10 A_{260nm} units); or no competitor DNA (for pure or nearly pure protein). For the S-300 fractions (10 μl), use 0.2 μl of 10 A_{260nm} unit poly(dI-dC).	0.2–1 μl
H_2O	Z μl
Total volume:	25 μl

Vortex the probe DNA mix thoroughly. The polyvinyl alcohol is viscous and complete mixing of the probe DNA solution is not attained until the mixture is extensively vortexed.

Note: (i) Polyvinyl alcohol may promote binding of factors to DNA. It probably functions as a molecular crowding agent ("volume excluder") that increases the effective concentration of macromolecules such as protein and DNA (imagine molecular sponges that soak up water and small ions but not large macromolecules). (ii) The use of competitor DNA is optional, but often helpful when using crude protein fractions. Note that the timing of competitor DNA addition may be an important parameter. Typically, the competitor DNA is added with the probe mix, as in this protocol for footprinting with AP-1. In some instances, however, it may be better to add the competitor to each individual tube after the addition of both the protein fraction and the probe mix. The optimal time of addition of the competitor should be determined experimentally.

3. Add appropriate amounts of buffer Z' + 0.1 M KCl and buffer Z' + 0.0 M KCl to each reaction tube.

Note: The final volume of the buffer Z' + protein fraction mixture should be 25 μl, and the final KCl concentration of the mixture should be 0.1 M KCl. For example, if you are footprinting 5 μl of a protein fraction that contains 0.3 M KCl, you would need to add 10 μl of buffer Z' + 0.0 M KCl and 10 μl of buffer Z' + 0.1 M KCl to make the final salt concentration 0.1 M KCl.

4. Add the protein fractions *directly* to the reaction tubes containing the appropriate amount and type (0.0 M KCl or 0.1 M KCl) of buffer Z'.

5. Add 25 μl of the probe DNA mix to each of the tubes. Mix the samples by flicking, and incubate on ice for 15 minutes.

6. Meanwhile, thaw an aliquot of the 2.5 mg/ml DNase I stock solution.

7. Just before the end of the 15-minute incubation of the probe DNA and protein fraction, dilute the DNase I in ice-cold H_2O. Mix thoroughly by inversion and gentle vortexing.

   Note: For negative control reactions without protein, 2 µl of a 1:2000 dilution of DNase I should work for most DNA probes. Depending upon the particular DNA sequence, the optimal amount of DNase I will vary. For reactions with impure protein, more DNase I is normally required because of the presence of DNase I inhibitors, such as monomeric actin. Crude protein fractions will need 20–100 times more DNase I. Partially purified fractions will require 3–10 times more DNase I. Pure protein fractions do not require any additional DNase I. Optimal DNase I dilutions must be determined for each protein fraction being tested.

8. Remove one sample of the probe DNA and protein fraction from the ice and let it stand for 1 minute at room temperature.

   Note: It is helpful when footprinting to have all necessary items (Pipetmen, solutions, timer, vortexer, DNase I) in close proximity. The smoother this procedure goes, the better (and more reproducible) your footprints will be.

9. Add 50 µl of 10 mM $MgCl_2$/5 mM $CaCl_2$ solution (at room temperature) to the test tube. Mix by flicking. Let the mixture stand for 1 minute at room temperature.

10. Add dilute DNase I (2 µl) to the test tube and quickly mix by flicking. Incubate for 1 minute at room temperature.

    Note: The endogenous nucleases in crude protein fractions could alter the DNase I ladder. When footprinting with crude extracts, include a control reaction that contains the extract without added DNase I.

11. Add 90 µl of the DNase I stop solution. Mix by vortexing.

    Note: Normally, three (or more) samples are footprinted per cycle. The following example demonstrates how one would footprint three samples simultaneously.

Time	Tube #	Procedure
0'	1, 2, 3	remove from ice bucket and let stand at room temperature
1' 00"	1	add 50 µl of 10 mM $MgCl_2$/5 mM $CaCl_2$
1' 20"	2	add 50 µl of 10 mM $MgCl_2$/5 mM $CaCl_2$
1' 40"	3	add 50 µl of 10 mM $MgCl_2$/5 mM $CaCl_2$
2' 00"	1	add 2 µl of appropriate DNase I dilution
2' 20"	2	add 2 µl of appropriate DNase I dilution
2' 40"	3	add 2 µl of appropriate DNase I dilution
3' 00"	1	add 90 µl of DNase I stop solution and vortex
3' 20"	2	add 90 µl of DNase I stop solution and vortex
3' 40"	3	add 90 µl of DNase I stop solution and vortex

12. *(Optional)* When all the samples have been footprinted, add 10 µl of 2.5 mg/ml proteinase K, mix by gentle vortexing, and let stand

for 5 minutes at room temperature. This step is useful when foot-printing with crude extracts but is not necessary with purified proteins.

13. To prepare the samples for electrophoresis, add 200 µl of 1:1 phenol/chloroform. Mix by vortexing. Spin for 5 minutes.

14. Transfer the upper layer to a new test tube. Add 800 µl of 100% ethanol and mix by inversion. Spin for 15 minutes to pellet the nucleic acids.

15. Remove and discard the supernatant. Add 800 µl of 75% ethanol and mix by vortexing. Spin for 5 minutes.

16. Remove and discard the supernatant. Dry the pellet in a Speed-Vac rotary concentrator.

17. Add 9 µl of formamide loading buffer and dissolve the pellet by vortexing.

18. Boil for 3 minutes and chill on ice.

19. Spin for 0.5 seconds to bring the liquid to the bottom of the tube. Mix by vortexing. Load 4 µl on a sequencing gel.

    Note: To determine the location of the protein-binding site, run the DNase I di-gestion ladder next to a Maxam-Gilbert sequencing ladder (prepared from the labeled footprint probe).

SPECIFIC INSTRUCTIONS FOR DNASE I FOOTPRINTING OF FRACTIONS IN THIS UNIT

S-300 Column

When footprinting the S-300 fractions, use the following amounts of DNase I and protein fractions:

	Volume of fraction (µl)	DNase I dilution (use 2 µl per reaction)
No protein control	0	1:2000
Crude nuclear extract (no DNase I control)	2	–
Crude nuclear extract	2	1:300
S-300 fractions	10	1:600
Purified AP-1 control (if available) (in 0.1 M KCl buffer)	5	1:2000 (do NOT add competitor DNA)

DNA Affinity Column

1. Save a 100-μl aliquot of the S-300 pooled peak fractions (i.e., the starting material for the affinity column).

2. Save both a 25-μl aliquot (for DNase I footprinting) and a 40-μl aliquot (for an SDS gel) of each of the affinity column fractions.

3. There are many other transcription factors in the flowthrough in addition to AP-1. Save all of the protein that flows through the DNA affinity column.

4. When footprinting the DNA affinity column fractions, use the following amounts of DNase I and protein fractions:

	Volume of fraction (μl)	DNase I dilution (use 2 μl per reaction)
No protein control	0	1:2000
S-300 pool (no DNase I control)	10	–
S-300 pool	10	1:600
Column flowthrough	10	1:600
DNA affinity fractions (0.2 M to 1.0 M fractions)	2.5 or 5	1:2000

• Experiment 5
Gel Mobility-shift Assay
•

INTRODUCTION

A brief protocol for the gel mobility-shift assay (Fried and Crothers 1981; Garner and Revzin 1981) is described here. This technique is also known as the gel retardation assay or the electrophoretic mobility-shift assay (EMSA). Some of the advantages and disadvantages of the gel mobility-shift assay versus the DNase I footprinting assay have been discussed throughout this unit (in particular, in the introduction to Experiment 4).

In this experiment, we perform a gel mobility-shift assay with AP-1 by using the same complementary oligonucleotides that were employed for DNA affinity chromatography (the exact sequences are given at the end of the introduction to Experiment 3). These oligonucleotides are 5'-phosphorylated with T4 polynucleotide kinase and [γ-^{32}P]ATP to give the mobility-shift probe. This probe is incubated with AP-1 and then subjected to electrophoresis under nondenaturing conditions. The mobility of the resulting protein-DNA complex through the gel is significantly less than that of the free probe. An example of results from a gel mobility-shift experiment with DNA affinity column fractions from an AP-1 purification is shown in Figure 6 (see p. 188).

MATERIALS

Acrylamide
Bisacrylamide
Ammonium persulfate (10%; w/v)
TEMED (*N,N,N',N'*-Tetramethylethylenediamine)
Glycerol (50%; v/v)
Competitor DNA (in TE) (The amount and type of competitor DNA will vary with the purity and type of protein; do not use competitor DNA with affinity-purified proteins)
Mobility-shift probe (Prepared by 5'-phosphorylation of complementary oligonucleotides with T4 polynucleotide kinase and [γ-^{32}P]ATP)

SAFETY NOTES

- Acrylamide and bisacrylamide are potent neurotoxins and are absorbed through the skin. Their effects are cumulative. Wear gloves and a mask when weighing acrylamide and bisacrylamide. Wear gloves when handling solutions containing these chemicals. Although polyacrylamide is considered to be nontoxic, it should be handled with care because of the possibility that it might contain small quantities of unpolymerized acrylamide.
- Ammonium persulfate is extremely destructive to tissue of the mucous membranes and upper respiratory tract, eyes, and skin. Inhalation may be fatal. Exposure can cause gastrointestinal disturbances and dermatitis. Wear gloves, safety glasses, respirator, and other protective clothing and work in a chemical fume hood. Wash thoroughly after handling.
- TEMED is extremely destructive to tissue of the mucous membranes and upper respiratory tract, eyes, and skin. Inhalation may be fatal. Prolonged contact can cause severe irritation or burns. Wear gloves, safety glasses, respirator, and other protective clothing and work in a chemical fume hood. Wash thoroughly after handling. Flammable: Vapor may travel a considerable distance to source of ignition and flash back.
- Wear gloves when handling radioactive substances. Consult the institutional environmental health and safety office for further guidance in the appropriate use of radioactive materials.

REAGENTS

TBE (10x)
Mobility-shift buffer (10x)
TE
(For recipes, see Preparation of Reagents, pp. 192–200)

PROCEDURE

1. Pour a 5% polyacrylamide gel (20 cm x 20 cm x 1.5 mm) by using the following recipe:

Acrylamide (30%; w/v)/bisacrylamide (0.8%; w/v)	16.2 ml
TBE (10x)	5.0 ml
H_2O	78.8 ml

   Mix, filter with a 0.45-μm filter, and then add 600 μl of 10% (w/v) ammonium persulfate and 48 μl of TEMED.

2. Let the gel polymerize for 30–60 minutes, and pre-run the gel at 100 V for at least 30 minutes prior to loading the samples.

3. For each reaction, combine the following in a tube on ice:

Mobility-shift buffer (10x)	1 µl
Glycerol (50%; v/v)	2 µl
Competitor DNA (if necessary; for purified proteins, add 1 µl of H_2O instead)	1 µl
Protein fraction (in buffer Z containing 0.1 M KCl)	5 µl
Mobility-shift probe (~20,000 cpu/µl)	1 µl
Total volume:	10 µl

   Mix gently by flicking the tube.

4. Incubate the samples for 10–15 minutes at room temperature.

5. Apply the samples directly to the gel. Because dyes can often inhibit the binding of proteins to DNA, it is recommended that dyes are not included in the samples.

6. Run the gel at 100 V at room temperature until a reference bromophenol blue dye (in a lane of the gel that is distinct from lanes containing protein) migrates approximately 10 cm down the gel.

7. Dry the gel and then subject it to autoradiography (typically, for several hours or overnight at –80ºC).

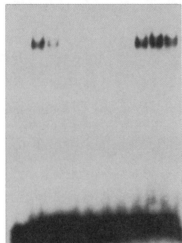

Probe only (no protein control)
Purified AP-1 (positive control)
S-300 pooled fractions (starting material for affinity resin)
DNA affinity resin flowthrough
0.2 M KCl fraction
0.3 M KCl fraction
0.4 M KCl fraction
0.5 M KCl fraction
0.6 M KCl fraction
0.7 M KCl fraction
0.8 M KCl fraction

◄ AP-1–DNA Complex

Free (unbound) Probe

Figure 6
Gel mobility-shift assay of AP-1. DNA-binding activity in fractions from the DNA affinity purification of AP-1 was assayed by using a probe containing the AP-1 recognition site. The free probe is at the bottom of the gel, whereas the slower-migrating AP-1/DNA complexes are near the top of the gel, as indicated by the arrow. This experiment was performed during the 1995 Cold Spring Harbor Laboratory Protein Purification and Characterization Course (courtesy of A. Gravel, C. Michels, R. Burk, and A. Ansari).

• Experiment 6
Preparation of Heparin-Sepharose CL-2B

●

MATERIALS

Sepharose® CL-2B (Pharmacia Biotech, Inc.)
Acetonitrile
Cyanogen bromide (CNBr) (Aldrich Chemical Co., Inc. C9 149-2)
Glycine
NaOH
Heparin (sodium salt; USP grade; from porcine intestinal mucosa; 140
    units/mg) (Life Technologies, Inc. [GIBCO/BRL] 15077-027)
    (amount required per preparation = 500,000 units)

SAFETY NOTES

- Acetonitrile is very volatile and extremely flammable. It is an irritant and a chemical asphyxiant that can exert its effects by inhalation, ingestion, or absorption through the skin. Cases of severe exposure are treated as cyanide poisoning. Handle acetonitrile in a chemical fume hood. Wear gloves and safety glasses.
- Cyanogen bromide is highly toxic and volatile. Wear gloves and always handle this compound in a fume hood.
- Sodium azide is extremely toxic. Wear gloves and safety glasses and work in a chemical fume hood. Sodium azide will explode when heated.

REAGENTS

Na_2CO_3 (2 M)
$NaHCO_3$ (0.1 M; pH 9.5)
$NaHCO_3$ (0.2 M; pH 8.5)
Ethanolamine-HCl (1 M; pH 8.0)
NaOAc (0.1 M; pH 4.0)/NaCl (0.5 M)
Urea (2 M)/NaCl (0.5 M)
$NaHCO_3$ (0.1 M; pH 10.0)/NaCl (0.5 M)
Tris-HCl (100 mM; pH 7.9)/EDTA (2 mM)/sodium azide (0.04%, w/v)
(For recipes, see Preparation of Reagents, pp. 192–200)

PROCEDURE

This protocol is adapted from March et al. (1974).

1. Wash 250 ml of Sepharose CL-2B (measure by settled bed volume) with at least 1 liter of double-distilled H_2O.

   Note: Handle the Sepharose CL-2B gently to avoid damaging the agarose beads.

2. Combine 250 ml of washed Sepharose CL-2B with 750 ml of 2 M Na_2CO_3 in a 2-liter plastic beaker. Stir with a magnetic stirrer.

3. In a fume hood, add 12.5 ml of acetonitrile to 25 g of CNBr. Stir with a glass rod to dissolve.

4. Using a pasteur pipette, transfer the CNBr solution to the stirring Sepharose CL-2B at room temperature.

5. Let the mixture stir for 2 minutes at room temperature.

6. Transfer the mixture to a 600-ml coarse sintered glass funnel and wash *quickly* and *gently* with 1 liter of 0.1 M $NaHCO_3$ (pH 9.5), 1 liter of double-distilled H_2O, and 1 liter of 0.2 M $NaHCO_3$ (pH 8.5).

   Note: DO NOT let the CNBr-activated resin dry out to a cake!

   Add 20 g of glycine and 20 g of NaOH to the filtrate and let it stand overnight in a fume hood before discarding.

7. Dissolve 3 g of heparin (500,000 units) in 250 ml of 0.2 M $NaHCO_3$ (pH 8.5) in a 500-ml plastic bottle.

   Note: Different preparations of heparin from different manufacturers have vastly different properties when used for heparin-agarose chromatography. In fact, some preparations of heparin are completely ineffective for heparin-agarose chromatography. Furthermore, we do not necessarily endorse the use of the specific source (GIBCO/BRL) of the heparin listed in the Materials section.

8. Transfer the CNBr-activated resin to the 500-ml plastic bottle containing the heparin solution (all solutions should be at room temperature).

9. Mix for 20 hours at 4°C.

10. Collect the resin by filtering through a sintered glass funnel. Suspend the resin in 400 ml of 1 M ethanolamine-HCl (pH 8.0) and mix for at least 4 hours at room temperature.

11. Wash the resin with 2 liters of 0.1 M NaOAc (pH 4.0)/0.5 M NaCl, 2 liters of 2 M urea/0.5 M NaCl, 2 liters of 0.1 M NaHCO$_3$ (pH 10.0)/0.5 M NaCl, and 2 liters of double-distilled H$_2$O.

12. Suspend the resin in 250 ml of 100 mM Tris-HCl (pH 7.9)/2 mM EDTA/0.04% sodium azide.

13. Add H$_2$O to a final volume of 500 ml. Store the resin at 4°C.

    Note: Sodium azide, which is both toxic and explosive (see Safety Note, p. 189), is included in the storage buffer at a concentration of 0.04% (w/v) to inhibit microbial growth. In this buffer, the heparin-Sepharose resin should be stable at 4°C for at least 1 year.

Preparation of Reagents

● _____

Benzamidine-HCl (0.5 M)
(protease inhibitor)

Prepare a stock solution of 0.5 M benzamidine-HCl (Sigma Chemical Co. B 6506; M.W. of benzamidine·HCl·1.5H$_2$O is 156.6 + 27 = 193.6). Store at –20°C.

Buffer D

50 mM Tris-HCl (pH 7.5)
20% (v/v) Glycerol
10% (w/v) Sucrose
0.42 M KCl
5 mM MgCl$_2$
0.1 mM EDTA
2 mM Dithiothreitol (freshly added from a 0.5 M stock solution
 [see p. 196] just before use)
1 mM PMSF (freshly added from a 100 mM stock solution in ethanol
 [see p. 198] just before use)
1 mM Sodium metabisulfite (freshly added from a 0.5 M stock solution
 [see p. 199] just before use)
1 mM Benzamidine-HCl (freshly added from a 0.5 M stock solution
 [see above] just before use)

Store at 4°C.

Note: The protease inhibitors that are used in the purification of AP-1 were somewhat arbitrarily chosen, based in part on their relatively low cost. The efficacy of a set of protease inhibitors must be determined experimentally for each specific protein.

Buffer G

50 mM Tris-HCl (pH 7.9)
1 mM EDTA
0.5 mM Dithiothreitol
30% (v/v) Glycerol

Store at 4°C. Use within one day of preparation.

Buffer H

10 mM Tris-HCl (pH 7.9)
10 mM KCl
1.5 mM $MgCl_2$
1 mM Dithiothreitol (freshly added from a 0.5 M stock solution
[see p. 196] just before use)
1 mM PMSF (freshly added from a 100 mM stock solution in ethanol
[see p. 198] just before use)
1 mM Sodium metabisulfite (freshly added from a 0.5 M stock solution
[see p. 199] just before use)
1 mM Benzamidine-HCl (freshly added from a 0.5 M stock solution
[see p. 192] just before use)

Store at 4°C.

Buffer Z
(for DNA affinity chromatography)

25 mM HEPES (K^+; pH 7.6)
Variable KCl, as indicated in the protocol
12.5 mM $MgCl_2$
1 mM Dithiothreitol (freshly added from a 0.5 M stock solution
[see p. 196] just before use)
20% (v/v) Glycerol
0.1% (v/v) Nonidet P-40

Adjust the pH of 1x buffer Z to 7.6 by the addition of KOH. Do not
make a 10x buffer. Store at 4°C.

Buffer Z[e]
(for DNA affinity chromatography)

25 mM HEPES (K^+; pH 7.6)
Variable KCl, as indicated in the protocol
1 mM Dithiothreitol (freshly added from a 0.5 M stock solution
[see p. 196] just before use)
20% (v/v) Glycerol
0.1% (v/v) Nonidet P-40

Adjust the pH of 1x buffer Z[e] to 7.6 by the addition of KOH. Do not
make a 10x buffer. Store at 4°C.

Buffer Z^e
(optimal for Sp1 footprinting)

	For 1 liter	Stock solutions
25 mM HEPES (K$^+$; pH 7.6)	25 ml	1 M HEPES (K$^+$; pH 7.6)
Variable KCl	variable	KCl
20% (v/v) Glycerol	200 ml	glycerol
0.1% (v/v) Nonidet P-40	10 ml	10% (v/v) Nonidet P-40
10 µM ZnSO$_4$	100 µl	0.1 M ZnSO$_4$
1 mM Dithiothreitol (freshly added)	2 ml	0.5 M dithiothreitol (see p. 196)

For footprinting of most factors, 100 mM KCl works well. The ZnSO$_4$ is optional. The Nonidet P-40 can be used at 0.01% (v/v). Store at 4°C. Add dithiothreitol just before use.

Buffer Z′
(generic footprinting buffer; good for AP-1; for some proteins, such as Sp1, MgCl$_2$ might reduce the affinity of the binding of the factors to DNA)

25 mM HEPES (K$^+$; pH 7.6)
Variable KCl
12.5 mM MgCl$_2$
1 mM Dithiothreitol (freshly added from a 0.5 M stock solution
    [see p. 196] just before use)
10 µM ZnSO$_4$
20% (v/v) Glycerol
0.1% (v/v) Nonidet P-40

For footprinting of most factors, 100 mM KCl works well. The ZnSO$_4$ is optional—it appears to have no effect upon proteins that do not contain Zn(II) and may enhance the activity of Zn(II)-containing proteins, such as those with Zn finger motifs. The Nonidet P-40 can be used at 0.01% (v/v). Store at 4°C. Add dithiothreitol just before use.

Calf intestinal phosphatase buffer (10x)

500 mM Tris-HCl (pH 9.0)
10 mM MgCl$_2$
1 mM ZnCl$_2$
10 mM Spermidine

Store at –20°C. Before use, add dithiothreitol to the 10x stock solution to give a concentration of 10 mM.

Column regeneration buffer

	For 500 ml	Stock solutions
10 mM Tris-HCl (pH 7.8)	2.5 ml	2 M Tris-HCl (pH 7.9)
1 mM EDTA	1 ml	0.5 M EDTA (Na+; pH 8.0)
2.5 M NaCl	73.05 g	NaCl
1% (v/v) Nonidet P-40	50 ml	10% (v/v) Nonidet P-40

Store at room temperature. This solution will be cloudy and will separate into two phases (Nonidet P-40 and aqueous) upon storage. Just before use, mix by swirling and shaking.

Column storage buffer

	For 500 ml	Stock solutions
10 mM Tris-HCl (pH 7.6)	2.5 ml	2 M Tris-HCl (pH 7.9)
1 mM EDTA	1 ml	0.5 M EDTA (Na+; pH 8.0)
0.3 M NaCl	30 ml	5 M NaCl
0.04% (w/v) Sodium azide	5 ml	4% (w/v) sodium azide

Store at room temperature *without sodium azide*. The sodium azide is freshly added before use.

SAFETY NOTE

- Sodium azide is extremely toxic. Wear gloves and safety glasses and work in a chemical fume hood. Sodium azide will explode when heated.

Competitor DNA

i. 1 mg/ml sonicated calf thymus DNA in TE (average size is ~0.3–0.5 kbp).

ii. Dissolve poly(dI-dC), poly(dG-dC), or poly(dA-dT) to a final concentration of 10 A_{260nm} units in TE containing 100 mM NaCl. Heat to 90°C, and cool slowly over 30–60 minutes to room temperature before use. Sonicate to 0.3–0.5 kbp average length.

Store at –20°C.

Dithiothreitol (DTT) (0.5 M)
(reducing agent)

Prepare a stock solution of 0.5 M dithiothreitol and store at –20°C.

DNase I

Dissolve DNase I (Worthington Biochemical Corp.; DPFF grade) in H_2O to a concentration of 2.5 mg/ml. Store frozen in 10-µl aliquots at –20°C or –70°C.

DNase I stop solution

20 mM EDTA (pH 8.0)
1% (w/v) Sodium dodecyl sulfate
0.2 M NaCl
250 µg/ml Glycogen (Sigma Chemical Co. G 0885; glycogen is used as a carrier to promote the precipitation of nucleic acids)

Store at room temperature. Do not refrigerate.

Ethanolamine-HCl (1 M; pH 8.0)

Dissolve 61.08 g of ethanolamine in 1 liter of H_2O. Adjust the pH to 8.0 with concentrated HCl. If necessary, clarify the solution by filtration. Store at room temperature.

Formamide loading buffer (10x)
(100 ml)

Deionized formamide	90 ml
10x TBE (see p. 199)	10 ml
Xylene cyanol (*optional*)	40 mg
Bromophenol blue	40 mg

Store at –20°C.

Preparation of deionized formamide

Combine 200 ml of formamide with 5 g of AG501-X8 (D) (Bio-Rad Laboratories) in a 250-ml Erlenmeyer flask. Cover the mouth of the flask with Parafilm, and gently stir the mixture at room temperature for 30 minutes. Avoid aeration of the formamide when stirring the mixture. Filter the solution through a coarse sintered glass funnel, and store the deionized formamide at –20°C.

Linker-kinase buffer (10x)

660 mM Tris-HCl (pH 7.6)
100 mM MgCl$_2$
150 mM Dithiothreitol
10 mM Spermidine

Store at –20°C. Add extra 10 mM dithiothreitol to the 10x stock solution just before use.

MgCl$_2$ (10 mM)/CaCl$_2$ (5 mM)

Store at room temperature.

Mobility-shift buffer (10x)

100 mM HEPES (K$^+$; pH 8.0)
0.6 M KCl
40 mM MgCl$_2$
1 mM EDTA
1 mg/ml Bovine serum albumin
2.5 mM Dithiothreitol

Na$_2$CO$_3$ (2 M)

Dissolve 424 g of anhydrous Na$_2$CO$_3$ (M.W. 105.49) in 2 liters of H$_2$O. Store at room temperature. Use within one day of preparation.

NaHCO$_3$ (0.1 M; Na$^+$; pH 9.5)

Dissolve 16.8 g of NaHCO$_3$ (M.W. 84.01) in 2 liters of H$_2$O. Adjust the pH to 9.5 with NaOH. Store at room temperature. Use within one day of preparation.

NaHCO$_3$ (0.2 M; Na$^+$; pH 8.5)

Dissolve 33.6 g of NaHCO$_3$ (M.W. 84.01) in 2 liters of H$_2$O. Adjust the pH to 8.5 with NaOH. Store at room temperature. Use within one day of preparation.

NaHCO$_3$ (0.1 M; Na$^+$; pH 10.0)/NaCl (0.5 M)

Dissolve 16.8 g of NaHCO$_3$ and 58.44 g of NaCl in 2 liters of H$_2$O. Adjust the pH to 10.0 with NaOH. Store at room temperature. Use within one day of preparation.

NaOAc (0.1 M; pH 4.0)/NaCl (0.5 M)

Dissolve 27.2 g of NaOAc and 58.44 g of NaCl in 2 liters of H_2O. Adjust the pH to 4.0 with HOAc. Store at room temperature. Use within one day of preparation.

Phenylmethylsulfonyl fluoride (PMSF) (100 mM) (protease inhibitor)

Prepare a 100 mM stock of PMSF in ethanol and store at –20°C.

SAFETY NOTE

- PMSF is extremely destructive to the mucous membranes of the respiratory tract, the eyes, and the skin. It may be fatal if inhaled, swallowed, or absorbed through the skin. It is a highly toxic cholinesterase inhibitor. It should be used in a chemical fume hood. Gloves and safety glasses should be worn.

Phosphate-buffered saline (PBS) (10x)

NaCl	80 g
KCl	2 g
Na_2HPO_4 (anhydrous)	9.2 g
KH_2PO_4	2 g

Dissolve in H_2O and adjust the volume to 1 liter. Store at 4°C.

Polyvinyl alcohol (10%; w/v)
(Sigma Chemical Co. P 8136; average molecular weight = 10,000)

Polyvinyl alcohol is not always necessary, but is nevertheless recommended. Store at 4°C (or at –20°C for longer-term storage [>1 week]). There will occasionally be microbial growth in 10% polyvinyl alcohol stored at 4°C.

Proteinase K

Dissolve proteinase K (Boehringer Mannheim Corp.) in TE to a concentration of 2.5 mg/ml. Store in aliquots at –20°C.

Sodium metabisulfite (0.5 M) (protease inhibitor)

Dissolve 1 g of sodium metabisulfite in H_2O to give a final volume of 10 ml and a concentration of 0.5 M. Store this solution at 4°C and use within 1 day.

T4 Polynucleotide kinase buffer (10x)

500 mM Tris-HCl (pH 7.6)
100 mM $MgCl_2$
50 mM Dithiothreitol
1 mM Spermidine
1 mM EDTA

Store at –20°C. Add extra 10 mM dithiothreitol to the 10x stock solution just before use.

TBE (10x)

0.89 M Tris base
0.89 M Boric acid
25 mM EDTA·(Na_2)

Dissolve 432 g of Tris base, 220 g of boric acid, and 37.2 g of EDTA·Na_2·$2H_2O$ in distilled H_2O. Add distilled H_2O to 4 liters final volume. The pH of the resulting solution should be 8.3. Store at room temperature.

TBE loading buffer (5x)

10x TBE (see above)	5 ml
Glycerol	3 ml
H_2O	2 ml
Xylene cyanol	25 mg
Bromophenol blue	25 mg

TE

10 mM Tris-HCl (pH 7.8)
1 mM EDTA

TM buffer + 0.1 M KCl

50 mM Tris-HCl (pH 7.9)
100 mM KCl
12.5 mM MgCl$_2$
1 mM EDTA
10% (v/v) Glycerol
1 mM Dithiothreitol (freshly added from a 0.5 M stock solution
  [see p. 196] just before use)
0.1 mM PMSF (freshly added from a 100 mM stock solution in ethanol
  [see p. 198] just before use)
1 mM Sodium metabisulfite (freshly added from a 0.5 M stock solution
  [see p. 199] just before use)
1 mM Benzamidine-HCl (freshly added from a 0.5 M stock solution
  [see p. 192] just before use)

Store at 4°C.

Tris-HCl (100 mM; pH 7.9)/EDTA (2 mM)/sodium azide (0.04%)

Add 12.5 ml of 2 M Tris-HCl (pH 7.9), 1 ml of 0.5 M EDTA, and 5 ml of 2% sodium azide (see Safety Note, p. 195) to H$_2$O and adjust the volume to 250 ml with H$_2$O. Store at room temperature. Use within one day of preparation.

Urea (2 M)/NaCl (0.5 M)

Dissolve 240 g of urea and 58.44 g of NaCl in 2 liters of H$_2$O. Store at room temperature. Use within one day of preparation.

References

Alberts, B. and G. Herrick. 1971. DNA-cellulose chromatography. *Methods Enzymol.* **21:** 198–217.

Arndt-Jovin, D.J., T.M. Jovin, W. Bähr, A.-M. Frischauf, and M. Marquardt. 1975. Covalent attachment of DNA to agarose: Improved synthesis and use in affinity chromatography. *Eur. J. Biochem.* **54:** 411–418.

Croston, G.E., L.A. Kerrigan, L. Lira, D.R. Marshak, and J.T. Kadonaga. 1991. Sequence-specific antirepression of histone H1-mediated repression of basal RNA polymerase II transcription. *Science* **251:** 643–649.

Curran, T. and B.R. Franza, Jr. 1988. Fos and Jun: The AP-1 connection. *Cell* **55:** 395–397.

Dignam, J.D., R.M. Lebovitz, and R.G. Roeder. 1983. Accurate transcription initiation by RNA polymerase II in a soluble extract from isolated mammalian nuclei. *Nucleic Acids Res.* **11:** 1475–1489.

Dong, B., D.S. Horowitz, R. Kobayashi, and A.R. Krainer. 1993. Purification and cDNA cloning of HeLa cell p54^{nrb}, a nuclear protein with two RNA recognition motifs and extensive homology to human splicing factor PSF and *Drosophila* NONA/BJ6. *Nucleic Acids Res.* **21:** 4085–4092.

Dynan, W.S. and R. Tjian. 1983. The promoter-specific transcription factor Sp1 binds to upstream sequences in the SV40 early promoter. *Cell* **35:** 79–87.

Fried, M. and D.M. Crothers. 1981. Equilibria and kinetics of lac repressor-operator interactions by polyacrylamide gel electrophoresis. *Nucleic Acids Res.* **9:** 6505–6525.

Galas, D. and A. Schmitz. 1978. DNase footprinting: A simple method for the detection of protein-DNA binding specificity. *Nucleic Acids Res.* **5:** 3157–3170.

Garner, M.M. and A. Revzin. 1981. A gel electrophoresis method for quantifying the binding of proteins to specific DNA regions: Application to components of the *Escherichia coli* lactose operon regulatory system. *Nucleic Acids Res.* **9:** 3047–3060.

Gorski, K., M. Carneiro, and U. Schibler. 1986. Tissue-specific in vitro transcription from the mouse albumin promoter. *Cell* **47:** 767–776.

Hager, D.A. and R.R. Burgess. 1980. Elution of proteins from sodium dodecyl sulfate-polyacrylamide gels, removal of sodium dodecyl sulfate, and renaturation of enzymatic activity: Results with sigma subunit of *Escherichia coli* RNA polymerase, wheat germ DNA topoisomerase, and other enzymes. *Anal. Biochem.* **109:** 76–86.

Jackson, S.P. and R. Tjian. 1988. O-glycosylation of eukaryotic transcription factors: Implications for mechanisms of transcriptional regulation. *Cell* **55:** 125–133.

———. 1989. Purification and analysis of RNA polymerase II transcription factors using wheat germ agglutinin affinity chromatography. *Proc. Natl. Acad. Sci.* **86:** 1781–1785.

Johnson, P.F. and S.L. McKnight. 1989. Eukaryotic transcriptional regulatory proteins. *Ann. Rev. Biochem.* **58:** 799–839.

Kadonaga, J.T. 1991. Purification of sequence-specific DNA binding proteins by DNA affinity chromatography. *Methods Enzymol.* **208:** 10–23.

Kadonaga, J.T. and R. Tjian. 1986. Affinity purification of sequence-specific DNA binding proteins. *Proc. Natl. Acad. Sci.* **83:** 5889–5893.

Kamakaka, R.T. and J.T. Kadonaga. 1994. The soluble nuclear fraction, a highly efficient transcription extract from *Drosophila* embryos. *Methods Cell Biol.* **44:** 225–235.

Kamakaka, R.T., C.M. Tyree, and J.T. Kadonaga. 1991. Accurate and efficient RNA polymerase II transcription with a soluble nuclear fraction derived from *Drosophila* embyros. *Proc. Natl. Acad. Sci.* **88:** 1024–1028.

Kaufman, P.D., R.F. Doll, and D.C. Rio. 1989. *Drosophila* P element transposase recognizes internal P element DNA sequences. *Cell* **59:** 359–371.

Lee, W., P. Mitchell, and R. Tjian. 1987. Purified transcription factor AP-1 interacts with TPA-inducible enhancer elements. *Cell* **49:** 741–752.

March, S.C., I. Parikh, and P. Cuatrecasas. 1974. A simplified method for cyanogen bromide activation of agarose for affinity chromatography. *Anal. Biochem.* **60:** 149–152.

Mimori, T., J.A. Hardin, and J.A. Steitz. 1986. Characterization of the DNA-binding protein antigen Ku recognized by autoantibodies from patients with rheumatic disorders. *J. Biol. Chem.* **261:** 2274–2278.

Mitchell, P.J. and R. Tjian. 1989. Transcriptional regulation in mammalian cells by sequence-specific DNA binding proteins. *Science* **245:** 371–378.

Patton, J.G., E.B. Porro, J. Galceran, P. Tempst, and B. Nadal-Ginard. 1993. Cloning and characterization of PSF, a novel pre-mRNA splicing factor. *Genes Dev.* **7:** 393–406.

Rosenfeld, P.J. and T.J. Kelly. 1986. Purification of nuclear factor I by

DNA recognition site affinity chromatography. *J. Biol. Chem.* **261:** 1398–1408.

Shapiro, D.J., P.A. Sharp, W.W. Wahli, and M.J. Keller. 1988. A high-efficiency HeLa cell nuclear transcription extract. *DNA* **7:** 47–55.

Slattery, E., J.D. Dignam, T. Matsui, and R.G. Roeder. 1983. Purification and analysis of a factor which suppresses nick-induced transcription by RNA polymerase II and its identity with poly(ADP-ribose) polymerase. *J. Biol. Chem.* **258:** 5955–5959.

Soeller, W.C., S.J. Poole, and T. Kornberg. 1988. In vitro transcription of the *Drosophila engrailed* gene. *Genes Dev.* **2:** 68–81.

Ueda, K. and O. Hayaishi. 1985. ADP-ribosylation. *Ann. Rev. Biochem.* **54:** 73–100.

Yang, Y.-S., J.H. Hanke, L. Carayannopoulos, C.M. Craft, J.D. Capra, and P.W. Tucker. 1993. NonO, a non-POU-domain-containing, octamer-binding protein, is the mammalian homolog of *Drosophila nonA*[diss]. *Mol. Cell. Biol.* **13:** 5593–5603.

Zhang, W.-W., L.-X. Zhang, R.K. Busch, J. Farrés, and H. Busch. 1993. Purification and characterization of a DNA-binding heterodimer of 52 and 100 kDa from HeLa cells. *Biochem. J.* **290:** 267–272.

UNIT III

Purification of a Recombinant Protein Overproduced in *Escherichia coli*

The purpose of this unit is to give students experience at purifying proteins that have been overexpressed in the bacterium *Escherichia coli*. It is now quite common to have access to the gene for a protein or enzyme of interest. The advent of inducible expression systems, especially the bacteriophage T7 RNA polymerase-based system developed by Bill Studier and colleagues (Studier 1990), allows nearly routine overexpression at levels of 2% to as high as 50% of the cell protein. In this unit, we describe a purification strategy for the sigma-32 (σ^{32}) subunit of *E. coli* RNA polymerase, which has been over-expressed using the pET11 T7-based system.

E. coli RNA POLYMERASE SUBUNIT σ^{32}

The *E. coli* RNA polymerase holoenzyme is made up of two parts, a core RNA polymerase ($\alpha_2\beta'\beta\omega$) capable of RNA synthesis but lacking DNA-binding specificity, and a sigma (σ) factor capable of binding to the core and directing specific binding to promoter DNA and efficient RNA chain initiation. Six different *E. coli* σ factors have now been identified, each with its own DNA sequence recognition properties. These factors are involved in global gene regulation at the level of transcription: σ^{70} is the major σ factor involved in the transcription of the majority of *E. coli* genes; σ^{54} is involved in regulating nitrogen metabolism; σ^{32} is specific for heat-shock promoters; σ^E is involved in high-temperature transcription from the *rpoH* promoter; σ^F is involved in the synthesis of flagellar and chemotactic proteins; and σ^S is the product of the *katF* gene and is involved in the expression of a number of genes at stationary phase due to carbon source starvation. These σ factors and the apparent promoter consensus sequences that they recognize are shown in Table 1.

Table 1 Summary of *E. coli* σ Factors

σ factor	Gene	MW (kD)	Consensus Sequence -35	Consensus Sequence -10	Genes recognized
σ^{70}	*rpoD*	70	TTGACA	TATAAT	most genes
σ^{54}	*rpoN, ntrA*	54	CTGGCACN$_5$TTGCA		nitrogen-regulated genes
σ^{32}	*rpoH, htpR*	32	CTTGAA	CCCCAT_TA	heat-shock-regulated genes
σ^{E}	*rpoE*	24	GAACTT	TCTGA	*rpoH*
σ^{F}	*fliA*	28	TAAA	GCCGATAA	genes for flagellar and chemotactic proteins
σ^{S}	*rpoS, katF*	40	not known		genes expressed during carbon starvation

GENERAL STRATEGY

In *E. coli* cells overexpressing σ^{32}, most of the overexpressed protein is found in an insoluble form called an inclusion body. Experiment 1 describes procedures for breaking *E. coli* cells by sonication and separating the inclusion bodies from the soluble extract. Since inclusion bodies are dense, they are easily pelleted and can be washed with deoxycholate to yield a substantially pure preparation. The technical challenge here is not so much purification of σ^{32}, but rather that of solubilizing the inclusion bodies and then removing the solubilizing agent to allow refolding of active σ^{32} without protein aggregation. In Experiment 2, we solubilize the inclusion bodies with the anionic detergent Sarkosyl (SKL), and remove the SKL by dialysis. We also explore the use of other solubilizing agents and refolding regimes. The refolded protein is "polished" by ion-exchange chromatography to remove trace contaminants and multimers.

A portion of the overexpressed σ^{32} is found in the soluble extract, some free and some bound to the core RNA polymerase to form a core RNA polymerase–σ^{32} complex. In Experiment 3, we partially purify the complex by precipitating it with polyethyleneimine (PEI) and eluting it from the PEI pellet with 0.9 M NaCl. We then purify the complex using immunoaffinity chromatography, which is a powerful separation technique. The antibody we use binds to the β′ subunit of the core RNA polymerase, and the complex is eluted from the column under very mild conditions (see the Introduction to Experiment 3 for more details about immunoaffinity chromatography and the use of "polyol-responsive" monoclonal antibodies).

A flowchart illustrating the purification strategies employed in this unit is shown in Figure 1. At each stage of the procedure, samples are taken to monitor the progress and effectiveness of the purification. In Experiments 4 and 5, we provide protocols for the quantitation and characterization of the purified protein. Additional samples can be taken at various stages of the preparation, and these can be used for protocol development as described in the last section of the unit.

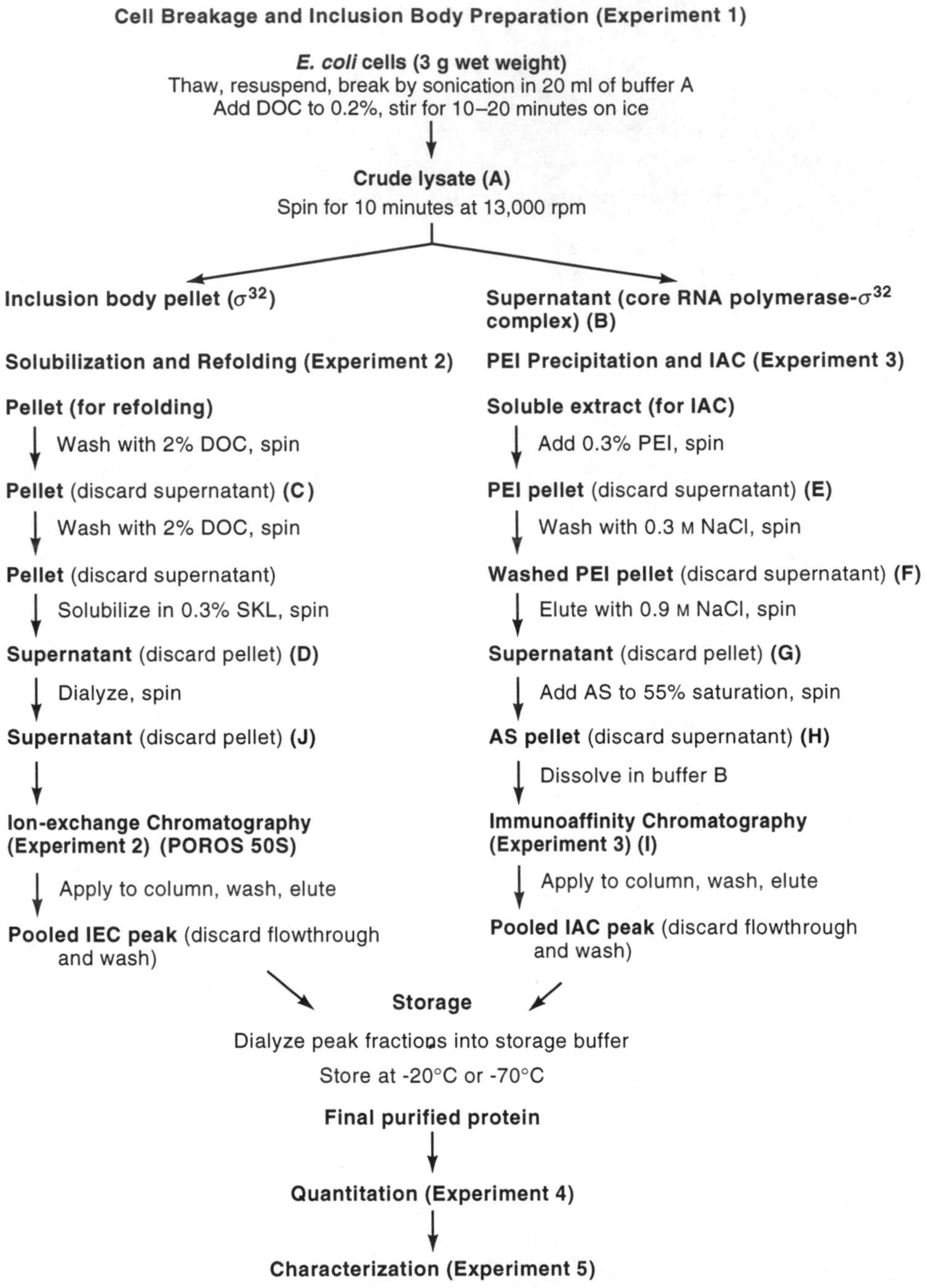

Cell Breakage and Inclusion Body Preparation (Experiment 1)

E. coli cells (3 g wet weight)
Thaw, resuspend, break by sonication in 20 ml of buffer A
Add DOC to 0.2%, stir for 10–20 minutes on ice

↓

Crude lysate (A)
Spin for 10 minutes at 13,000 rpm

Inclusion body pellet (σ^{32})

Solubilization and Refolding (Experiment 2)

Pellet (for refolding)
↓ Wash with 2% DOC, spin

Pellet (discard supernatant) (C)
↓ Wash with 2% DOC, spin

Pellet (discard supernatant)
↓ Solubilize in 0.3% SKL, spin

Supernatant (discard pellet) (D)
↓ Dialyze, spin

Supernatant (discard pellet) (J)
↓

Ion-exchange Chromatography (Experiment 2) (POROS 50S)
↓ Apply to column, wash, elute

Pooled IEC peak (discard flowthrough and wash)

Supernatant (core RNA polymerase-σ^{32} complex) (B)

PEI Precipitation and IAC (Experiment 3)

Soluble extract (for IAC)
↓ Add 0.3% PEI, spin

PEI pellet (discard supernatant) (E)
↓ Wash with 0.3 M NaCl, spin

Washed PEI pellet (discard supernatant) (F)
↓ Elute with 0.9 M NaCl, spin

Supernatant (discard pellet) (G)
↓ Add AS to 55% saturation, spin

AS pellet (discard supernatant) (H)
↓ Dissolve in buffer B

Immunoaffinity Chromatography (Experiment 3) (I)
↓ Apply to column, wash, elute

Pooled IAC peak (discard flowthrough and wash)

Storage
Dialyze peak fractions into storage buffer
Store at -20°C or -70°C

Final purified protein
↓

Quantitation (Experiment 4)
↓

Characterization (Experiment 5)

Figure 1
Flowchart for the purification of the σ^{32} subunit of *E. coli* RNA polymerase.

Breakage of *E. coli* Cells and Preparation of Inclusion Bodies

INTRODUCTION

Popular Methods for Breaking E. coli for Purification of Expressed Proteins

A variety of methods (including the sonication process used in this experiment) can be used to break cells, and each has advantages and disadvantages.

Sonication. Cells are sonicated hard on ice, sodium deoxycholate (DOC) is added, and the cells are spun to obtain a pellet and supernatant. DNA is sheared during the sonication, so DNase I is not required. This method is good for small- to medium-scale preparations, but it is not suitable for large-scale preparations.

Tris/EDTA/DOC/lysozyme. Cells are treated with lysozyme in the presence of DOC or Triton X-100. The lysozyme attacks the cell membranes, while the DOC helps to solubilize some of the proteins. EDTA is added as an antioxidant and protease inhibitor and to chelate magnesium that stabilizes the cell wall. When cells are lysed this way, a lot of DNA is often liberated and this can interfere with the purification, depending on whether the protein of interest is soluble or insoluble. DNase I is often used to reduce the viscosity of the preparation, but it can also interfere with subsequent purification steps (especially for DNA-binding transcription factors!) This method works on any scale, but the lysozyme and DNase I can get expensive for large-scale preparations. The DNase I can be omitted if the lysate is sheared vigorously in a Waring blendor (Burgess and Jendrisak 1975).

Manton-Gaulin homogenizer. Cells are subjected to pressure shock and shear force as they pass through a small orifice under high pressure (~10,000 psi). Two passes through the homogenizer shear the DNA nicely. This procedure can be scaled up to very large volumes (the Manton-Gaulin homogenizer was originally used for milk homogenization).

Cell disruption bomb. This is a small pressure cell which is sold by Parr Instrument Co. (model no. 4639). A cell suspension (e.g., 0.5 g in 25 ml of buffer) is introduced into the chamber and the pressure is increased to 2000 psi with the use of a nitrogen tank. The valve is then released, resulting in a rapid pressure drop that disrupts the cells.

Resuspending Pellets

In this unit, we often wash pellets by resuspending them in an appropriate buffer and then repelleting them by centrifugation. This is an important step since unwanted material in the pellet that is physically trapped or solubilized by the wash buffer must be effectively removed. Inadequate resuspension will allow unwanted material to be carried through to the next stage of the purification procedure and decrease the purity of the σ^{32} at a subsequent stage. We encounter two pellets that are rather difficult to resuspend: inclusion bodies and polyethyleneimine (PEI) precipitates. Effective resuspension breaks up the pellet into very small particles. Several common methods for resuspending pellets are listed below.

Stirring with a glass rod and vortexing. Simple vortexing is usually not adequate with sticky pellets. A large pellet can be broken into smaller pieces with a glass rod, but it is difficult to resuspend thoroughly this way.

Sucking material up and down with a pipette. Although this method is simple, problems can occur if chunks of the pellet clog the tip of the pipette. For small-scale preparations, significant losses of particulate protein bound to the inside of the pipette can occur.

Use of a Dounce glass homogenizer. This works very well. Partially resuspended material is transferred into a 100-ml glass homogenizer vessel and thoroughly resuspended by forcing the glass pestle up and down, shearing the chunks of pellet between the pestle and the vessel wall. The disadvantage is that sticky particulate material often coats the inside of the homogenizer, resulting in significant losses of protein.

Use of a mechanical homogenizer. A convenient mechanical homogenizer is called a Tissue-Tearor, which is available from Fisher Scientific (15-338-55). It consists of a small, variable-speed electric motor that rotates a shaft within a stationary stainless steel housing, creating a strong mixing action. Because the tip is narrow (7 mm in diameter), it conveniently fits into the centrifuge tube so that resuspension can be done within the original tube without transfer to another tube and the resulting losses. Usually pellets can be resuspended effectively in 2–3 seconds. It is important to wash the homogenizer well between uses. This is most easily accomplished by operating the homogenizer for a few seconds in each of two beakers of H_2O immediately after use.

MATERIALS AND EQUIPMENT

E. coli cells from a σ^{32} overproducing strain (BL21[DE3]/pLysS, pLHN16)
Chloramphenicol
Ampicillin
Isopropylthio-β-D-galactoside (IPTG)
Rifampicin
Oak Ridge tubes (40 ml)
Graduated conical polypropylene centrifuge tubes (50 ml)
Tissue-Tearor™ homogenizer (Fisher Scientific 15-338-55)
Sonicator

REAGENTS

LB medium
SDS sample buffer (2x)
Buffer A
Sodium deoxycholate (DOC) (20% stock solution)
(For recipes, see Preparation of Reagents, pp. 266–272)

PROCEDURE

Preparation of Starting Material

The *E. coli* cell strain used in this unit (σ^{32} overexpression plasmid pLHN16 in BL21[DE3]/pLysS) was constructed as described in Nguyen et al. (1993) (see also the Novagen publication *pET™ System Manual* [Novagen, Inc. 1995] on the use of the pET11 expression system).

1. Grow the *E. coli* cells at 37°C in two 2-liter shaker flasks using 500 ml of LB medium in each flask and chloramphenicol (25 µg/ml)/ ampicillin (100 µg/ml) selection until an A_{550nm} of 0.9 is attained.

2. Add IPTG to a final concentration of 1 mM to induce the expression of the T7 RNA polymerase. 0.5 hours later, add rifampicin to a final concentration of 150 μg/ml to achieve maximal overexpression.

3. Harvest the cells 3.5 hours after adding rifampicin by spinning at 8000 rpm for 30 minutes at 4°C. Resuspend the cell pellet in 30 ml of LB medium per liter of culture, and spin again in a 40-ml Oak Ridge tube at 13,000 rpm for 10 minutes at 4°C. Freeze the cells on dry ice, and store at −70°C until use.

   Note: Although frozen cells are used in this unit, for an unknown protein it is much safer to work with fresh cells, especially when refolding is needed. It is best if the cells are frozen for less than 5 days.

Sampling of Steps to Monitor Purification Procedure

In order to follow the progress and effectiveness of the purification, it is essential to perform the following steps at each stage of the purification and for each fraction.

1. Measure the volume.

   Note: It is very convenient to prepare a set of calibrated tubes for each size tube used (e.g., Eppendorf tube, Oak Ridge tube, etc.) by carefully adding H_2O and marking the level corresponding to each volume to allow rapid measurement of the volumes of solutions. Graduated conical tubes are also convenient to use for this purpose.

2. Add a 36-μl sample to 84 μl of 2x SDS sample buffer. Heat in a 70–90°C water bath for 2–5 minutes and store at 4°C.

3. Save a portion (150 μl) for protein determination and immuno-quantitation. Record this information on a balance sheet and use it to create a purification summary table.

Care must be taken to save a *representative* sample. This means that the whole fraction should be mixed well just prior to removing the sample. This is particularly critical for fractions containing precipitated or resuspended nonsoluble material. It is convenient to prepare a table listing samples A–J, their description, their volume, and two columns to be checked as samples for SDS gels and samples for protein determination are taken. You will also be instructed to take samples at various stages of the purification (as indicated in each experiment) that will be used for protocol development as described in the last section of this unit.

Breakage of Cells by Sonication

1. Thaw 3 g of *E. coli* cells (BL21[DE3]/pLysS, pLHN16) at room temperature. Resuspend the cells in 20 ml of buffer A in a 40-ml Oak Ridge tube by briefly homogenizing with the Tissue-Tearor.

   Note: For the purification of σ^{32}, buffer A contains no reducing agent since σ^{32} contains no cysteine residues. Normally one would use 0.1–0.5 mM dithiothreitol in all buffers to prevent oxidation of protein.

2. Sonicate for 90 seconds on ice using a macrotip at a setting of 8 and a 50% service cycle.

   Note: The BL21DE3 cells harbor pLysS, which expresses T7 lysozyme. The lysozyme cannot attack the cell walls from the inside, however, so this gene is not lethal. When the cells are subjected to freeze-thaw, the lysozyme gains access to the cell walls and lyses them. In some cases, this is sufficient for cell breakage, but the viscosity of the liberated DNA must be dealt with. One way is to digest with fairly large quantities of DNase I, but this can be expensive and will add another protein to the mixture that can be troublesome (e.g., if you are purifying a DNA-binding protein). For this reason, and to ensure complete cell breakage, we are using sonication. This will shear the DNA to a considerable degree and make it easier to pellet the inclusion bodies.

3. Add DOC to give a concentration of 0.2% (i.e., approximately 240 µl of the 20% stock solution). Mix well, and allow to stand for 10 minutes.

   Note: (i) The 0.2% DOC is used to help liberate slightly insoluble proteins, and at higher levels (2.0%) it releases membrane components (see Experiment 2). DOC goes into solution quite slowly, so the stock solution should be prepared 1 day in advance. (ii) If one were just isolating inclusion bodies and did not wish to carry out further fractionation on the soluble proteins in the supernatant (e.g., sample B below), one could add DOC to 2% at this step and omit the second DOC wash described in Experiment 2.

4. Take the first sample (**sample A**) as described above (see p. 212).

Preparation of Inclusion Bodies and Soluble Extract

1. To pellet the inclusion bodies, spin the cell lysate in a small rotor (Sorvall SS-34 or Beckman JA20) at 13,000 rpm for 10 minutes at 4°C.

2. Decant the supernatant (take **sample B**) and save it on ice for purification of the core RNA polymerase–σ^{32} complex by PEI precipitation and immunoaffinity chromatography (IAC) (see Experiment 3). To solubilize and renature the overexpressed σ^{32} in the inclusion body pellet, see Experiment 2.

• Experiment 2
Solubilization, Refolding, and Ion-exchange Chromatography of the Inclusion Body Pellet (σ^{32})

MATERIALS AND EQUIPMENT

Inclusion body pellet (see Experiment 1, p. 213)
Tissue-Tearor™ homogenizer (Fisher Scientific 15-338-55)
Dialysis tubing (Spectra/Por™ 6; 25,000 M.W. cutoff)
POROS® 50S cation-exchange column (PerSeptive Biosystems)
SDS-PAGE apparatus

REAGENTS

Buffer A
Buffer A + 1 M NaCl
Buffer A + 50% glycerol
Sodium deoxycholate (DOC) (20% stock solution)
Sarkosyl (SKL) (20% stock solution)
(For recipes, see Preparation of Reagents, pp. 266–272)

PROCEDURE

Solubilization of the Inclusion Body Pellet with Sarkosyl

1. Add 18 ml of buffer A and 2 ml of the 20% DOC stock solution to the inclusion body pellet (net DOC concentration is 2%). Resuspend the pellet thoroughly using the Tissue-Tearor and allow to stand for at least 10 minutes at room temperature.

   Note: Prior to this wash, the inclusion body pellet has a white bull's-eye which is the inclusion body protein. The brown layer above consists of all sorts of cellular debris. 2% DOC is quite effective at solubilizing this debris. 2% DOC will form hydrogels below pH 8.0 in the absence of protein and in the cold. If you get gels, increase the pH and the temperature.

2. Spin the suspension at 13,000 rpm for 10 minutes at 4°C. Take a sample from the supernatant (**sample C**) before discarding. To ensure the pellet is fully washed, resuspend the pellet again using the procedure described in step 1. Divide the suspension into two equal portions (tubes #1 and #2) and spin at 13,000 rpm for 10 minutes at 4°C (you do not need to sample the supernatant a second time).

   / *Protocol development:* Before the second spin at 13,000 rpm, transfer 6 x 50 μl portions into Eppendorf tubes for use in determining how much SKL is needed to solubilize an inclusion body pellet (see p. 249). /

   Note: The pellet is washed a second time to try to deal with any debris that was trapped in the pellet during the first spin. The orange color of the pellet is due to the rifampicin used during cell growth. When rifampicin is not used, the pellet should be nearly white. If the pellet is brownish or butterscotch in color, it is likely that there are some unbroken cells remaining.

3. To the pellet in tube #1, add 19.7 ml of buffer A and 0.3 ml of 20% SKL stock solution (net SKL concentration is 0.3%). The pellet should slowly dissolve with vigorous agitation. Allow to stand for at least 30 minutes.

   Note: (i) At this point, the insoluble protein is substantially denatured, so do not be afraid to agitate vigorously. (ii) SKL is a mild anionic detergent that solubilizes many inclusion body proteins and allows renaturation when it is removed from the protein by dialysis or chromatography. Since SKL becomes bound to the protein, enough SKL must be added to titrate the protein—at least 1 mg of SKL/mg protein appears to be required. When the protein concentration is high, concentrations of SKL above the nominal critical micelle concentration (CMC; ~0.4%) may be needed.

   / *Protocol development:* The pellet in tube #2 will be used to test other methods for solubilization and refolding proteins (see pp. 259–262). /

4. Spin the solubilized protein suspension in tube #1 at 13,000 rpm for 10 minutes. Collect the supernatant (take **sample D**), and discard the pellet (the pellet should not be large).

Refolding of the Solubilized Protein by Removal of Detergent by Dialysis

1. Perform a protein determination on the solubilized material (for the standard curve, make sure you use bovine serum albumin [BSA] containing 0.3% SKL). Adjust the solubilized protein concentration to 1 mg/ml by diluting with buffer A + 0.3% SKL.

2. Dilute the solubilized protein preparation tenfold with buffer A to give a final protein concentration of approximately 0.1 mg/ml and a final SKL concentration of approximately 0.03%.

3. Dialyze the solubilized protein preparation (which is approximately 200 ml in volume) against 2 liters of buffer A with good mixing for 8 hours at 4°C. Change to fresh buffer and repeat.

   / Protocol development: Every 4 hours, take a 150-μl sample for detergent analysis by reverse-phase high performance liquid chromatography (HPLC). This will allow you to determine how long it takes to remove SKL by dialysis and how much detergent is present in the sample that goes onto the ion-exchange column (see p. 253). /

   Note: Dialysis of solutions containing SKL (or many other detergents) creates a slow gradient of detergent removal, which is highly conducive to allowing the protein time to sort among a variety of conformational states and thus to fold properly, while at the same time blocking unwanted hydrophobic aggregation. It appears that σ^{32}, and some other proteins, will aggregate if all the SKL is removed by dialysis. Therefore, the dialysis procedure recommended here is not adequate to remove SKL completely, only to lower it slowly to 0.01–0.02%. The remaining detergent is removed in the next step when the σ^{32} is bound to the ion-exchange column, washed, and then eluted with a salt gradient.

Ion-exchange Chromatography

1. Remove the dialyzed protein solution from the dialysis tubing and spin it at 8000 rpm for 20 minutes at 4° C to remove any aggregated material.

2. Retain the supernatant for final fractionation on a POROS 50S cation-exchange column (take **sample J**).

   Note: σ^{32} is negatively charged at pH 7.9 (the sum of –46 and +40; for the titration curve of σ^{32}, see Introduction, Fig. 2, p. 4). With a net charge of –6, σ^{32} will bind to the positively charged quaternary amine groups of a POROS 50Q anion-exchange column. One could also use other anion-exchange columns such as Q Sepharose Fast Flow, Mono Q, etc. Any residual SKL would be expected to bind to the POROS 50Q. Since σ^{32} has a large number of positively charged residues, it will also bind to cation-exchange columns. As a result, one can also purify σ^{32} on a negatively charged column such as POROS 50S, S-Sepharose Fast Flow, or Mono S. A cation-exchange column is better than an anion-exchange column for the purification of σ^{32} because residual SKL or SKL that dissociates from the bound protein should flow through and not bind to the column. In fact, it is even possible to avoid the dialysis entirely and simply put the diluted protein on the POROS 50S column.

3. Wash the column resin in buffer A, and then pour it into a glass column fitted with a flow adapter to produce a column of 5 ml total volume. Wash the column with buffer A + 1 M NaCl and equilibrate it with buffer A.

4. If the dialysis was performed in the presence of low salt, as in this experiment, apply the protein sample directly to the column at 4 ml/minute at room temperature.

5. Wash the column with buffer A for 15 minutes. Elute with a gradient of 0–1 M NaCl in buffer A for 60 minutes at 4 ml/minute. Collect 4-ml fractions and monitor the absorbance at 260 nm and 280 nm.

6. Analyze the fractions by SDS-PAGE (see Appendix 5) and pool the peak fractions for further analysis. The pooled peak fractions can be prepared for storage by dialysis against buffer A + 50% glycerol as described below. See Figure 2 for typical SDS gels illustrating the results obtained in this experiment.

Storage of Purified Protein

1. Dialyze the pooled peak fractions against one change of buffer A + 50% glycerol overnight at 4°C.

2. Determine the protein concentration by measuring the A_{280nm} and using the extinction coefficient determined as described in Experiment 5 (pp. 240–241).

3. Store for short periods of time (days to weeks) at –20°C; at this temperature the sample will not freeze because of the presence of the 50% glycerol. Store frozen at –70°C for longer periods of time.

Note: This method of storage has several advantages. First, it results in an approximately threefold concentration of the sample due to water exiting the dialysis tubing faster than the glycerol can enter. Second, most enzymes are stable for years under these conditions at –70°C. One disadvantage of this method is that the glycerol may have to be removed before some enzymes can be used for enzymatic studies or protein chemistry. If the protein concentration is high enough, the material can be diluted until the glycerol becomes negligible. Otherwise, the sample can be dialyzed to remove the glycerol. Another disadvantage is the high cost of pure reagent grade glycerol (~$31/liter). A trick for conserving glycerol is to dialyze initially in a tall graduated cylinder without stirring. The water inside the dialysis bag will rapidly exit the bag (this is the reason for the observed threefold concentration) and because it is less dense than the 50% glycerol storage buffer, it will float to the top of the cylinder. The top 10–20% of the buffer can be poured off carefully to remove most of the water and then the buffer in the cylinder is mixed to equilibrium. This effectively gives a buffer change without using any more glycerol.

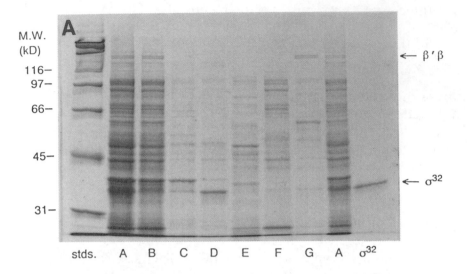

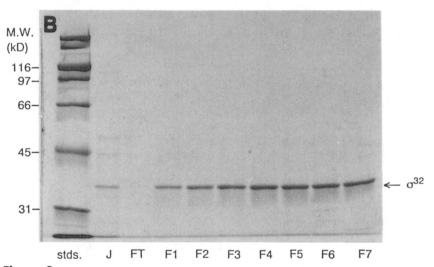

Figure 2
SDS gels of the various fractions isolated during the purification of σ^{32}. Fractions were prepared as described above and analyzed on 10% SDS gels. (*Panel A*) M.W. standards (stds.) and samples A, B, C, D, E, F, G, A, and pure σ^{32}. (*Panel B*) M.W. standards, sample J (i.e., dialyzed fraction that was applied to the POROS 50S column), flowthrough from the POROS 50S column (FT), and fractions across the peak that eluted from the column (1–7).

• Experiment 3

Polyethyleneimine Precipitation and Immunoaffinity Chromatography of the Soluble Extract (Core RNA Polymerase–σ^{32} Complex)

• ───────────────────────────────────────

INTRODUCTION

Differences between AMS and PEI in Protein Purification

Ammonium Sulfate (AMS)

AMS has a multivalent charge, and therefore it dissolves in H_2O to produce solutions of very high ionic strength. In solutions with high ionic strength, the hydrophobic effect is enhanced, and proteins in such solutions will tend to aggregate and precipitate as their solubility limits are reached. In devising protein purification strategies, most researchers do not fully use the power of AMS precipitation; they take cuts that are too broad. An increase of only 6% AMS is sufficient to decrease the solubility of a given protein by at least tenfold! In this experiment, we use AMS merely to concentrate protein. We add solid AMS to give a 55% saturated solution, which effectively precipitates all of the protein present in our sample. Since AMS alters the solubility threshold of a protein, the amount of AMS required to precipitate a protein varies with the protein concentration in a solution. Dilute protein solutions require higher AMS concentrations for effective precipitation than do more concentrated protein solutions. Despite the fact that AMS precipitates proteins, it is not thought to denature them. Often, proteins (especially antibodies) are transiently stored as AMS pellets.

Polyethyleneimine (PEI, Polymin P)

PEI is a cationic polymer that forms insoluble complexes with acidic macromolecules. Thus, PEI precipitates DNA and RNA, proteins bound to DNA and RNA, and acidic proteins. PEI precipitation is a stoichiometric titration, so the same absolute amount of PEI is required to precipitate a given amount of protein, no matter what the protein concentration is.

The binding of PEI is salt-dependent. DNA and RNA remain bound at up to approximately 1.5 or 1.6 M NaCl. Proteins usually elute from PEI well before this (by 1 M NaCl). Remember that if a protein is precipitated with PEI, it may be riding on DNA; but even under these circumstances, the protein should elute from the DNA at or before 1 M NaCl. When the salt concentration is raised, the PEI is solubilized at the same time as the protein. This means that if you collect the supernatant from a PEI elution and then dilute or dialyze to decrease the salt concentration, the free PEI and the eluted protein will recomplex and precipitate again. For this reason, AMS precipitation (high salt) is often used after PEI precipitation and elution; the protein will precipitate, and the PEI will remain in the supernatant.

Even if your protein does not bind to PEI, using such a step still can be very useful if your intent is to remove the DNA from a protein sample. In such cases, take care not to add too much PEI so that it does not interfere with subsequent steps. Good references to PEI precipitation can be found in Burgess and Jendrisak (1975) and Burgess (1991).

Immunoaffinity Chromatography

In many cases, the power of immunoaffinity chromatography (IAC) as a purification procedure has not yet been realized because the enzyme being purified is not stable under the harsh buffer conditions (e.g., buffers with a pH of 3.0 or 10.0 and containing 4 M urea or other denaturing agents) often used to elute the enzyme tightly bound to the immobilized antibody. Polyclonal antibodies are antibodies with a variety of specificities and affinities, requiring elution with sufficiently stringent conditions to disrupt the tightest antigen-antibody complex. The advent of monoclonal antibodies (MAbs) enabled purification of large quantities of antibody with homogeneous antigen-binding properties. We have discovered a method of screening for hybridomas that produce MAbs that are ideally suited for immunoaffinity purification of enzymes, particularly those that are labile and cannot survive exposure to the harsh elution conditions typically required. These MAbs are called "polyol-responsive" MAbs. They have the property of binding tightly to antigen under one condition, but releasing the antigen when eluted under mild conditions (a mixture of salt and a polyol such as glycerol, ethylene glycol, or propylene glycol). Approximately 5–10% of the positive hybridomas from a typical fusion produce a MAb that is polyol-responsive. A typical elution condition might be 30% propylene glycol and 0.75 M NaCl or 0.5 M AMS. In this experiment, we use a MAb called NT73, which binds to the RNA polymerase β' subunit and can be eluted with 30% propylene glycol and 0.75 M NaCl (Thompson et al. 1990, 1992).

●———————————————————————————————————————

Fractionation of the Soluble Extract
by PEI Precipitation

MATERIALS AND EQUIPMENT

Soluble extract (0.2% sodium deoxycholate [DOC] supernatant; see
     Experiment 1, p. 213)
Tissue-Tearor™ homogenizer (Fisher Scientific 15-338-55)
Ammonium sulfate (AMS)

REAGENTS

Polyethyleneimine (PEI) (10% stock solution, pH 7.9)
Buffer A
Buffer A + 0.3 M NaCl
Buffer A + 0.9 M NaCl
Dithiothreitol (DTT) (0.1 M)
(For recipes, see Preparation of Reagents, pp. 266–272.)

PROCEDURE

1. Add 0.75 ml of the 10% PEI solution to the bulk of the soluble ex-
    tract (0.2% DOC supernatant), which is approximately 24 ml in
    volume, to give a final PEI concentration of 0.3%. Mix, and allow
    to stand for 15 minutes at 4°C.

    / *Protocol development:* Before adding the PEI, take 6 x 50 μl portions
    of the 0.2% DOC supernatant to determine how much PEI is
    needed to precipitate σ^{32} and RNA polymerase (see p. 250). After
    adding PEI, take 6 x 50 μl portions of the PEI suspension to
    determine how much salt is needed to elute σ^{32} and RNA
    polymerase from the PEI pellet (see p. 252). /

2. Spin the suspension at 5000 rpm for 10 minutes at 4°C. Take a
    sample from the supernatant (**sample E**) before discarding. Save the
    pellet.

3. Wash the PEI pellet at a low salt concentration by adding 20 ml of
    buffer A + 0.3 M NaCl to the pellet. Resuspend the pellet vigorous-
    ly using the Tissue-Tearor and allow to stand for at least 10 min-
    utes at 4°C.

4. Spin the suspension at 5000 rpm for 10 minutes at 4°C. Take a sample from the supernatant (**sample F**) before discarding. Save the pellet.

   Note: The low-salt wash elutes some protein and leaves free σ^{32} and σ^{32} complexed to core RNA polymerase in the PEI pellet. This is roughly equivalent to doing a low-resolution step salt elution off DEAE-Sepharose.

5. Perform a high-salt elution of the PEI pellet by adding 20 ml of buffer A + 0.9 M NaCl to the pellet. Resuspend the pellet vigorously using the Tissue-Tearor and allow to stand for at least 10 minutes at 4°C.

6. Spin the suspension at 13,000 rpm for 10 minutes at 4°C. Decant and retain the supernatant (this is the high-salt eluate). Take a sample (**sample G**).

   Note: The high-salt elution releases the σ^{32} complexed to core RNA polymerase and leaves other materials (mostly nucleic acids) in the pellet. There should be a sizable pellet.

7. To remove the PEI from the high-salt eluate, slowly add 7.6 g of AMS per 20 ml to give a 55% saturated solution of AMS. Continue mixing until all the AMS is dissolved. Allow to stand on ice overnight (or for at least 30 minutes). Add 20 µl of 0.1 M DTT to give a final concentration of 0.1 mM DTT.

8. Spin at 13,000 rpm for 10 minutes at 4°C. Take a sample from the supernatant (**sample H**) before discarding. Store the pellet in the refrigerator overnight.

   Note: AMS precipitates proteins through enhancement of hydrophobic interactions. A 55% saturated solution of AMS precipitates most proteins and leaves the PEI and a few proteins in the supernatant. The amount of AMS needed to achieve precipitation will vary with the protein and its concentration.

Results

For a typical SDS gel illustrating the results obtained in this experiment, see Figure 2, panel A (p. 218). Note that the β′β bands present in sample B are not in sample E (PEI supernatant) or in sample F (0.3 M NaCl wash of the PEI pellet), but they are found in sample G (0.9 M NaCl eluate of the PEI pellet). For the results of the protocol development PEI titration and NaCl elution experiments, see Figure 5 (p. 251).

•

Immunoaffinity Chromatography

MATERIALS AND EQUIPMENT

Immunoaffinity resin (with immobilized MAb NT73; see below)
Cyanogen bromide (CNBr)-activated Sepharose® 4B (Sigma Chemical
     Co. C 9142)
HCl (1 mM)
55% saturated AMS pellet (see p. 222)
Econo-Column® (Bio-Rad Laboratories)
SDS-PAGE apparatus

REAGENTS

Coupling buffer
Ethanolamine (1 M)
Buffer B
IAC elution buffer
Dithiothreitol (DTT) (0.1 M)
Potassium thiocyanate (KSCN) (2 M)
Sodium azide (2%)
(For recipes, see Preparation of Reagents, pp. 266–272)

SAFETY NOTE

• Sodium azide is extremely toxic. Wear gloves and safety glasses and
  work in a chemical fume hood. Sodium azide will explode when
  heated.

PROCEDURE

Preparation and Storage of Immunoaffinity Resin

The MAb-producing mouse hybridomas utilized in this procedure
were prepared according to standard protocols (see Harlow and Lane
1988). The MAbs were purified from mouse ascites fluid by precipitating with 45% saturated AMS and by exploiting their inability to bind
to a DEAE-cellulose column at pH 7.0 and 25 mM NaCl. Many mouse
IgG MAbs flow through the DEAE column under these conditions,
resulting in a MAb preparation that is greater than 80% pure and

quite suitable for immunoaffinity chromatography. (Many procedures for MAb purification are described in Harlow and Lane 1988.) The MAbs were covalently coupled to cyanogen bromide (CNBr)-activated Sepharose using the method outlined below, which is also described in the Pharmacia publication *Affinity Chromatography: Principles and Methods* (Pharmacia LKB Biotechnology 1993).

1. Swell and wash 1 g of CNBr-activated Sepharose 4B resin (~3.5 ml of gel volume) in 1 mM HCl.

2. Mix approximately 10 mg of MAb dissolved in coupling buffer with the washed resin for 2 hours at room temperature.

3. Block the remaining reactive groups on the resin by exposing to 1 M ethanolamine for 2 hours at room temperature.

4. Wash away excess protein and blocking agent. The immuno-affinity resin normally contains 2–3 mg of covalently bound MAb per milliliter of packed resin. Store the immunoaffinity resin at 4°C in a buffer containing 0.02% sodium azide to prevent bacterial growth.

Immunoaffinity Chromatography

In this experiment, we use an immunoaffinity column to bind core RNA polymerase and any bound σ factors. Since σ^{32} has been over-produced in our starting cells, most of the core RNA polymerase will contain bound σ^{32}. (Normally σ^{32} would be a minor component of RNA polymerase.) The core RNA polymerase–σ^{32} complex is acidic and will precipitate with PEI.

1. Wash the immunoaffinity resin before use by resuspending 2 ml of the slurry in 10 ml of buffer B. Spin gently at 1000 rpm for 1–2 minutes at room temperature. It is essential to spin gently because at higher speeds centrifugal forces can crush the resin. Repeat this step once. These washes remove the sodium azide and any MAb that has leached off the resin during storage.

2. Dissolve the 55% saturated AMS pellet in 20 ml of buffer B and spin at 13,000 rpm for 10 minutes at room temperature to remove any insoluble material (there should be very little if any pellet). Take a sample (**sample I**).

3. Add the dissolved, clarified AMS pellet to the pelleted resin and mix gently on a rocker for 30 minutes at room temperature.

/ Protocol development: Remove 100-μl samples at 0, 5, 15, and 30 minutes. Spin each sample immediately and analyze the supernatants by SDS-PAGE to determine how long it takes for the protein to bind to the immunoaffinity resin (see p. 258). /

Note: It is necessary to use lower concentrations of reducing agent (DTT) in the buffers that come in contact with the immunoaffinity resin because the disulfide bridges of the immunoglobulin (IgG) can be reduced and result in loss of the IgG heavy and light chains from the resin. For this reason, we use buffer B (no DTT). RNA polymerase can survive brief exposure to buffers lacking DTT, but it should be added back to the column fractions as soon as possible. This can be conveniently done by placing 1 μl of 0.1 M DTT in each empty fraction tube. The 5% glycerol is omitted from buffer B; if it were present, some enzyme would wash off the column during the wash steps because of the polyol-responsive nature of the MAb used in this procedure.

4. Gently spin down the resin, remove the supernatant (IAC flow-through), resuspend the resin in 10 ml of buffer B, and pour the slurry into a Bio-Rad Econo-Column.

5. Collect 10 ml (1st wash), add 5 ml more of buffer B, and collect a further 5 ml (2nd wash).

Note: The washing of the resin and the elution of the σ factor from the resin can be done in batch mode in a tube, adding the appropriate buffer, mixing gently for 15–30 minutes, and gently spinning down the resin. It is more efficient to bind σ^{32} to the resin and to remove the unbound material in batch mode, but to do subsequent washing and elution in a column. During exposure of the resin to elution buffer, σ^{32} will dissociate from the antibody but must diffuse out of the large 100 μm Sepharose beads in a three-dimensional random walk that may take many minutes. Once out of the beads, σ^{32} is more effectively washed away from the beads if buffer is flowing by in the column mode.

6. Add 10 x 1 ml portions of IAC elution buffer to the column at room temperature, collecting the fractions into Eppendorf tubes containing 1 μl of 0.1 M DTT. Put the fractions (1–10) on ice and assay them by rapid western dot blots or SDS gels (see Fig. 3) to determine which fractions to pool.

Note: The density of the IAC elution buffer is greater than the immunoaffinity resin in buffer B. When added, it can cause disruption of the column (the resin floats!). Therefore, it is necessary to let the top of the column pack down slightly at the end of the wash and to add very slowly the first 1-ml portion of elution buffer (it is best to add 200 μl, let that sink in, and then add the rest gently). If the column slows down when the viscous elution buffer is applied, a 6–10 cm portion of plastic tubing can be attached to the bottom of the column to increase the hydrostatic pressure drawing the buffer through the column.

7. After use, treat the column with 2 M KSCN (a strongly chaotropic, denaturing salt that does not irreversibly inactivate antibodies) to strip off remaining noncovalently bound protein. Wash the column with buffer B, and store it in buffer B containing 0.02% sodium azide at 4°C. If columns are carefully washed and stored, they can be reused dozens of times.

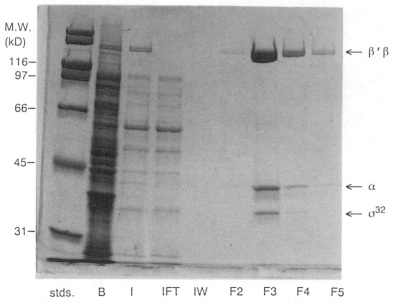

Figure 3

SDS gel of the immunoaffinity chromatography (IAC) experiment. Fractions were prepared as described in this experiment and analyzed on a 10% SDS gel. The gel shows M.W. standards (stds.), sample B (soluble extract), sample I (sample loaded onto IAC column), IAC flowthrough (IFT), IAC wash (IW), and fractions 2–5 from the IAC column. Note that all of the β'β bands present in sample I are missing in the IFT, indicating that all of the RNA polymerase bound to the IAC column. Fraction 3 shows only β'β, α, and σ^{32}.

Optional POROS 50Q Anion-exchange Chromatography

If one wanted to achieve even greater purity of the core RNA polymerase–σ^{32} complex, one could dilute the peak fractions from the IAC tenfold with 50 mM Tris (pH 7.9) to lower the propylene glycol concentration to 3% and the NaCl concentration to 0.075 M. The diluted sample could be subjected to ion-exchange chromatography, as described on pp. 216–217, except that a POROS 50Q column would be used in place of a POROS 50S column. The final pooled fractions can be dialyzed against storage buffer (buffer A + 50% glycerol) as described on p. 217.

• *Experiment 4*

Quantitation and Summary of Preparation

•

Protein Determination

INTRODUCTION

It is very desirable to have a rapid and accurate method to determine the protein concentration of a sample. This allows one to follow recovery of protein during a purification procedure. Although there is no ideal method, one that is very popular is the method of Bradford (1976). When Coomassie Blue G 250 is dissolved in acid at a pH below 1.0, it turns a red-brown color, but when it binds to protein, the blue color is restored due to a shift in the pK_a of the bound Coomassie Blue. One simply measures the increase in A_{595nm} that occurs when a protein sample is added to the dye reagent. Always construct a calibration curve with a standard protein of known concentration. Bovine serum albumin (BSA) is most commonly used as a standard. Depending on the content of hydrophobic and arginine residues in the protein of interest, the color yield per milligram of protein may be as much as 40% higher or lower than that of BSA.

MATERIALS AND EQUIPMENT

Bovine serum albumin (BSA) standard solution (2 mg/ml in H_2O)
Bradford reagent (Coomassie® Plus, Pierce Chemical Co.)
Spectrophotometer that reads at 595 nm or a microtiter dish reader
    with a 595-nm filter
Microtiter dishes (Immulon™ 2, Dynatech Laboratories, Inc.)

REAGENTS

Tris-buffered saline (TBS)
(For recipe, see Preparation of Reagents, pp. 266–272)

PROCEDURE

1. Prepare a series of dilutions of the BSA standard solution containing 2000, 1000, 500, 250, 125, 62.5, and 31.25 µg/ml in TBS. Prepare a set of twofold dilutions in TBS of each unknown sample to be assayed.

2. Add 5 µl of each of the BSA dilutions and each of the unknown sample dilutions to 1 ml of Bradford reagent. Mix, incubate for 5 minutes at room temperature, and read the A_{595nm} within 1 hour. If a microtiter dish reader is available, reading the A_{595nm} can be facilitated. In the microtiter dish procedure, add 7 µl of each sample to 200 µl of Bradford reagent, mix with a Pipetman tip, and make sure that no bubbles are present in microtiter dish wells. If bubbles are present, break them with a dry 22-gauge needle. Incubate for 5 minutes at room temperature and read the A_{595nm}.

3. Two kinds of controls can be performed. First, assay the various buffers present in the samples to see if any give color development themselves. Second, assay a mid-range concentration of BSA standard in the presence of the various buffers to see if any of them interfere with color development of the BSA.

4. Plot a standard curve and determine the protein concentration of the unknown samples.

   Note: Since several components of the σ^{32} purification procedure (e.g., Sarkosyl, sodium deoxycholate, and polyethyleneimine) show some interference with this assay, we have found that a microprocedure can be followed using BSA standards of 0, 5, 10, 15, and 25 µg/ml and 100-, 200-, and 400-fold dilutions of samples from the preparation. 100 µl of each diluted sample is added to 100 µl of Bradford reagent in a microtiter dish and processed as above.

Quantitative SDS Gel Staining and Scanning

INTRODUCTION

Very often, sodium dodecyl sulfate (SDS) gels are stained with Coomassie Brilliant Blue (CBB) and then rapidly destained, often using mixed-bed resins or other materials to absorb free dye as it diffuses out of the stained gel. Although this method allows one to see polypeptides in the various fractions analyzed, it does not allow one to obtain quantitative information (this fact is not widely recognized!). In order to detect protein bands quantitatively on an SDS gel, one must: (i) completely soak the gel in stain solution to ensure that SDS (which inhibits CBB binding to protein) has diffused out of the gel and that enough CBB has diffused into the gel to saturate the protein with dye; (ii) destain the gel to remove most unbound, background dye without causing dissociation of bound dye from the protein; and (iii) scan the destained gel such that the absorbance is proportional to the amount of bound dye. Overdestaining results in selective loss of stain from minor bands and from more diffuse bands, such as are often obtained with low-molecular-weight proteins. A simple method to ensure quantitative results is to avoid overdestaining by allowing the proteins in the gel to come to equilibrium with a dilute dye solution that contains free dye at a concentration above the binding constant of the protein-dye complex. One can only be sure that conditions for quantitative measurement have been met if the areas under scanned bands, when plotted against the amount of sample applied to the gel, fall on a straight line that extrapolates through zero. It should be noted that although most proteins bind approximately the same amount of dye per microgram of protein, dye binding can vary by 10% or more between different proteins. Therefore, the values obtained by this method are not very accurate unless one is measuring the concentration of a protein using the same protein as the standard. However, in general, CBB staining is *much* more accurate than silver staining.

EQUIPMENT

SDS-PAGE apparatus
Gel scanning apparatus

REAGENTS

Coomassie® Brilliant Blue (CBB) dye solution
Destaining solution
(For recipes, see Preparation of Reagents, pp. 266–272)

PROCEDURE

1. Carefully apply a series of increasing amounts of a protein sample to the lanes of an SDS gel. Also apply a series of increasing amounts of a sample of pure protein to serve as a standard for quantitation. Run the gel as usual (see Appendix 5).

2. Remove the gel from the apparatus. Rinse the gel in destaining solution for 1 minute to remove some of the SDS, and then soak it in CBB dye solution with gentle mixing (such as on a rocking platform) at 20°C. Soak a 0.75-mm thick gel for 1 hour and a 1.5-mm thick gel for approximately 4 hours.

3. Pour off the CBB dye solution and soak the gel in destaining solution with gentle mixing for 1–4 hours, depending on the thickness of the gel (use a sponge or a Kimwipe to absorb free dye). When most of the dye has diffused out of the gel, remove the absorbant material from the tray and add CBB dye solution to the destaining solution to give an A_{650nm} reading of 0.1 (light blue). At A_{650nm} = 0.1, the concentration of CBB is above the average binding constant for CBB binding to protein. Allow the gel to equilibrate with the dilute dye solution overnight and store in dilute dye until the gel is scanned.

4. Scan the stained and destained gel at 650 nm and measure the amount of bound dye in each protein band.

5. For each band, plot the amount of dye bound versus the amount of sample applied to the gel. Compare the slope of the line to that of the standard and calculate the concentration of target protein in each sample.

6. Integrate the entire scan of the gel of the starting material or any other step in the purification and calculate what fraction of the total protein is present in the σ^{32} band.

   Note: This estimate is a maximum estimate of purity. Often, there are many bands below the limit of detection that, when added together, are significant. Most researchers overestimate the purity of their proteins.

Quantitative Western Dot Blots

INTRODUCTION

It is now quite common to attempt the purification of a protein that: (i) does not have an enzymatic activity (e.g., a structural protein); (ii) does not have a well-defined quantitative assay (e.g., a transcription factor); (iii) has not yet been associated with an activity (e.g., a newly cloned gene of unknown function); or (iv) has an activity but cannot be assayed until it is quite pure because of interfering substances present in early fractions of the preparation. Nevertheless, it is highly desirable to determine how much of the protein is present in the starting material and in some of the main preparation fractions. One method, based on quantitative scanning of properly destained SDS gels, is described on pp. 229–230.

Another common method is the use of western blotting to measure the amount of a particular protein immunologically. Western blotting involves: (i) transferring proteins from SDS gels to a nitrocellulose membrane; (ii) blocking the nitrocellulose to prevent nonspecific protein binding; (iii) exposing the blocked blot to a first antibody specific for the protein being measured (e.g., a monoclonal antibody [MAb] to σ^{32}); (iv) washing the blot; (v) exposing the blot to a second antibody specific for the first antibody (e.g., a rabbit anti-mouse immunoglobulin G [IgG] antibody) and to which an enzyme such as horseradish peroxidase (HRP) has been covalently attached; (vi) washing the blot; and (vii) exposing the blot to substrates that react with the HRP enzyme to produce a measurable reaction.

Western blot data are generally thought of as merely qualitative. It is possible, however, to obtain quantitative measurements using this technique. The main problems include: (i) inconsistent transfer of proteins of different sizes out of the gel and onto the nitrocellulose; (ii) inconsistent absolute results from one experiment to another due to uncontrolled variations in the enzyme reaction conditions; (iii) lack of linearity of the signal produced versus the amount of protein present; and (iv) different affinities of different antibody-protein complexes.

Most of these problems can be solved if: (i) a dilution series of each sample is run to ensure that some data are in the linear region of the assay; (ii) a standard curve is included in each experiment; (iii) one only attempts quantitation of a single protein so that only one protein-antibody complex is being studied; and (iv) the enzymatically produced signal is proportional to the amount of enzyme over a wide range. All of these can be accomplished by the protocol below, using the enhanced chemiluminescence (ECL) assay developed by Amersham Life Science, Inc.

MATERIALS AND EQUIPMENT

Samples from various purification steps
Nitrocellulose membrane (0.45 μm, 8 x 11.5 cm rectangle) (Schleicher & Schuell, Inc.)
Dot blot apparatus (Minifold® I, Schleicher & Schuell, Inc. 27510)
Mouse anti-σ^{32} monoclonal antibody 3RH2 (MAb 3RH2)
Goat anti-mouse immunoglobulin G with horseradish peroxidase covalently attached (IgG-HRP) (Amersham Life Science, Inc.)
ECL™ reagents #1 and #2 (Amersham Life Science, Inc.)
ECL™ HYPERFILM® (Amersham Life Science, Inc.) or Kodak X-ray film

REAGENTS

Buffer A
Sarkosyl (SKL) (20% stock solution)
Tris-buffered saline (TBS)
TBS + 0.1% Tween-20 (TBST; to prevent nonspecific protein binding)
TBS + 1% bovine serum albumin (BSA)
(For recipes, see Preparation of Reagents, pp. 266–272)

PROCEDURE

1. Make a twofold dilution series of the most important samples from the purification procedure according to the following scheme. Dilute 20 μl of each sample into 180 μl of buffer A + 0.3% SKL. Mix well and then make eight successive twofold dilutions by transferring 100 μl of each dilution into 100 μl of buffer A (use a different pipette tip for each dilution). The twofold dilutions are conveniently performed in a microtiter dish that has been blocked by incubating with 100 μl of TBS + 1% BSA per well for 10 minutes and washed with TBST. The eight wells for each sample represent dilutions of 20-, 40-, 80-, 160-, 320-, 640-, 1280-, and 2560-fold. Reasonable fractions to assay are **sample A** (crude lysate), **sample B** (0.2% DOC supernatant), **sample C** (first 2% DOC wash), **sample D** (inclusion bodies dissolved in SKL), **sample E** (PEI supernatant),

sample F (0.3 M NaCl wash), sample G (0.9 M NaCl eluate), sample I (sample loaded onto immunoaffinity chromatography [IAC] column), fraction 3 from IAC, sample J (dialyzed SKL extract), a peak fraction from the POROS 50S column, and a σ^{32} standard of known concentration (~0.5 mg/ml).

Note: The first dilution is into buffer A + 0.3% SKL to solubilize the inclusion bodies present in sample A. Unsolubilized inclusion bodies result in sequestered σ^{32}, which, in our experience, leads to an eightfold underestimation of σ^{32} in sample A!

2. Pre-wet the nitrocellulose in Milli-Q H_2O for 2 minutes and in TBS for 5 minutes. Assemble the dot blot apparatus, making sure that the plates fit very tightly so that samples will not leak from one slot to another (first put a rectangle of filter paper and then a rectangle of nitrocellulose).

3. Spot 40 μl of each dilution (from 20-fold to 2560-fold) into the appropriate slot (you can use the same pipette tip for a dilution series if you start with the most dilute). Let sit for 3 minutes. Apply a gentle vacuum. Wash three times with 100 μl of TBST (apply with the vacuum off and then turn it on).

4. Remove the nitrocellulose from the manifold. Incubate it in TBS + 1% BSA for 30 minutes and then in 14 ml of the first antibody solution (14 ml of TBS + 1% BSA and 5 μl of MAb 3RH2) for 1 hour. The MAb solution can be poured off and stored at 4°C for several days for reuse.

5. Wash the nitrocellulose four times with TBST for 5 minutes each.

6. Incubate the nitrocellulose in 14 ml of the second antibody solution (14 ml of TBS + 1% BSA and 7 μl of goat anti-mouse IgG-HRP) for 1 hour. Pour off the second antibody solution and save for future use. Wash the nitrocellulose four times with TBST for 5 minutes each.

7. Mix 7 ml of ECL reagent #1 and 7 ml of ECL reagent #2 (i.e., 0.15 ml of mix per cm^2 of nitrocellulose) and pour onto the filter. Mix well, incubate for 1 minute, and drain off the excess reagent. Wrap the nitrocellulose in Saran Wrap. Expose to ECL Hyperfilm for 2, 10, and 60 seconds. Develop the film (2 minutes in developer, 0.5 minutes in H_2O to rinse, 2 minutes in fixer, and 10 minutes in H_2O to rinse). Let the film dry.

8. Quantitate the film by scanning it or by visually estimating which dilution of each sample gives a signal equal to a signal of the σ^{32}

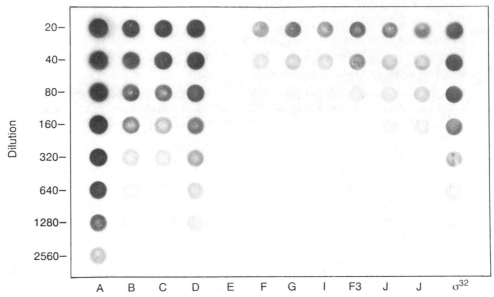

Figure 4

Results from quantitative western dot blots. Samples and dilutions were prepared as described on pp. 232–233. The blotting procedure was as described on p. 233. Film was exposed for 10 seconds. The undiluted σ^{32} standard was 0.47 mg/ml. F3 is the third fraction from the IAC column.

standard. For example, if the σ^{32} standard gives a signal of intermediate intensity at the 640-fold dilution and **sample D** gives the same intensity at the 1280-fold dilution, then you would estimate that **sample D** is twice as concentrated in σ^{32} as the standard (see Fig. 4).

•

Enzyme Assay

INTRODUCTION

Normally one would assay σ^{32} by its ability to stimulate the transcription of core RNA polymerase from a heat-shock promoter (Nguyen et al. 1993). This assay is complex and involves in vitro transcription from a DNA restriction fragment and then analysis of the synthesized RNA by gel electrophoresis to measure the amount of RNA of the correct size. In this unit, we use a simpler assay—the stimulation of transcription of core RNA polymerase from a nonspecific template, poly(dAT). We measure incorporation of the RNA precursor, $[\alpha\text{-}^{32}P]UTP$, into RNA by the ability of the RNA, but not the UTP, to bind to DEAE-cellulose paper. Portions of the σ^{32} preparation are added to a reaction mixture (containing core RNA polymerase, DNA or poly(dAT), ATP, and $[\alpha\text{-}^{32}P]UTP$, and appropriate salt, pH, and Mg^{++}), and the reaction is allowed to proceed for 10 minutes at 37°C. The amount of label (measured by scintillation counting) that remains on the DEAE-cellulose disk after the salt wash is a measure of the RNA synthesized.

MATERIALS AND EQUIPMENT

Core RNA polymerase (2.3 mg/ml)
Pure σ^{32} standard (0.8 mg/ml)
Sample of purified σ^{32} eluted from the POROS® 50S cation-exchange
    column
Sample of core RNA polymerase–σ^{32} complex eluted from the im-
    munoaffinity column
$[\alpha\text{-}^{32}P]UTP$ (use 2.5 μCi/ml of reaction solution)
Water bath set at 37°C
Stopping solution (0.2 M EDTA)
DEAE-cellulose (DE81) disks
PO$_4$ washing buffer (5% Na$_2$HPO$_4$)
Ethanol (95%)

SAFETY NOTE

• Wear gloves when handling radioactive substances. Consult the institutional environmental health and safety office for further guidance in the appropriate use of radioactive materials.

REAGENT

Reaction solution
(For recipe, see Preparation of Reagents, pp. 266–272)

PROCEDURE

1. Pipette 50-μl aliquots of reaction solution (containing 2.5 μCi of [α-^{32}P]UTP/ml) into tubes on ice.

2. Add 5 μl of appropriately diluted σ^{32} samples, and mix. One sample should be a standard σ^{32} preparation and another sample should be the purified core RNA polymerase–σ^{32} complex eluted from the immunoaffinity column. Make sure that you include a "no σ^{32}" control to determine the incorporation by core RNA polymerase alone, and a "no incubation" control (add stopping solution to a tube on ice without incubation at 37°C) to determine the background.

3. Add 5 μl of diluted core RNA polymerase (1 μg total) to each tube, except those containing core RNA polymerase–σ^{32} complex and one tube containing pure σ^{32} standard.

4. Incubate the tubes for 10 minutes at 37°C and stop the reactions by adding 10 μl of stopping solution.

5. Spot 25 μl of each reaction onto a DEAE-cellulose disk.

6. Place the disks into a flask and wash them four times for 5 minutes each with 100 ml of cold PO$_4$ washing buffer. Pour the first two washes into the radioactive waste container. Finally, wash once with H$_2$O and once with 95% ethanol.

7. Let the disks dry and count the radioactivity.

8. Plot incorporation (with "no incubation" background subtracted) versus amount of σ^{32} added for each σ^{32} sample. Determine the activity of each sample relative to the known σ^{32} standard. On the basis of the protein concentration of each sample, one can calculate a relative specific activity.

   Note: Another activity of σ^{32} is its ability to bind to core RNA polymerase. One can therefore assay for the conversion of core RNA polymerase to core RNA polymerase–σ^{32} complex on nondenaturing gels as described in Experiment 5, pp. 243–244.

● _____

Balance Sheet

It is useful, especially when the final yield is low, to determine where your enzyme went during the preparation. Therefore, if desired, a balance sheet can be prepared that indicates how protein and enzyme fractionated at each step. This level of detail is usually not reported in a publication, but it is extremely useful in deciding retrospectively how to improve the preparation the next time.

Fraction	Sample	Vol.	Protein conc.	σ^{32} conc.	% Total protein	% Total σ^{32}	Fold purification
Cell Breakage							
Crude lysate + 0.2% DOC	**A**						
Solubilization/ Refolding							
Pellet + 2% DOC							
2% DOC supernatant	**C**						
Pellet+ 2% DOC							
2% DOC supernatant							
Pellet + 0.3% SKL							
0.3% SKL pellet							
0.3% SKL supernatant	**D**						
Supernatant dialyzed	**J**						
IEC flowthrough							
IEC wash							
IEC pooled peak							
PEI Precipitation/ Immunoaffinity Chromatography							
0.2% DOC supernatant	**B**						
0.3% PEI supernatant	**E**						
0.3 M NaCl wash	**F**						
0.9 M NaCl eluate	**G**						
55% AMS supernatant	**H**						
55% AMS pellet diluted to 20 ml	**I**						
IAC flowthrough							
IAC wash							
IAC pooled peak							

Protein Purification Summary Table and Summary Photograph of Main Fractions

A summary table such as the one below is considered almost essential when publishing a purification paper. It should include the main fractions containing the majority of the protein being purified. If a quantitative enzyme assay is available, it should also include a column for specific activity (the activity units per milligram of protein). Note that sometimes activity cannot be determined at the crude lysate stage.

Sample	Fraction	Vol.[a]	Protein conc.[b]	σ^{32} conc.[c]	Total protein[d]	Total σ^{32}[e]	Estimated purity[f]	Yield[g]
A	Crude lysate							
D	Resuspended inclusion bodies							
J	Dialyzed SKL extract							
	Pooled IEC peak							
B	0.2% DOC supernatant							
G	0.9 M NaCl PEI eluate							
I	Applied to IAC							
	Pooled IAC peak							

[a]Volume of fraction (ml).
[b]Measured by Bradford (mg/ml).
[c]Estimated by western blot (mg/ml).
[d]Volume x protein concentration (mg).
[e]Volume x σ^{32} concentration (mg).
[f]Based on SDS gel analysis (%).
[g]Recovery of initial σ^{32} (%).

Run an SDS gel on the fractions summarized above. It is ideal if the same proportion of the sample is loaded for each fraction; this facilitates visual comparison of the intensity of the stained band representing the σ^{32}. In a published paper, a summary table containing this level of detail and a summary gel photograph give an excellent record of the preparation. Also, include a lane with at least 10 µg of the purest sample.

• Experiment 5
Protein Characterization

UV Spectrum of the Pure Protein—A_{280nm}/A_{260nm}

INTRODUCTION

A relatively simple and useful measure of protein purity is obtained by determining the ultraviolet (UV) spectrum of a purified protein. Even though sodium dodecyl sulfate (SDS) gels may not show contaminating proteins, the protein may contain contaminating nucleic acid. A rough estimate of the amount of nucleic acid can be obtained from the ratio of absorbance at 280 nm and 260 nm. This is based on the fact that a typical protein solution at a concentration of 1 mg/ml has an A_{280nm} of 1, an A_{260nm} of 0.5, and an A_{280nm}/A_{260nm} of approximately 2.0. On the other hand, a DNA solution at a concentration of 1 mg/ml has an A_{280nm} of 10, an A_{260nm} of 20, and an A_{280nm}/A_{260nm} of approximately 0.5. Even a 1% or 3% nucleic acid contamination can decrease the A_{280nm}/A_{260nm} of a protein from approximately 2.0 to 1.57 or 1.18, respectively.

PROCEDURE

1. Carefully determine the UV spectrum of a protein solution from 210 nm to 340 nm using an appropriate buffer blank.

2. If no absorbance is seen from 310 nm to 340 nm (proteins do not absorb in this region), then simply measure the absorbance at 280 nm and 260 nm. The ratio of A_{280nm}/A_{260nm} should be 1.8–2.0.

3. If apparent absorbance is seen from 310 nm to 340 nm, this is due to light scattering (either because of a large protein or as a result of aggregation) and the A_{280nm} and A_{260nm} must be corrected using the method of Leach and Sheraga (1960). This method involves plotting the logarithm of the absorbance versus the logarithm of the wavelength. The absorbance is extrapolated from 310 nm to 340 nm to determine the amount of the absorbance at 280 nm and 260 nm that is due to light scattering. The corrected absorbance values at 280 nm and 260 nm can be used to determine the A_{280nm}/A_{260nm} and the protein concentration from the $E(1 mg/ml)_{280nm}$ (see pp. 240–241).

•

Determination of the Extinction Coefficient (Method of Scopes)

INTRODUCTION

Scopes has published a convenient method for determining the extinction coefficient (E) of a protein (Scopes 1974). It is based on the fact that whereas most of the absorbance at 205 nm is due to the peptide bond, some absorbance is dependent on the amino acids present in the protein. He developed an empirical equation that relates $E(1 \text{ mg/ml})_{280nm}$ to $E(1 \text{ mg/ml})_{205nm}$, A_{280nm}, and A_{205nm}.

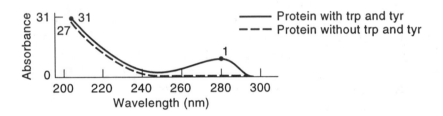

MATERIALS AND EQUIPMENT

Bovine serum albumin (BSA) or σ^{32} solution at a concentration of
    approximately 1 mg/ml
Clean quartz cuvettes
Spectrophotometer that reads at 205 nm and 280 nm

REAGENTS

Dialysis buffer
(For recipe, see Preparation of Reagents, pp. 266–272)

PROCEDURE

1. Dialyze a solution of BSA (~1 mg/ml) or an unknown concentration of the pure protein of interest against 2 x 400 ml of dialysis buffer with good mixing for 3–5 hours.

2. Read the A_{280nm} (which should be in the range 0.25–1.0).

3. Carefully dilute the protein solution 30-fold into dialysis buffer (e.g., 200 μl sample plus 5.8 ml of buffer) and read the A_{205nm}.

4. Using the equation $E(1 \text{ mg/ml})_{205nm} = 27.0 + 120(A_{280}/A_{205})$, calculate $E(1 \text{ mg/ml})_{205nm}$.

5. Calculate the protein concentration = $A_{205}/E(1 \text{ mg/ml})_{205nm}$ =

6. Calculate the $E(1 \text{ mg/ml})_{280nm} = A_{280}/\text{protein concentration}$ =

Alternative Method: Calculating Extinction Coefficient from Amino Acid Sequence

The extinction coefficient can also be calculated from the amino acid composition deduced from a gene sequence. This method has been described by Gill and von Hippel (1989) and more recently refined by Pace et al. (1995). It exploits the fact that the A_{280} is dominated by the absorbance of tryptophan and tyrosine, and to a lesser extent, by cystine. As an example, the extinction coefficient of σ^{32} is calculated below.

Amino acid	Individual amino acid M extinction coefficient at 280 nm	No. of residues in σ^{32}	Molecular weight	M extinction coefficient at 280 nm
Tryptophan	5500	6		33,000
Tyrosine	1490	7		10,430
Cystine	125	0		0
Total		284	32,448	43,430

A 1 M solution of σ^{32} would be 32,448 g/l = 32,448 mg/ml and would have an A_{280nm} of 43,430. Therefore, a 1 mg/ml solution of σ^{32} would have an A_{280nm} of 43,430/32,448 = 1.34. Therefore, the $E(1 \text{ mg/ml})_{280nm} = 1.34$.

Estimation of Purity by Scanning an Overloaded Stained SDS Gel

INTRODUCTION

Due to the high-resolution separation of proteins on SDS gels and the sensitive staining of proteins by Coomassie Brilliant Blue (CBB), one can obtain an estimate of protein purity by staining and destaining a protein preparation analyzed on an SDS gel as described in Experiment 4 of this unit. This method assumes: (i) that no impurities have polypeptide subunits that migrate identically to the target protein and (ii) that all proteins bind CBB to the same extent per microgram of protein. SDS gels must be overloaded to visualize minor contaminants.

REAGENTS

Coomassie® Brilliant Blue (CBB) dye solution
Destaining solution
(For recipes, see Preparation of Reagents, pp. 266–272.)

PROCEDURE

1. Run several dilutions of a relatively pure protein sample (containing approximately 1, 3, 10, and 30 µg of total protein) on a 10% polyacrylamide SDS minigel and stain and destain as described in in Experiment 4 (pp. 229–230).

2. Scan the destained gels and determine the amount of dye-binding material in the main band (presumed to be the target protein) and in the minor bands (presumed to be the most significant impurities).

3. Calculate the relative amounts of the major and minor bands assuming that all of the proteins bind CBB to the same extent per microgram of protein. Some of the minor contaminants can only be seen on the overloaded gel lanes and are not visible when only 1 µg of total protein is loaded.

●

Assessment of Homogeneity by Mobility on Nondenaturing Gel Electrophoresis

INTRODUCTION

The mobility of a protein during electrophoresis under conditions in which the protein retains its native configuration can be a measure of homogeneity. Since mobility is a function of both charge and shape, one would expect to be able to resolve monomeric, dimeric, etc., forms from each other. It is also often possible to resolve conformational isomers of a protein by native gel electrophoresis due to differences in the shapes of the isomers. Basically, the same gel recipes are used as for SDS and urea denaturing gels, namely, the Tris-glycine discontinuous gel system of Ornstein (1964) and Davis (1964).

MATERIALS AND EQUIPMENT

Core RNA polymerase
Core RNA polymerase–σ^{32} complex eluted from the immunoaffinity column
σ^{32} eluted from the POROS® 50S cation-exchange column
Nondenaturing gel electrophoresis apparatus

REAGENTS

Nondenaturing gel sample buffer (2x) (This is the same as SDS sample buffer but without the SDS.)
Storage buffer
Coomassie® Brilliant Blue (CBB) dye solution
Destaining solution
(For recipes, see Preparation of Reagents, pp. 266–272.)

PROCEDURE

1. Assemble a nondenaturing slab gel (e.g., a 4–12% gel) with 10 lanes.

   Note: A number of manufacturers (e.g., NOVEX) sell gradient Tris-glycine mini-gels for SDS-PAGE that actually lack SDS. Normally, the SDS electrophoreses in from the reservoir buffer and sample buffer. By omitting the SDS from these buffers, these gels can be run in the nondenaturing or native mode rather easily.

2. Add 1–10 µl of each protein sample to 5–9 µl of storage buffer and 10–20 µl of 2x nondenaturing gel sample buffer. Mix. In the table below, we suggest a list of samples and appropriate amounts of protein:

Lane	Core (µg)	σ^{32} (µg)	Core-σ^{32} complex (µg)
1	1	-	-
2	3	-	-
3	3	1	-
4	3	3	-
5	3	9	-
6	-	1	-
7	-	3	-
8	-	9	-
9	-	-	3
10	-	-	6

3. Apply 20 µl of each sample to a lane, run the gel, stain with CBB, and destain.

   Note: High-performance liquid chromatography (HPLC) gel-exclusion chromatography can also be used to measure size heterogeneity as described in the Protocol Development Trials section of this unit.

• *Protocol Development Trials*

Purification of σ³² from a Bacterial Overexpresser

• ─────────────────────────────────────

INTRODUCTION

Although the laboratory protocol for the purification of σ^{32} has already been developed and will be used to process most of the preparation, in parallel we will explore some of the key variables and learn how to do protocol development trials. During the main purification, samples were taken that will allow us to answer key protocol development questions. The process of protocol development can be used for any overexpressed protein you may want to purify, even if it behaves somewhat differently from σ^{32}.

• ——

Rapid Dot Blot Western Assays

In standard dot blot western assays, the membrane is blocked for 1 hour, exposed to a first antibody for 1 hour, and then exposed to a second antibody for 1 hour. In cases where lesser sensitivity is allowable, the blocking, first antibody, and second antibody steps can be combined and accelerated to take less than 15 minutes. This is particularly useful when it is necessary to determine rapidly which fractions from a column (for example) contain σ^{32}.

MATERIALS AND EQUIPMENT

Nitrocellulose membrane (Schleicher & Schuell, Inc.)
Mouse anti-σ^{32} monoclonal antibody 3RH2 (MAb 3RH2)
Rabbit anti-mouse immunoglobulin G (IgG)-alkaline phosphatase
    conjugate

REAGENTS

Tris-buffered saline (TBS)
TBS + 1% bovine serum albumin (BSA)
TBS + 0.1% Tween-20 (TBST)
5-Bromo-4-chloro-3-indolyl phosphate/nitro blue tetrazolium
    (BCIP/NBT) color reagent
(For recipes, see Preparation of Reagents, pp. 266–272.)

PROCEDURE

1. Mark and number a grid on a small square of nitrocellulose membrane. Place the nitrocellulose on a piece of paper towel and wet the nitrocellulose and towel with TBS.

2. Use a spatula or pipette tip to smooth the nitrocellulose against the towel, then spot 1-μl samples onto the nitrocellulose at positions indicated by the grid.

3. Allow the nitrocellulose to stand for 2 minutes after the dots are pulled through the membrane by capillary action, then place it in the antibody/BSA solution (mouse anti-σ^{32} MAb 3RH2 and rabbit anti-mouse IgG-alkaline phosphatase conjugate, each at 1/1000 dilution in TBS + 1% BSA).

   Note: We have found that excess polyethyleneimine (PEI) in a sample (e.g., samples from PEI precipitation curve at high PEI additions) can cause a false positive reaction, probably by binding the MAb. This can be diminished by blocking the blot for 2 minutes in TBS + 1% BSA prior to incubating with the mixed antibodies.

4. Allow the antibodies to bind with gentle agitation for at least 6 minutes, then aspirate off the supernatant (save for future blots) and wash the nitrocellulose twice quickly with TBST.

5. Wash the nitrocellulose three more times with TBST for at least 1 minute each, then rinse quickly with H_2O, and add BCIP/NBT color reagent.

6. Allow the spots to develop for 5–20 minutes, then rinse the nitrocellulose with H_2O, pat it dry, and allow it to dry completely before taping it to a protocol sheet.

● ───

Is the σ^{32} Soluble or Insoluble?

In this case the answer is both, but mostly insoluble. Since it is more efficient in a course setting to answer this question when other samples are available, in Experiment 1 we just save samples (native and SDS-containing samples) of the cell lysate (**sample A**) and the 0.2% DOC supernatant (**sample B**) for later analyses.

Note: In cases where the protein is found in both the soluble and insoluble forms, often the proportion of soluble material can be increased by growing and inducing the cells at 30°C instead of 37°C. Quite often, however, the soluble material is somewhat multimeric and possibly less active.

●──

How Much Sarkosyl Is Needed to Dissolve the Inclusion Body Pellet?

MATERIALS AND EQUIPMENT

Apparatus for SDS-PAGE
Polyacrylamide minigel (10%)
Molecular weight markers

REAGENTS

Buffer A
Sarkosyl (SKL) (20% stock solution in H_2O)
Coomassie Brilliant Blue (CBB) dye solution
Destaining solution
Reagents for rapid dot blot western assays (see p. 246)
(For recipes, see Preparation of Reagents, pp. 266–272.)

PROCEDURE

1. Take 6 x 50 μl aliquots of the second 2% DOC suspension before it is spun down (see p. 215). Spin these samples in a microcentrifuge for 1 minute at full speed and discard the supernatants.

2. Add to the pellets 0, 0.1, 0.2, 0.3, 0.4, and 0.6% SKL in 100 μl of buffer A. Resuspend the pellets vigorously, allow to stand for 10 minutes, spin in a microcentrifuge for 1 minute, and sample the supernatants for rapid dot blot western analysis (see pp. 246–247) and observe the size of the pellets.

3. Run an SDS gel of each supernatant and do rapid dot blot western assays on these samples along with **samples A** and **B**.

4. For the gel analysis, load 20 μl each of **samples A, B, C,** and **D,** 0.1% SKL supernatant, 0.2% SKL supernatant, 0.3% SKL supernatant, 0.4% SKL supernatant, 0.6% SKL supernatant, and 3 μl of molecular weight markers on 10% SDS gels. Run at 120 V (20 mA) for approximately 60 minutes.

5. Stain for 30 minutes with CBB dye solution, rinse in destaining solution, and destain until bands appear.

●

How Much Polyethyleneimine Is Needed to Precipitate σ^{32} and RNA Polymerase?

MATERIALS AND EQUIPMENT

Apparatus for SDS-PAGE
Polyacrylamide minigel (10%)

REAGENT

Polyethyleneimine (PEI) (6% stock solution; pH 7.9)
(For recipe, see Preparation of Reagents, pp. 266–272.)

PROCEDURE

1. Take 6 x 50 µl aliquots of the 0.2% DOC supernatant (see p. 221). Add 0, 1, 2, 3, 4, and 5 µl of 6% PEI stock solution to the aliquots (to give 0, 0.12, 0.24, 0.36, 0.48, and 0.6% PEI), mix well, and incubate for 5–10 minutes.

2. Spin down the precipitates for 1 minute in a microcentrifuge, and sample the supernatants for rapid dot blot western assays (see pp. 246–247) or SDS gels, if desired. Process dot blots immediately.

Results

For a typical SDS gel showing the PEI titration experiment, see Figure 5.

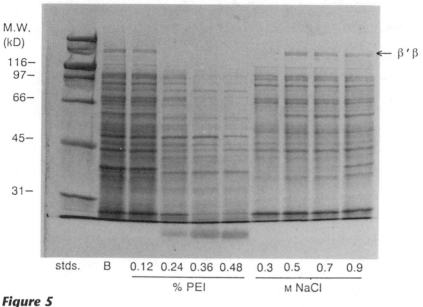

Figure 5

SDS gel of PEI titration and NaCl elution experiments. The samples were prepared as described on p. 250 and p. 252 and were analyzed on a 10% SDS gel.
Note that the β'β bands (indicating the RNA polymerase) are removed by
concentrations of PEI ≥0.24%. The last four lanes show a 0.3% PEI pellet
eluted with 0.3 M, 0.5 M, 0.7 M, and 0.9 M NaCl. The β'β bands are not eluted
by 0.3 M NaCl, but they are eluted by concentrations of NaCl ≥0.5 M.

How Much Salt Is Needed to Elute σ^{32} and RNA Polymerase from the PEI Pellet?

MATERIALS AND EQUIPMENT

Apparatus for SDS-PAGE
Polyacrylamide minigel (10%)

REAGENTS

Buffer A
Buffer A containing 0, 0.3, 0.5, 0.7, 0.9, and 1.1 M NaCl
(For recipe, see Preparation of Reagents, pp. 266–272.)

PROCEDURE

1. Take 6 x 50 µl aliquots of the PEI suspension before it has been spun down (see p. 221). Spin these samples in a microcentrifuge for 1 minute, then resuspend the pellets in 50 µl of buffer A containing 0, 0.3, 0.5, 0.7, 0.9, and 1.1 M NaCl.

2. Mix well and allow to stand for 10–15 minutes. Spin in a microcentrifuge for 1 minute, sample the supernatants, and carry out rapid dot blot western assays (see pp. 246–247) and SDS-PAGE, if desired.

Results

For a typical SDS gel showing the NaCl elution experiments, see Figure 5 (p. 251).

• ───

How Long Does It Take to Remove the Sarkosyl by Dialysis?

MATERIALS AND EQUIPMENT

Apparatus for reverse-phase high-performance liquid chromatography (HPLC)
C_{18} reverse-phase HPLC column (VYDAC™, 4.6 x 250 mm)
Glacial acetic acid
Trifluoroacetic acid (TFA) (2% stock solution in H_2O)
Acetonitrile
Solvent A (0.1% TFA) (filter through a 0.2-μm nylon filter)
Solvent B (80% acetonitrile + 0.086% TFA) (filter through a 0.2-μm nylon filter)

SAFETY NOTES

- Glacial acetic acid and trifluoroacetic acid are volatile and should be used in a chemical fume hood. Concentrated acids should be handled with great care; gloves and a face protector should be worn.
- Acetonitrile is very volatile and extremely flammable. It is an irritant and a chemical asphyxiant that can exert its effects by inhalation, ingestion, or absorption through the skin. Cases of severe exposure are treated as cyanide poisoning. Handle acetonitrile in a chemical fume hood. Wear gloves and safety glasses.

PROCEDURE

1. Assay the samples taken during or after dialysis (see p. 216) by reverse-phase HPLC.

2. To 100 μl of each sample, add 5 μl of glacial acetic acid, and mix.

   Note: If a sample is extremely turbid or precipitates, spin in a microcentrifuge prior to injecting.

3. Inject 50 μl of acetic-acid-adjusted sample onto a C_{18} column being run in a 0.1% TFA/water/acetonitrile system, with detection at 215 nm. After injection, wash the column with solvent A for 5

minutes at 1 ml/minute. Elute with a linear gradient of 100% solvent A to 100% solvent B for 10 minutes. Wash with solvent B for 3 minutes and with solvent A for 7 minutes.

4. Also inject a dilution series of Sarkosyl (SKL) (0.005–0.075%) standards, and plot the height of the SKL peaks as a function of concentration. From the peak height of your samples, calculate and plot the concentration of Sarkosyl in the sample as a function of time.

5. After use, wash the column with 20 ml of MilliQ H_2O, followed by 20 ml of 20% methanol, and store at room temperature.

Note: Prepare a blank sample of 100 μl of buffer A and 5 μl of glacial acetic acid and run as above. This may be used to correct for any solvent peaks eluting from the column.

Results

For a typical reverse-phase HPLC profile, see Figure 6.

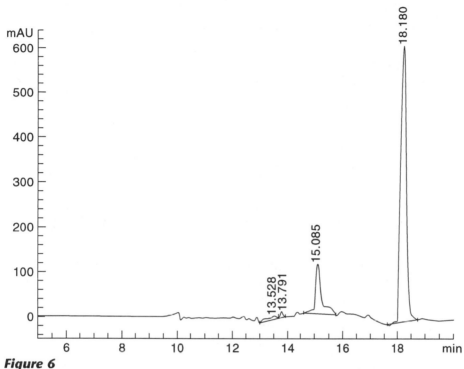

Figure 6

Detection of σ^{32} and Sarkosyl by reverse-phase HPLC. A portion of **Sample J** (Sarkosyl-solubilized inclusion body pellet that has been diluted and dialyzed) was prepared as described on pp. 215–216 and analyzed by reverse-phase HPLC as described on pp. 253–254. The σ^{32} peak elutes at 15.08 minutes, and the Sarkosyl elutes at 18.18 minutes. After chromatography on POROS 50S, the peak of eluted σ^{32} contains no detectable Sarkosyl.

• ──

What Dialysis Conditions Will Result in the Highest Yields of Refolded, Soluble Monomeric σ^{32}?

The dialysis conditions suggested on pp. 215–216 are just one of many possible conditions. The goal is to refold the protein as rapidly and conveniently as possible and to obtain the highest yield of refolded, soluble, monomeric, and active σ^{32}. Some of the variables that can be tested include:

• Vary the protein concentration during refolding from 1–2 mg/ml to less than 0.1 mg/ml. The lower the protein concentration, the less likely it is that aggregation will occur.

• Vary the temperature from 25°C to 4°C.

• Vary the salt concentration from 50 mM to 250 mM.

• Vary the pH. Aggregation is more likely to occur as the pH approaches the pI.

• Vary additives such as polyethylene glycol, etc.

MATERIALS AND EQUIPMENT

Centricon™-10 concentrator (Amicon, Inc.)
High-performance liquid chromatography (HPLC) size exclusion
    column TSK-GEL® G3000 PWXL (7.8 x 300 mm) (TosoHaas)
50 mM Tris (pH 7.9) + 200 mM NaCl

PROCEDURE

Monitoring the Formation of Soluble Monomer by HPLC Size Exclusion Chromatography

1. Dialyze a sample under whichever conditions you wish to try.

2. Remove the dialyzed sample from the dialysis tube, and spin at 13,000 rpm for 10 minutes to clarify. Retain the supernatant.

3. If the sample was dialyzed at a very low protein concentration, concentrate using a Centricon-10 concentrator. Add 2.0 ml of dialyzed sample to the Centricon-10 tube and spin at 5,000 rpm for 90 minutes or until the volume has been reduced to 1/5 to 1/10 of the original volume.

   Note: One needs to choose a Centricon tube with a pore size such that water and salts will pass through the membrane under the centrifugal pressure while the σ^{32} is retained. Centricon-30 or Centricon-100 have larger pores and concentrate faster, but a Centricon-10, with a nominal molecular weight cutoff of 10,000, is used here because σ^{32} has a molecular weight of 32,000 and some σ^{32} would pass through larger pores. Centricon tubes can also be used to change the salt concentration of a sample. You simply concentrate your sample tenfold and then bring back to the original volume with a different buffer. Concentrators that process smaller (0.5 ml; Microcon) and larger (20 ml; Centriprep) volumes are also available from Amicon, Inc.

4. Apply 100–400 µl of the supernatant to a 7.8 x 300-mm TSK-GEL G3000 PWXL size exclusion column that has been equilibrated at room temperature with 50 mM Tris (pH 7.9) + 200 mM NaCl at 1 ml/minute and develop the column under the same conditions, collecting 0.5-ml fractions for 30 minutes.

   Note: The salt is added to prevent weak ionic binding of proteins to the polymer matrix, which would distort the elution times and prevent pure size exclusion chromatography.

5. Monitor the column outflow with an ultraviolet detector at 280 nm. Estimate the proportion of the material running as soluble monomer.

   Note: The HPLC size exclusion column should be calibrated by running a set of proteins with known native molecular weights through the column under the same elution conditions. By plotting the elution positions of the standards versus the log of their molecular weights, one can estimate, by interpolation, the molecular weight of the protein species eluting when dialyzed σ^{32} is analyzed.

6. If necessary, analyze selected fractions by SDS-PAGE to confirm the identity of eluting peaks.

How Long Does It Take for Protein to Bind to the Immunoaffinity Resin?

MATERIALS AND EQUIPMENT

Apparatus for SDS-PAGE
Polyacrylamide minigel (10%)

PROCEDURE

1. Take 100-μl samples at 0, 5, 15, and 30 minutes after mixing the dissolved, diluted AMS pellet with the washed immunoaffinity resin (see p. 225).

2. Spin the samples immediately and retain the supernatants for SDS-PAGE analysis to assess the rate of binding of the core RNA polymerase–σ^{32} complex to the antibody.

   Note: Free σ^{32} will not bind to the immunoaffinity column. The core RNA polymerase–σ^{32} complex will bind and can be monitored by the removal of the core $\beta'\beta$ subunits (a doublet of ~155 kD on the SDS gel) from the supernatant fraction.

•

Alternative Procedures for Refolding Denatured σ^{32}

Although previous work has established Sarkosyl (SKL) to be a good refolding agent for σ^{32}, it may not be best for another protein. Here we describe a procedure for testing other methods for solubilizing and refolding proteins. Although some of these conditions may also work for σ^{32}, it is likely that some will not. The intent of this section is to demonstrate how these conditions can be easily and systematically screened.

Although the information required for the proper folding of a protein is encoded in the primary sequence, even in vivo, proteins need assistance in order to fold properly. A set of enzymes that assist the folding of nascent polypeptide, called chaperonins, perform this function in vivo, and in some cases, these enzymes have been used successfully to assist the refolding of proteins in vitro as well. Until consistent and inexpensive means to use these enzymes in a preparative mode can be developed, the challenge for an experimenter wishing to refold a protein is to mimic the assistance provided by chaperonins. One of the functions of these enzymes is to assist with the proper formation of disulfide bonds. Treatment of this problem is beyond the scope of this course. The other main function of some chaperonins is, as the protein starts to fold, to prevent local hydrophobic patches on the protein's surface from sticking to hydrophobic patches on other proteins, leading to the formation of an aggregate or precipitate.

When an inclusion body protein is solubilized with a denaturant, such as guanidine-HCl or urea, most of the normal secondary structure (i.e., helices, β sheets, etc.) are disrupted. When the denaturant is removed, these structures start to reform and create the types of sticky patches mentioned above. These sticky patches need to be given time to associate intramolecularly, and to try out a number of possible arrangements, without aggregating. There are several ways to help this to happen:

1. Determine at what concentration of denaturant the protein is undergoing refolding (the folding midpoint), and proceed through this region in a defined fashion.

2. Perform folding at low protein concentration (typically <50 μg/ml) (Hager and Burgess 1980).

3. Add a cosolvent such as polyethylene glycol or detergent near the critical micelle concentration to reversibly mask hydrophobic groups (Tandon and Horowitz 1987; Cleland et al. 1992).

4. Use a detergent as a denaturant and protective agent (Nguyen et al. 1993).

5. Perform refolding while protein monomers are immobilized on chromatographic resins (Creighton 1986).

6. Add a known substrate or ligand for the native protein.

In general, it is difficult to predict exactly which of these strategies will work for a new protein, so it is important to develop an easy method to test a variety of protocols and to analyze the results. The following scheme allows the determination of an approximate folding midpoint and screening for folding conditions.

It should be noted that the products of a refolding reaction commonly consist of two pools: monomer (usually folded properly and active) and aggregate or precipitate (usually less active or inactive). Some of the aggregated material may not appear turbid, so it is important to check the aggregation state either with a native gel or by size exclusion chromatography.

Note: Since in a number of high-level protein expression systems, the protein production exceeds the capacity of the chaperonin system, fair amounts of aggregated protein are often produced, even when the protein appears to be soluble! Thus, checking for aggregate is prudent, even when inclusion bodies are not observed. Sometimes, researchers have found that growing cells at a lower temperature allows soluble expression of a protein formerly found in insoluble form. Much of this soluble material may be aggregated.

Freshly isolated inclusion bodies from freshly grown cells tend to give the best folding yields. Also, the cleaner the inclusion body protein is, in general, the better the folding.

Screen for Solubility in Urea (Tube #2)

1. First, you need to find out how soluble the protein is in 8 M urea. To do this, prepare a 100-ml batch of 8 M urea in buffer A (dissolve 48 g of solid urea in buffer A and adjust the volume to 100 ml). This may require mild warming.

2. Resuspend the pellet in tube #2 (from p. 215) in 10 ml of the 8 M urea solution using a Tissue-Tearor washed in 8 M urea. Let it stand for 15 minutes. Spin at 13,000 rpm for 10 minutes at 4°C and sample the supernatant for subsequent protein assay.

3. Do not remove the supernatant from the pellet. Dilute the volume to 20 ml by adding a further 10 ml of 8 M urea. Resuspend the pellet, repeat the spin, and sample the supernatant. Dilute the volume to 40 ml and repeat this step.

4. Assay the supernatants for protein, and calculate the concentration and the amount of protein solubilized.

Screen for Approximate Folding Midpoint (Tube #2)

1. Prepare a serial twofold dilution series of the urea-solubilized σ^{32} in buffer A. (Do this in microcentrifuge tubes.)

2. Let the samples stand for approximately 15 minutes. Spin in a microcentrifuge for 2 minutes at room temperature and assay the supernatants for protein.

3. Also, look at the pellets—where does the protein start to fall out of solution?

Attempt to Fold the Protein by Dilution with/without Added Agents

Here we describe a dilution scheme that slowly takes the protein through the folding midpoint.

1. Adjust the protein concentration of the urea-solubilized σ^{32} to approximately 1 mg/ml or 0.3 mg/ml (by adding 8 M urea in buffer A), then place 2.0 ml of the protein solution in each of five 25-ml glass test tubes (A–E).

2. Take each sample through the following dilution protocol, with or without additives as noted for each group.

Starting volume (ml)	Volume of buffer A added (ml)	Final volume (ml)	Net urea concentration (M)	Wait time (min)
2.0	3.35	5.35	3.0	10
5.35	0.50	5.85	2.75	10
5.85	0.60	6.45	2.50	10
6.45	0.70	7.15	2.25	10
7.15	0.90	8.05	2.0	20
8.05	1.15	9.20	1.75	20
9.20	1.55	10.75	1.5	20
10.75	2.15	12.90	1.25	20
12.90	3.25	16.15	1	20
16.15	5.35	21.50	0.75	20

Set up the dilution experiments according to the scheme above so that protein concentrations are as indicated in the table below (in mg/ml) and the indicated amounts of additives are present at the indicated levels after the first dilution (for group 4, add PEG before the first dilution).

Group #	Tube A	Tube B	Tube C	Tube D	Tube E
1	prot=1.0	prot=1.0 SKL= 0.2%	prot=0.3 SKL=0.2%	prot=1.0 SKL=0.05%	prot=0.3 SKL=0.05%
2	prot=1.0	prot=1.0 TRT=0.2%	prot=0.3 TRT=0.2%	prot=1.0 TRT=0.05%	prot=0.3 TRT=0.05%
3	prot=1.0	prot=1.0 ZWT=0.2%	prot=0.3 ZWT=0.2%	prot=1.0 ZWT=0.05%	prot=0.3 ZWT=0.05%
4	prot=1.0	prot=1.0 PEG=0.2%	prot=0.3 PEG=0.06%	prot=1.0 PEG=0.05%	prot=0.3 PEG=0.015%

Where: SKL = Sarkosyl (20% stock solution)
TRT = Triton X-100 (20% stock solution)
ZWT = Zwittergent 3-14 (20% stock solution)
PEG = Polyethylene glycol 3350 (20% stock solution)
protein concentrations are expressed in mg/ml

Note: You could easily test other additives, wait times, temperatures, etc.

3. Observe the turbidity of the end of each wait period. If you wish, transfer 100-μl samples at each point into a microtiter dish. Reading them at >400 nm can give a more precise reading of the folding midpoint by turbidimetry.

4. After finishing the dilution series, take 1-ml samples of each dilution and spin in a microcentrifuge for 10 minutes. Assay the supernatants for protein. If 100% of the protein is soluble, you should obtain results of approximately 0.1 mg/ml or 0.03 mg/ml. Dialyze 20-ml samples of any condition that looks promising against 1 liter of buffer A overnight.

Note: The dilution trials described above could be repeated using buffer A + 6 M guanidinium hydrochloride (GuHCl) instead of buffer A + 8 M urea to dissolve the inclusion body pellet in tube #2.

●————————————————————————————————

Strategies for Rapid Development of a New Protocol for Purification from Bacterial Overexpresser (Assumes No Disulfide Bridges)

The intent of this section is to provide a brief sketch of how to use a series of experiments similar to those described in this unit to lead rapidly to a preliminary purification protocol for a new protein over-expressed in bacteria. Many experimenters forget to use one of the best attributes of bacterial expression systems in developing a purification protocol, namely, the ready ability to make more starting material. They often will only prepare cells once, and perform serial purification trials for up to several weeks with the original material. By doing this, one is vulnerable to all sorts of artifacts as the enzyme preparation ages.

In general, it tends to be more efficient to plan to grow and induce cells every day for several days, and to use each batch of material to move a little farther through the purification. For instance, the objective of the workup of the first culture is to determine solubility and screen simple workup steps. After this is done, most materials should be discarded. The next day, the cells are rapidly taken through the steps defined the day before, and trials are done to determine the next steps. After a few iterations, a robust basic workup is obtained which can rapidly afford partially purified protein. This, then, is the appropriate time to settle in and work at the final purification steps.

PROCEDURE

Day 1

The objectives are to test induction conditions for expression of T7 RNA polymerase, to determine supernatant/pellet distribution, and to make a preliminary evaluation of secondary workup steps.

1. Start one 50-ml culture from a low-density overnight culture of *E. coli* cells.

2. At an A_{600nm} of 0.3–0.7, induce expression of the T7 RNA polymerase with 0.8 mM IPTG and split the culture.

3. After 30 minutes, add rifampicin to a final concentration of 150 μg/ml to one portion of the culture.

4. During induction, take time course samples for SDS-PAGE analysis by spinning 1 ml of culture and solubilizing the pellet in 100 μl of 2x SDS sample buffer per A_{600nm} unit. Follow the inductions for 2–4 hours.

5. After the last sample has been taken, pool the cultures and work up the cells with the sonication/DOC protocol (see p. 213). This should answer the question of whether or not the protein will be soluble or be found in the pellet.

6. If the protein is in the pellet, screen in a preliminary way for Sarkosyl solubilization (see pp. 214–215 and p. 249). If the protein is in the supernatant, try screening the supernatant for PEI precipitation/elution conditions (see pp. 221–222 and pp. 250–252). After finishing these experiments, toss the whole thing in the trash and prepare for a larger (1 liter) culture the next day.

Day 2

The objectives are to take the protein rapidly through the first few steps of the protocol and screen for later column steps. Use a fresh 1-liter culture using the conditions determined to be best on Day 1.

1. If the protein is in the soluble fraction, take it through PEI precipitation/elution (pp. 221–222), then screen for binding conditions to various chromatographic resins. Generally, it is suggested that one try ion exchangers (Q and S) and a hydrophobic interaction resin (phenyl Sepharose). Screen binding first, then elution using the best binding conditions. Adsorb the protein to the column in batch mode, then pour into the column and elute.

2. If the protein is in the pellet fraction, split into batches and dissolve in previously defined Sarkosyl levels at several protein concentrations. Dialyze overnight. You can also try some guanidinium hydrochloride (GuHCl) or urea folding trials on some aliquots of the pellet. If the pellet is not as pure as you would like, try washing some pellet with other detergents (e.g., Triton X-100, Tween-20, Brij-35), or low concentrations of urea or GuHCl. The next day, use gel filtration to determine the fraction of monomeric material as a function of protein concentration and other parameters. Prepare for one more 1-liter culture.

Day 3

The objectives are to take the protein through the main line procedure and to try further chromatographic steps. Start activity assays, and consider two-dimensional gels to look for electrophoretic isoforms and/or comigrating impurities.

1. If the protein is soluble, you should have material of fair purity and it is probably time to check for soluble aggregate and modified protein, and to try activity assays.

2. If the protein was in the pellet, you will likely have to use some chromatography in order to remove residual detergent.

Preparation of Reagents

5-Bromo-4-chloro-3-indolyl phosphate/nitro blue tetrazolium
(BCIP/NBT) color reagent
(for detecting alkaline-phosphatase-conjugated antibodies
in western blots)

0.1 M Tris-HCl (pH 9.5)
0.1 M NaCl
5 mM $MgCl_2$

Prepare the buffer according to the recipe above and add 330 mg of BCIP and 170 mg of NBT per liter. Store in the dark. (This reagent is commercially available as Western Blue Reagent from Promega Corp.)

Buffer A
(1 liter)

		Final concentration
1 M Tris-HCl (pH 7.9) (see p. 272)	50 ml	50 mM
0.5 M EDTA (see p. 268)	1 ml	0.5 mM
5 M NaCl (see p. 269)	10 ml	50 mM
100% Glycerol	50 ml	5%

Adjust the volume to 1 liter with H_2O. For the purification of σ^{32}, buffer A contains no reducing agent since σ^{32} contains no cysteine residues. Normally one would use 0.1–0.5 mM dithiothreitol in all buffers to prevent oxidation of protein.

Buffer A + 0.3 M NaCl
(for polyethyleneimine pellet extraction)

18.8 ml of buffer A plus 1.2 ml of 5 M NaCl

Buffer A + 0.9 M NaCl
(for polyethyleneimine pellet extraction)

16.4 ml of buffer A plus 3.6 ml of 5 M NaCl

Buffer A + 1 M NaCl
(for ion-exchange chromatography)
(1 liter)

		Final concentration
1 M Tris-HCl (pH 7.9) (see p. 272)	50 ml	50 mM
0.5 M EDTA (see p. 268)	1 ml	0.5 mM
5 M NaCl (see p. 269)	200 ml	1 M
100% Glycerol	50 ml	5%

Adjust the volume to 1 liter with H_2O. For the purification of σ^{32}, buffer A contains no reducing agent since σ^{32} contains no cysteine residues. Normally one would use 0.1–0.5 mM dithiothreitol in all buffers to prevent oxidation of protein.

Buffer A + 50% glycerol
(for use in storage)
(1 liter)

		Final concentration
1 M Tris-HCl (pH 7.9) (see p. 272)	50 ml	50 mM
0.5 M EDTA (see p. 268)	1 ml	0.5 mM
5 M NaCl (see p. 269)	10 ml	50 mM
100% Glycerol	500 ml	50%

Adjust the volume to 1 liter with H_2O. For the purification of σ^{32}, buffer A contains no reducing agent since σ^{32} contains no cysteine residues. Normally one would use 0.1–0.5 mM dithiothreitol in all buffers to prevent oxidation of protein.

Buffer B
(500 ml)

		Final concentration
1 M Tris-HCl (pH 7.9) (see p. 272)	25 ml	50 mM
0.5 M EDTA (see p. 268)	0.5 ml	0.5 mM
5 M NaCl (see p. 269)	5 ml	50 mM

Adjust the volume to 500 ml with H_2O.

Coomassie® Brilliant Blue (CBB) dye solution
(0.025% CBB R-250 in ethanol/acetic acid/H_2O [5:1:5])

Add 0.275 g of CBB R-250 to 500 ml of ethanol and mix until dissolved. Add 100 ml of acetic acid, mix, and add 500 ml of H_2O. Filter through a medium sintered glass filter (or paper, but it is slower). Be sure to dissolve the CBB in the ethanol first—it is much faster than trying to dissolve it in the 5:1:5 mixture.

Coupling buffer
(for coupling MAb to Sepharose® 4B)

0.1 M $NaHCO_3$ (pH 8.3; adjust the pH with NaOH)
0.5 M NaCl

Dissolve 8.4 g of $NaHCO_3$ and 29.2 g of NaCl in H_2O. Adjust the volume to 1 liter with H_2O. Prepare fresh before use.

Destaining solution
(7.5% glacial acetic acid in H_2O)

Add 75 ml of glacial acetic acid to 925 ml of H_2O.

SAFETY NOTE

- Glacial acetic acid is volatile and should be used in a chemical fume hood. Concentrated acids should be handled with great care; gloves and a face protector should be worn.

Dialysis buffer
(for determination of extinction coefficient)

50 mM Na_2SO_4
5 mM KPO_4 (pH 7.0)

Dithiothreitol (DTT) (0.1 M)

Dissolve 154 mg of DTT (DL-dithiothreitol, anhydrous M.W. = 154.2; Sigma Chemical Co. D 0632) in H_2O and adjust the volume to 10 ml. Store in the dark (wrapped in aluminum foil) at $-20^{\circ}C$.

EDTA (0.5 M; pH 7.9)

Dissolve 18.6 g of EDTA $\cdot$ Na_2 $\cdot$ $2H_2O$ and 2 g of NaOH in H_2O and adjust the volume to 100 ml.

Ethanolamine (1 M)

Add 6 ml of 98% ethanolamine (Sigma Chemical Co. E 9508) to 50 ml of coupling buffer (for recipe, see above). Adjust the pH to 8.0 with concentrated HCl and adjust the volume to 100 ml with coupling buffer. If the ethanolamine is yellow, do not use it.

IAC elution buffer
(100 ml)

		Final concentration
1 M Tris-HCl (pH 7.9) (see p. 272)	5 ml	50 mM
0.5 M EDTA (see p. 268)	0.1 ml	0.5 mM
Propylene glycol	30 ml	30%
5 M NaCl (see below)	15 ml	0.75 M

Adjust the volume to 100 ml with H_2O.

LB medium
(1 liter)

Bacto tryptone	10 g
Yeast extract	5 g
NaCl	5 g

Dissolve in H_2O and adjust the volume to 1 liter. Autoclave.

NaCl (5 M)

Dissolve 146.1 g of NaCl in H_2O and adjust the volume to 500 ml.

Polyethyleneimine (PEI) (10% v/v in H_2O; pH 7.9)

Add 10 ml of PEI (also called by its trade name, Polymin P; BASF) to 70 ml of H_2O. Titrate to pH 7.9 with concentrated HCl, and adjust the final volume to 100 ml with H_2O.

Polyethyleneimine (PEI) (6% v/v in H_2O; pH 7.9)

Add 6 ml of 10% PEI (pH 7.9) to 4 ml of H_2O.

Potassium thiocyanate (KSCN) (2 M)
(for stripping the immunoaffinity column)

Dissolve 19.44 g of KSCN (Aldrich Chemical Co. 20,779-9) in H_2O and adjust the volume to 100 ml. Store at 4°C.

Reaction solution
(for enzyme assay)

10 µg/ml poly(dAT)
0.2 mM ATP
0.05 mM UTP
10 mM $MgCl_2$
2 mM EDTA
1 mM Dithiothreitol
100 mM NaCl
25 mM Tris-HCl (pH 7.9)

Sarkosyl (SKL) (20% v/v in H_2O)

Dissolve 10 g of Sarkosyl (*N*-lauroylsarcosine, sodium salt, anhydrous M.W. = 293.4; Sigma Chemical Co. L 5125) in H_2O and adjust the volume to 50 ml.

SDS gel running buffer

Dilute coldroom Tris-glycine 1:1 with H_2O and add 1/100 volume of 10% SDS stock solution.

Coldroom Tris-glycine (4x Tris-glycine)

Dissolve 460.8 g of glycine and 96 g of Tris base in 8 liters of H_2O. Adjust the pH to 8.5.

Sodium dodecyl sulfate (SDS) (10% w/v in H_2O)

Dissolve 10 g of SDS in H_2O and then adjust the volume to 100 ml with H_2O.

SDS sample buffer (2x)

Dissolve 12 g of SDS in 50 ml of 4x Upper Tris (for recipe, see p. 272). Add 20 ml of 2-mercaptoethanol and adjust the volume to 100 ml with 100% glycerol. Add a trace of bromophenol blue as a marker dye.

SAFETY NOTE

- 2-Mercaptoethanol may be fatal if swallowed and is harmful if inhaled or absorbed through the skin. High concentrations are extremely destructive to the mucous membranes, upper respiratory tract, skin, and eyes. Use only in a chemical fume hood. Gloves and safety glasses should be worn.

Sodium azide (2%)

Dissolve 200 mg of sodium azide in H_2O and adjust the volume to 10 ml.

SAFETY NOTE

- Sodium azide is extremely toxic. Wear gloves and safety glasses and work in a chemical fume hood. Sodium azide will explode when heated.

Sodium deoxycholate (DOC) (20% w/v in H_2O)

Dissolve 10 g of DOC (deoxycholic acid, sodium salt, anhydrous M.W. = 414.5; Sigma Chemical Co. D 7650) in H_2O and adjust the volume to 50 ml. DOC dissolves slowly, so prepare the solution several days before it is required. Store at room temperature for a few days or at 4°C for longer periods. It may be necessary to warm to 37°C briefly to obtain a clear solution.

Storage buffer

Buffer A containing 50% glycerol and 0.1 mM dithiothreitol.

Tris-buffered saline (TBS)

		Final concentration
1 M Tris-HCl (pH 7.9) (see p. 272)	10 ml	10 mM
5 M NaCl (see p. 269)	20 ml	100 mM

Adjust the volume to 1 liter with H_2O.

TBS + 0.1% Tween-20 (TBST)
(for washing western blots)

		Final concentration
1 M Tris-HCl (pH 7.9)	10 ml	10 mM
5 M NaCl (see p. 269)	20 ml	100 mM
Tween-20	1 ml	0.1%

Adjust the volume to 1 liter with H_2O.

TBS + 1% bovine serum albumin (BSA)
(for blocking nitrocellulose in westerns, antibody incubations)

Dissolve 500 mg of BSA in 50 ml of TBS. Add sodium azide (see Safety Note, p. 271) to 0.02% if desired storage exceeds 3 days at 4°C.

Tris-HCl (1 M; pH 7.9 at 25°C)

Dissolve 242.2 g of Trizma base in 1800 ml of H_2O. Add approximately 108 ml of concentrated HCl and let the solution cool to 25°C. Adjust the pH to 7.9 and adjust the volume to 2 liters with H_2O.

SAFETY NOTE

- Concentrated acids should be handled with great care; gloves and a face protector should be worn.

Upper Tris (4x)

Add 60.6 g of Tris to 40 ml of 10% SDS stock solution. Adjust the volume to 1 liter with H_2O, and adjust the pH to 6.8 with 12 N HCl.

Sodium dodecyl sulfate (SDS) (10% w/v in H_2O)

Dissolve 10 g of SDS in H_2O and then adjust the volume to 100 ml with H_2O.

References

Bradford, M.M. 1976. A rapid and sensitive method for the quantitation of microgram quantities of protein utilizing the principle of protein-dye binding. *Anal. Biochem.* **72:** 248–254.

Burgess, R. 1991. The use of polyethyleneimine in the purification of DNA binding proteins. *Methods Enzymol.* **208:** 3–10.

Burgess, R. and J. Jendrisak. 1975. A procedure for the rapid, large-scale purification of *E. coli* DNA-dependent RNA polymerase involving Polymin P precipitation and DNA-cellulose chromatography. *Biochemistry* **14:** 4634–4638.

Cleland, J.L., S.E. Builder, J.R. Swartz, M. Winkler, J.Y. Chang, and D.I.C. Wang. 1992. Polyethylene glycol enhanced protein folding. *Bio/Technology* **10:** 1013–1019.

Creighton, T. 1986. Patent W086/05809.

Davis, B.J. 1964. Disc electrophoresis. II. Methods and applications to human serum proteins. *Ann. N.Y. Acad. Sci.* **121:** 404–427.

Gill, S. and P. von Hippel. 1989. Calculation of protein extinction coefficients from amino acid sequence data. *Biochemistry* **182:** 319–326.

Hager, D.A. and R.R. Burgess. 1980. Elution of proteins from SDS-polyacrylamide gels, removal of SDS, and renaturation of enzymatic activity: Results with sigma subunit of *E. coli* RNA polymerase, wheat germ DNA topoisomerase, and other enzymes. *Anal. Biochem.* **109:** 76–86.

Harlow, E. and D. Lane. 1988. *Antibodies: A laboratory manual.* Cold Spring Harbor Laboratory, Cold Spring Harbor, New York.

Leach, S.J. and H.A. Sheraga. 1960. Effect of light scattering on ultraviolet difference spectra. *J. Am. Chem. Soc.* **82:** 4790–4792.

Nguyen, L., D. Jensen, and R. Burgess. 1993. Overproduction and purification of σ^{32}, the *E. coli* heat shock transcription factor. *Protein Expression Purif.* **4:** 425–433.

Novagen publication. 1995. *pET® System manual*, 5th edition. Novagen, Inc., Madison, Wisconsin.

Ornstein, L. 1964. Disc electrophoresis. I. Background and theory. *Ann. N.Y. Acad. Sci.* **121:** 321–349.

Pace, C.N., F. Vagdos, L. Fee, G. Grimsley, and T. Gray. 1995. How to measure and predict the molar absorption coefficient of a protein. *Protein Science* **4:** 2411–2423.

Pharmacia publication. 1993. *Affinity chromatography: Principles and methods*, pp. 26–30. Pharmacia LKB Biotechnology, Piscataway, New Jersey.

Scopes, R. 1974. Measurement of protein by spectrophotometry at 205 nm. *Anal. Biochem.* **59:** 277–282.

Studier, W., A. Rosenberg, J. Dunn, and J. Dubendorff. 1990. Use of T7 RNA polymerase to direct expression of cloned genes. *Methods Enzymol.* **185:** 60–89.

Tandon, S. and P.M. Horowitz. 1987. Detergent-assisted refolding of guanidinium chloride-denatured rhodanese. *J. Biol. Chem.* **262:** 4486–4491.

Thompson, N.E., D.B. Aronson, and R.R. Burgess. 1990. Purification of eukaryotic RNA polymerase II by immunoaffinity chromatography. *J. Biol. Chem.* **265:** 7069–7077.

Thompson, N.E., D.A. Hager, and R.R. Burgess. 1992. Isolation and characterization of a polyol-responsive monoclonal antibody useful for gentle purification of *E. coli* RNA polymerase. *Biochemistry* **31:** 7003–7008.

UNIT IV

Solubilization and Purification of the Rat Liver Insulin Receptor

Cell surface proteins are important for transmitting information from the outside to the inside of cells and for maintaining membrane potential. To understand the mechanisms by which membrane proteins accomplish these functions, it is often necessary to know the structures of these proteins. Purifying membrane proteins is a prerequisite to studying their structures and functions. A specific membrane protein usually constitutes less than 0.1% of the total amount of membrane protein. Their low abundance makes the isolation of membrane proteins a major task. Purification of membrane proteins is further complicated by the fact that these molecules are embedded in phospholipid bilayers and so must be solubilized from the membranes. Therefore, selecting a detergent that will solubilize the protein without denaturing it is a crucial step for membrane protein purification. There are now a variety of detergents for solubilizing membrane proteins. The amount and type of detergent need to be carefully selected for each individual membrane protein. After solubilization, most membrane proteins can be purified by the techniques used to purify soluble proteins. However, because of the low abundance of most membrane proteins, a membrane protein is seldom purified without affinity chromatography with a specific ligand or a specific inhibitor.

GENERAL STRATEGY

In this unit, we describe the purification of insulin receptors from rat liver as an example of the isolation of a low-abundance membrane protein. With any protein purification scheme, one needs a specific assay to follow the protein of interest throughout the purification steps. Here we use a simple two-point insulin binding assay that works with both crude membranes and detergent-solubilized receptors. First, plasma membranes are purified from rat liver by sucrose density gradient centrifugation. This yields a highly enriched plasma-membrane fraction that is used for affinity labeling of the insulin receptor as well as insulin binding. The plasma membranes are then solubilized in Triton X-100. The detergent extract is passed through a wheat germ agglutinin (WGA)-agarose column, which binds glycoproteins rich in terminal sialic acid and N-acetylglucosamine residues, including the insulin receptor. After the WGA column is washed, the bound glycoproteins are eluted with a competing sugar, N-acetylglucosamine, and the fractions are assayed for insulin binding and protein content. This step provides a partially purified (~10–20-fold) fraction that can be used for insulin-stimulated autophosphorylation experiments. The fractions with the highest insulin binding activity are pooled and applied to an insulin-agarose affinity column. The insulin receptors are eluted from this column by changing the detergent from Triton X-100 to octyl β-glucoside, which dissociates the insulin-receptor complex without denaturing the receptors (Ridge et al. 1988). Then, the column fractions are assayed for insulin binding to identify the peak of insulin-receptor elution. The column fractions are also analyzed by sodium dodecyl sulfate–polyacrylamide gel electrophoresis (SDS-PAGE) and silver staining. This isolation method yields an insulin receptor fraction purified 2000–3000-fold. A flow-chart illustrating the purification strategies employed in this unit is shown in Figure 1.

Most of the techniques described in this unit are generally applicable to the purification of other membrane receptors and perhaps other membrane proteins as well. The most important step is finding a detergent that will solubilize the protein without compromising its activity. Guidelines for selecting and using detergents for membrane-protein solubilization are included in the text.

INSULIN RECEPTOR

The insulin receptor is a heterotetrameric membrane protein composed of two identical α-subunits that bind insulin and two identical β-subunits that span the membrane. After insulin binds to the extracellular α-subunit of the receptor, the protein kinase activity of the β-subunit is activated. How an interaction on the outside of a cell is transmitted through the single membrane domain in the lipid bilayer is unknown. There is evidence that the protein kinase activity of the insulin receptor is essential for the physiological consequences of extracellular insulin action, which include stimulation of glucose up-

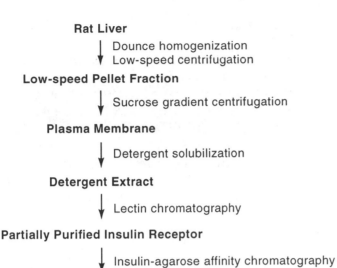

Rat Liver

↓ Dounce homogenization
↓ Low-speed centrifugation

Low-speed Pellet Fraction

↓ Sucrose gradient centrifugation

Plasma Membrane

↓ Detergent solubilization

Detergent Extract

↓ Lectin chromatography

Partially Purified Insulin Receptor

↓ Insulin-agarose affinity chromatography

Purified Insulin Receptor

Receptor Characterization

(1) Cross-linking of insulin receptors with [^{125}I]insulin
(2) Ligand-stimulated receptor autophosphorylation
(3) Receptor glycosylation analysis

Figure 1
Flowchart for the purification of insulin receptor from rat liver.

take, glycogen synthesis, and thymidine incorporation into DNA. Purification of the insulin receptor has allowed detailed biochemical studies of the tyrosine kinase activity of the receptor as well as its molecular cloning. The precise details of insulin action via the receptor are still emerging.

In this unit, we purify the insulin receptor from rat liver plasma membrane and characterize its properties, which include insulin binding, insulin-stimulated receptor autophosphorylation of the β-subunit, cross-linking of insulin to the insulin receptor α-subunit, and receptor glycosylation. The insulin receptor was selected as an example of membrane protein purification for the following reasons. First, the insulin receptor is a well-known hormone receptor. It possesses the hormone-binding properties and ligand-dependent tyrosine kinase activity typical of growth-hormone receptors. Second, it is one of the best studied receptors in terms of purification. The purification scheme for the insulin receptor was developed and improved over the past 20 years. As a result, it is now possible routinely to isolate the insulin receptor in a highly purified and active form. The procedures used for the solubilization and purification of the insulin receptor may represent one of the "optimized" conditions for most membrane proteins.

Insulin receptors are present in all mammalian (and many non-mammalian) cells, although their abundance varies widely. Rat liver is a convenient source for the insulin receptor as it is present at approximately 0.2 pmol/mg of membrane protein. Other good sources for insulin receptors include human placenta (from which the receptor has been cloned) and cell lines overexpressing insulin receptors. The advantage of liver as the starting material is that a protein highly homologous to the insulin receptor, insulin-like growth factor-1 receptor, is expressed at a negligible level.

Isolation of Plasma Membranes from Rat Liver

•

INTRODUCTION

In this experiment, we describe a procedure for the preparation of plasma membranes from rat liver that is adapted from Neville (1968). The rat livers are homogenized in a hypotonic buffer containing 1 mM $CaCl_2$ to enhance aggregation of plasma membranes (Ray 1970). The large membrane pieces, together with unbroken cells and nuclei, are then collected by low-speed centrifugation. The pellets are resuspended in a sucrose solution and then subjected to sucrose density gradient centrifugation. The liver plasma membranes are removed from the top of the sucrose gradient, resuspended in buffer, and subjected to centrifugation to remove the sucrose. This method yields a highly purified preparation of liver plasma membranes, as judged by biochemical, enzymatic, and electron microscopic analysis (Ray 1970), with good recovery. Approximately 100 mg of plasma membrane protein can be obtained from one rat liver, which weighs approximately 25 g. The total amount of protein in the plasma membrane preparation is determined before detergent solubilization.

Before describing the procedure, we discuss some of the general problems of membrane protein purification. For a more extensive description of protein purification, the reader is referred to Deutscher (1990).

Use of Protease Inhibitors

A crucial aspect to be considered in any protein isolation protocol is how to control the activity of the cellular proteases liberated upon homogenization of the cells or tissues. Since most proteins are present in very low abundance, any proteolytic degradation of the target protein will make the purification even more difficult or impossible. Therefore, it is necessary to inhibit endogenous protease activity as much as possible. There are a number of general precautions that can minimize the adverse effects of endogenous proteases on the protein being isolated (for a good overview, see Beynon and Bond 1989).

pH effects.   Many cellular proteases are only maximally active at the relatively acidic pH of the lysosome. Maintaining the pH of the isolation buffer at neutral values will therefore help minimize protease activity.

Temperature.   In general, performing the isolation protocol at temperatures near 4°C will reduce endogenous protease activity. It should be noted, however, that a small number of proteins are destabilized at low temperature, and therefore activity-based purification schemes will show loss of activity due to temperature alone.

Protease inhibitors.   Protease inhibitors are by far the most important tools we have to control undesirable proteolysis. The following are some general guidelines to aid in the selection and use of commercially available protease inhibitors. Proteases can be divided into four major groups according to the functional groups in their active sites: serine proteases, thiol proteases, metalloproteases, and acid proteases. Accordingly, protease inhibitors can be categorized into four groups (see Table 1). Some have very broad inhibitory actions within a class of proteases; for example, EDTA inhibits a large number of metallo-proteases. In contrast, other protease inhibitors, such as trypsin inhib-

Table 1 Commonly Used Protease Inhibitors

Inhibitor	Class	Proteases inhibited	Soluble in	Effective concentration
Aprotinin	serine	trypsin, plasmin, kallikrein	H_2O	1–2 µg/ml
Benzamidine	serine	trypsin	H_2O	15 µg/ml
EDTA	metallo	many metallo-proteases	H_2O	1 mM
Leupeptin	serine and thiol	papain, plasmin, cathepsin B, trypsin	H_2O	1–2 µg/ml
PMSF [a]	serine and thiol	chymotrypsin, plasmin, kallikrein, thrombin, trypsin	DMSO	0.1–1.0 mM
Pepstatin	acid	cathepsin D, pepsin, renin, chymosin	methanol	1 µg/ml

[a]PMSF (phenylmethylsulfonyl fluoride) has a short half-life (only a few minutes) in buffer. A stock solution of 100 mM PMSF in DMSO (dimethyl sulfoxide) should be made and diluted into buffer immediately before use.

itor, have a very narrow specificity. In a typical cell or tissue homogenate, it is safe to assume that proteases of all four classes are present and, consequently, one needs to use a combination of inhibitors to prevent proteolysis of the target protein.

Although no single inhibitor can inhibit all four classes of proteases, one can prepare a protease inhibitor cocktail that has sufficiently broad specificity to limit protease activities to an acceptable level. Often, prior knowledge of protease activity in a given tissue or cell can be obtained from the literature and so specific inhibitors can be chosen. It is dangerous to assume from a given isolation protocol that a given inhibitor mixture will be adequate to protect your protein. Conversely, it is not wise to add every protease inhibitor available in the hope that they will prevent proteolysis. Not only is this approach wasteful and expensive, but it can also create problems in measuring the activity of the protein being isolated. Some inhibitors that we have found to be effective are shown in Table 1.

Selecting protease inhibitors by empirical methods is time consuming and costly. A more rational approach is to use a protease activity detection kit (e.g., from Boehringer Mannheim Corp.). This kit allows one to assess the level of endogenous protease activity in a tissue or cell homogenate before beginning large-scale protein purification. Furthermore, the kit can be used to determine the most effective protease inhibitor cocktail to combat the proteases detected in the homogenate. There is also a batch or column procedure kit that uses immobilized α_2-macroglobulin, a general endoprotease inhibitor, to remove many proteases from cell homogenates (Boehringer Mannheim Corp.).

Sucrose Density Gradient Centrifugation

In isolating insulin receptors from rat liver, purified plasma membranes are used as a starting material. This procedure involves the use of a sucrose density gradient to separate cellular membranes and organelles. This is a common approach for isolating membranes. The concentration of sucrose is usually expressed as w/w%. For example, to prepare a 44% sucrose solution, add 44 g of sucrose to 56 g (56 ml) of distilled H_2O. This simple procedure is usually good enough for membrane isolation. To be more accurate, one would need a refractometer because sucrose can contain variable amounts of water that would give lower than expected concentrations. Refractometers are available from several commercial suppliers. Some instruments have multiple scales that can read % solutions directly. For those that do not, the refractive index data can be converted to % solution by using tables in the *CRC Handbook of Chemistry and Physics* (Weast et al. 1986).

● ───

Neville's Procedure for the Isolation of Liver Plasma Membranes

MATERIALS AND EQUIPMENT

Powdered rat liver (~25 g; keep frozen until use)

> **Note:** Human placenta is an excellent source of insulin receptors. Unfortunately, researchers at institutions not affiliated with a medical center may have difficulty obtaining placentas.

Dounce homogenizer (glass; 15-ml) with pestles A and B
Cheesecloth
Centrifuge bottles (250-ml)
Refractometer (No. 13-947; Fisher Scientific or any other brand)
SW-28 rotor and thin-wall polyallomer SW-28 tubes

REAGENTS

Solution A
Sucrose (69% [w/w] and 42.3% [w/w])
Solution B
(For recipes, see Preparation of Reagents, pp. 337–343.)

PROCEDURE

This procedure is adapted from Neville (1968). *Perform all steps at 4ºC.*

1. Place approximately 6 g (about one quarter) of the powdered liver in a medium-sized glass (15-ml) Dounce homogenizer. Add 8 ml of ice-cold solution A and homogenize the liver on ice with eight strokes using the loose pestle B. Go slowly so as not to splatter the homogenate. Add the homogenate to 500 ml of solution A on ice. Repeat the procedure with the remaining 18 g of liver in three batches, adding the homogenates to the same 500 ml of solution A. Stir the final mixture for 3 minutes. Filter it through two layers of cheesecloth into a 2-liter flask.

    > **Note:** Twisting the pestle is of little use; up and down strokes provide the shearing force to homogenize the tissue. If the pestle gets very hard to move, remove it slowly and wipe with a tissue to remove any strips of connective tissue on the ball of the pestle. Do not apply downward force to an unsupported homogenizer or it will break. Hold the homogenizer firmly in one hand while supporting it in an ice bucket. Avoid making bubbles in the homogenate.

2. Place the filtered homogenate into six 250-ml centrifuge bottles and spin them at 1500g (3200 rpm in JA-14 rotor) for 10 minutes at 4°C. Using a suction apparatus, apply gentle suction to remove the supernatant solution but do not disturb the loose pellets. Pour the pellets into a 15-ml Dounce homogenizer on ice.

3. Homogenize the pellets with three gentle strokes using the loose pestle B. Measure the volume of the homogenate.

4. Pour the homogenate into a beaker. Add an equal volume of 69% (w/w) sucrose. Mix by stirring on a stirring plate until no schlieren patterns are visible. Check the sucrose concentration of the solution in the refractometer. Adjust with H_2O or 69% sucrose until the sucrose-homogenate mixture contains 44% (w/w) sucrose (refractive index = 1.4076).

    Note: Mix the homogenate well between refractometer readings.

5. Pour 20 ml of the homogenate into each of several SW-28 tubes.

6. Carefully overlay each aliquot of the homogenate with 10 ml of ice-cold 42.3% (w/w) sucrose (refractive index = 1.4042).

7. Balance the tubes by adding ice-cold 42.3% (w/w) sucrose.

8. Load the tubes into a cold SW-28 rotor and spin them at 25,000 rpm (90,000g) for 2 hours. Check the vacuum grease on the O-rings to make sure there are no leaks in the rotor.

9. Remove the 2–4-mm layer of membranes floating at the top of each tube with a spatula and transfer them to a single SW-28 tube. Fill the tube with solution B and mix gently. Spin the mixture at 25,000 rpm for 30 minutes at 4°C to collect the membranes. This step is to remove sucrose. Remove the supernatant and add 3 ml of solution B to the pellet. Gently homogenize the pellet in a 15-ml Dounce homogenizer using pestle A, and distribute the suspension in 0.25-ml aliquots in microcentrifuge tubes. Freeze at –20°C.

Alternative Procedure for the Isolation of a Crude Membrane Fraction from Tissues

Although the procedure described by Neville (1968) is good for isolating rat liver plasma membranes, it may not be suitable for isolating membranes from other tissues. Here we describe a procedure for preparing a crude membrane fraction from other tissues.

EQUIPMENT

Dounce homogenizer (glass; 15-ml) with pestle A

REAGENT

Homogenization buffer
(For recipe, see Preparation of Reagents, pp. 337–343.)

PROCEDURE

Perform all steps at 0–4ºC.

1. Mince the tissue in ice-cold homogenization buffer to remove any blood. Rinse the tissue pieces with homogenization buffer and allow them to settle on ice. Repeat the mincing until the tissue is in 1-mm^3 pieces with no visible blood.

2. Add five parts buffer to one part tissue (v/v) and homogenize the tissue in a 15-ml glass Dounce homogenizer on ice with 10–20 strokes using pestle A.

3. Spin the homogenate at 600*g* for 10 minutes at 4ºC. The pellet contains unbroken cells and nuclei, and the supernatant contains cellular membranes, mitochondria, and cytosol. Discard the pellet.

4. Spin the supernatant at 8000*g* for 10 minutes at 4ºC to pellet the mitochondria. Discard the pellet.

5. Spin the supernatant in a fixed-angle rotor at 100,000*g* for 20 minutes at 4ºC. Discard the supernatant.

6. Resuspend the pellet in homogenization buffer. Homogenize in a small Dounce homogenizer, and spin the mixture again at 100,000g for 20 minutes at 4°C. Discard the supernatant.

7. Thoroughly rehomogenize the pellet in a small volume of appropriate buffer.

8. Take a small aliquot for protein determination. The crude membranes can be stored at –85°C after rapid freezing in a dry ice/ethanol bath.

● ———

Determination of Protein Concentration in the Presence of Interfering Substances

Traditionally, protein concentration was determined using Folin-Ciocalteau reagent according to the procedure of Lowry and co-workers (Lowry et al. 1951). However, salt or detergent in the sample interferes with this method. A modified procedure that partially overcomes these problems was described by Peterson (1977). In the Peterson assay, proteins are first precipitated with deoxycholate and trichloroacetic acid. This step gives rapid and almost quantitative isolation of soluble and membrane proteins from interfering substances, even in very dilute solutions (<1 µg/ml). Subsequently, the protein concentration is determined by the sequential addition of reagent A (a solution containing copper sulfate, potassium tartrate, sodium carbonate, and sodium dodecyl sulfate [SDS]) and reagent B (diluted Folin-Ciocalteau reagent). Including SDS in reagent A alleviates possible interference by nonionic and cationic detergent and lipid and also provides conditions for rapid denaturation of membrane and proteolipid proteins (Peterson 1977). The drawback of this procedure is that it requires more steps and takes longer to perform than the fast, dye-binding assay.

Several companies sell protein-binding dyes for determining protein concentration. Many of these dyes are compatible with certain amounts of salts, buffers, and detergents. These dye-binding procedures usually involve few steps and so are fast. They have therefore become popular for protein determination. However, during the purification of a membrane protein, the detergent concentrations vary during the various solubilization and purification steps. In addition, samples may become very dilute as the purification progresses. The latter situation requires that a large sample volume be used for protein determination, and the amount of detergent in this large volume may exceed the limit of a specific dye-binding assay. To avoid this problem toward the end of a purification, it is important to select a protein measurement method that can be used throughout the entire purification procedure. Although it is more tedious than the dye-binding assay, Peterson's method is commonly used during the purification of membrane proteins. The Peterson protein assay is generally suitable for measuring 1–50 µg of protein in a total volume of 1 ml. If necessary, this protocol can be scaled down to a smaller volume (e.g., 0.1 ml) to increase the sensitivity to the range of 0.1–10 µg (see below). A protocol for Peterson's protein assay is given below.

MATERIALS

Bovine serum albumin (BSA)
Sodium deoxycholate (0.15%)
Trichloroacetic acid (TCA; 72%)

REAGENTS

Reagent A
Reagent B
(For recipes, see Preparation of Reagents, pp. 337–343.)

PROCEDURE

1. Prepare a 1 mg/ml solution of BSA in distilled H_2O. Freeze aliquots at $-20°C$ for future assays.

2. To prepare a standard curve, set up the following mixtures in 1.5-ml microcentrifuge tubes:

BSA (1 mg/ml) (μl)	Distilled H_2O (μl)	Final amount of protein (μg)
0	1000	0
2.5	997.5	2.5
5	995	5
10	990	10
20	980	20
40	960	40

3. Dilute the membrane samples with distilled H_2O (1:10) and take 5-μl, 10-μl, and 20-μl aliquots for assay. For solubilized membrane samples and WGA column fractions, use 10 μl of the undiluted sample. Include a blank tube with 10 μl of buffer to measure the absorbance of the buffer components.

    Note: Steps 4–8 can be omitted if interfering substances are absent, in negligible quantities, or appropriately controlled for. Under these circumstances, dilute each sample to 0.4 ml with distilled H_2O.

4. Dilute each membrane sample to 1 ml with distilled H_2O.

5. Add 0.1 ml of 0.15% sodium deoxycholate to each tube. Mix, and allow the solutions to stand for 10 minutes at room temperature.

6. Add 0.1 ml of 72% TCA to each tube. Mix, and spin in a microcentrifuge for 15 minutes at room temperature.

7. Discard the supernatants. These can be removed efficiently by suction.

8. Add 0.4 ml of distilled H_2O to each tube.

9. Add 0.4 ml of reagent A to each tube. Vortex, and allow the solutions to stand for 10 minutes at room temperature.

10. Add 0.2 ml of reagent B to each tube and mix immediately. Incubate for 30 minutes at room temperature.

11. Read the absorbance at 750 nm.

    Note: Read the absorbance within 2 hours unless standard protein samples are included with the group of tubes. Color loss is 1–2% per hour at room temperature. This procedure can easily be converted to a microassay by scaling down steps 8–10 tenfold to increase the sensitivity. Steps 1–7 remain the same as in the standard assay, except that the total protein per sample in the standard curve should be reduced to 0.1–10 µg.

12. Plot the amounts of protein in the standard tubes versus the absorbance at 750 nm to obtain a standard curve.

13. Compare the absorbance of each sample at 750 nm with the standard curve to obtain the amount of protein in the sample.

•

Determination of the Number
of Insulin Receptors in a Membrane

The ability of insulin to bind to its receptor with high affinity (K_D ~10^{-9} M) allows one to estimate the number of insulin receptors even in fairly crude preparations. Precise quantitation of insulin receptor binding properties requires a relatively elaborate and time-consuming competition binding assay (see Experiment 2). Here we describe a simple, two-point binding assay that is useful for estimating the number of insulin receptors in membrane samples and WGA column fractions. Samples are incubated with trace amounts of [^{125}I]insulin with or without a saturating concentration of unlabeled insulin. The radioactive insulin alone gives the total insulin binding, whereas the radioactive plus unlabeled insulin gives the nonspecific binding. Subtracting the nonspecific binding from the total binding gives specific insulin binding. The first binding assay should be performed with a purified plasma membrane preparation to determine the quality of the starting material. Typically, the ratio of specific to nonspecific binding is 2 or 3 to 1.

MATERIALS

Bovine serum albumin (BSA; 1%)
Porcine insulin (17.5 µM [0.1 mg/ml] in 0.001 N HCl) (e.g., Sigma Chemical Co. I 3505)
[^{125}I]Insulin (receptor grade) (DuPont NEN® NEX 196) (2200 µCi/nmol; 35.5 nM)

REAGENT

Binding buffer (for two-point binding assay)
(For recipe, see Preparation of Reagents, pp. 337–343.)

SAFETY NOTE

• The isotope ^{125}I accumulates in the thyroid and is a potential health hazard. Wear gloves when handling radioactive substances. Consult the institutional environmental health and safety office for further guidance in the appropriate use of radioactive materials.

PROCEDURE

1. Add 40 μl of rat liver membranes (20 mg/ml) to each of two micro-centrifuge tubes (labeled #1 and #2).

2. Add 30 μl of 1% BSA to each tube.

3. Add 140 μl of binding buffer to each tube.

4. Add 60 μl of 17.5 μM porcine insulin to tube #2 (to give a final insulin concentration of 3.5 μM). Add 60 μl of distilled H_2O to tube #1.

5. Add 30 μl of 5 nM [^{125}I]insulin to each tube (to give a final [^{125}I]insulin concentration of 0.5 nM).

6. Incubate the tubes on a rotary shaker for 2 hours at room temperature or for 16 hours at 4°C.

7. Spin the tubes in a microcentrifuge for 20 minutes. Remove as much of the supernatant as possible.

   Note: The pellet can be washed now to remove residual free ligand if the ligand has a high affinity for receptor (e.g., $K_D = 10^{-11}$). However, washing may partially dissociate the complex if the ligand has only a low or moderate affinity for its receptor.

8. Count the radioactivity in the tubes in a γ-counter. Subtract the cpm in tube #2 (nonspecific and trapped counts) from the cpm in tube #1 (total cpm) to give the specific cpm.

INSULIN-BINDING CALCULATION

The standard formula for hormone-receptor interaction is usually expressed as

$$[H] + [R] \rightleftarrows [HR]$$

where [H] is the free ligand concentration, [R] is the free receptor concentration, and [HR] is the concentration of the hormone-receptor complex. At equilibrium, the dissociation constant is

$$K_D = \frac{[H]\,[R]}{[HR]}$$

Thus, $[H] = [H]_t - [HR]$ (where $[H]_t$ is the total ligand concentration) and $[R]_t = [R] + [HR]$ (where $[R]_t$ is the total receptor concentration). Rearranging the equation for K_D yields

$$K_D = \frac{[H] \, ([R]_t - [HR])}{[HR]}$$

For the two-point binding assay, one can assume that the rat liver insulin receptor has a K_D of 10^{-9} M. One then measures [HR] and [H] to calculate the total receptor concentration, $[R]_t$.

$$[HR] = \frac{\text{specific binding cpm}}{\text{total cpm in tube}} \times \text{ insulin concentration in tube}$$

$$[H] = (1 - \frac{\text{specific binding cpm}}{\text{total cpm in tube}}) \times \text{ insulin concentration in tube}$$

$$[R]_t = \frac{[HR] \, (K_D + [H])}{[H]}$$

amount of insulin bound = $[R]_t \times$ volume

To determine specific activity, one can either divide "amount of insulin bound" by the amount of protein in the sample or divide $[R]_t$ by the concentration of protein in the tube. The result of this calculation is usually expressed as pmol of insulin bound/mg of protein.

•

Determination of the Affinity of Insulin Receptor for Insulin

To use this method of estimating binding for insulin receptors in tissues other than liver, it is necessary first to determine the K_D. This is usually done by performing a cold-ligand displacement experiment, in which a constant amount of radioactively labeled ligand is displaced by increasing concentrations of unlabeled ligand. The binding data are then transformed into concentrations by dividing the specific cpm at each dilution of ligand by the specific activity of the ligand mixture (labeled and unlabeled) at each concentration of ligand. The data obtained by this method can be plotted or analyzed by any number of binding programs to calculate B_{max} and K_D (Munson and Rodbard 1980; Klotz 1982). Here is an example of how to determine the affinity of insulin receptor for insulin.

MATERIALS

[^{125}I]Insulin (receptor grade) (DuPont NEN® NEX 196)
Porcine insulin (e.g., Sigma Chemical Co. I 3505)
Bovine serum albumin (BSA; 1%)

REAGENT

Binding buffer (for cold-ligand displacement experiment)
(For recipe, see Preparation of Reagents, pp. 337–343.)

SAFETY NOTE

- The isotope ^{125}I accumulates in the thyroid and is a potential health hazard. Wear gloves when handling radioactive substances. Consult the institutional environmental health and safety office for further guidance in the appropriate use of radioactive materials.

PROCEDURE

1. Set up the following reactions in microcentrifuge tubes:

Tube no.	Membranes (20 mg per ml) (μl)	[125I] insulin (5 nM) (μl)	Porcine insulin (20 nM) (μl)	Porcine insulin (600 nM) (μl)	Binding buffer (μl)	1% BSA (μl)	Total insulin conc. (nM)[a]
1	40	30	0	0	200	30	0.50
2	40	30	5	0	195	30	0.83
3	40	30	20	0	180	30	1.83
4	40	30	60	0	140	30	4.50
5	40	30	0	5	195	30	10.50
6	40	30	0	10	190	30	20.50
7	40	30	0	100	100	30	200.50

[a]Total ligand concentrations should include several concentrations above and below K_D.

2. Incubate the tubes on a shaker for 2 hours at room temperature.

3. Spin the tubes in a microcentrifuge for 20 minutes. Remove the supernatants.

4. Count the radioactivity in the tubes in a γ-counter. Subtract the cpm in tube 7 (nonspecific and trapped cpm) from the cpm in tubes 1–6 to determine the specific cpm.

5. Divide the specific cpm in each tube by the total cpm to give the fraction of insulin bound to the membranes. Multiply this value by the concentration of insulin in each tube to give the concentration of the ligand-receptor complex ([HR], also called [B], which stands for bound ligand).

6. Determine the free ligand concentration ([H], also called [F], which stands for free ligand) by subtracting [HR] from the concentration of insulin in the tube.

7. At this point, one can analyze the results using several approaches. If a computer program is available, it is preferable to fit the data directly to the equation

$$[HR] = \frac{[R]_t \, [H]}{K_D + [H]}$$

One can also analyze the data by plotting [HR] versus log[H]. This plot should give a sigmoidal curve. The total number of receptors and K_D can then be obtained from the maximal value of [HR] and the inflection point, respectively (Klotz 1982). A third approach is to use a Scatchard plot to analyze the data. A Scatchard plot is a graph of

$$\frac{[HR]}{[H]} \text{ (or } \frac{[B]}{[F]}) \quad \text{versus} \quad [HR] \text{ (or } [B])$$

If there is only one type of binding site, this graph gives a straight line. To make a Scatchard plot, first determine [HR]/[H] for every [H]. Then, plot [HR]/[H] versus [HR]. The slope of this line is $-1/K_D$, and the abscissa intercept is the total number of receptors ($[R]_t$). If there is more than one kind of binding site and they have different affinities, the Scatchard plot will be a curve instead of a straight line.

Solubilization of the Insulin Receptor from Membranes

• —————————————————————————————

INTRODUCTION

Solubilization of proteins from membranes with detergent is the most critical step in membrane protein purification. In this experiment, the purified plasma membranes from Experiment 1 are solubilized in the nonionic detergent Triton X-100. A detergent extract is made by ultracentrifugation of the protein-detergent mixture, and the binding of insulin to the solubilized insulin receptor is determined to assess the activity of insulin receptors at this stage. Before describing the protocol, it is worthwhile discussing general guidelines for choosing detergents.

Detergents are amphipathic molecules that form micelles rather than bilayers in aqueous solution. In a micelle, the hydrophobic part of the detergent molecule is removed from contact with water (Tanford 1973). Detergents are useful for solubilizing membrane proteins because they disrupt the structure of the phospholipid bilayer and replace some of the phospholipids that are in contact with the transmembrane regions of membrane proteins. In this way, a protein that is an intrinsic part of a membrane can be solubilized as a protein-lipid-micelle complex. The aim of solubilization is to allow purification of an active protein, so the best detergent to use is one that allows the solubilized protein to retain its activity and be purified. The literature (e.g., Helenius et al. 1979) and catalogs of biochemical suppliers indicate that a large number of diverse detergents are available for the solubilization of membrane proteins. However, they are not universally applicable, and one must consider the specific properties of a particular detergent when devising a strategy for membrane protein solubilization.

Properties of Detergents

Detergents have three distinguishing characteristics: the structure of the molecule, the size of the micelle, and the critical micellar concentration (cmc), that is, the concentration above which micelles form.

Structure. The structures of some common detergents (Hjelmeland and Chrambach 1984; Hjelmeland 1986) are shown in Figure 2. It is evident that both nonpolar and polar parts of the detergents are highly variable. The nonpolar parts can be: (i) steroidal and relatively rigid (as in cholate, CHAPS, BigCHAP, and digitonin); (ii) composed of alkyl chains of 8–14 carbons (as in octyl glucoside, dodecyl maltoside, Lubrol PX, and Zwittergent 3–14); or (iii) a substituted phenyl group (as in Triton X-100). The polar regions can be: (i) a carboxylic acid with negative charge (as in cholate); (ii) zwitterionic-substituted sulfobetaines (as in CHAPS and Zwittergent 3–14); (iii) nonionic sugar derivatives such as glucose (as in octyl glucoside and BigCHAP), maltose (as in dodecyl maltoside), or a pentasaccharide (as in digitonin); or (iv) poly(ethoxy)ethanol (as in Lubrol PX and Triton X-100). The shape of the molecule determines the packing arrangement and thus the size of the micelle; the interaction between the polar groups determines the cmc.

cmc. Detergent molecules exist as monomers and micelles in aqueous solutions. The micelles are aggregates of detergent molecules in which the hydrophobic parts of the molecules face the center and the polar groups face the outside. At low detergent concentrations, only monomers exist. As the concentration of detergent increases, micelles start to form and exist in equilibrium with the monomers. The concentration above which micelles start to form is called the cmc. Beyond the cmc, most of the excess detergent will form micelles rather than monomers. Therefore, a detergent with a high cmc has a high concentration of monomer in a monomer/micelle mixture. This is desirable when one wants to dialyze away the detergent or replace one detergent with another. In dialysis, only monomers and very small micelles can diffuse across the membrane. When monomers are removed by dialysis, new equilibria between monomers and micelles are established when the micelles disaggregate to maintain the monomer concentration near the cmc. This dynamic equilibrium continues until no micelles are left. Since the efficiency of dialysis depends on the concentration gradient across the membrane, detergents with a higher monomer concentration will dialyze faster. This is why detergents with high cmc values are easier to remove by dialysis than detergents with low cmc values.

In general, detergents with a cholanoic acid group (e.g., cholate, CHAPS, and BigCHAP) have small micellar sizes and cmc values above 2 mM (see Table 2). These detergents have the advantage that they can be removed readily by dialysis and usually do not cause loss of activity of the proteins. The use of digitonin is complicated by the impurity of the preparation; although it has large micelles, its cmc is not known. Detergents with alkyl chains at least 12 carbons long (e.g.,

Zwittergent 3–14, dodecyl maltoside, and Lubrol PX) have large micellar sizes (30,000–64,000 daltons) and small cmc values (0.1–0.3 mM), irrespective of the structure of the polar part of the molecule.

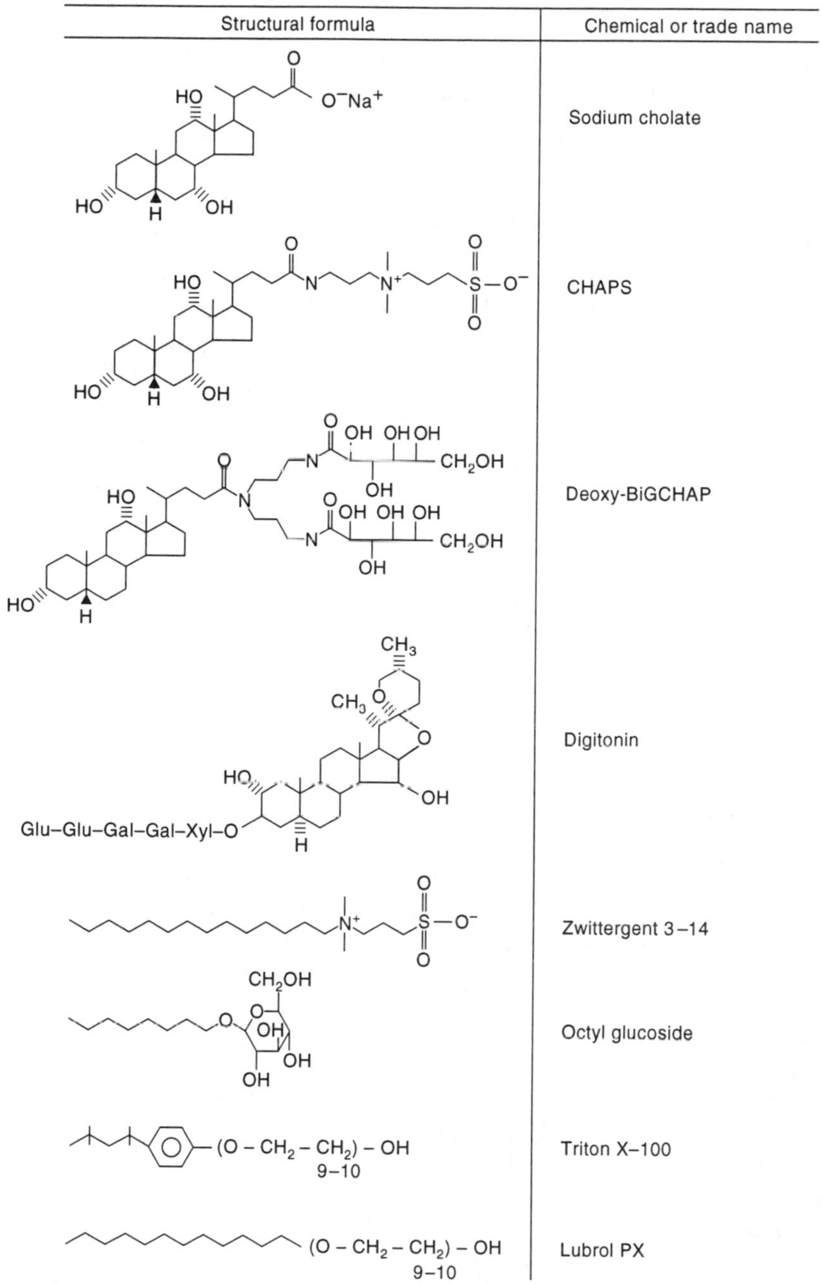

Structural formula	Chemical or trade name
	Sodium cholate
	CHAPS
	Deoxy-BiGCHAP
	Digitonin
	Zwittergent 3–14
	Octyl glucoside
	Triton X–100
	Lubrol PX

Figure 2

Structures and conventional names of detergents useful for the solubilization of membrane proteins. (Reproduced, with permission of Academic Press, Inc., from Hjelmeland and Chrambach 1984.)

Table 2 Properties of Detergents

Detergent	Molecular weight	Aggregation[a] number	cmc[b] (mM)
Nonionic			
BigCHAP	862	10	3.4
Brij 35	1200 (n=23)	40	0.09
C12E8	540	120–125	0.07–0.1
C12E9	583	–	0.07–0.1
Decyl-β-glucoside	322	–	2–3
Decyl-β-maltoside	483	–	1.6
Deoxy-BigCHAP	862	8–16	1.1–1.4
Digitonin	1229	60	–
Dodecyl-β-glucoside	348	130	0.13
Dodecyl maltoside	511	98	0.1–0.6
Lubrol PX	582	110	0.1
Nonidet P-40	606	149	0.05–0.3
Octyl-β-glucoside	292	27	20–25
Octyl-β-maltoside	455	–	–
Octyl-β-thiogalactoside	308	–	–
Octyl-β-thioglucoside	308	–	9
PLURONIC F-127	12,600	–	–
Triton X-100	625	100–155	0.2–0.9
Tween-20	1228	–	0.06
Tween-80	1310	58	0.02
Zwitterionic			
CHAPS	615	4–14	6–10
CHAPSO	631	11	8
Zwittergent 3–08	280	–	330
Zwittergent 3–10	308	41	25–40
Zwittergent 3–12	336	55	3.6
Zwittergent 3–14	364	83	0.33
Ionic			
Cholate, Na^+	431	2	9–15
CTAB	365	170	1
Deoxycholate, Na^+	415 (pH >8)	3–12	2–6
Dodecyl sulfate, Na^+	289	62	8.3
Dodecyl sulfate, Li^+	272	–	6–8
Taurocholate, Na^+	538	4	3–11
Taurodeoxycholate, Na^+	522	6	1–4

[a]Average number of monomers in one micelle. The molecular weight of the detergent multiplied by the aggregation number will give the molecular weight of the micelle of that detergent.
[b]cmc varies with salts, salt concentrations, temperature, and pH.

The tetramethylbutylphenyl chain of Triton X-100 is also highly hydrophobic and results in a small cmc (0.2–0.9 mM) and a large micelle size (62,000–100,000 Daltons). These detergents have the disadvantage that they cannot be easily removed by dialysis because the micelle is too large and the cmc is too low for effective removal in a reasonable time. On the other hand, octyl glucoside, which is easily removed by dialysis, has a cmc of 25 mM and a micellar size of 8000 Daltons, consistent with the view that the size of the alkyl chain is the main determinant of the strength of the interaction between the nonpolar chains and thus of the cmc.

Choosing a Detergent

In spite of the substantial amount of information available about the structure of detergents, choosing a detergent for a particular task is still an empirical endeavor. Hjelmeland and Chrambach (1984) have suggested that several different detergents should be screened for their ability to solubilize a protein while preserving its activity. The list of detergents they suggest includes CHAPS, cholate, digitonin, Lubrol PX or $C_{12}E_9$, and an alkyl glucoside. In general, detergents with large cmc values and thus a high concentration of detergent monomer in solution will denature proteins more readily than detergents with small cmc values. Therefore, it is somewhat risky to use detergents like octyl glucoside, sodium dodecyl sulfate, and Zwittergent 3–10. On the other hand, detergents with small cmc values may be unable to solubilize the protein.

When selecting a detergent to solubilize a specific protein, the most important criterion is the ability to solubilize and retain the activity of the specific protein. Other factors may also affect the choice of detergent. If the detergent must be removed after solubilization, for example, if the protein is to be reconstituted into phospholipid vesicles by dialysis, detergents with high cmc values should be used. Triton X-100 and other detergents that have absorbance at 280 nm should be avoided if the protein assay involves reading the absorbance at 280 nm. Charged detergents should be avoided if ion-exchange chromatography or electrophoresis is to be performed.

Solubilization of Membrane with Detergents

For practical purposes, a membrane protein is "solubilized" by detergent if the activity of the protein remains in the supernatant fraction after centrifugation of the detergent/membrane mixture at 100,000g for 1 hour. How much detergent should be used to solubilize a membrane? Membrane solubilization depends on the ratio of nonmonomeric detergent to the lipid and protein components of the membrane (Silvius 1992).

A diagrammatic representation of the solubilization process is shown in Figure 3. At low detergent-to-protein ratios, the detergent monomers partition into the membrane and perturb its structure, causing an increase in permeability. As the ratio increases, the bilayer becomes saturated with detergent, and mixed micelles of detergent, lipid, and protein form. The membrane is entirely in mixed micelles when the detergent-to-protein ratio is between 2 and 4. As the ratio increases further, the system shifts toward a composition of protein-detergent, lipid-detergent, and pure detergent micelles. An idealized profile of the process is shown in Figure 4.

Before applying a detergent to membranes, one must have a reliable assay for soluble membrane protein activity. If the protein is an enzyme, one can use assay procedures similar to those used for membranes except that the assay solution needs to contain a small concentration of detergent. However, the presence of detergent in the solubilized sample may interfere with the methods of detection in the assay. Under such circumstances, previous assay conditions must be modified. If the protein is a membrane receptor, a method for separating the receptor-ligand complex from free ligand in solution needs to

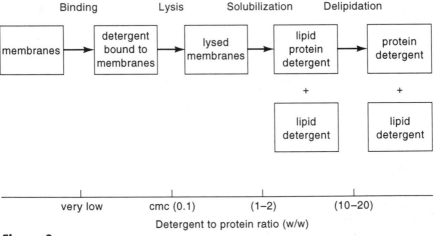

Figure 3
Progressive solubilization of whole membranes to form protein-detergent complexes as a function of the ratio of detergent to protein. (Reproduced, with permission of Academic Press, Inc., from Hjelmeland and Chrambach 1984.)

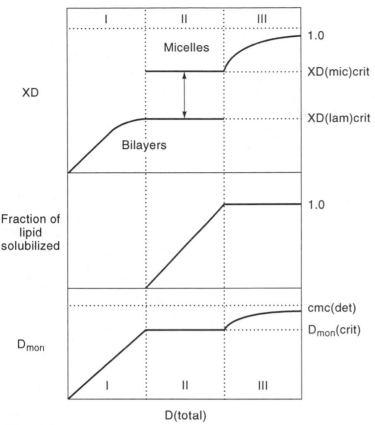

Figure 4

Stages in the solubilization of a homogeneous lipid bilayer by increasing concentrations of a detergent (D[total]). The regions designated I, II, and III correspond respectively to ranges of total detergent concentration in which bilayers only, bilayers and micelles, or micelles only are present. (*Top panel*) Mole fraction(s) of detergent in bilayers XD(lam) and/or micelles XD(mic). (*Middle panel*) Fraction of total lipid incorporated into mixed micelles. (*Bottom panel*) Concentration of monomeric detergent (D_{mon}). For simplicity, the variation of the monomeric detergent concentration with the total detergent concentration in region I is shown as linear but it may also be nonlinear, particularly at higher detergent levels. (Reproduced, with permission, from Silvius 1992 [© Annual Reviews Inc.].)

be determined. Precipitating receptor-ligand complex with polyethylene glycol is a commonly used method in the soluble receptor binding assay. If the protein is an ion transporter, a protocol for reconstituting the transporter into liposomes to measure transport activity may be required before solubilization and purification can take place.

Detergent Exchange

Sometimes it is desirable to change the detergent in a protein-detergent micelle. For instance, solubilization may be most effective with a charged detergent, but a later step in the purification may involve ion-exchange chromatography, which requires an uncharged detergent. There are several ways to accomplish this change (Furth et al. 1984). If the protein (for instance, the insulin receptor) can be absorbed onto an affinity support such as WGA-agarose, the detergents can be exchanged by washing the absorbed protein with two column volumes of buffer containing the new detergent. The eluted protein is equilibrated with the new detergent. Alternatively, the original protein-detergent complex can be loaded onto a sucrose density gradient made with a buffer containing the second detergent and ultracentrifuged in a swinging-bucket rotor at 90,000g for 16 hours. The protein peak collected from the gradient is equilibrated with the second detergent. A third procedure is possible if the protein is in a detergent with a high cmc value and a small micelle size. The protein solution is concentrated with a Centricon cartridge (Amicon, Inc.) of the proper size to allow the micelle of the detergent to pass through the pores. The concentrated solution is then passed through a column of Sephadex G-75 (2 ml) equilibrated with the new detergent. The protein equilibrated with the new detergent appears at the excluded (void) volume of the column.

Impurities in Detergents

Highly purified detergents can be obtained from several sources (e.g., Pierce Chemical Co. and Boehringer Mannheim Corp.) and should be used in preference to unpurified compounds. Nevertheless, even pure preparations of detergents can develop impurities with time.

A frequent problem is the presence of peroxidized compounds in detergents with poly(ethoxy)ethanol groups; these substances can inactivate proteins by direct oxidation or through free-radical formation. Accordingly, it is advisable to store the stock solutions of these detergents under nitrogen. Alkyl glycoside detergents are often contaminated with long-chain alcohols produced by hydrolysis of the glycosidic bond; these can denature proteins. Stock solutions of these detergents should be made just before use. In many cases, detergents are mixtures of homologous molecules; for instance, detergents like polydodecanol contain several alkyl groups (C_8, C_{10}, C_{14}, and C_{16}) in addition to the preponderant C_{12} group, and the length of the poly-(ethoxy)ethanol chain is also variable. As the cmc is related to the length of the alkyl chain, the behavior of these detergents can be quite variable, depending on the composition of the mixture. It is possible to avoid this problem by obtaining or purifying homogeneous species.

Other Things to Keep in Mind When Using Detergents

- After solubilizing a protein with a detergent, always include the same detergent in buffers used during purification to prevent the proteins from aggregating.

- Avoid using purification steps that use hydrophobic interactions as the principle for separation.

- The molecular weight estimated from gel filtration columns is the sum of the molecular weights of the protein plus the detergent micelles. The molecular weight of a detergent micelle can be calculated by multiplying the detergent molecular weight with the aggregation number (see Table 2). Many detergent-protein complexes contain up to 50% detergent by weight, a significant contribution. Calibration of such columns with water-soluble protein standards can lead to erroneous results since these proteins do not interact with the detergent in the same manner as solubilized membrane proteins.

- Solubilization by detergent may change the properties of a protein; for example, the affinity of a receptor for its ligand may be changed or a multimeric complex may be dissociated. Compare the properties of the protein after solubilization with those of the protein in the membrane to make sure that the detergent has not altered the protein.

● ———

Solubilization of the Insulin Receptor and Assessment of Activity

MATERIALS AND EQUIPMENT

Purified rat liver plasma membranes (from Experiment 1)
Ti 70 rotor and polypropylene tubes with caps
Bovine serum albumin (BSA; 1%)
[^{125}I]Insulin (receptor grade) (DuPont NEN® NEX 196)
Porcine insulin (17.5 μM [0.1 mg/ml] in 0.001 N HCl) (e.g., Sigma
     Chemical Co. I 3505)
Bovine γ-globulin (0.4% in solution B) (Miles Laboratories, Inc. 82-
     041-2)
Polyethylene glycol 6000 (20% in H$_2$O)

REAGENTS

Solution B
Solution C
Binding buffer (for solubilized receptor)
(For recipes, see Preparation of Reagents, pp. 337–343.)

PROCEDURE

Solubilization of the Insulin Receptor Using Triton X-100

For results comparing the efficacy of Triton X-100 with various other detergents in solubilizing insulin receptors from rat liver plasma membranes, see Table 3.

1. Mix 100–150 mg of purified rat liver plasma membranes in 10 ml of solution B. Add 4 ml of solution C and incubate for 30 minutes at 4°C.

2. Spin the suspension at 200,000*g* (45,000 rpm in a Ti 70 rotor) for 30 minutes and collect the supernatant with a pasteur pipette, taking care not to disturb the pellet.

   Note: A pellet of Triton X-100-insoluble material is usually present, adhering tightly to the bottom of the tube.

Table 3 **Effects of Various Detergents in Solubilizing Insulin Receptors from Rat Liver Plasma Membranes**

Detergent	Specific activity (pmol insulin bound/mg protein)[a]
Triton X-100	7.0
CHAPS	4.0
Octyl glucoside	3.5
Nonidet P-40	1.7
Deoxycholate, Na+	0.1

The data were generated during the 1995 Cold Spring Harbor Laboratory Protein Purification and Characterization Course (courtesy of A. Ansari, R. Burk, C. Michels, and A. Gravel).
[a]From WGA-agarose column.

Measurement of Insulin Binding to Solubilized Receptors

1. Set up the following reactions in microcentrifuge tubes:

Tube	Binding buffer (μl)	Solubilized receptor (μl)	1% BSA (μl)	[^{125}I]insulin (5 nM) (μl)	Porcine insulin (17.5 μM) (μl)	Distilled H$_2$O (μl)
A	140	40	30	30	–	60
B	140	40	30	30	60	–

The results from tube A give total binding and those from tube B give nonspecific binding. Specific binding = total binding – nonspecific binding.

Note: The receptor grade [^{125}I]insulin (NEX 196) from DuPont NEN has a specific activity of 2200 $\mu Ci/nmol$. The concentration of insulin is 35.5 nM. For this assay, it is necessary to dilute the stock [^{125}I]insulin to 5 nM with binding buffer. The desired final concentration of [^{125}I]insulin in the binding assay for solubilized receptors is 500 pM, which is equivalent to 30 μl of the 5 nM solution in a 300-μl reaction.

2. Incubate these reactions for 16 hours at 4°C or for 2 hours at room temperature.

3. Separate the receptor-bound insulin from free insulin by precipitation. Add 75 μl of 0.4% bovine γ-globulin in solution B and incubate for 5 minutes at 4°C. Add 375 μl of 20% polyethylene glycol 6000 and incubate for 10 minutes at 4°C. Collect the precipitates by spinning the mixtures in a microcentrifuge for 10 minutes. Remove as much of each supernatant as possible and count the radioactivity in the pellets.

Note: Although polyethylene glycol precipitation is a convenient method for measuring insulin-receptor number during purification, it probably underestimates the absolute number of binding sites since only a fraction of the insulin-receptor complex is precipitated (Finn et al. 1984). For determining the affinity of insulin for insulin-receptor, add several concentrations of unlabeled insulin to give final insulin concentrations of 500 pM to 200 nM as described in Experiment 1.

•

Screening Detergents for Membrane Protein Solubilization

Although Triton X-100 is a good detergent for solubilizing insulin receptors from rat liver plasma membranes, it may not be suitable for solubilizing other membrane proteins. Here we describe a strategy for screening detergents to determine which is suitable for solubilizing a particular membrane protein of interest.

PROCEDURE

1. Suspend the membrane preparation in the buffer of choice (e.g., phosphate buffer or HEPES buffer). The concentration of the buffer should be 50 mM and the pH should be close to the pK_a of the buffer. The final protein concentration should be approximately 10 mg/ml. Keep the membrane suspension at 4°C.

2. Make 10% (100 mg/ml) stock solutions of the detergents to be tested. Dilute each detergent stock solution with buffer to obtain the following detergent concentrations: 0.2%, 1%, 2%, and 6%.

   Notes: (i) Digitonin is only soluble up to 4%. (ii) Boehringer Mannheim Corp. has a detergent kit that is a sampler of nine nonionic and three zwitterionic detergents frequently used to purify and analyze membrane proteins.

3. Mix equal volumes of each detergent solution (from step 2) with aliquots of the membrane preparation (from step 1). The final concentration of membrane protein will be 5 mg/ml in each case and the detergent concentrations will be 0.1%, 0.5%, 1%, 3%, and 5%. Also prepare a sample diluted in buffer without detergent. You will thus have tubes containing detergent to protein ratios (i.e., milligram of detergent per milligram of protein) of 0, 0.2, 1, 2, 6, and 10.

4. Stir the mixtures for 1 hour at 4°C.

   Note: Avoid foaming because it may denature the protein.

5. Spin the mixtures at 100,000*g* for 1 hour at 4°C.

6. Transfer the supernatants to clean tubes. Resuspend each pellet in an equal volume of buffer.

7. Assay the activity of the protein in each supernatant and pellet.

   Note: Compare the activity of the protein in the supernatant and pellet to see whether the detergent can solubilize the protein from the membrane as the detergent concentration is increased. The activity should be plotted against the detergent-to-protein ratio.

OPTIMIZING SOLUBILIZATION CONDITIONS

Several results are possible depending on the proteins and the detergents used in the experiment described above. If the activity remains associated with pellet, the detergent cannot solubilize the protein of interest. However, one can take advantage of this situation to remove some unwanted proteins using this detergent. If all of the activity is lost upon solubilization, the detergent causes inactivation of the protein and should not be used. If the soluble activity increases and reaches a plateau as the detergent concentration is increased, the detergent is suitable for solubilizing the protein from the membrane. In this case, one should use a detergent-to-protein ratio in the plateau region for solubilization. If the soluble activity of a protein increases and then decreases as the detergent concentration is increased, the detergent-to-protein ratio that gives the maximal activity should be used for solubilization. The decrease in solubilized activity with a high detergent-to-protein ratio is most likely due to inactivation of the protein by a high concentration of the detergent.

The most important parameter for protein solubilization is the detergent-to-protein ratio rather than the detergent concentration per se. However, this ratio may change slightly depending on protein concentrations. Therefore, one may want to find the optimal detergent to protein ratio for a specific protein concentration and work at this protein concentration.

Other factors besides detergent may also affect the activity during solubilization. For example, a different buffer or addition of protease inhibitors, dithiothreitol, EDTA, or glycerol may help to preserve the activity. However, this must be determined experimentally.

• Experiment 3
Lectin Affinity Chromatography of Solubilized Receptors

INTRODUCTION

After solubilization with Triton X-100, the solubilized proteins are mixed with the lectin wheat germ agglutinin (WGA), which is coupled to agarose beads. A column is poured, washed, loaded, and eluted with the competing sugar N-acetylglucosamine. The WGA column fractions are analyzed for protein content using a micro-protein assay, and the peak protein fractions are pooled for use in further experiments in which WGA-purified insulin receptors are required. The binding of insulin to the WGA column fractions is determined to assess the content of insulin receptors at this stage of the purification.

Lectin Affinity Chromatography

Lectins are sugar-binding proteins. They were first isolated from plants, although their function in plants is still unknown. These proteins have tremendous experimental utility due to their highly specific interactions with glycoconjugates. In addition, many lectins are potent mitogens and activators of the cell cycle. In this experiment, we use lectin affinity chromatography as an initial purification step for the insulin receptor by taking advantage of the capacity of a specific lectin to bind to the oligosaccharide moieties of the receptor. This is an extremely useful technique for nearly all membrane proteins, since, with only a few exceptions, membrane proteins are glycosylated. In the past 20 years, over 100 lectins have been purified and their carbohydrate specificity determined. Table 4 lists the carbohydrate specificity of commonly used lectins. It is now possible to find a lectin that binds to virtually any membrane protein and many cytoplasmic proteins. Coupling lectins to solid phase supports such as agarose provides a convenient method for performing chromatography (Cuatrecasas and Parikh 1972; Fujita-Yamaguchi et al. 1983).

In a typical application, membrane proteins are solubilized with an appropriate detergent and allowed to bind to the immobilized lectin in a batch process or applied directly to a column containing

Table 4 Lectins and Their Carbohydrate Binding Specificities

Lectins	Carbohydrate binding specificity
Concanavalin A (Con A)	α-Man, α-Glc, α-GlcNAc
Wheat germ agglutinin (WGA)	β-GlcNAc, sialic acid
Dolichos biflorus (DBA)	α-GalNAc
Ricinus communis (RCA-I)	β-Gal
Ulex europaeus (UEA-I)	α-fucose
Arachis hypogaea (PNA)	β-Gal
Glycine max (SBA)	α-GalNAc, β-GalNAc
Limulus polyphemus (LPA)	sialic acid
Helix aspersa (HAA)	α-GlcNAc, α-GalNAc

Abbreviations: (Man) mannose; (Glc) glucose; (GlcNAc) *N*-acetylglucosamine; (Gal) galactose; (GalNAc) *N*-acetylgalactosamine

the immobilized lectin. After thorough washing of the lectin column, an eluting sugar is applied, and the fractions are collected and assayed for activity or protein. In most cases, lectin chromatography provides an initial 10–20-fold purification of a membrane protein. Importantly, this chromatography step also considerably reduces the amount of cytosolic protein (including proteases) in the detergent extract.

There is no a priori way to determine which lectin will bind to a specific glycoprotein. EY Laboratories, Inc. produces a kit that contains a variety of immobilized lectins that allow you to screen lectin binding of a protein on a small scale. To scale up the lectin purification step, one needs several milliliters of lectin coupled to agarose or Sepharose. If the immobilized lectin is not available commercially, there are several coupling procedures by which one can covalently attach purified lectin to a solid support (see Experiment 4) (Cuatrecasas and Parikh 1972).

It is usually more convenient to run lectin chromatography in small disposable columns (Bio-Rad Laboratories), either by gravity flow or under low pressure with a pump. The nature of the solid support (agarose beads) precludes their use in moderate- or high-pressure chromatography systems. Regardless of how the column is run, it is important to apply the sample, wash, and elute the resin at the same temperature to avoid anomalous flow and bubbles. These steps are usually performed at 4°C. With some care, it is possible to reuse a lectin column several times. After eluting the sample, wash the column extensively and store it in a neutral buffer containing the eluting sugar (10 mM) and sodium azide (0.05%) to maintain the integrity of the immobilized lectin and inhibit bacterial growth. Detergents should be avoided as they will eventually denature the lectin. Even with these precautions, the lectin will leach out of the gel with extended use, leading to decreased glycoprotein binding.

MATERIALS AND EQUIPMENT

Wheat germ agglutinin (WGA)-agarose (~2.5 ml of settled beads) (Vector Laboratories, Inc. ALI023 or EY Laboratories, Inc. A2101)

Solubilized insulin receptors (from Experiment 2)

Disposable plastic minicolumns (Bio-Rad Laboratories)

Bovine serum albumin (BSA; 1%)

[^{125}I]Insulin (receptor grade) (DuPont NEN® NEX 196)

Porcine insulin (17.5 μM [0.1 mg/ml] in 0.001 N HCl) (e.g., Sigma Chemical Co. I 3505)

Bovine γ-globulin (0.4% in solution B) (Miles Laboratories, Inc. 82-041-2)

Polyethylene glycol 6000 (20% in H_2O)

REAGENTS

Solution D
Solution E
Binding buffer (for solubilized receptor)
(For recipes, see Preparation of Reagents, pp. 337–343.)

PROCEDURE

Lectin Affinity Chromatography

1. Wash 2.5 ml of WGA-agarose with 25 ml of solution D to remove any uncoupled WGA.

2. Mix 10–15 mg of solubilized insulin receptors (~5 ml) with 2.5 ml of washed WGA-agarose and rock the mixture gently for 16 hours at 4°C or for 1 hour at room temperature.

3. Pour the agarose into a disposable plastic minicolumn and wash it with 15 ml of solution D.

4. Elute the insulin receptors with 15 ml of solution E. Collect 0.5-ml fractions and determine the protein concentration of each using a microprotein assay. Combine the fractions containing the peak of protein concentration; this usually yields approximately 3 ml of 0.3 mg/ml protein.

   Note: The major peak of protein is usually seen in fractions 3–6 or approximately 1/2 column volume and is fairly sharp. Keep the lectin column reagents (buffers and agarose) at the same temperature. Using reagents at different temperatures will cause bubbles and produce inhomogeneities in the column, leading to poor resolution of the eluted protein.

Measurement of Insulin Binding to Partially Purified Receptors

1. Set up the following reactions in microcentrifuge tubes:

Tube	Binding buffer (μl)	WGA-purified receptor (μl)	[^{125}I]insulin (5 nM) (μl)	Porcine insulin (17.5 μM) (μl)	Distilled H_2O (μl)	1% BSA (μl)
A	140	40	30	–	60	30
B	140	40	30	60	–	30

   The results from tube A give total binding and those from tube B give nonspecific binding. Specific binding = cpm in tube A – cpm in tube B.

   Note: The receptor grade [^{125}I]insulin (NEX 196) from DuPont NEN has a specific activity of 2200 μCi/nmol. The concentration of insulin is 35.5 nM. For this assay, it is necessary to dilute the stock [^{125}I]insulin to 5 nM with buffer (50 mM HEPES, 0.1% Triton X-100, 0.1% BSA, pH 7.4). The desired final concentration of [^{125}I]insulin in the binding assay for partially purified receptors is 500 pM, which is equivalent to 30 μl of the 5 nM solution in a 300-μl reaction.

2. Incubate these reactions for 16 hours at 4°C or for 2 hours at room temperature.

3. Separate the receptor-bound insulin from free insulin by precipitation. Add 75 μl of 0.4% bovine γ-globulin and incubate for 5 minutes at 4°C. Add 375 μl of 20% polyethylene glycol 6000 and incubate for 10 minutes at 4°C.

4. Collect the precipitates by spinning the mixtures in a microcentrifuge for 10 minutes.

5. Remove as much of each supernatant as possible and count the pellets for radioactivity.

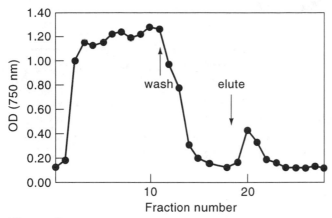

Figure 5
WGA-agarose column elution profile of Triton X-100-solubilized insulin receptors. Plasma membranes were solubilized with Triton X-100 and the detergent extract was applied to a WGA-agarose column. Fractions of 1 ml were collected. Arrows indicate when competing sugar, N-acetylglucosamine, was applied. The protein concentration in each fraction was determined. This profile was generated during the 1995 Cold Spring Harbor Laboratory Protein Purification and Characterization Course (courtesy of E. Miyoshik, T. Wang, A. Stunnikov, and A. Cheung).

Results

Typical results from the purification of solubilized insulin receptors by WGA-agarose chromatography are shown in Figure 5 and Table 5.

Table 5 Purification of Insulin Receptors from Rat Liver Plasma Membranes

Purification steps	Total protein (mg)	Total activity (pmol insulin bound)	Specific activity (pmol/mg protein)	Fold purification	Yield
Plasma membrane	200	25	0.125	1	100%
WGA-agarose	2.66	18.6	7	56	73%

These data were generated during the 1995 Cold Spring Harbor Laboratory Protein Purification and Characterization Course (courtesy of K. High, G. Lukacs, K. Dietmeier, and R. Jiang).

CONCANAVALIN A–SEPHAROSE CHROMATOGRAPHY

In addition to WGA, concanavalin A (Con A) is also a commonly used lectin for glycoprotein purification. Con A has a binding specificity for α-mannose, α-glucose, and α-N-acetylglucosamine. Procedures for purification are identical to those described for WGA-agarose, except that elution is achieved with α-methyl glucoside or α-methyl mannoside. If the membrane proteins were solubilized with octyl glucoside (or a related glucoside detergent), then a Con A column should not be used because the detergent will compete with the glycoproteins for binding to Con A.

• Experiment 4
Insulin Affinity Chromatography of Partially Purified Receptors

INTRODUCTION

The ability to couple small ligands to a solid support as a means of binding a specific receptor is an extremely useful form of affinity chromatography. In this experiment, we use an insulin agarose column as the final step in purifying the insulin receptor. This method takes advantage of the high affinity binding of the insulin receptor for its ligand ($K_D = 10^{-9}$ M).

Cuatrecasas (1972) introduced the use of insulin affinity chromatography in his protocol for insulin receptor purification. Preparing an insulin column involves coupling 3,3'-diaminodipropylamine to cyanogen-bromide (CNBr)-activated Sepharose 4B and adding succinic anhydride. The succinylaminodipropylamino agarose is activated to the N-hydrosuccinimide ester, which allows direct coupling to insulin. By using this method, it is possible to couple 0.2–1.0 mg of insulin per milliliter of packed gel (35–175 nmol/ml), which is equivalent to 6–30 mg of insulin receptor protein (assuming two moles of insulin bound per mole of receptor and 100% binding).

Initial attempts by Cuatrecasas and coworkers (1972) to purify insulin receptors from rat liver yielded a preparation with insulin binding activity of 2–3 µg/mg of receptor protein. Assuming that the insulin receptor ($M_r = 350,000$) binds one or two moles of insulin per mole of receptor, then the receptor should theoretically bind approximately 16–32 µg of insulin per milligram of receptor protein. This large discrepancy in insulin binding in the affinity-purified receptor could be due to many factors, such as residual impurities and partially denatured receptor.

Fujita-Yamaguchi et al. (1983) introduced a different elution method for the insulin affinity column. They replaced the 4.5 M urea and pH 6.0 acetate buffer of Cuatrecasas (1972) with 1 M NaCl and 50 mM acetate (pH 5.0), which is immediately neutralized with Tris buffer as the fractions are collected. This elution technique increases the specific activity of the purified receptor to 28.5 µg of insulin bound per milligram of receptor protein.

Despite the near-theoretical binding activity achieved by Fujita-

Yamaguchi et al. (1983), the insulin-stimulated tyrosine kinase activity of the receptor remained very low. Finn and colleagues (Finn et al. 1984; Hofmann et al. 1987) developed a series of affinity ligands using biotinylated insulin derivatives and succinylavidin agarose. With this technology, they were able to attain high-specific-activity insulin binding and, more importantly, significantly higher insulin-stimulated tyrosine kinase activity (Hofmann et al. 1987) than in previous studies. In this experiment, we take advantage of many of these improvements in the purification of the insulin receptor from rat liver.

General Application of Affinity Chromatography

Affinity chromatography procedures involve three steps: preparation of the affinity matrix, binding, and elution.

Preparation of the affinity matrix. The steps involved in the preparation of insulin agarose are as follows: First, the agarose is activated by cyanogen bromide, which makes it reactive to amino groups. Second, a linker group is attached to the agarose via an amino group. In the case of insulin agarose, a diamino compound is used to allow attachment of a succinyl group to extend the linker. The linker serves to stretch the ligand out from the solid support in order to minimize the possible steric hindrance. Third, the carboxyl group on the linker is activated to an *N*-hydroxysuccinamide ester. Finally, the agarose with activated carboxyl groups on the linker reacts with the amino groups of the ligand (insulin).

Nowadays, preactivated affinity matrices are available from various suppliers, and researchers only have to couple the ligand to the solid support. A variety of activated solid supports are available for coupling with various functional groups on the ligands (see Table 6). Most of these supports are designed for coupling with amino groups on the ligands, and they can react with both the α-amino group of

Table 6 Activated Beads That Are Available Commercially

Source	Beads	Activated group	Ligand attachment
Bio-Rad Laboratories	Affi-Gel® 10	hydroxysuccinimide ester	$-NH_2$
Pierce Chemical Co.	Reacti-Gel® 6X	carbonyl imidazole	$-NH_2$
Pharmacia Biotech, Inc.	CNBr-activated Sepharose®	isocyanate	$-NH_2$

the amino terminus and the ε-amino groups of lysine side chains of the peptide or protein. If the coupling occurs via a lysine side chain that is part of the binding site, the coupling reaction will result in inactivation of the ligand. To minimize this possibility, the coupling reaction is typically carried out at pH 7.5–8.0. Under these conditions, some α-amino groups (pK_a 8.5) exist in free amino reactive form, but the ε-amino group (pK_a 10.0) of lysine is in the protonated unreactive form. A procedure for coupling the ligand to an activated support is provided in this experiment.

Binding of receptors (or proteins) to the affinity matrix. Several factors affect the binding reaction. Sometimes the ligand coupled to the beads may not be in an active conformation (see above). If this is suspected to be responsible for the failure of protein to bind the affinity gel, it might be necessary to immobilize the ligand using a new coupling strategy. Another potential problem is that binding between protein and the immobilized ligand may be rather slow. To avoid this complication, it is advisable to allow enough time for the protein to interact with the immobilized ligand. This is usually achieved by mixing the sample and the gel in a batchwise manner.

Elution of bound receptors (or proteins). For elution, it is necessary to break the interactions between the protein and the immobilized ligand. This can be accomplished by several methods, for example: (i) changing the affinity of the protein for the ligand by altering pH, ionic strength, or temperature; (ii) adding a large excess of ligand, which either competes directly for the same binding site or acts indirectly at allosteric sites to reduce the affinity of the proteins for the immobilized ligand; (iii) denaturing the proteins by adding urea, guanidine, or SDS.

● ───

Insulin Affinity Chromatography

MATERIALS AND EQUIPMENT

Partially purified insulin receptors from the WGA-agarose column (see
    Experiment 3)
NaCl (5 M)
Insulin agarose (~2 ml of packed gel) (Sigma Chemical Co.)
Disposable plastic minicolumns (Bio-Rad Laboratories)
Centricon™ concentrators (Amicon, Inc.)
Silver Stain Plus Kit (Bio-Rad Laboratories 161-0449)

REAGENTS

Solution F
Solution G
Solution H
(For recipes, see Preparation of Reagents, pp. 337–343.)

PROCEDURE

1. Adjust the solution of partially purified insulin receptors from the
   WGA-agarose column (~3 ml) to 1 M NaCl by adding 0.75 ml of 5
   M NaCl.

2. Wash the insulin agarose with 40 ml of solution F to remove any
   uncoupled insulin which might interfere with the immobilizing
   step.

3. Incubate the mixture from step 1 with the insulin agarose (0.5 ml
   of insulin agarose per milliliter of receptor solution) for 18 hours
   at 4°C.

4. After bringing the agarose to room temperature, pour it into a disposable plastic minicolumn. Wash the column with 15 ml of solution F at room temperature.

5. Elute the insulin receptor with 10 ml of solution G. Collect 1-ml
   fractions.

6. Identify which fractions contain insulin receptors using the insulin binding assay described in Experiment 2 (see pp. 305–306).

7. Pool the fractions with insulin-binding activity and concentrate them using a Centricon. This will remove much of the water and detergent (octyl β-glucoside has a micelle molecular size of ~8000).

8. Reintroduce Triton X-100 to the concentrated receptor solution by mixing it with an equal volume of solution H. Replacing the octyl β-glucoside with Triton X-100 is necessary to obtain high-affinity insulin binding and insulin-stimulated autophosphorylation (Ridge et al. 1988).

9. To confirm the identity and purity of the insulin receptors, check the size of the isolated protein on a 7.5% SDS-polyacrylamide gel (see Appendix 5). Load approximately 50 μl of sample in each lane, and include a lane with molecular weight standards. After electrophoresis, silver stain the gel using the Silver Stain Plus Kit.

•————————————————————————————————————

Coupling of Ligands to Activated Beads

Here we describe coupling to Affi-Gel 10 as an example of this procedure.

MATERIALS

Phosphate buffer (50 mM; pH 7.5–8.0)
Affi-Gel® 10 (Bio-Rad Laboratories)
Sodium phosphate (50 mM) containing NaCl (1 M) (PBS)
Ethanolamine (100 mM)

PROCEDURE

1. Prepare a 1–10 mg/ml solution of the protein (ligand) in 50 mM phosphate buffer (pH 7.5–8.0). The protein preparation must not contain other amino compounds. Thus, Tris buffer or buffers containing ammonium salt should not be used. Suitable buffers include phosphate, MES, MOPS, and HEPES. If the protein preparation contains other amino compounds, dialyze it against 0.5 M phosphate buffer (pH 7.5–8.0). Save a small portion of the protein sample for determining the coupling efficiency.

2. Affi-Gel 10 is supplied in isopropanol suspension. It is necessary to remove this alcohol to avoid denaturing protein ligands. Pour the Affi-Gel 10 suspension into a sintered glass funnel. Quickly wash the gel several times with deionized H_2O at 4°C. Do not allow the gel to dry. If the gel dries out, the air trapped in the beads will make some linking sites unavailable.

3. Add the washed beads to the protein solution (~1 ml of beads per 0.5 ml of ligand solution). Mix gently on a rocker overnight at room temperature.

4. Separate the beads by filtration. Save the filtrate. Determine the protein concentrations in the filtrate and the protein sample saved in step 1 in order to calculate the coupling efficiency. Protein concentrations can be determined by several methods. If the protein concentrations are to be determined by OD_{280}, it is necessary to

lower the pH of the solution to <6.0 by adding 0.1 N HCl. Otherwise, *N*-hydroxysuccinimide released during coupling will absorb at 280 nm at neutral or high pH. Coupling efficiency only affects the capacity of the gel.

5. Wash the beads with phosphate-buffered saline (PBS).

6. Incubate the beads in 100 mM ethanolamine for 4 hours or overnight to block the remaining reactive sites.

7. Wash the beads with PBS. The affinity matrix is now ready to use.

• Experiment 5
Cross-linking of Insulin Receptors with [^{125}I]Insulin
•

INTRODUCTION

Affinity labeling is a powerful method for examining the subunit structure of a receptor protein. A radioactive ligand is allowed to bind to the receptor and is covalently attached by chemical or photochemical cross-linking. The reaction products are then analyzed by SDS-polyacrylamide gel electrophoresis (SDS-PAGE) and the apparent molecular weight of the ligand-binding subunit can be deduced. This general scheme has been successfully used for a wide variety of receptor peptides, including angiotensin, bradykinin, enkephalin, epidermal growth factor, insulin, and nerve growth factor (Eberle and deGraan 1985). The receptor protein can be identified from relatively crude preparations by comparing labeling patterns in the presence and absence of saturating concentrations of unlabeled ligand.

There are two different approaches to affinity labeling. One method is photoaffinity labeling, in which photoreactive aryl azide derivatives of a ligand are cross-linked to the receptor by exposure to a high-energy (usually ultraviolet) light source. The aryl nitrenes produced by photolysis are highly reactive. They can form stable covalent attachments to the binding site faster than they can diffuse away from it. Yip and Yeung (1985) have used photoaffinity labeling extensively to analyze the subunit structure of the insulin receptor with excellent results. However, there are some practical limitations to this technique. One is that the preparation and purification of the photoaffinity ligand may be laborious. It also requires radioactive labeling of the derivatized ligand. Furthermore, one must have a high-energy ultraviolet light source for the photolysis reaction.

Another approach to affinity labeling is to bind radioactively labeled ligands to the receptor and cross-link them with bifunctional reagents. These reagents react with free amino groups in the ligand and receptor to form covalent associations between the receptor and the ligand. The use of bifunctional reagents was first reported by Pilch and Czech (1979), who used disuccinimidyl suberate to label the insulin and insulin-like growth factor receptors (Massague and Czech 1985).

Many varieties of bifunctional reagents have been developed;

they differ in their spacer lengths, cleavability, solubility, and reactive properties, which make them useful for analyzing the structure of nearly any peptide receptor. (The Pierce Chemical Co. catalog contains an extensive list of these reagents.) In this experiment, disuccinimidyl suberate is used to affinity label insulin receptors with [125I]insulin and the labeled proteins are examined with SDS-PAGE.

Note: The efficiency of cross-linking with disuccinimidyl suberate can vary from 2% to 15% of the total receptor population. Before loading the gel, it is useful to count an aliquot of the labeled membranes to determine the amount of [125I]insulin in the sample. Even though 85–98% of the counts are due to free [125I]insulin, you can use the total cpm data to estimate amount of labeled insulin covalently attached to its receptor and therefore the length of exposure of the X-ray film necessary to produce satisfactory results.

MATERIALS AND EQUIPMENT

Purified rat liver plasma membranes (see Experiment 1)
Partially purified insulin receptors from the WGA-agarose column (see Experiment 3)
Purified insulin receptors from the insulin agarose column (see Experiment 4)
[125I]Insulin (receptor grade) (DuPont NEN® NEX 196)
Porcine insulin (17.5 µM) (e.g., Sigma Chemical Co. I 3505)
Disuccinimidyl suberate (Pierce Chemical Co. 21555)
Dimethyl sulfoxide (DMSO)
NH_4Cl (1 M)
Glycerol (10%; v/v)
Protein gel electrophoresis apparatus (Bio-Rad Laboratories or Hoefer Scientific Instruments)
Gel dryer (Bio-Rad Laboratories or Hoefer Scientific Instruments)

REAGENT

SDS-PAGE sample buffer (5x)
(For recipe, see Preparation of Reagents, pp. 337–343.)

PROCEDURE

1. Set up the following reactions:

Tube	Plasma membranes (2–4 mg/ml) (μl)	WGA-agarose purified sample (μl)	Insulin-agarose purified sample (μl)	[^{125}I]insulin (35 nM) (μl)	Porcine insulin (17.5 μM) (μl)
1	50	0	0	5	0
2	50	0	0	5	5
3	0	50	0	5	0
4	0	50	0	5	5
5	0	0	50	5	0
6	0	0	50	5	5

2. Incubate the reactions for 2 hours at room temperature.

3. Dissolve disuccinimidyl suberate in DMSO to give a final concentration of 10 mM.

4. Add 6 μl of 10 mM disuccinimidyl suberate to each tube. Incubate for 1 minute at room temperature.

5. Quench the reactions by adding 1 μl of 1 M NH$_4$Cl.

6. Add 15 μl of 5x SDS-PAGE sample buffer.

7. Boil the samples for 5 minutes.

8. Load the samples onto a 7.5% SDS-polyacrylamide gel. Run the gel at 170 V until the dye front leaves the gel. (For further information on SDS-PAGE, see Appendix 5.)

9. Incubate the gel in 10% glycerol and dry the gel in a gel dryer.

   Note: The proteins can also be transferred to a nitrocellulose membrane as described in Experiment 6.

10. Identify the affinity-labeled insulin receptor by autoradiography.

Results

Typical results from a cross-linking experiment are shown in Figure 6.

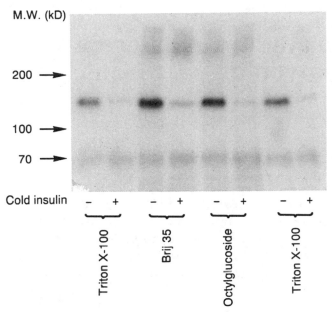

M.W. (kD)

200 →

100 →

70 →

Cold insulin   –   +   –   +   –   +   –   +

Triton X-100   Brij 35   Octylglucoside   Triton X-100

Figure 6

Cross-linking of [^{125}I]insulin to the insulin receptor α-subunit by disuc-cinimidyl suberate. Rat liver plasma membranes were solubilized with vari-ous detergents as shown and the detergent extracts were purified by lectin af-finity chromatography (WGA-agarose column) before performing the cross-linking experiments. These data were generated during the 1995 Cold Spring Harbor Laboratory Protein Purification and Characterization Course (cour-tesy of R. Jain, L. Hwang, T. Hughes, and M. Gong).

• *Experiment 6*
Insulin-stimulated Insulin Receptor Autophosphorylation

INTRODUCTION

The identification of the molecular events leading to insulin action has been, and continues to be, a major research effort in scores of laboratories. In the past 20 years, a few common findings have emerged. The recognition that insulin binds to a membrane receptor and the cloning of an insulin receptor cDNA confirmed many of the predictions about the receptor made from biochemical studies (Ebina et al. 1985; Ullrich et al. 1985). Before the cloning, several laboratories reported insulin-stimulated autophosphorylation and exogenous tyrosine kinase activity of the receptor toward artificial substrates (Rosen et al. 1981; Kasuga et al. 1982; Petruzzelli et al. 1982). This enzymatic function of the receptor is carried out by the β-subunit, a largely intracellular domain that contains six tyrosines. Findings in the past eight years support the idea that insulin-induced autophosphorylation is the beginning of a cascade of phosphorylation events that leads to many, if not all, of insulin's actions (Rosen 1987). The challenge of untangling this signal transduction pathway with all its details is still before us. In addition to the insulin receptor, many other receptors (e.g., EGF and PDGF receptors) have similar autophosphorylation activities which are activated by ligand binding.

In Experiment 5, we characterized the purified insulin receptor with regard to its binding properties. However, this physical process (binding) may or may not have a direct correlation with biological functions. It is often necessary to characterize the purified protein further in terms of its biological function. In this experiment, we examine the insulin-stimulated tyrosine kinase activity of insulin receptors. An antiphosphotyrosine antibody is used to detect the phosphorylated receptor, which is resolved by SDS-PAGE.

MATERIALS AND EQUIPMENT

Purified rat liver plasma membranes (see Experiment 1)
Partially purified insulin receptors from the WGA-agarose column (see Experiment 3)

Purified insulin receptors from the insulin agarose column (see Experiment 4)

Porcine insulin (17.5 μM [0.1 mg/ml] in 0.001 N HCl) (e.g., Sigma Chemical Co. I 3505)

ATP (20 mM; pH 7.4)

Protein gel electrophoresis apparatus (Bio-Rad Laboratories or Hoefer Scientific Instruments)

Whatman® 3MM filter paper

Nitrocellulose membrane (Schleicher and Schuell, Inc.)

Electrophoretic transfer cell (Bio-Rad Laboratories or Hoefer Scientific Instruments)

Primary antibody (antiphosphotyrosine antibody) (monoclonal IgG2bk; Upstate Biotechnology, Inc. 05-321)

Secondary antibody (horseradish peroxidase (HRP)-conjugated anti-mouse IgG; Bio-Rad Laboratories)

ECL™ western blotting detection Kit (Amersham Life Science, Inc.)

REAGENTS

Autophosphorylation buffer (10x)
Starter solution (10x)
SDS-PAGE sample buffer (5x)
Western blot transfer solution
Blocking buffer
Tris-HCl (10 mM; pH 7.4)
NaCl (150 mM)
Tween-20 (0.1%) (TBST)
(For recipes, see Preparation of Reagents, pp. 337–343.)

PROCEDURE

Autophosphorylation

1. Set up the following mixtures:

Tube	Plasma membranes (2–4 mg/ml) (μl)	WGA-agarose purified sample (μl)	Insulin-agarose purified sample (μl)	Autophosphorylation buffer (10x) (μl)	Porcine insulin (17.5 μM) (μl)	Distilled H$_2$O (μl)
1	25	0	0	4	0	5
2	25	0	0	4	5	0
3	0	25	0	4	0	5
4	0	25	0	4	5	0
5	0	0	25	4	0	5
6	0	0	25	4	5	0

2. Incubate the mixtures for 15 minutes at room temperature.

3. Start the phosphorylation reaction by adding 2 µl of 20 mM ATP and 4 µl of 10x starter solution. Mix and incubate for 15 minutes at room temperature.

4. Terminate the reactions by adding 10 µl of 5x SDS-PAGE sample buffer.

5. Boil the samples for 5 minutes.

6. Load the samples onto a 7.5% SDS polyacrylamide gel. Run the gel at 170 V until the dye front leaves the gel. (For further information on SDS-PAGE, see Appendix 5.)

Transfer of Proteins to Nitrocellulose

1. Place a fiber pad and then a piece of wet Whatman 3MM filter paper on one side of a gel holder.

2. Put the gel on top of the filter paper.

3. Wet a piece of nitrocellulose membrane with H_2O and place it over the gel. Remove any bubbles trapped between the filter and the gel.

4. Lay another piece of wet Whatman 3MM filter paper across the top of the nitrocellulose membrane.

5. Finish the "sandwich" with another fiber pad.

6. Close the gel holder.

7. Set the holder in the buffer tank with the nitrocellulose facing the positive side of the chamber. The sandwich should be assembled in the following manner:

> cathode (black)
> fiber pad
> 3MM filter paper
> gel
> nitrocellulose membrane
> 3MM filter paper
> fiber pad
> anode (red)

8. Fill the chamber with western blot transfer solution.

9. Run electrophoresis transfer at 100 V for 2 hours in the cold room.

Western Blot

1. Incubate the nitrocellulose membrane in blocking buffer for 1 hour at 37°C.

2. Place the nitrocellulose membrane in a tray with enough TBST (see p. 343) containing primary antibody (10,000-fold dilution of antiphosphotyrosine antibody) to keep the membrane wet. Ensure that the side of the nitrocellulose membrane that had faced the gel is now facing up.

3. Rock the tray for 1–2 hours at room temperature.

4. Wash the nitrocellulose membrane for 5 minutes with 5 ml of TBST. Repeat four times.

5. Add enough secondary antibody (5000-fold dilution of HRP-conjugated anti-mouse IgG) to keep the nitrocellulose membrane wet.

6. Incubate for 1 hour at room temperature.

7. Wash the nitrocellulose membrane for 5 minutes with 5 ml of TBST. Repeat four times.

8. Prepare a chemiluminescence detection cocktail by mixing equal amounts of reagent 1 and reagent 2 from the ECL Western blotting detection kit.

9. Pour the detection cocktail over the nitrocellulose membrane. Let the reaction proceed for 1 minute.

10. Immediately drain the excess reagent.

11. Wrap the nitrocellulose membrane in plastic wrap.

12. Apply phosphorescent orientation dots.

    Note: Polymark Natural Glow No. PM 501, which can be purchased from arts and crafts supply stores, works well for this purpose.

13. Expose the blot to film for 5 seconds, 1 minute, or increasing periods of time until the desired result is obtained.

• Experiment 7
Analysis of Insulin Receptor Glycosylation

• ———————————————————————————————

INTRODUCTION

The growing awareness of the importance of protein-linked oligosaccharides in biological systems has led to a dramatic increase in the analysis of these carbohydrate moieties with the hope of elucidating their functional significance (for a review, see Hart 1992). The bewildering complexity of the sugar side chains promises to yield a wealth of biological information. With the advent of molecular biology techniques, the first step in the analysis of protein-linked oligosaccharides has become finding the consensus sequence for potential glycosylation sites in a cloned protein. The question that is frequently asked is whether the putative glycosylation sites are actually occupied by sugars. Before attempting to analyze the carbohydrate sequence of glycoproteins, useful information about the extent and types of glycosylation of a specific protein can be obtained by removing the sugars with deglycosylases. Furthermore, complete deglycosylation is required before the molecular weight of the protein core can be determined. In purifying a protein, knowing its lectin binding properties can be of great help in designing initial purification steps. For example, insulin receptors from all tissues except brain contain terminal N-acetylneuraminic acid (NeuNAc; sialic acid) groups that are sensitive to neuraminidase. The ability of WGA to bind sialic acid makes this lectin a good choice for the initial purification of insulin receptors from all cells except brain. In this experiment, we analyze the major protein-linked oligosaccharides present on the insulin receptor by using a combination of specific deglycosylase enzymes and SDS-PAGE.

The carbohydrate composition of a glycoprotein can be analyzed by treating the radioactively labeled protein with commercially available endoglycosidases and analyzing the reaction products by SDS-PAGE gel electrophoresis. In the case of the insulin receptor, affinity labeling with [125I]insulin provides a convenient marker for following the action of the glycosidases. The insulin-binding subunit (α-chain) migrates at 135 kD in SDS gels and contains approximately 30 kD of carbohydrate. Receptors can be labeled in a crude membrane fraction and then subjected to the action of specific endoglycosidases.

An alternative to enzymatic methods is chemical deglycosylation. This technique generally involves the use of anhydrous acids such as hydrogen fluoride or trifluoromethane sulfonic acid that attack the oligosaccharide-peptide bond to yield a free protein. Chemical deglycosylation may give a more accurate estimate of protein molecular weight than deglycosylases since all glycosylation sites are potentially accessible to hydrogen fluoride. Herzberg et al. (1985) performed chemical deglycosylation on insulin receptors and found the molecular weights of the α and β subunits to be 98 kD and 80 kD, respectively. This matches the molecular weight of the insulin receptor derived from cDNA (Ebina et al. 1985). A disadvantage of chemical deglycosylation is that the reaction conditions must be carefully controlled to yield an intact, deglycosylated protein. In addition, the acids used are hazardous. Also, the nature of the specific oligosaccharides present in the sample cannot be determined by this technique.

Asparagine (or *N*-) linked oligosaccharides can be detected by treating the labeled receptors with endoglycosidase F (peptide *N*4-*N*-acetyl-β-glucosaminyl asparagine aminidase F; E.C. 3.5.1.52). This enzyme cleaves the sugar at the β-asparaginyl glycosyl bond between the innermost *N*-actylglucosamine and the asparagine residue on the protein backbone converting the asparagine to aspartic acid. A recombinant version of endoglycosidase F called *N*-glycanase is available from Genzyme Corp. and Boehringer Mannheim Corp. This enzyme is essentially free of the common contaminants present in natural enzyme preparations, such as exoglycosidases and proteases. Both endoglycosidase F and *N*-glycanase release the entire core oligosaccharide from complex, high mannose, sialylated, phosphorylated, and sulfated sugar chains. To assess the extent to which the *N*-linked oligosaccharide is of the high-mannose variety as opposed to the complex variety, the labeled protein is treated with the enzyme endoglycosidase H (endo-β-*N*-acetylglucosaminidase; E.C. 3.2.1.96), which specifically hydrolyzes the core of the high mannose asparagine-linked oligosaccharides. Examples of oligosaccharide structure and glycosidase cleavage sites are shown in Figure 7.

Glycosylation of serine or threonine residues through their hydroxyl moieties, termed *O*-linked glycosylation, can be detected by treatment with endo-α-*N*-acetylgalactosaminidase (E.C. 3.2.1.97), which is marketed by Genzyme Corp. as *O*-glycanase. This enzyme hydrolyzes the galactose-β-(1,3)-*N*-acetylgalactosamine core from serine or threonine residues in the protein.

A large number of glycoproteins contain terminal NeuNAc groups attached to the oligosaccharide core. Treating the labeled protein with neuraminidase (acylneuraminylhydrolase; E.C. 3.2.1.18) will hydrolyze NeuNAc moieties and increase the mobility of the protein on SDS-PAGE. An example of such an analysis of the glycosylation pattern of the insulin receptor is shown in Figure 8 (Brennan 1988).

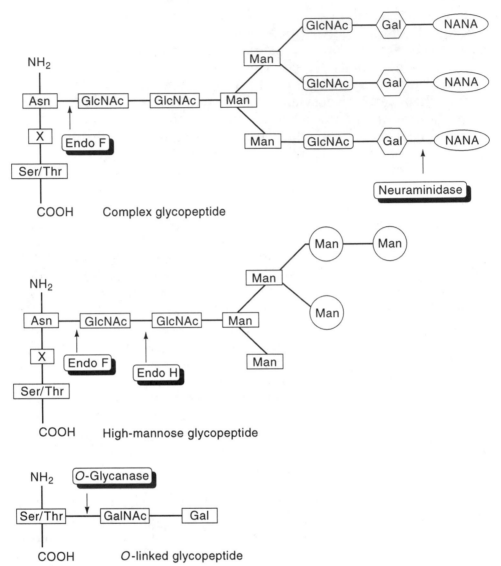

Figure 7
Examples of oligosaccharide structures and glycosidase cleavage sites. *N*-linked oligosaccharides are attached to the side chain of asparagine, which is part of the Asn-X-Ser/Thr consensus sequence. *N*-linked oligosaccharides typically have an identical core structure composed of two *N*-acetylglucosamines and three mannoses (as shown in square boxes). Various sugar units are attached to this core structure to give different types of *N*-linked oligosaccharides. Shown here are two examples, one complex variety and one high mannose variety. *O*-linked oligosaccharides are usually linked by an *N*-acetylgalactosamine to the hydroxyl group of serine or threonine. Abbreviations: (GlcNAc) *N*-acetylglucosamine; (Man) mannose; (Gal) galactose; (NANA) *N*-acetylneuraminic acid; (GalNAc) *N*-acetylgalactosamine.

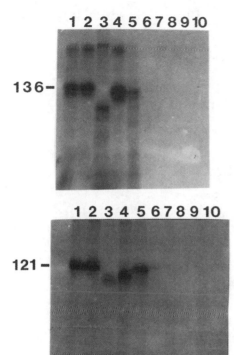

Figure 8

This autoradiogram of rat brain and liver insulin receptors was prepared after they were cross-linked to [^{125}I]insulin with disuccinimidyl suberate, treated with endoglycosidase F (endo F), endoglycosidase H (endo H), or neuraminidase, and then subjected to SDS-PAGE under reducing conditions. Lanes 1 and 6, 4°C control; lanes 2 and 7, 37°C control; lanes 3 and 8, endo F-treated membranes; lanes 4 and 9, endo H-treated membranes; lanes 5 and 10, neuraminidase-treated membranes. Lanes 6–10 correspond to nonspecific binding controls in which cross-linking to [^{125}I]insulin was carried out in the presence of a saturating concentration (5 mM) of porcine insulin. (*Top*) Adult liver insulin receptors; (*bottom*) adult brain insulin receptors. The numbers 136 and 121 are molecular mass in kDs. (Reproduced, with permission, from Brennan 1988 [© The Endocrine Society].)

MATERIALS AND EQUIPMENT

Purified insulin receptors from the insulin agarose column (see Experiment 4)

Endoglycosidase F (*N*-glycanase; Boehringer Mannheim Corp. 903329 or Genzyme Corp.)

Endoglycosidase H (Boehringer Mannheim Corp. 100117 or Genzyme Corp. ENDO H1)

Neuraminidase (Boehringer Mannheim Corp. 1080725 or Sigma
Chemical Co. type X, N 2133)
Gel electrophoresis unit (Bio-Rad Laboratories or Hoefer Scientific In-
struments)
Glycerol (10%)
X-ray film and cassette

REAGENTS

Protease inhibitors stock solution (100x) (for glycosylation experi-
ment)
Endoglycosidase F buffer (5x)
Endoglycosidase H buffer (10x)
Neuraminidase buffer (10x)
SDS-PAGE sample buffer (5x)
(For recipes, see Preparation of Reagents, pp. 337–343.)

PROCEDURE

1. Affinity label the insulin-agarose purified insulin receptors by following the procedure described in Experiment 5 for tube #5 (steps
1–5). Prepare four identical tubes. Label the tubes A, B, C, and D.

   Note: The total volume in each tube will be 62 μl.

2. Set up the following reactions:

   Sample A (control)

   a. Add 1 μl of 100x protease inhibitors stock solution.

   b. Add 17 μl of H_2O.

   Sample B (endo F-treated)

   a. Add 16 μl of 5x endoglycosidase F buffer.

   b. Add 2 μl of endoglycosidase F.

   c. Add 1 μl of 100x protease inhibitors stock solution.

   Sample C (endo H-treated)

   a. Add 8 μl of 10x endoglycosidase H buffer.

   b. Add 3 μl of endoglycosidase H.

   c. Add 1 μl of 100x protease inhibitors stock solution.

   d. Add 6 μl of H_2O.

Sample D (neuraminidase-treated)

a. Add 8 µl of 10x neuraminidase buffer.

b. Add 3 µl of neuraminidase.

c. Add 1 µl of 100x protease inhibitors stock solution.

d. Add 6 µl of H_2O.

3. Incubate the samples for 4 hours at 37°C.

4. Stop the reaction by adding 20 µl of 5x SDS-PAGE sample buffer.

5. Boil for 5 minutes.

6. Load the samples onto a 7.5% SDS polyacrylamide gel. Run the gel at 170 V until the dye front leaves the gel. (For further information on SDS-PAGE, see Appendix 5.)

7. Incubate the gel in 10% glycerol for 10 minutes and dry the gel in a gel dryer.

8. Identify the affinity-labeled insulin receptor by autoradiography.

PRACTICAL NOTES ON THE USE OF GLYCOSIDASE

Using affinity-labeled insulin receptors from rat liver as a substrate, the reaction conditions described above yield complete digestion with the two endoglycosidases, F and H, as well as with the exoglycosidase neuraminidase. In general, it is necessary to determine the optimum digestion conditions for each enzyme.

The most common reason for poor digestion by endoglycosidases is the substrate's lack of accessibility to the enzyme. This is due to folding of the protein and exclusion of endoglycosidase-sensitive sites in the native state. The accessibility of substrates to endoglycosidases can be improved by the following methods:

- Removal of terminal sugars like sialic acid and fucose from the protein before endoglycosidase treatment. Since sialic acid and fucose groups commonly block endoglycosidase-sensitive sites on the protein, treating the sample with neuraminidase and β-glucuronidase first can remove these carbohydrate moieties.

- Denaturation of glycoprotein by adding SDS (maximum concentration of 1%) and boiling for 10 minutes before adding the endoglycosidase. A nonionic detergent such as Triton X-100 or Nonidet P-40 should be added after boiling to prevent denaturation of the endoglycosidase by SDS. Alternatively, the SDS-denatured sample can be diluted to a concentration of 0.1% SDS.

- Many membrane samples and some exoglycosidase and endogly-cosidase preparations contain proteases. The protease inhibitor cocktail listed in the Reagents section for this experiment limits protease activity well in rat liver membranes. Other membrane preparations may require a wider spectrum of protease-inhibiting activity. A control sample containing only labeled membranes in reaction buffer should be incubated along with the glycosidase-containing samples. This will reveal the extent of endogenous protease activity in the sample.

Preparation of Reagents

Autophosphorylation buffer (10x)

500 mM HEPES (pH 7.4)
1 mg/ml Bovine serum albumin (BSA)
1% Triton X-100

Binding buffer
(for solubilized receptor)

0.2 M Na_2HPO_4
2 mM EGTA
2 mM EDTA
0.1% Triton X-100 (Pierce Chemical Co. 28314G or Boehringer
Mannheim Corp. 1332481)

Adjust the pH to 7.4 with NaOH.

Binding buffer
(for two-point binding assay or cold-ligand displacement experiment)

0.2 M Na_2HPO_4
2 mM EGTA
2 mM EDTA

Adjust the pH to 7.4 with NaOH.

Blocking buffer

TBST (see p. 343) containing 1 mg/ml bovine serum albumin (RIA
grade; Sigma Chemical Co. A 7888).

Endoglycosidase F buffer (5x)

500 mM Sodium phosphate (pH 6.1)
250 mM EDTA
5% Nonidet P-40 (Pierce Chemical Co. 28324G or Boehringer
    Mannheim Corp. 1332473)
5% β-mercaptoethanol
0.5% Sodium dodecyl sulfate (SDS) (Pierce Chemical Co. 28364G or
    Boehringer Mannheim Corp. 1358995)
5 mM Phenylmethylsulfonyl fluoride (PMSF) (see Safety Note, p. 338)

SAFETY NOTE

- β-Mercaptoethanol may be fatal if swallowed and is harmful if inhaled or absorbed through the skin. High concentrations are extremely destructive to the mucous membranes, upper respiratory tract, skin, and eyes. Use only in a chemical fume hood. Gloves and safety glasses should be worn.

Endoglycosidase H buffer (10x)

300 mM 2-Morpholinoethanesulfonic acid (pH 7.4)
10 mM Dithiothreitol (DTT)
2.5% Sodium dodecyl sulfate (SDS)
10 mM Phenylmethylsulfonyl fluoride (PMSF) (see Safety Note below)

Homogenization buffer

250 mM Sucrose
10 mM HEPES (pH 7.4)
1 mM EDTA
0.1 mM Phenylmethylsulfonyl fluoride (PMSF) (see Safety Note below)
 (for stock solution, see below) (and other appropriate protease
 inhibitors)

Add protease inhibitors immediately before use. PMSF has a short
half-life (only a few minutes) in buffer.

Neuraminidase buffer (10x)

500 mM Sodium acetate (pH 5.5)
1.4 M NaCl
10 mM Phenylmethylsulfonyl fluoride (PMSF) (see Safety Note below)
90 mM $CaCl_2$

Phenylmethylsulfonyl fluoride (PMSF) stock solution (100 mM

Dissolve 1.74 g of PMSF in 100 ml of dimethyl sulfoxide.

SAFETY NOTE

- PMSF is extremely destructive to the mucous membranes of the respiratory tract, the eyes, and the skin. It may be fatal if inhaled, swallowed, or absorbed through the skin. It is a highly toxic cholinesterase inhibitor. It should be used in a chemical fume hood. Gloves and safety glasses should be worn.

Protease inhibitors stock solution (100x)

		Final concentration
Benzamidine	1.57 g	1 M
Bacitracin	0.8 g	8%
Aprotinin	6 mg	600 μg/ml
Pepstatin	1.4 mg	0.2 mM
Leupeptin	0.95 mg	0.2 mM

Dissolve in distilled H_2O and adjust the volume to 10 ml.

Protease inhibitors stock solution (100x)
(for glycosylation experiment)

Leupeptin	0.1 mg/ml
Antipain	0.2 mg/ml
Benzamidine	1 mg/ml
Aprotinin	10^3 Kallikrein inhibitor units/ml
Chymostatin	0.1 mg/ml
Pepstatin	0.1 mg/ml

Reagent A
(for Peterson's protein assay)

Dissolve 0.2 g of copper sulfate and 0.4 g of potassium tartrate in 100 ml of distilled H_2O. Dissolve 20 g of sodium carbonate in 100 ml of distilled H_2O. Mix both solutions together by stirring. Store at room temperature. Combine a volume of this solution with equal volumes of 0.8 N NaOH, 10% sodium dodecyl sulfate, and distilled H_2O.

Reagent B
(for Peterson's protein assay)

Dilute one volume of Folin-Ciocalteau phenol reagent (Sigma Chemical Co. F 9252) with five volumes of distilled H_2O.

SDS-PAGE sample buffer (5x)

0.25 M Tris-HCl (pH 6.8)
5% Sodium dodecyl sulfate (SDS)
5% β-mercaptoethanol
50% Glycerol

SAFETY NOTE

- 2-Mercaptoethanol may be fatal if swallowed and is harmful if inhaled or absorbed through the skin. High concentrations are extremely destructive to the mucous membranes, upper respiratory tract, skin, and eyes. Use only in a chemical fume hood. Gloves and safety glasses should be worn.

Solution A
(1 liter)

		Final concentration
1 M HEPES (pH 7.4)	50 ml	50 mM
1 M CaCl$_2$	1 ml	1 mM
100 mM Phenylmethylsulfonyl fluoride (PMSF) (see p. 338)	10 ml	1 mM
100x Protease inhibitors (see p. 339)	10 ml	

Add protease inhibitors immediately before use. PMSF has a short half-life (only a few minutes) in buffer.

Solution B
(100 ml)

		Final concentration
1 M HEPES (pH 7.4)	5 ml	50 mM
100 mM Phenylmethylsulfonyl fluoride (PMSF) (see p. 338)	0.1 ml	0.1 mM
100x Protease inhibitors (see p. 339)	1 ml	

Add protease inhibitors immediately before use. PMSF has a short half-life (only a few minutes) in buffer.

Solution C
(10 ml)

		Final concentration
1 M HEPES (pH 7.4)	0.5 ml	47 mM
10% Triton X-100 (Pierce Chemical Co. 28314G or Boehringer Mannheim Corp. 1332481)	10 ml	10%
100 mM Phenylmethylsulfonyl fluoride (PMSF) (see p. 338)	0.01 ml	0.1 mM
100x Protease inhibitors (see p. 339)	0.1 ml	

Add protease inhibitors immediately before use. PMSF has a short half-life (only a few minutes) in buffer.

Solution D
(10 ml)

		Final concentration
1 M HEPES (pH 7.4)	0.5 ml	50 mM
10% Triton X-100 (Pierce Chemical Co. 28314G or Boehringer Mannheim Corp. 1332481)	0.1 ml	0.1%
1 M NaCl	1.5 ml	150 mM
1 M MgCl$_2$	0.1 ml	10 mM
100 mM Phenylmethylsulfonyl fluoride (PMSF) (see p. 338)	0.01 ml	0.1 mM
100x Protease inhibitors (see p. 339)	0.1 ml	

Add protease inhibitors immediately before use. PMSF has a short half-life (only a few minutes) in buffer.

Solution E
(10 ml)

		Final concentration
1 M HEPES (pH 7.4)	0.5 ml	50 mM
10% Triton X-100 (Pierce Chemical Co. 28314G or Boehringer Mannheim Corp. 1332481)	0.1 ml	0.1%
N-Acetylglucosamine	0.66 g	0.3 M
100 mM Phenylmethylsulfonyl fluoride (PMSF) (see p. 338)	0.01 ml	0.1 mM
100x Protease inhibitors (see p. 339)	0.1 ml	

Add protease inhibitors immediately before use. PMSF has a short half-life (only a few minutes) in buffer.

Solution F
(40 ml)

		Final concentration
1 M HEPES (pH 7.4)	2 ml	50 mM
10% Triton X-100 (Pierce Chemical Co. 28314G or Boehringer Mannheim Corp. 1332481)	0.4 ml	0.1%
NaCl	2.34 g	1 M
100 mM Phenylmethylsulfonyl fluoride (PMSF) (see p. 338)	0.04 ml	0.1 mM
100x Protease inhibitors (see p. 339)	0.4 ml	

Add protease inhibitors immediately before use. PMSF has a short half-life (only a few minutes) in buffer.

Solution G
(10 ml)

		Final concentration
1 M HEPES (pH 7.4)	0.5 ml	50 mM
Octyl glucoside	60 mg	0.6%
NaCl	0.585 g	1 M
100 mM Phenylmethylsulfonyl fluoride (PMSF) (see p. 338)	0.01 ml	0.1 mM
100x Protease inhibitors (see p. 339)	0.1 ml	

Add protease inhibitors immediately before use. PMSF has a short half-life (only a few minutes) in buffer.

Solution H
(10 ml)

		Final concentration
1 M HEPES (pH 7.4)	0.5 ml	50 mM
10% Triton X-100 (Pierce Chemical Co. 28314G or Boehringer Mannheim Corp. 1332481)	0.2 ml	0.2%
100 mM Phenylmethylsulfonyl fluoride (PMSF) (see p. 338)	0.01 ml	0.1 mM

Add PMSF immediately before use. PMSF has a short half-life (only a few minutes) in buffer.

Starter solution (10x)

100 mM $MgCl_2$
20 mM $MnCl_2$

Sucrose (42.3% w/w)

Sucrose	42.3 g
H_2O	57.7 ml

Dissolve 42.3 g of sucrose in 57.7 ml of distilled H_2O, or adjust to a refractive index of 1.4042.

Sucrose (69% w/w)

Sucrose	69 g
H_2O	31 ml

Add 69 g of sucrose to 31 ml of distilled H_2O in a large flask. Cover the flask with plastic wrap and stir the mixture on a hot plate to dissolve the sucrose. Cool the solution to room temperature before use.

TBST

10 mM Tris-HCl (pH 7.4)
150 mM NaCl
0.1% Tween-20

Western blot transfer solution

25 mM Tris-HCl (pH 8.3)
192 mM Glycine
20% Methanol

References

Beynon, R.J. and J.S. Bond. 1989. *Proteolytic enzymes: A practical approach.* IRL Press at Oxford University Press, England.

Brennan, W.A., Jr. 1988. Developmental aspects of the rat brain insulin receptor: Loss of sialic acid and fluctuation in number characterize fetal development. *Endocrinology* **122:** 2364–2370.

Cuatrecasas, P. 1972. Affinity chromatography and purification of the insulin receptor of liver cell membranes. *Proc. Natl. Acad. Sci.* **69:** 1277–1281.

Cuatrecasas, P. and I. Parikh. 1972. Absorbents for affinity chromatography. Use of N-hydroxy succinimide esters of agarose. *Biochemistry* **11:** 2291–2299.

Deutscher, M.P., ed. 1990. *Methods in Enzymology,* vol. 182. *Guide to protein purification.* Academic Press, New York.

Eberle, A.N. and P.N.E. deGraan. 1985. General principles for photoaffinity labeling of peptide hormone receptors. *Methods Enzymol.* **109:** 129–156.

Ebina, Y., L. Ellis, K. Jarnagin, M. Edery, L. Graf, E. Clauser, J.H. Ou, F. Masiarz, Y.W. Kan, I.D. Goldfine, R.A. Roth, and W.J. Rutter. 1985. The human insulin receptor cDNA: The structural basis for hormone-activated transmembrane signalling. *Cell* **40:** 747–758.

Finn, F.M., G. Titus, D. Horstman, and K. Hofmann. 1984. Avidin-biotin affinity chromatography: Application to the isolation of human placental insulin receptor. *Proc. Natl. Acad. Sci.* **81:** 7328–7332.

Fujita-Yamaguchi, Y., S. Choi, Y. Sakamoto, and K. Itakura. 1983. Purification of insulin receptor with full binding activity. *J. Biol. Chem.* **258:** 5045–5049.

Furth, A.J., H. Bolton, J. Potter, and J.D. Priddle. 1984. Separating detergents from protein. *Methods Enzymol.* **104:** 318–329.

Hart, G.W. 1992. Glycosylation. *Curr. Opin. Cell. Biol.* **4:** 1017–1023.

Helenius, A., D.F.R. McCaslin, and C. Tanford. 1979. Properties of detergents. *Methods Enzymol.* **56:** 734–749.

Herzberg, V.L., F. Grigorescu, A.S.B. Edge, R.G. Spiro, and C.R. Kahn. 1985. Characterization of insulin receptor carbohydrate by comparison of chemical and enzymatic deglycosylation. *Biochem. Biophys. Res. Commun.* **129:** 789–796.

Hjelmeland, L.M. 1986. The design and synthesis of detergents for membrane biochemistry. *Methods Enzymol.* **124:** 135–168.

Hjelmeland, L.M. and A. Chrambach. 1984. Solubilization of functional membrane proteins. *Methods Enzymol.* **104:** 305–318.

Hofmann, K., H. Romovacek, G. Titus, K. Ridge, J.A. Raffensperger, and F.M. Finn. 1987. The rat liver insulin receptor. *Biochemistry* **26:** 7384–7390.

Kasuga, M., F.A. Karlsson, and C.R. Kahn. 1982. Insulin stimulates the phosphorylation of the 95,000 dalton subunit of its own receptor. *Science* **215:** 185–187.

Klotz, I.M. 1982. Numbers of receptor sites from Scatchard graphs: Facts and fantasies. *Science* **217:** 1247–1249.

Lowry, O.H., N.J. Rosebrough, A.L. Farr, and R.J. Randall. 1951. Protein measurement with the Folin phenol reagent. *J. Biol. Chem.* **193:** 265–275.

Massague, J. and M.P. Czech. 1985. Affinity cross-linking of receptors for insulin and the insulin-like growth factors I and II. *Methods Enzymol.* **109:** 179–187.

Munson, P.J. and D. Rodbard. 1980. Ligand: A versatile computerized approach for characterization of ligand-binding systems. *Anal. Biochem.* **107:** 220–239.

Neville, D.M., Jr. 1968. Isolation of an organ specific protein antigen from cell surface membrane of rat liver. *Biochim. Biophys. Acta* **154:** 540–552.

Peterson, G.L. 1977. A simplication of the protein assay method of Lowry et al. which is more generally applicable. *Anal. Biochem.* **83:** 346–356.

Petruzzelli, L.M., S. Ganguly, C.J. Smith, M.H. Cobb, C.S. Rubin, and O.M. Rosen. 1982. Insulin activates a tyrosine-specific kinase in extracts of 3T3L1 adipocytes and human placenta. *Proc. Natl. Acad. Sci.* **79:** 6792–6796.

Pilch, P.F. and M.P. Czech. 1979. Interaction of cross-linking agents with insulin effector system of isolated fat cells. *J. Biol. Chem.* **254:** 3375–3381.

Ray, T.K. 1970. A modified method for the isolation of the plasma membrane from rat liver. *Biochim. Biophys. Acta* **196:** 1–9.

Ridge, K.D., K. Hofmann, and F.M. Finn. 1988. ATP sensitizes the insulin receptor to insulin. *Proc. Natl. Acad. Sci.* **85:** 9489–9493.

Rosen, O.M. 1987. After insulin binds. *Science* **237:** 1452–1458.

Rosen, O.M., C.S. Rubin, M.H. Cobb, and C.J. Smith. 1981. Insulin stimulates the phosphorylation of ribosomal protein S6 in a cell-free system derived from 3T3-L1 adipocytes. *J. Biol. Chem.* **256:** 3630–3633.

Silvius, J.R. 1992. Solubilization and functional reconstitution of biomembrane components. *Annu. Rev. Biophys. Biomol. Struct.* **21:** 323–348.

Tanford, C. 1973. *The hydrophobic effect: Formation of micelles and biological membranes*, pp. 36–44. John Wiley, New York.

Ullrich, A., J.R. Bell, E.Y. Chen, R. Herrera, L.M. Petruzzelli, T.J. Dull, A. Gray, L. Coussens, Y.C. Liao, M. Tsubokawa, A. Mason, P.H. Seeburg, C. Grunfeld, and O.M. Rosen. 1985. Human insulin receptor and its relationship to the tyrosine kinase family of oncogenes. *Nature* **313:** 756–761.

Weast, R.C., M.J. Astle, and W.H. Beyer, eds. 1986. *CRC handbook of chemistry and physics*, 67th edition, pp. E374–375. CRC Press, Boca Raton, Florida.

Yip, C.C. and C.W.T. Yeung. 1985. Photoaffinity labeling of the insulin receptor. *Methods Enzymol.* **109:** 170–179.

Appendices

Appendix 1
Measurement of pH

Measurement of pH is a fundamental skill required for research in a biochemical laboratory, but it is rarely taught specifically. A useful theoretical and practical discussion of pH measurements is found in *Principles of Instrumental Analysis* (1985). You should consult the manufacturer for technical information and specific instructions for your pH meter and electrode.

The term pH refers to the negative logarithm of the hydrogen ion concentration in the solution. The "p" denotes $-\log_{10}$ and "H" denotes the hydrogen ion concentration. This is a general notation: p is the $-\log_{10}$ of whatever follows. For example, pCa refers to the negative logarithm of the calcium ion concentration. Since the pH unit is a logarithm, each unit of pH corresponds to a tenfold change in absolute concentration units. In the calmodulin experiment, for example, the pH of the ion-exchange step is 8.0, whereas the isoelectric point of the protein is just above 4.0. In other words, the hydrogen ion concentration of the ion-exchange buffer is 10,000-fold lower than that required to bring the calmodulin to a net charge of zero. In the earlier step of precipitation, the hydrogen ion concentration changed by this same four orders of magnitude to effect the precipitation. This is a very large change in the environment of the protein. For some proteins, pH change can result in unfolding and inactivation. As you adjust the pH of a solution and transfer proteins from one pH to another, remember that this change in environment can result in dramatic changes in the behavior of the protein. By analogy, imagine the difference between drinking a spoonful of bicarbonate of soda (sodium bicarbonate) or a spoonful of vinegar (acetic acid)!

A pH meter consists of an electrode connected to the meter itself, which contains the electronic circuits required to amplify the measured voltage and convert it to understandable units (based on prior calibration) on a digital display. The electrode is the business end of the pH meter and comprises two galvanic half cells, one dependent on hydrogen ion concentration and the other a reference, theoretically independent of the sample solution. The body of the electrode is usually glass or plastic, and the tip contains a pH-sensitive glass membrane that permits hydrogen ions to exchange with the inner and outer surfaces, establishing a potential across the membrane. The interior of the glass electrode contains a standard solution and half-cell assembly that produces a small voltage proportional to the potential. The electrode is usually filled with a saturated solution of KCl to permit free transmission of current through the solution. The pH measurement is performed by recording the flow of metal ions across the junction in response to the equilibrium hydrogen ion concentration. The most popular electrodes in a modern protein chemistry laboratory are of the "combination" type, which incorporate the reference and measurement electrodes into a single unit. The metal ions used are usually derived from either Ag/AgCl or Hg/Hg_2Cl_2. It is important that the filling solution is saturated, so that the chloride concentration does not change. It is also important not to use buffers that will chelate the metal ions. Specifically, Tris buffers chelate silver ions effectively, so pH measurements of Tris buffers using silver chloride electrodes can be inaccurate. More importantly, constant use of a silver chloride electrode for Tris buffers can result in the inability to measure pH at all. Typically, we use a "calomel" or mercurous/ mercurous chloride electrode to avoid this problem. However, calomel electrodes can be affected by large amounts of sulfhydryl compounds.

The pH of a solution is dependent on temperature, and this temperature dependence varies with different buffers. Tris buffers, for instance, are highly temperature-dependent. It is therefore important to make pH measurements consistently at the same temperature. Usually, one should use the temperature of the experiment. That is, if the ion-exchange column is to be run at 4°C, then all buffers should be adjusted and their pH measured at that temperature. Many modern pH meters have temperature compensation adjustments that allow correction for temperature. Always calibrate a pH meter with standard solutions covering the pH range of the buffer to be adjusted. Do not calibrate in a linear fashion between pH 7.00 and 10.01, and try to measure a buffer at pH 5.5! Instead, calibrate with standards at 7.00 and 4.01, for example. Do not assume the pH meter is calibrated. This should be done before each measurement. Clean and store the electrode properly, usually in a saturated solution of KCl. There should be a visible KCl precipitate, showing that there is indeed a saturated solution of the salt. Some electrodes are gel-filled, so they will not evaporate or need refilling. These are convenient, but make sure they are working properly before use. Finally, solutions containing a lot of protein (e.g., the ammonium sulfate supernatant from the calmodulin preparation) can leave residue that clogs the porous portion of the pH electrode tip. Be sure to clean off the electrode properly; distilled water is usually adequate. It is tempting to wipe the excess water off of the electrode with a Kimwipe, but resist this temptation. Rubbing paper along the glass electrode body can set up static charges that can affect measurements. Instead, let the water drip off the end, and use the corner of a Kimwipe to wick the excess from the tip.

REFERENCE

Skoog, D.A. 1985. *Principles of insrumental analysis*, 3rd edition, pp. 600–624. Saunders College Publishing, Philadelphia, Pennsylvania.

Appendix 2
Preparation of Buffers

TRIS BUFFER

Prepare the following:

Stock solution A	0.2 M Tris
Stock solution B	0.2 M HCl

Add 50 ml of A to x ml of B and adjust the volume to 200 ml with H_2O.

x ml	pH		x ml	pH
5.0	9.0		26.8	8.0
8.1	8.8		32.5	7.8
12.2	8.6		38.4	7.6
16.5	8.4		41.4	7.4
21.9	8.2		44.2	7.2

PHOSPHATE BUFFER

Prepare the following:

Stock solution A	0.2 M monobasic sodium phosphate
Stock solution B	0.2 M dibasic sodium phosphate

Add x ml of A to y ml of B and adjust the volume to 200 ml with H_2O.

x ml	y ml	pH	x ml	y ml	pH
93.5	6.5	5.7	45.0	55.0	6.9
92.0	8.0	5.8	39.0	61.0	7.0
90.0	10.0	5.9	33.0	67.0	7.1
87.7	12.3	6.0	28.0	72.0	7.2
85.0	15.0	6.1	23.0	77.0	7.3
81.5	18.5	6.2	19.0	81.0	7.4
77.5	22.5	6.3	16.0	84.0	7.5
73.5	26.5	6.4	13.0	87.0	7.6
68.5	31.5	6.5	10.5	90.5	7.7
62.5	37.5	6.6	8.5	91.5	7.8
56.5	43.5	6.7	7.0	93.0	7.9
51.0	49.0	6.8	5.3	94.7	8.0

GOOD'S BUFFERS

Structure	Name	pK_a at 20°C
$O \overset{+}{N}HCH_2CH_2SO_3^-$	MES	6.15
$H_2NCOCH_2\overset{+}{N} \overset{CH_2COO^-}{\underset{CH_2COONa}{}}$ H	ADA	6.60
$NaO_3SCH_2CH_2N \overset{+}{N}HCH_2CH_2SO_3^-$	PIPES	6.80
$H_2NCOCH_2\overset{+}{N}H_2CH_2CH_2SO_3^-$	ACES	6.90
$(CH_3)_3\equiv\overset{+}{N}-CH_2CH_2NH_2Cl^-$	Cholamine chloride	7.10
$(HOCH_2CH_2)_2\equiv\overset{+}{N}HCH_2CH_2SO_3^-$	BES	7.15
$(HOCH_2)_3\equiv\overset{+}{N}HCH_2CH_2SO_3^-$	TES	7.50
$HOCH_2CH_2\overset{+}{N} NCH_2CH_2SO_3^-$ H	HEPES	7.55
$(HOCH_2)_3\equiv\overset{+}{C}NH_2CH_2COO^-$	Tricine	8.15
$H_2NCOCH_2NH_2$	Glycinamide	8.20
$(HOCH_2CH_2)_2\equiv\overset{+}{N}HCH_2COO^-$	Bicine	8.35

REFERENCES

Ferguson, W.J., K.I. Braunschweiger, W.R. Braunschweiger, J.R. Smith, J.J. McCormick, C.C. Wasmann, N.P. Jarvis, D.H. Bell, and N.E. Good. 1980. Hydrogen ion buffers for biological research. *Anal. Biochem.* **104:** 300–310.

Gomori, G. 1955. General preparative procedures. Preparation of buffers for use in enzyme studies. *Methods Enzymol.* **I:** 138–146.

Good, N.E., G.D. Winget, W. Winter, T.N. Connolly, S. Izawa, and R.M.M. Singh. 1966. Hydrogen ion buffers for biological research. *Biochemistry* **5:** 467–477.

Appendix 3
Measurement of Conductivity

In an ion-exchange chromatography experiment, it is critical to know both the ionic strength and the pH of the protein solution that is to be loaded on the column. The ionic strength of the protein solution must be at or below the ionic strength of the starting buffer. Ionic strength is determined using a conductivity meter, which measures the overall conductivity of the solution as the current passing across platinum electrodes in a glass measuring cell. Units of conductivity are Siemens/cm, which is a cgs standard unit. It is also important to measure the ionic strength of the fractions eluted from the ion-exchange column. It is theoretically possible to calculate the concentration of solute from the measured conductivity. In practice, however, it is more convenient to compare the conductivity of the sample to known standards prepared in the same buffer. This permits accurate estimates of ionic strength without knowing all of the apparent dissociation constants for all of the ionizable groups in the sample. If you do not want to waste much of a precious sample and you do not want to dip a conductivity meter electrode into a pure protein solution, an acceptable method is to dilute 20 µl of sample into 1 ml of pure water, mix well, and read the conductivity.

Conductivity is very dependent on temperature as shown in the table below. Most modern conductivity meters have temperature compensation adjustments that allow correction for temperature.

Temperature (°C)	Conductivity (milliSiemens/cm)			
	pure H_2O	0.01 M KCl	0.01 M KCl	1.0 M KCl
0	0.14×10^{-4}	0.77	7.1	65.2
18	0.40×10^{-4}	1.22	11.2	97.8
25	0.58×10^{-4}	1.41	12.9	111.3
34	0.89×10^{-4}	–	–	–
50	1.76×10^{-4}	–	–	–

Ions vary in their equivalent ionic conductances (i) at infinite dilution. Some examples are given in the table below.

Cation	i_+	Anion	i_-
K^+	73.5	Cl^-	76.4
Na^+	50.1	Br^-	78.4
Li^+	38.7	I^-	76.8
NH_4^+	73.4	HCO_3^-	44.5
$1/2\ Mg^{++}$	53.1	OAc^-	40.9
		$1/2\ SO_4^=$	79.8

As a result, for instance, a 0.01 M solution of sodium acetate (50.1 + 40.9 = 91) will have a lower conductivity than a 0.01 M solution of potassium chloride (73.5 + 76.4 = 149.9).

Appendix 4
Fractionation with Solid Ammonium Sulfate

For the principles of ammonium sulfate precipitation, see Unit I. The following table is adapted, with permission, from Oxford University Press (Oxford) from *Data for Biochemical Research*, 2nd edition (R.M.C. Dawson et al., eds.) (© Oxford University Press [1969]).

Final concentration of ammonium sulfate (% saturation at 0°C)

Initial concentration of ammonium sulfate (% saturation at 0°C)	20	25	30	35	40	45	50	55	60	65	70	75	80	85	90	95	100
	solid ammonium sulfate to add to 100 ml of solution																
0	10.6	13.4	16.4	19.4	22.6	25.8	29.1	32.6	36.1	39.8	43.6	47.6	51.6	55.9	60.3	65.0	69.7
5	7.9	10.8	13.7	16.6	19.7	22.9	26.2	29.6	33.1	36.8	40.5	44.4	48.4	52.6	57.0	61.5	66.2
10	5.3	8.1	10.9	13.9	16.9	20.0	23.3	26.6	30.1	33.7	37.4	41.2	45.2	49.3	53.6	58.1	62.7
15	2.6	5.4	8.2	11.1	14.1	17.2	20.4	23.7	27.1	30.6	34.3	38.1	42.0	46.0	50.3	54.7	59.2
20	0	2.7	5.5	8.3	11.3	14.3	17.5	20.7	24.1	27.6	31.2	34.9	38.7	42.7	46.9	51.2	55.7
25		0	2.7	5.6	8.4	11.5	14.6	17.9	21.1	24.5	28.0	31.7	35.5	39.5	43.6	47.8	52.2
30			0	2.8	5.6	8.6	11.7	14.8	18.1	21.4	24.9	28.5	32.3	36.2	40.2	44.5	48.8
35				0	2.8	5.7	8.7	11.8	15.1	18.4	21.8	25.4	29.1	32.9	36.9	41.0	45.3
40					0	2.9	5.8	8.9	12.0	15.3	18.7	22.2	25.8	29.6	33.5	37.6	41.8
45						0	2.9	5.9	9.0	12.3	15.6	19.0	22.6	26.3	30.2	34.2	38.3
50							0	3.0	6.0	9.2	12.5	15.9	19.4	23.0	26.8	30.8	34.8
55								0	3.0	6.1	9.3	12.7	16.1	19.7	23.5	27.3	31.3
60									0	3.1	6.2	9.5	12.9	16.4	20.1	23.9	27.9
65										0	3.1	6.3	9.7	13.2	16.8	20.5	24.4
70											0	3.2	6.5	9.9	13.4	17.1	20.9
75												0	3.2	6.6	10.1	13.7	17.4
80													0	3.3	6.7	10.3	13.9
85														0	3.4	6.8	10.5
90															0	3.4	7.0
95																0	3.5
100																	0

Note: The pH of the solution may decrease significantly on addition of ammonium sulfate.

Appendix 5
Polyacrylamide Gel Electrophoresis of Proteins in Sodium Dodecyl Sulfate

This appendix covers the fundamentals of polyacrylamide gel electrophoresis (PAGE) in the presence of the ionic detergent sodium dodecyl sulfate (SDS). It is intended to provide basic instructions and recipes for successful protein analysis that is common to all of the units in this volume. There are other books and journals dedicated solely to the theory and practice of electrophoresis (e.g., Andrews 1986; Hames and Rickwood 1990; *Electrophoresis*), and you should refer to those for more detailed reviews of the field. Proteins can be thought of as dipolar ions (Cohen and Edsall 1943) and, as such, will migrate in an electric field. The electrophoresis of proteins was first performed in the 1930s by Tiselius in solution and later, in the 1950s, by Smithies in starch gels and Raymond in polyacrylamide gels (for a review of the early days of electrophoresis, see Andrews 1986). The use of gel matrices for electrophoresis allowed scientists to take advantage of the molecular sieving properties of the cross-linked gel to retard the mobility of proteins and trap them in a conveniently handled material (Van Holde 1985).

Modern SDS-PAGE is the culmination of three innovations that permit the correlation of electrophoretic mobility with a protein's molecular mass and therefore allows researchers to estimate molecular weight (Weber and Osborn 1969; Swank and Munkres 1971; Chrambach and Rodbard 1971). First was the use of discontinuous (disc) buffer systems in which the sample and the running buffer have very different pH values (e.g., 6.8 and 8.3) and counterions (e.g., chloride and glycine) to allow the proteins to enter the separating gel as more focused bands (Davis 1964). Second was the use of SDS along with reducing agents to denature the proteins and endow them with relatively uniform charge per unit mass (Shapiro and Maizel 1969). Third was the union of these two procedures in a simple buffer system, such as Tris-glycine containing SDS (Laemmli 1970). More recently, the Tris-tricine buffer system has been demonstrated to be very effective for separating proteins (Schägger and von Jagow 1987; Patton et al. 1991).

Preparation of Gels

It is most common today to use a slab gel (rectangular or square) format, but tubes and capillary formats are also useful for single samples in preparative and analytical modes, respectively. Many of the reagents for polyacrylamide slab gel electrophoresis are available in formats that make electrophoresis very easy. For example, pre-mixed acrylamide/bisacrylamide solutions and concentrated (10%; w/v) SDS solutions are useful because the dry powder forms of these compounds are dangerous if inhaled. Pre-cast/pre-poured gels are also available from a variety of vendors in several styles, such as gradients of increasing acrylamide concentration (4–20% is popular) or fixed acrylamide concentration. These are useful in situations when there is limited preparation time, as in a laboratory classroom, or when documentation of lot-to-lot consistency and certification of analysis are useful, as in an industrial quality assurance setting. Pre-cast/pre-poured gels are expensive, and the shelf life is finite. Also, highly discontinuous gel systems with stacking gels are usually not provided in a pre-cast/pre-poured format because diffusion would rapidly (24–48 hours) cause the stacking buffer to lose its effective advantage by mixing at the interface with the separating gel buffer. Therefore, it is often preferable in a research laboratory setting to cast your own gels. They are fresh when used; they can be prepared in the optimal size, format, and percentage acrylamide; they can be layered with a stacking gel to aid in large-volume sample applications; and the acts of designing and casting the gel are instructive.

Selection of Reagents

The selection of reagents is very important. Many vendors now sell the individual components for gel electrophoresis in a highly purified form. This was not always the case, and one should check that the reagents used are of the highest purity available. For example, preparations of dodecyl sulfate may be contaminated with sulfated aliphatic chains of lengths other than 12 carbons (dodecyl), such as myristyl sulfate (14 carbons). Some separations are altered by the presence of a small percentage of such contaminants. Although these alterations can be advantageous or disadvantageous, the most problematic parts of the contaminations are variability by lot number, manufacturer, and time. Differences in the SDS can be minimized by using the same vendor continually and verifying that the dodecyl content is very high and unchanging. Recrystallization of SDS is usually unnecessary. Similarly, purity and consistency of the acrylamide is essential to successful electrophoresis. Filtration of the acrylamide solutions is highly recommended to remove particulates and clumps, especially those not readily visible.

Preparation of Solutions and Buffers

Be sure that all buffer solutions are prepared correctly and are not stored for long periods of time. Sulfhydryl reagents (dithiothreitol, 2-mercaptoethanol) should be added fresh each time a working solution aliquot is made, usually daily. If you store SDS as a concentrated (10%; w/v) solution, keep it at room temperature (above 20°C) because it will precipitate in the cold. Always check that the SDS is in solution, just in case someone lowered the heat in your laboratory overnight. Note that you should use a clear bottle to store the concentrated SDS so that you will notice a precipitate if one occurs. Always make sure to wear gloves when handling the gels, both for personal safety and to avoid contamination of the gels.

SAFETY NOTES

- Sulfhydryl reagents (dithiothreitol, 2-mercaptoethanol) are harmful if inhaled or absorbed through the skin. High concentrations are extremely destructive to the mucous membranes, upper respiratory tract, skin, and eyes. Use only in a chemical fume hood. Gloves and safety glasses should be worn.
- Acrylamide and bisacrylamide are potent neurotoxins and are absorbed through the skin. Their effects are cumulative. Wear gloves and a mask when weighing acrylamide and bisacrylamide. Wear gloves when handling solutions containing these chemicals. Although polyacrylamide is considered to be nontoxic, it should be handled with care because of the possibility that it might contain small quantities of unpolymerized acrylamide.
- APS (ammonium persulfate) is extremely destructive to tissue of the mucous membranes and upper respiratory tract, eyes, and skin. Inhalation may be fatal. Exposure can cause gastrointestinal disturbances and dermatitis. Wear gloves, safety glasses, respirator, and other protective clothing and work in a chemical fume hood. Wash thoroughly after handling.
- TEMED (*N,N,N',N'*-tetramethylethylenediamine) is extremely destructive to tissue of the mucous membranes and upper respiratory tract, eyes, and skin. Inhalation may be fatal. Prolonged contact can cause severe irritation or burns. Wear gloves, safety glasses, respirator, and other protective clothing and work in a chemical fume hood. Wash thoroughly after handling. Flammable: Vapor may travel a considerable distance to source of ignition and flash back.
- A respirator or mask should be worn when handling powdered sodium dodecyl sulfate (SDS).

● ——

Electrophoresis

The solution volumes are adjusted for use with a mini-slab gel apparatus, which holds gels that are approximately 8 x 10 x 0.15 cm. Several formats are available in this size range. All contain glass plates, plastic spacers (usually 0.1–0.2 cm thick), and Teflon combs to form the wells of the gel during casting. Below are step-by-step instructions for successful SDS-PAGE.

CASTING THE SEPARATING GEL (LOWER GEL)

Washing the Equipment

To minimize contamination by keratins, soak the gel plates, combs, and spacers in strong alkaline detergent (2% solution of RBS 35 [Pierce Chemical Co.]) concentrate in water (20 ml of concentrate per liter of water). You can maintain a covered tub of detergent solution and suspend the plates on a rack in the tub for storage for at least 10 minutes (or overnight). Also, try to keep the gel materials and solutions as dust-free as possible. It is sometimes useful to pre-rinse pipettes with buffers to remove dust particles that may have settled in the pipettes. Always wear gloves and change them frequently. Use paper wipes that do not leave particles (e.g., Kimwipes) to dry plates, or rinse plates with methanol or acetone and allow to air-dry in a fume hood.

Mixing the Lower Gel

On the basis of your best estimate of the size of the protein(s) of interest, you will want to choose an appropriate acrylamide concentration. The following table summarizes the mixtures of components needed for several percentages of acrylamide/bisacrylamide mixtures. The molecular mass is given for the smallest size protein of interest on the gel.

	Molecular mass of protein			
	>50 kD	30–40 kD	20–30 kD	<20 kD
	Total percent of acrylamide/bisacrylamide			
Solution	8%	10%	12%	15%
30:0.8 Acrylamide/ bisacrylamide	2.13 ml	2.67 ml	3.20 ml	4.00 ml
H_2O	3.87 ml	3.33 ml	2.80 ml	2.00 ml
Separating gel buffer (4x)	2.00 ml	2.00 ml	2.00 ml	2.00 ml
	8.00 ml	8.00 ml	8.00 ml	8.00 ml
10% (w/v) APS	+ 45 μl	+ 45 μl	+ 45 μl	+ 45 μl
TEMED	+ 12 μl	+ 12 μl	+ 12 μl	+ 12 μl

(For recipes, see Preparation of Solutions and Buffers, pp. 366–368.)

Pouring the Lower Gel

See Safety Notes, p. 361.

1. Combine the acrylamide/bisacrylamide, H_2O, and 4x separating gel buffer in a small (25 ml) Erlenmeyer flask with a sidearm port.

2. Place a stopper in the flask, and de-gas the mixture for 10 minutes under vacuum.

3. Add the APS, and mix gently, but thoroughly. Try to avoid the formation of bubbles.

4. Add the TEMED. Mix gently, but quickly.

5. Pour the gel with a pre-rinsed (with water) pasteur pipette until the height of the liquid is about 1 cm from the top of the gel plates.

6. Layer isobutanol (2-methyl-1-propanol) evenly on top of the gel material using a pre-rinsed pasteur pipette. The isobutanol layer should be about 2 mm high.

7. Let the gel polymerize for at least 1 hour.

CASTING THE STACKING GEL (UPPER GEL)

Mixing the Stacking Gel

	Final 3% (w/v) acrylamide/bisacrylami total concentration
30:0.8 Acrylamide/bisacrylamide	0.75 ml
Distilled/deionized H_2O	3.00 ml
Stacking gel buffer (4x)	1.25 ml
	5.00 ml
10% (w/v) APS	+ 30 µl
TEMED	+ 8 µl

(For recipes, see Preparation of Solutions and Buffers, pp. 366–368.)

Pouring the Upper Gel

See Safety Notes, p. 361.

1. Combine the acrylamide/bisacrylamide, H_2O, and 4x stacking gel buffer in a small (25 ml) Erlenmeyer flask with a sidearm port.

2. Place a stopper in the flask, and de-gas the mixture for 10 minutes under vacuum.

3. After the separating gel has polymerized, pour off the upper liquid layer of isobutanol and unpolymerized acrylamide.

4. Rinse the upper portion of the gel with distilled, deionized H_2O.

5. Rinse the upper portion of the gel with a small portion (<0.5 ml) of the stacking gel mix.

6. Insert the comb between the gel plates.

7. Add the APS, and mix gently, but thoroughly. Try to avoid the formation of bubbles.

8. Add the TEMED. Mix gently, but quickly.

9. Pour the upper gel with a pasteur pipette (pre-rinsed with H_2O).

The gel should polymerize within 10 minutes. Use the gel within 2 hours.

RUNNING THE GEL

Preparing the Samples

See Safety Notes, p. 361.

1. Add 5–20 µl of sample buffer (1x) containing 2-mercaptoethanol (see p. 368 for recipe) to each sample of precipitated or dried protein 1.5-ml polypropylene microcentrifuge tubes with caps. Mix by vortexing briefly and place immediately into a rack in a boiling water bath for 5 minutes.

2. Cool samples to room temperature and give a brief spin in a microcentrifuge (~10 seconds).

Loading the Samples

1. Remove the comb from the polymerized gel and mount into the electrophoresis chamber. Add running buffer (1x) (see p. 367 for recipe) into each reservoir, making sure that each sample well is filled. Take care to remove any bubbles or extraneous polyacrylamide fragments from the wells.

2. Load each sample in the appropriate volume, usually a maximum of 15 µl on a gel that is 0.15 cm thick. Because the sample buffer contains 10% glycerol, the sample will settle down through the buffer in the well to the bottom.

3. Take care that samples do not mix by spillage across the well divider. Use very narrow bore tips for automatic pipettors, and change the tips for each sample.

Running the Gel

1. Attach the electrode leads to the power supply, black to the negative pole and red to the positive pole. Proteins with SDS bound at pH 8.3 are negatively charged, and they will migrate toward the positive (red) electrode.

2. Run the stacking gel at 8 mA (constant current) per gel. If two gels are running simultaneously in one apparatus, run the gels at 16 mA. The protein samples will form a narrow band at the stacking/separating gel interface.

3. When the bromophenol blue enters the separating gel, increase the current to 18 mA per gel.

4. Stop the electrophoresis by shutting off the power supply when the bromophenol blue reaches the bottom of the gel. Do not let the dye run out the bottom.

PREPARATION OF SOLUTIONS AND BUFFERS

Acrylamide/bisacrylamide stock solution (30:0.8)
(1 liter)

30% (w/v) Acrylamide	300 g
0.8% (w/v) Bisacrylamide	8 g

Add distilled, deionized H_2O to a final volume of 1 liter. Filter through a 0.22-μm membrane. Store at 4°C in the dark. *See Safety Notes, p. 361.*

Separating gel buffer (4x)

1.5 M Tris-HCl (pH 8.8)
0.4% (w/v) SDS

	For 500 ml	For 1 liter
Tris base	90.8 g	181.7 g
10% (w/v) SDS	20 ml	40 ml

Add distilled, deionized H_2O to the desired final volume. Adjust pH to 8.8 at room temperature with HCl. Filter through a 0.22-μm membrane. Store at 4°C.

Stacking gel buffer (4x)

0.5 M Tris-HCl (pH 6.8)
0.4% (w/v) SDS

	For 500 ml	For 1 liter
Tris base	30.3 g	60.6 g
10% (w/v) SDS	20 ml	40 ml

Add distilled, deionized H_2O to the desired final volume. Adjust pH to 6.8 with HCl at room temperature. Filter through a 0.22-μm membrane. Store at 4°C.

Electrode buffer (4x)

0.1 M Tris
0.768 M Glycine

	For 4 liters	For 8 liters
Tris base	48.4 g	96.9 g
Glycine	230.6 g	461.2 g

Add distilled, deionized H_2O to the desired final volume. It is not necessary to adjust the pH. The proportions of Tris base and glycine give pH 8.3. Store at room temperature in a large vessel (carboy).

SDS (10%; w/v)
(0.1 liter)

Dissolve 10 g of SDS in distilled, deionized H_2O to a 0.1-liter final volume. Store at room temperature in a clear bottle. *See Safety Notes, p. 361.*

Running buffer (1x)

Combine 1/4 volume of 4x electrode buffer and 3/4 volume of distilled, deionized H_2O. Then add 1/100 volume of 10% SDS to a final concentration of 0.1% (w/v) SDS. An example is given below:

	For 800 ml
Electrode buffer (4x)	200 ml
Distilled, deionized H_2O	592 ml
10% (w/v) SDS	8 ml
	800 ml

Stock sample buffer (2x)

0.25 M Tris-HCl (pH 6.8)
4% (w/v) SDS
20% (v/v) Glycerol
Trace bromophenol blue

When preparing this buffer, be very careful to wear gloves and to avoid contamination of the buffer with keratins (proteins that are found on skin).

	For 100 ml
Stacking gel buffer (4x)	50 ml
SDS (solid-dry powder)	4 g
Glycerol	20 ml
Bromophenol blue (solution is deep blue)	2 mg

Add H_2O to 100 ml final volume. This buffer can be stored at room temperature or frozen in aliquots, but it must be warmed before use to ensure that the SDS is in solution. Be sure that repeated use of a common stock of this solution does not result in contamination. Aliquots will help avoid this problem. *See Safety Notes, p. 361.*

Sample buffer (1x) with 2-mercaptoethanol

Before use, make a working solution of sample buffer by diluting the 2x stock sample buffer (see above) and adding 2-mercaptoethanol to a final concentration of 5% (v/v) (*see Safety Notes, p. 361*). Typically:

2x Stock sample buffer	100 µl
H_2O	90 µl
2-Mercaptoethanol	10 µl
	200 µl

Ammonium persulfate (APS) (10%; w/v)

Dissolve 3 g of ammonium persulfate in distilled, deionized H_2O to a final volume of 30 ml. This solution may be stable for brief periods of days at 4°C, but it is recommended that you prepare it freshly for each new set of gels. *See Safety Notes, p. 361.*

●　───────────────────────────────

Staining of Gels

SILVER STAINING OF GELS

Reagents

Methanol (50% and 5% v/v)
10 μM Dithiothreitol (DTT) (*See Safety Notes, p. 361.*)
$AgNO_3$ (0.1% w/v)
Citric acid (solid)
Developer solution
(For recipes, see Preparation of Reagents, p. 370.)

Procedure

This procedure is modified from Merril (1987). Perform the steps at room temperature with slow shaking of the gel on a rotating platform.

1. Soak the gel in 50% methanol two times for 15 minutes each.

2. Soak the gel in 5% methanol for 10 minutes.

3. Rinse the gel quickly three times with H_2O.

4. Soak the gel in 10 μM DTT for 20 minutes.

5. Soak the gel in 0.1% $AgNO_3$ for 20 minutes.

6. Rinse the gel quickly (<15 seconds per rinse) first in H_2O and then two times in developer solution.

7. Soak the gel in developer solution for a few minutes until the protein bands appear.

8. Stop the development by adding solid citric acid (dihydrate) (about 10 g of citric acid per 200 ml of developer solution).

9. Cover the gel with aluminum foil (to keep out light) and soak for 10 minutes.

10. Rinse gel extensively with H_2O. Soak in H_2O for 10 minutes under aluminum foil (in the dark). The gel will develop colors in the protein bands overnight in H_2O (in the dark).

If desired, the gel can be soaked for >1 hour in 4% (v/v) glycerol and then dried.

Preparation of Reagents

Methanol
(500 ml)

	For 50% v/v	For 5% v/v
Methanol	250 ml	25 ml
H_2O	250 ml	475 ml

Dithiothreitol (DTT) (10 µM)

0.5 M DTT	10 µl
H_2O	500 ml

See Safety Notes, p. 361.

AgNO₃ (0.1% w/v)

$AgNO_3$	0.5 g
H_2O	500 ml

Developer solution

Sodium carbonate solution
37% (w/v) Formaldehyde

First, prepare sodium carbonate solution by dissolving 15 g of anhydrous sodium carbonate in 500 ml of H_2O. Then, *just before use*, add 250 µl of 37% (w/v) formaldehyde to the sodium carbonate solution to give the complete developer solution.

SAFETY NOTE

- Formaldehyde is toxic and is also a carcinogen. It is readily absorbed through the skin and is irritating or destructive to the skin, eyes, mucous membranes, and upper respiratory tract. Wear gloves and safety glasses.

COOMASSIE BLUE STAINING OF POLYACRYLAMIDE GELS

Materials and Equipment

Polyacrylamide gel of interest
Glycerol (4%; v/v)
Gel dryer
Whatman® No. 1 and Whatman® 3MM filter papers

Solutions

Staining solution
High-methanol destain
Standard (low-methanol) destain
(For recipes, see Preparation of Solutions, p. 372.)

Procedure

1. Stain the gel in approximately 100 ml of staining solution. Incubate at room temperature on either a platform rocker or a rotating platform for at least 20 minutes.

2. Discard the staining solution (*carefully*, it splashes easily) and rinse the gel with approximately 100 ml of high-methanol destain.

3. Destain the gel in 100–200 ml of high-methanol destain. Change the destain solution when the intensity of the color of the destain equals that of the gel. It should take approximately 2–3 hours and 3–4 changes of the destain. Change the solution often until most of the blue color is gone.

4. Complete the destaining by placing the gel in approximately 100 ml of the standard (low-methanol) destain for 4–6 hours or overnight. The background on the gel should now be essentially clear. Leaving the gel in destain too long (several days to weeks) will decrease the intensity of the stained protein bands. After destaining, the gel can be stored in distilled H_2O at room temperature.

5. Equilibrate the gel in glycerol (4%; v/v) in H_2O for at least 60 minutes (acetic acid tends to gum up the gel dryer and vacuum pump, and the glycerol helps to keep the gel from cracking when it is dried). The gel can now be stored at 4°C for extended periods of time or dried in a gel dryer.

6. Dry the gel as follows. First, soak two rectangular pieces of cellophane (which are slightly larger than the gel) in H_2O for a few

minutes to hydrate the cellophane. Place the gel between the two pieces of cellophane and make sure that there are *no bubbles* between the gel and the cellophane. Then place on the gel dryer in the following order (from top to bottom): plastic wrap (e.g., Saran Wrap); cellophane; polyacrylamide gel of interest; cellophane; Whatman 3MM paper; Whatman 3MM paper. *Make sure that there is no plastic wrap between the gel and the gel dryer.* Dry in the gel dryer with heat for approximately 1 hour.

Note: If photographs are desired, it is best to take them before the gel is dried.

Preparation of Solutions

Store all solutions at room temperature.

Staining solution
(1 liter)

Coomassie® Brilliant Blue R250	2.5 g
Methanol	454 ml
Glacial acetic acid	92 ml
H_2O	454 ml

Filter through Whatman #1 paper.

SAFETY NOTE

- Glacial acetic acid is volatile and should be used in a chemical fume hood. Concentrated acids should be handled with great care; gloves and a face protector should be worn.

High-methanol destain

	For 1 liter	For 2 liters
Methanol	454 ml	908 ml
Glacial acetic acid	75 ml	150 ml
(*See Safety Note above.*)		
H_2O	471 ml	942 ml

Standard (low-methanol) destain

	For 1 liter	For 2 liters
Methanol	50 ml	100 ml
Glacial acetic acid	75 ml	150 ml
(*See Safety Note above.*)		
H_2O	875 ml	1750 ml

• ———

Sample Preparation by Precipitation

PRECIPITATION WITH TRICHLOROACETIC ACID

Materials and Equipment

Acetone (Aldrich Chemical Co. Inc.)

> **Note:** Store at room temperature. Do not place in freezer.

Polypropylene microcentrifuge tubes (1.5-ml)

> **Note:** (i) Always wash the tubes before use. (ii) When handling very low levels of protein (<100 ng), it might be necessary to siliconize the tubes according to the following procedure: Soak the tubes briefly (5 minutes) in 5% (v/v) dichlorodimethylsilane (Aldrich Chemical Co. Inc.) in methylene chloride, and then rinse with ethanol (100%) and then with glass-distilled H_2O. Let the tubes dry for at least one day at room temperature. Some proteins bind more tightly to polypropylene following siliconization. Unfortunately, this property is relatively empirical, and one does not know a priori if the protein of interest should reside in a washed polypropylene or siliconized tube.

Molecular mass markers (*optional*)

Reagent and Buffer

TCA + DOC
Sample buffer (1x) with and without 2-mercaptoethanol
(For recipes, see Preparation of Reagent and Buffer, p. 374.)

Procedure

1. Add 1/4 volume of TCA + DOC to the protein fraction (in a 1.5-ml polypropylene microcentrifuge tube) to a final TCA concentration of 20% (w/v). Mix by vortexing.

2. Incubate on ice for 20 to 30 minutes.

3. Spin 15 minutes in a microcentrifuge at room temperature. The pellet, if visible, is a sticky yellow-tan colored gel. Remove the supernatant with a finely drawn pasteur pipette. *Try to remove as much of the supernatant as possible.* The pellet will be visible if 100 µl of sample is precipitated.

4. Add 3 volumes (of the original sample volume) of acetone (at room temperature). Let the samples stand at room temperature for approximately 10 minutes to allow the TCA + DOC to dissolve in the acetone.

5. Spin 15 minutes at room temperature. The pellet is now similar in size and physical characteristics to a speck of dust. Approximately 10 µg or more of protein can be seen. Sometimes a white pellet of salt (KCl, etc.) is obtained. Remove the supernatant with a *very* finely drawn pasteur pipette. Let the pellet dry for 10 minutes on ice (leave the cap of the 1.5-ml tube open). The dry pellet can be stored at –20°C for an indefinite period of time (>1 month).

6. Dissolve the pellet in sample buffer (1x) containing 2-mercapto-ethanol (use 6 µl with the standard mini-slab gel apparatus). If a small residue of TCA remains, the bromophenol blue will turn yellow. This does not matter, as there is enough buffering capacity in the electrophoresis to neutralize traces of TCA. If there is a residue of KCl in the pellet, a flocculent white precipitate (potassium dodecyl sulfate) will form upon addition of sample buffer to the precipitated protein. If potassium dodecyl sulfate precipitates, it will be difficult to load the samples on the SDS gel, but once the samples are loaded, the gel should run well.

7. If molecular mass markers are desired, then use a stock solution of 0.5 mg total protein per milliliter of molecular mass marker proteins in 1x SDS sample buffer *without* 2-mercaptoethanol. Store at –20°C in small (50 µl) aliquots. For silver stained gels, use 2 µl of MW standards + 4 µl of sample buffer *with* 2-mercaptoethanol to a final volume of 6 µl.

Preparation of Reagent and Buffer

TCA + DOC
(10 ml)

Trichloroacetic acid (TCA) (100%; w/v)	10 ml
Deoxycholate, Na salt (DOC) (Sigma Chemical Co.)	40 mg

Store at room temperature. This solution, which is normally colorless, will turn light yellow upon standing 2–3 weeks. The deoxycholate acts like a carrier that assists in the precipitation of protein. It is soluble in 100% (w/v) TCA, but not in 20% (w/v) TCA. Thus, it precipitates out of solution upon dilution of the TCA + DOC mixture. Deoxycholate is soluble in acetone, and it is extracted from the protein sample along with the TCA in the acetone wash.

Trichloroacetic acid (TCA) (100%; w/v)
(100 ml)

TCA (Gold Label; Aldrich Chemical Co. Inc.)	100 g
H_2O	41 ml

Sample buffer (1x) with 2-mercaptoethanol

Before use, make a working solution of sample buffer by diluting 2x stock sample buffer (see p. 367 for recipe) and adding 2-mercapto-ethanol to a final concentration of 5% (v/v) (*see Safety Notes, p. 361*). Typically:

2x Stock sample buffer	100 µl
H$_2$O	90 µl
2-Mercaptoethanol	10 µl
	200 µl

PRECIPITATION WITH ACIDIFIED ACETONE/METHANOL

A useful alternative to TCA precipitation is the use of acidified acetone mixed with methanol. The acidification helps to remove any SDS in the sample by solubilizing the detergent in the organic phase while precipitating the protein. Acetone and methanol are both mis-cible with water, so there should be no phase separation. At least a fivefold excess of organic is required to precipitate most proteins. The pellet is only visible with approximately >10 µg quantities of protein.

Materials

Hydrochloric acid (high purity; e.g., Ultrex brand from J.T. Baker)
Acetone (high purity; e.g., Gold Label brand from Aldrich)
Methanol (high purity; e.g., Aldrich or Burdick & Jackson highest grade available)

Procedure

This procedure is modified from *Current Protocols in Molecular Biology* by D.R. Marshak and J.A. Smith.

1. Prepare acidified acetone:

Acetone	120 ml
HCl	10 µl

   Mix together to produce a 1 mM solution.

2. Prepare precipitation reagent: Mix equal volumes of acidified acetone and methanol. Chill in the freezer at –20ºC.

3. Concentrate the protein solution to less than 0.1 ml by vacuum centrifugation.

4. Add a fivefold excess (by volume) of precipitation reagent to the aqueous protein solution. Mix thoroughly and incubate overnight in the freezer at −20°C.

5. Centrifuge the sample at 4°C for 30 minutes at the highest speed in a microcentrifuge.

6. Remove the supernatant carefully with a finely drawn pasteur pipette. Let the pellet dry under nitrogen gas in a fume hood for 1 hour.

REFERENCES

Andrews, A.T. 1986. *Electrophoresis: Theory, techniques, and biochemical and clinical applications*. Oxford University Press, New York.

Chrambach, A. and Rodbard, D. 1971. Polyacrylamide gel electrophoresis. *Science* **172:** 440–450.

Cohn, E.J. and J.T. Edsall, eds. 1943. *Proteins, amino acids, and peptides as ions and dipolar ions*. Reinhold, New York.

Current Protocols in Molecular Biology (ed. F.M. Ausabel et al.), vol. 2, pp. 10.19.4–10.19.5 (Supplement 10). Greene/Wiley, New York.

Davis, B.J. 1964. Disc electrophoresis II. Method and application to human serum proteins. *Ann. N.Y. Acad. Sci.* **121:** 404–427.

Hames, B.D. and D. Rickwood, eds. 1990. *Gel electrophoresis of proteins, a practical approach*. Oxford University Press, New York.

Laemmli, U.K. 1970. Cleavage of structural proteins during the assembly of the head of bacteriophage T4. *Nature* **227:** 680–685.

Merril, C.R. 1987. Detection of proteins separated by electrophoresis. In *Advances in electrophoresis*, vol. 1 (A. Chrambach, M.J. Dunn, and B.J. Radola, eds.), pp. 111–140. VGH, New York.

Patton, W.F., N. Chung-Welch, M.F. Lopez, R.D. Cambria, B.L. Utterback, and W.M. Skea. 1991. Tris-tricine and tris-borate buffer systems provide better estimate of human mesothelial cell intermediate filament molecular weight than the standard tris-glycine system. *Anal. Biochem.* **197:** 25–33.

Schägger, J. and G. von Jagow. 1987. Tricine-sodium dodecyl sulfate-polyacrylamide gel electrophoresis for the separation of proteins in the range of 1 to 100 kDa. *Anal. Biochem.* **166:** 368–379.

Shapiro, A.L. and J.V. Maizel. 1969. Molecular weight estimation of polypeptides by SDS-polyacrylamide gel electrophoresis. *Anal. Biochem.* **29:** 505–514.

Swank, R.T. and K.D. Munkres. 1971. Molecular weight analysis of oligopeptides by electrophoresis in polyacrylamide gel with sodium dodecyl sulfate. *Anal. Biochem.* **39:** 462–477.

Van Holde, K.E. 1985. *Physical biochemistry*, 2nd edition, chapter 6. Prentice Hall, Englewood Cliffs, New Jersey.

Weber, K. and M. Osborn. 1969. The reliability of molecular weight determinations by dodecyl sulfate-polyacrylamide gel electrophoresis. *J. Biol. Chem.* **244:** 4406–4412.

Appendix 6
Oxidation of Proteins with Performic Acid

Oxidation of proteins with performic acid is a useful and easy way to partially denature the protein and stabilize the sulfur-containing amino acids. Performic acid oxidation quantitatively converts cysteine residues to cystine and methionine residues to methionine sulfone. These structures are stable to acid hydrolysis.

Cysteic acid

$$NH_2-CH-COOH$$
$$|$$
$$CH_2$$
$$|$$
$$SO_3H$$

Methionine sulfone

$$NH_2-CH-COOH$$
$$|$$
$$CH_2$$
$$|$$
$$CH_2$$
$$|$$
$$O=S=O$$
$$|$$
$$CH_3$$

The oxidation breaks down any disulfide bonds in the protein and disrupts hydrophobic interactions that are mediated by methionines. In addition, the procedure often renders the target protein more soluble in aqueous media. The reagents are all completely volatile, so it is very convenient to carry out the oxidation in the tube that is to be used for any further procedures, such as acid hydrolysis or preparation for electrophoresis.

The formation of the performic acid reagent is highly time- and temperature-dependent. Therefore, it is important to follow the protocol exactly to obtain optimum results. Use highly purified, fresh reagents for this procedure. Formic acid is frequently contaminated with formaldehyde, which can modify the protein of interest in distinct and undesirable ways (e.g., reaction with amines), so always use highly purified or redistilled formic acid that has been stored in glass under nitrogen gas. The hydrogen peroxide should be fresh and stored at 4°C in a tightly closed container. All glassware and plasticware should be washed carefully and rinsed with pure water.

MATERIALS AND EQUIPMENT

Hydrogen peroxide (fresh) (30%)
Formic acid (highest grade available)
Ice/water bath

PROCEDURE

This procedure is adapted from Hirs (1967).

1. Prepare the performic acid reagent by mixing hydrogen peroxide and formic acid together in a ratio of 1:19 (v/v) (e.g., 0.5 ml of hydrogen peroxide and 9.5 ml of formic acid). Let the mixture stand in a tightly covered container for *exactly 2 hours* at room temperature (25°C).

2. Place the performic acid reagent in an ice/water bath. Dissolve the protein sample to be oxidized in formic acid (usually concentrations of 1 mg/ml are satisfactory). Place the dissolved protein sample in the ice/water bath. Allow both the protein sample and the performic acid reagent to stand in the ice/water bath for 30 minutes so they are ice-cold.

   Note: Ice alone will not chill the tubes as well as the ice/water bath.

3. Add a 2–3-fold excess (by volume) of performic acid reagent to the protein sample. Incubate the reaction mixture in the ice/water bath for 2.5 hours.

4. Add a small volume (10% of total) of pure H_2O (distilled or deionizied) to the reaction mixture and mix thoroughly. Remove the formic acid, performic acid, and H_2O by evaporating to dryness in a vacuum centrifuge. Redissolve the protein sample in H_2O and redry in the vacuum centrifuge.

   Note: Upon drying from an organic acid such as formic acid, the protein sample does not appear as a white or crystalline material but rather as a "glass" that is clear. Therefore, do not expect to see the dry protein at the bottom of the tube easily. If held up to the light in a clear tube, the dry protein can be seen by changes in the transmitted light.

REFERENCE

Hirs, C.H.W. 1967. Performic acid oxidation. *Methods Enzymol.* **11**: 59–62.

Appendix 7
Isolation of Phosphopeptides Using Iminodiacetic Acid (Iron-chelating) Sepharose 6B

Phosphorylation of proteins is a very common occurrence, conveying structural changes and regulatory information. During the structural and functional analysis of a phosphorylated protein, it is very helpful to be able to separate the phosphopeptides from the unmodified (un-phosphorylated) peptides following proteolytic cleavage. One of the most useful methods available is the use of metal-chelate resins loaded with iron (ferric ions). The phosphopeptides bind specifically to the iron chelate, and they can be eluted with a soluble metal chelator (e.g., EDTA). This procedure was adapted by H. Michal and C. Anderson from Muszynska et al. (1986) and Lees-Miller and Anderson (1989). The protocol is optimal for isolating 50–200 nmoles of phosphoprotein. The procedure can be scaled down to a batch isolation of phosphopeptides using <100 µl of iron-chelate resin in a 1.5-ml polypropylene microcentrifuge tube. Although probably not quantitative at that level, it is possible to isolate usable amounts of phosphopeptides at 10–50 pmoles. Analysis by chemical methods and mass spectrometry are recommended for phosphorylated peptides.

MATERIALS AND EQUIPMENT

Column (1 x 6 cm; ~5 ml) containing iminodiacetic acid (iron-chelating) Sepharose® 6B (Pharmacia Biotech Inc.) (theoretical capacity of the column is ~2 µmoles of phosphoprotein)
Tris-HCl (50 mM; pH 7.6) containing EDTA (100 mM) and NaCl (500 mM)
Ferric chloride (50 mM)
Acetic acid (0.1 M)
Sodium acetate (0.1 M; pH 5.0) (i.e., 0.1 M acetic acid adjusted to pH 5.0 with NaOH)
Ammonium acetate (1%; pH 6.3 and pH 8.3)
SpeedVac® rotary concentrator (Savant Instruments, Inc.)
EDTA (0.2 M; pH 8.0)

PROCEDURE

Perform all procedures at room temperature.

1. Wash the iminodiacetic acid Sepharose 6B column with 4 volumes (20 ml) of H_2O.

2. Wash the column with 4 volumes of 50 mM Tris-HCl (pH 7.6) containing 100 mM EDTA and 500 mM NaCl.

3. Wash the column with 4 volumes of H_2O.

4. Wash the column with 4 volumes of 50 mM ferric chloride to saturate the column with iron.

5. Wash the column with 2 volumes (10 ml) of 0.1 M acetic acid to remove loosely bound iron.

6. Load the peptide mixture (dissolved in ~4 ml of 0.1 M acetic acid) onto the column.

7. Wash the column with 2 volumes of 0.1 M acetic acid to remove unbound peptides.

8. Wash the column with 2 volumes of 0.1 M sodium acetate (pH 5.0).

9. Wash the column with 3 volumes (15 ml) of 1% ammonium acetate (pH 6.3).

10. Elute the phosphopeptides with 4 volumes of 1% ammonium acetate (pH 8.3).

11. Collect 0.5–1.0-ml samples. Pool the samples according to pH (do spot tests on paper). Concentrate using a SpeedVac rotary concentrator and analyze for phosphopeptides.

12. After elution, wash the column immediately with 4 volumes of 0.2 M EDTA (pH 8.0). Metal-free columns can be stored in 0.2 M EDTA (pH 8.0) at room temperature and reused many times.

REFERENCES

Lees-Miller, S.P. and C.W. Anderson. 1989. Two human 90-kDa heat shock proteins are phosphorylated *in vivo* at conserved serines that are phosphorylated *in vivo* by casein kinase II. *J. Biol. Chem.* **264:** 2431–2437.

Muszynska, G., L. Andersson, and J. Porath. 1986. Selective adsorption of phosphoproteins on gel-immobilized ferric chelate. *Biochemistry* **25:** 6850– 6853.

Appendix 8
Isolation and Separation of Peptide Fragments for Internal Sequence Analysis of Protein

One of the most important links in molecular biology is the analysis of minute amounts of protein to enable the cloning of a cDNA sequence encoding the protein of interest. To do this effectively, the internal sequence of a protein is usually required because the amino terminus of a protein is often blocked (i.e., refractory to Edman degradation) and because sequence information is needed at several points in the primary structure. Efficient isolation of peptides is very important in this respect because accuracy in sequence determination and the length of the valid sequence both contribute to the ultimate success of cloning procedures, using either conventional oligonucleotide probes or polymerase chain reaction products. Often a protein is easily isolated by polyacrylamide gel electrophoresis (see Appendix 5) but is difficult to purify in solution. Therefore, the development of direct methods of proteolytic digestion within a piece of the stained gel followed by isolation of the peptides by reverse-phase HPLC has been a timely innovation. It also avoids the time and potential losses incurred during blotting transfer procedures. The following procedure was developed by Ryuji Kobayashi at Cold Spring Harbor Laboratory as a modification of that described by Rosenfeld et al. (1992). Earlier methods by Kawasaki et al. (1990) also contributed to the evolution of the present protocol. The procedures of Kobayashi have been used very successfully for structural analysis of proteins found in vanishingly small quantities as natural products.

MATERIALS AND EQUIPMENT

Coomassie® Brilliant Blue G (0.05% in 1% acetic acid prepared in 20% methanol)
Acetic acid (5% in 10% methanol)
Methanol (50% in H_2O and 10% in H_2O)
SpeedVac® rotary concentrator (Savant Instruments, Inc.)
Achromobacter protease I (lysylendopeptidase; 50 ng/μl in 0.1 M Tris-HCl [pH 9.0])

Tween-20 (0.1% in 0.1 M Tris-HCl [pH 9.0])
Ultrafree™ MC filter (22 μm; Millipore Corp.)
Trifluoroacetic acid (TFA; 0.1% in 50% acetonitrile)
C18 reverse-phase HPLC column (2.1 x 250 mm; 5 μm; 300 Å)
    (VYDAC)
Acetonitrile
2-Propanol

SAFETY NOTES

- Trifluoroacetic acid is volatile and should be used in a chemical fume hood. Concentrated acids should be handled with great care; gloves and a face protector should be worn.
- Acetonitrile is very volatile and extremely flammable. It is an irritant and a chemical asphyxiant that can exert its effects by inhalation, ingestion, or absorption through the skin. Cases of severe exposure are treated as cyanide poisoning. Handle acetonitrile in a chemical fume hood. Wear gloves and safety glasses.

PROCEDURE

1. Separate the proteins of interest by SDS-PAGE (see Appendix 5).

2. Stain the gel with 0.05% Coomassie Brilliant Blue G for 15–30 minutes.

3. Destain the gel with 5% acetic acid in 10% methanol.

4. Soak the gel in H_2O for 10 minutes.

5. Excise the protein bands from the gel and transfer them to microcentrifuge tubes. Excise a piece of gel that does not contain protein to use as a control. If necessary, cut the gel pieces into smaller fragments so that they fit easily into the bottom of the microcentrifuge tubes.

6. Add 1 ml of 50% methanol to each tube. Incubate for 20 minutes at room temperature. Discard the supernatant.

7. Add 1 ml of 10% methanol to each tube. Incubate for 20 minutes at room temperature. Discard the supernatant.

8. Dry the gel pieces in a SpeedVac rotary concentrator for 2 minutes.

9. Add 10 µl of *Achromobacter* protease I to each tube.

10. Add a minimum volume of 0.1% Tween-20 in 0.1 M Tris-HCl (pH 9.0) to each tube—just enough to cover the gel pieces.

    Note: The gel pieces will swell, so it is important to ensure that they remain covered in the detergent-containing buffer.

11. Incubate the tubes for 24 hours at 30°C.

12. Spin the tubes in a microcentrifuge and transfer each supernatant to a 22-µm Ultrafree MC filter. Spin at 12,000 rpm for 2 minutes. Retain the filtrates.

13. Add a volume of 0.1% TFA in 50% acetonitrile to the remaining gel pieces in each tube—enough to cover the gel pieces. Incubate for 30 minutes at 4°C.

14. Repeat steps 12 and 13. Combine the filtrates from each sample.

15. Spin the samples in a SpeedVac rotary concentrator until the volume is less than 100 ml. Add the appropriate HPLC equilibration solution to prepare the samples for HPLC.

16. Separate the peptide fragments in the digest by reverse-phase HPLC on a C18 column. Elute the peptides with an increasing gradient of acetonitrile/2-propanol (3:1) containing 0.09% TFA. Monitor the UV absorbance of the peptides at 214 nm (for the peptide bond) and at 295 nm (for tryptophan).

REFERENCES

Kawasaki, H., Y. Emori, and K. Suzuki. 1990. Production and separation of peptides from proteins stained with Coomassie brilliant blue R-250 after separation by sodium dodecyl sulfate-polyacrylamide gel electrophoresis. *Anal. Biochem.* **191:** 332–336.

Rosenfeld, J., J. Capdevielle, J.C. Guillemot, and P. Ferrara. 1992. In-gel digestion of proteins for internal sequence analysis after one- or two-dimensional gel electrophoresis. *Anal. Biochem.* **203:** 173–179.

Appendix 9
Recommended Reading

Literature

Burgess, R.R. 1987. Protein purification. In *Protein engineering* (ed. D. Oxender and C.F. Fox), pp. 71–82. Alan R. Liss, New York.

———, ed. 1987. *Protein purification: Micro to macro. Proceedings of the Cetus-UCLA Symposium.* Alan R. Liss, New York.

Cohn, E.J. and J.T. Edsall, eds. 1943. *Proteins, amino acids, and peptides as ions and dipolar ions.* Reinhold, New York.

Creighton, T.E. 1993. *Proteins: Structures and molecular properties*, 2nd edition. W.H. Freeman, San Francisco.

Deutscher, M.P., ed. 1990. *Methods in Enzymology*, vol. 182. *Guide to protein purification.* Academic Press, New York. (Entire volume deals with protein purification techniques.)

Fleischer, S. and B. Fleischer, eds. 1989. *Methods in Enzymology*, vol. 172. *Biomembranes part R transport theory: Cells and model membranes.* Academic Press, New York. Many useful techniques for membrane protein purification and characterization.

Gross, E. 1967. Cleavage of peptide chains. The cyanogen bromide reaction. *Methods Enzymol.* **11:** 238–255.

Harris, E.L.V. and S. Angal, eds. 1989. *Protein purification methods: A practical approach.* IRL Press at Oxford University Press, England.

———, eds. 1989. *Protein purification applications: A practical approach.* IRL Press at Oxford University Press, England.

Harris, T.J.R., ed. 1990. *Protein production by biotechnology.* Elsevier Applied Science, New York.

Hermanson, G.T., A.K. Mallia, and P.K. Smith. 1992. *Immobilized affinity ligand techniques*. Academic Press, San Diego. An excellent guide to affinity chromatography methods.

Jacoby, W., ed. 1971. *Methods in Enzymology*, vol. 22. *Enzyme purification and related techniques*. Academic Press, New York.

———, ed. 1984. *Methods in Enzymology*, vol. 104. *Enzyme purification and related techniques, part C*. Academic Press, New York.

Janson, J.-C. and L. Ryden. 1989. *Protein purification: Principles, high resolution methods, and applications*. VCH Publishers, New York.

Sauer, R., ed. 1991. *Methods in Enzymology*, vol. 208. *Protein-DNA interactions*. Academic Press, New York.

Scopes, R.K. 1994. *Protein purification: Principles and practice*, 3rd edition. Springer-Verlag, New York.

Suelter, C.H. 1985. *A practical guide to enzymology*. John Wiley and Sons, New York.

Software

Protein Purification: A Strategic Approach (A.G. Booth, Ph.D., University of Leeds, IRL Press). Available for both Macintosh and IBM. Contact Oxford University Press Customer Service for information at 1-800-451-7556.

Purify It (Alan Place and Tom Schmidt, University of Maryland) Module copyright 1990, The BioQUEST Library, Beloit College, Wisconsin, Version 1.0 B7. For information, call (301) 405-7600.

Techniques Index

Subject Index